Honda CBR900RR
Service and Repair Manual

by Penny Cox and Matthew Coombs

(2161-240-8Y3)

Models covered
Honda CBR900RR FireBlade. 893cc. UK 1992 through 1995
Honda CBR900RR FireBlade. 919cc. UK 1996 through 1999
Honda CBR900RR. 893cc. US 1993 through 1995
Honda CBR900RR. 919cc. US 1996 through 1999

ABCDE
FGHIJ
KLMN

© Haynes Publishing 1999

A book in the **Haynes Service and Repair Manual Series**

ISBN 1 85960 709 8

Library of Congress Catalog Card Number 99-75446

British Library Cataloguing in Publication Data
A catalogue record for this book is available from the British Library.

Printed by **J H Haynes & Co Ltd, Sparkford, Nr Yeovil, Somerset BA22 7JJ, England**

Haynes Publishing
Sparkford, Nr Yeovil, Somerset BA22 7JJ, England

Haynes North America, Inc
861 Lawrence Drive, Newbury Park, California 91320, USA

Editions Haynes S.A.
Tour Aurore - La Défense 2, 18 Place des Reflets,
92975 PARIS LA DEFENSE Cedex, France

Haynes Publishing Nordiska AB
Box 1504, 751 45 UPPSALA, Sweden

Contents

LIVING WITH YOUR HONDA CBR

Introduction

Daily (pre-ride) checks

MAINTENANCE

Routine maintenance and servicing

Contents

REPAIRS AND OVERHAUL

Engine, transmission and associated systems

Chassis components

Electrical system

Wiring diagrams

REFERENCE

Index

The Birth of a Dream

by Julian Ryder

There is no better example of the Japanese post-War industrial miracle than Honda. Like other companies which have become household names, it started with one man's vision. In this case the man was the 40-year old Soichiro Honda who had sold his piston-ring manufacturing business to Toyota in 1945 and was happily spending the proceeds on prolonged parties for his friends. However, the difficulties of getting around in the chaos of post-War Japan irked Honda, so when he came across a job lot of generator engines he realised that here was a way of getting people mobile again at low cost.

A 12 by 18-foot shack in Hamamatsu became his first bike factory, fitting the

Honda C70 and C90 OHV-engined models

generator motors into pushbikes. Before long he'd used up all 500 generator motors and started manufacturing his own engine, known as the 'chimney', either because of the elongated cylinder head or the smoky exhaust or perhaps both. The chimney made all of half a horsepower from its 50 cc engine but it was a major success and became the Honda A-type. Less than two years after he'd set up in Hamamatsu, Soichiro Honda founded the Honda Motor Company in September 1948. By then, the A-type had been developed into the 90 cc B-type engine, which Mr Honda decided deserved its own chassis not a bicycle frame. Honda was about to become Japan's first post-War manufacturer of complete motorcycles. In August 1949 the first prototype was ready. With an output of three horsepower, the 98 cc D-type was still a

simple two-stroke but it had a two-speed transmission and most importantly a pressed steel frame with telescopic forks and hard tail rear end. The frame was almost triangular in profile with the top rail going in a straight line from the massively braced steering head to the rear axle. Legend has it that after the D-type's first tests the entire workforce went for a drink to celebrate and try and think of a name for the bike. One man broke one of those silences you get when people are thinking, exclaiming 'This is like a dream!' 'That's it!' shouted Honda, and so the Honda Dream was christened.

> 'This is like a dream!'
> 'That's it'
> shouted Honda

Mr Honda was a brilliant, intuitive engineer and designer but he did not bother himself with the marketing side of his business. With hindsight, it is possible to see that employing Takeo Fujisawa who would both sort out the home market and plan the eventual expansion into overseas markets was a masterstroke. He arrived in October 1949 and in 1950 was made Sales Director. Another vital new name was Kiyoshi Kawashima, who along with Honda himself, designed the company's first four-stroke after Kawashima had told them that the four-stroke opposition to Honda's two-strokes sounded nicer and therefore sold better. The result of that statement was the overhead-valve 148 cc E-type which first ran in July 1951 just two months after the first drawings were made. Kawashima was made a director of the Honda Company at 34 years old.

The E-type was a massive success, over 32,000 were made in 1953 alone, but Honda's lifelong pursuit of technical innovation sometimes distracted him from commercial reality. Fujisawa pointed out that they were in danger of ignoring their core business, the motorised bicycles that still formed Japan's main means of transport. In May 1952 the F-type Cub appeared, another two-stroke despite the top men's reservations. You could buy a complete machine or just the motor to attach to your own bicycle. The result was certainly distinctive, a white fuel tank with a circular profile went just below and behind the saddle on the left of the bike, and the motor with its horizontal cylinder and bright red cover just below the rear axle on the same side of the bike. This was the machine that turned Honda into the biggest bike maker in Japan

The CB250N Super Dream became a favorite with UK learner riders of the late seventies and early eighties

ready for the TT. In 1959 the factory entered five riders in the 125. They did not have a massive impact on the event being benevolently regarded as a curiosity, but sixth, seventh and eighth were good enough for the team prize. The bikes were off the pace but they were well engineered and very reliable.

The TT was the only time the West saw the Hondas in '59, but they came back for more the following year with the first of a generation of bikes which shaped the future of motorcycling - the double-overhead-cam four-cylinder 250. It was fast and reliable - it revved to 14,000 rpm - but didn't

with 70% of the market for bolt-on bicycle motors, the F-type was also the first Honda to be exported. Next came the machine that would turn Honda into the biggest motorcycle manufacturer in the world.

The C100 Super Cub was a typically audacious piece of Honda engineering and marketing. For the first time, but not the last, Honda invented a completely new type of motorcycle, although the term 'scooterette' was coined to describe the new bike which had many of the characteristics of a scooter but the large wheels, and therefore stability, of a motorcycle. The first one was sold in August 1958, fifteen years later over nine-million of them were on the roads of the world. If ever a machine can be said to have brought mobility to the masses it is the Super Cub. If you add in the electric starter that was added for the C102 model of 1961, the design of the Super Cub has remained substantially unchanged ever since, testament to how right Honda got it first time. The Super Cub made Honda the world's biggest manufacturer after just two years of production.

Honda's export drive started in earnest in 1957 when Britain and Holland got their first bikes, America got just two bikes the next year. By 1962 Honda had half the American market with 65,000 sales. But Soichiro Honda had already travelled abroad to Europe and the USA, making a special point of going to the Isle of Man TT, then the most important race in the GP calendar. He realised that no matter how advanced his products were, only racing success would convince overseas markets for whom 'Made in Japan' still meant cheap and nasty. It took five years from Soichiro Honda's first visit to the Island before his bikes were

handle anywhere near as well as the opposition. However, Honda had now signed up non-Japanese riders to lead their challenge. The first win didn't come until 1962 (Aussie Tom Phillis in the Spanish 125 GP) and was followed up with

The GL1000 introduced in 1975, was the first in Honda's line of Goldwings

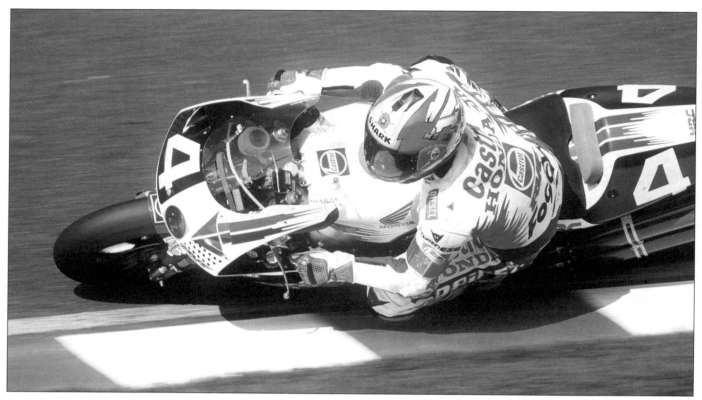

Carl Fogarty in action at the Suzuka 8 Hour on the RC45

An early CB750 Four

a world-shaking performance at the TT. Twenty-one year old Mike Hailwood won both 125 and 250 cc TTs and Hondas filled the top five positions in both races. Soichiro Honda's master plan was starting to come to fruition, Hailwood and Honda won the 1961 250 cc World Championship. Next year Honda won three titles. The other Japanese factories fought back and inspired Honda to produce some of the most fascinating racers ever seen: the awesome six-cylinder 250, the five-cylinder 125, and the 500 four with which the immortal Hailwood battled Agostini and the MV Agusta.

When Honda pulled out of racing in '67 they had won sixteen rider's titles, eighteen manufacturer's titles, and 137 GPs, including 18 TTs, and introduced the concept of the modern works team to motorcycle racing. Sales success followed racing victory as Soichiro Honda had predicted, but only because the products advanced as rapidly as the racing machinery. The Hondas that came to Britain in the early '60s were incredibly sophisticated. They had overhead cams where the British bikes had pushrods, they had electric starters when the Brits relied on the kickstart, they had 12V electrics when even the biggest British bike used a 6V system. There seemed no end to the technical wizardry and when in 1968 the first four-cylinder CB750 road bike arrived the world changed for ever. They even had to invent a new word for it: superbike. Honda raced again with the CB750 at Daytona and won the World Endurance title with a prototype DOHC version that became the CB900 roadster. There was the six-cylinder CBX, the first turbocharged production bike, they invented the full-dress tourer with the Goldwing and came back to GPs with the revolutionary oval-pistoned NR500 four-stroke, a much-misunderstood bike that was more rolling experiment than racer. It was true, though, that Mr Honda was not keen on two-strokes - early motocross engines had to be explained away to him as lawnmower motors! However, in 1982 Honda raced the NS500, an agile three-cylinder lightweight against the big four-cylinder opposition in 500 GPs. The bike won in the first year and in '83 took the world title for Freddie Spencer. In four-stroke racing the V4 layout took over from the straight four, dominating TT, F1 and Endurance championships and when Superbike arrived Honda were ready with the RC30. On the roads the VFR V4 became an instant classic while the CBR600 invented another new class of bike on its way to becoming a best-seller.

And then there was the NR750. This limited-edition technological tour-de-force embodied many of Soichiro Honda's ideals. It used the latest techniques and materials in every component, from the oval-piston, 32-valve V4 motor to the titanium coating on the windscreen, it was - as Mr Honda would have wanted - the best it could possibly be. A fitting memorial to the man who has shaped the motorcycle industry and motorcycles as we know them today.

The 1997 CBR900RR-V model

Honda CBR900RR (FireBlade)

Never underestimate what the mighty Honda Corporation can do with a concept you thought was way past its sell-by date. Across the frame four? First there was the CB750, then the DOHC CB900, and then the CB1100R. Then the R and water-cooling was added to produce the CBR1000 and 600, thus inventing the Supersports 600 category. Add another R and we have the CBR900RR, the mighty FireBlade (as it's known in the UK), the punch of a litre bike in a package the size and weight of a Supersports 600. How do they do that?

The answer is the way Honda usually do these things, with obsessive attention to detail. Internal friction of each component was minimised, weight was shaved off every internal component until a 185 kg motorcycle was left with 126 bhp on tap. The result was astonishing acceleration. The top speed was amazing too but it was the way it got there that was so outrageously addictive.

The first FireBlade, the N-model, arrived in early 1992 to a chorus of disbelief. It was like turning back the clock to the first days of bikes like the Z900 Kawasaki, here was a bike with outrageous power but an edge to it. It wasn't a luxury cruiser like the ZZ-R1100 Kawasaki, it was a hard-edged sportster with a riding position that made your wrists and forearms seize up at legal speeds. In another throwback to the days when men were men, there was a wicked powerband at 8000 rpm which could turn wheelies into embarrassing loop-the-loops. Allied to a frisky front end and ultra-quick steering, this made for a motorbike that was usually in charge of its rider rather than the other way round.

None of this catalogue of intimidation put the buyers off. Far from it, there was one year, 1995, when the FireBlade was the top selling two-wheeler in the UK. Not the top-selling sports bike or litre bike, but the top selling bike: Period. If there was a down-side to this very single-minded motorcycle it was the finish which was not quite up to the near-perfection we have come to expect of Honda. The lightweight bodywork, no doubt designed that way to keep weight down, added to the slightly flimsy feel.

When Honda thought they sensed the opposition catching up they revamped the bike for 1996 under the watchword 'total control'. The 1996 'Blade looked the same but, typically, Honda had changed around 60% of it. The frame was new, with thinner walls and fewer internal compartments, the motor was bored out by 1 mm, the compression ratio upped a fraction and a host of other internal mods, major and minor, incorporated. The bodywork was deprived of those strange holes Honda bored in everything for a while and lightened, but the most significant changes were to the riding position which was transformed from tortuous racer crouch to relaxed stoop. Overall, the effect was to civilise the FireBlade. The monstrous performance was still there but the powerband was gone. The bike now behaved more like a CBR600 that had taken a course of steroids.

For the first five years of its model life the FireBlade was the undisputed boss sportster. The reintroduced Isle of Man Production TT saw the 'Blade dominate, and win the UK's new Production series. Not many sportsters stay top of the heap for more than a couple of years but the 'Blade managed longer than most, only being usurped towards the end of its model run.

Acknowledgements

Our thanks are due to Paul Branson Motorcycles of Yeovil who supplied the machines featured in the photographs throughout this manual and to Mel Rawlings A.I.R.T.E. of MHR Engineering who carried out the mechanical work. We would also like to thank the Avon Rubber Company, who kindly supplied information and technical assistance on tyre fitting, and NGK Spark plugs (UK) Ltd for information on spark plug maintenance and electrode conditions.

Thanks are also due to Honda (UK) Ltd and Kel Edge for supplying color transparencies. The introduction, "The Birth of a Dream" was written by Julian Ryder.

About this Manual

The aim of this manual is to help you get the best value from your motorcycle. It can do so in several ways. It can help you decide what work must be done, even if you choose to have it done by a dealer; it provides information and procedures for routine maintenance and servicing; and it offers diagnostic and repair procedures to follow when trouble occurs.

We hope you use the manual to tackle the work yourself. For many simpler jobs, doing it yourself may be quicker than arranging an appointment to get the motorcycle into a dealer and making the trips to leave it and pick it up. More importantly, a lot of money can be saved by avoiding the expense the shop must pass on to you to cover its labour and overhead costs. An added benefit is the sense of satisfaction and accomplishment that you feel after doing the job yourself.

References to the left or right side of the motorcycle assume you are sitting on the seat, facing forward.

We take great pride in the accuracy of information given in this manual, but motorcycle manufacturers make alterations and design changes during the production run of a particular motorcycle of which they do not inform us. No liability can be accepted by the authors or publishers for loss, damage or injury caused by any errors in, or omissions from, the information given.

Professional mechanics are trained in safe working procedures. However enthusiastic you may be about getting on with the job at hand, take the time to ensure that your safety is not put at risk. A moment's lack of attention can result in an accident, as can failure to observe simple precautions.

There will always be new ways of having accidents, and the following is not a comprehensive list of all dangers; it is intended rather to make you aware of the risks and to encourage a safe approach to all work you carry out on your bike.

Asbestos

● Certain friction, insulating, sealing and other products - such as brake pads, clutch linings, gaskets, etc. - contain asbestos. Extreme care must be taken to avoid inhalation of dust from such products since it is hazardous to health. If in doubt, assume that they do contain asbestos.

Fire

● Remember at all times that petrol is highly flammable. Never smoke or have any kind of naked flame around, when working on the vehicle. But the risk does not end there - a spark caused by an electrical short-circuit, by two metal surfaces contacting each other, by careless use of tools, or even by static electricity built up in your body under certain conditions, can ignite petrol vapour, which in a confined space is highly explosive. Never use petrol as a cleaning solvent. Use an approved safety solvent.

● Always disconnect the battery earth terminal before working on any part of the fuel or electrical system, and never risk spilling fuel on to a hot engine or exhaust.

● It is recommended that a fire extinguisher of a type suitable for fuel and electrical fires is kept handy in the garage or workplace at all times. Never try to extinguish a fuel or electrical fire with water.

Fumes

● Certain fumes are highly toxic and can quickly cause unconsciousness and even death if inhaled to any extent. Petrol vapour comes into this category, as do the vapours from certain solvents such as trichloro-ethylene. Any draining or pouring of such volatile fluids should be done in a well ventilated area.

● When using cleaning fluids and solvents, read the instructions carefully. Never use materials from unmarked containers - they may give off poisonous vapours.

● Never run the engine of a motor vehicle in an enclosed space such as a garage. Exhaust fumes contain carbon monoxide which is extremely poisonous; if you need to run the engine, always do so in the open air or at least have the rear of the vehicle outside the workplace.

The battery

● Never cause a spark, or allow a naked light near the vehicle's battery. It will normally be giving off a certain amount of hydrogen gas, which is highly explosive.

● Always disconnect the battery ground (earth) terminal before working on the fuel or electrical systems (except where noted).

● If possible, loosen the filler plugs or cover when charging the battery from an external source. Do not charge at an excessive rate or the battery may burst.

● Take care when topping up, cleaning or carrying the battery. The acid electrolyte, evenwhen diluted, is very corrosive and should not be allowed to contact the eyes or skin. Always wear rubber gloves and goggles or a face shield. If you ever need to prepare electrolyte yourself, always add the acid slowly to the water; never add the water to the acid.

Electricity

● When using an electric power tool, inspection light etc., always ensure that the appliance is correctly connected to its plug and that, where necessary, it is properly grounded (earthed). Do not use such appliances in damp conditions and, again, beware of creating a spark or applying excessive heat in the vicinity of fuel or fuel vapour. Also ensure that the appliances meet national safety standards.

● A severe electric shock can result from touching certain parts of the electrical system, such as the spark plug wires (HT leads), when the engine is running or being cranked, particularly if components are damp or the insulation is defective. Where an electronic ignition system is used, the secondary (HT) voltage is much higher and could prove fatal.

Remember...

x **Don't** start the engine without first ascertaining that the transmission is in neutral.

x **Don't** suddenly remove the pressure cap from a hot cooling system - cover it with a cloth and release the pressure gradually first, or you may get scalded by escaping coolant.

x **Don't** attempt to drain oil until you are sure it has cooled sufficiently to avoid scalding you.

x **Don't** grasp any part of the engine or exhaust system without first ascertaining that it is cool enough not to burn you.

x **Don't** allow brake fluid or antifreeze to contact the machine's paintwork or plastic components.

x **Don't** siphon toxic liquids such as fuel, hydraulic fluid or antifreeze by mouth, or allow them to remain on your skin.

x **Don't** inhale dust - it may be injurious to health (see Asbestos heading).

x **Don't** allow any spilled oil or grease to remain on the floor - wipe it up right away, before someone slips on it.

x **Don't** use ill-fitting spanners or other tools which may slip and cause injury.

x **Don't** lift a heavy component which may be beyond your capability - get assistance.

x **Don't** rush to finish a job or take unverified short cuts.

x **Don't** allow children or animals in or around an unattended vehicle.

x **Don't** inflate a tyre above the recommended pressure. Apart from overstressing the carcass, in extreme cases the tyre may blow off forcibly.

✔ **Do** ensure that the machine is supported securely at all times. This is especially important when the machine is blocked up to aid wheel or fork removal.

✔ **Do** take care when attempting to loosen a stubborn nut or bolt. It is generally better to pull on a spanner, rather than push, so that if you slip, you fall away from the machine rather than onto it.

✔ **Do** wear eye protection when using power tools such as drill, sander, bench grinder etc.

✔ **Do** use a barrier cream on your hands prior to undertaking dirty jobs - it will protect your skin from infection as well as making the dirt easier to remove afterwards; but make sure your hands aren't left slippery. Note that long-term contact with used engine oil can be a health hazard.

✔ **Do** keep loose clothing (cuffs, ties etc. and long hair) well out of the way of moving mechanical parts.

✔ **Do** remove rings, wristwatch etc., before working on the vehicle - especially the electrical system.

✔ **Do** keep your work area tidy - it is only too easy to fall over articles left lying around.

✔ **Do** exercise caution when compressing springs for removal or installation. Ensure that the tension is applied and released in a controlled manner, using suitable tools which preclude the possibility of the spring escaping violently.

✔ **Do** ensure that any lifting tackle used has a safe working load rating adequate for the job.

✔ **Do** get someone to check periodically that all is well, when working alone on the vehicle.

✔ **Do** carry out work in a logical sequence and check that everything is correctly assembled and tightened afterwards.

✔ **Do** remember that your vehicle's safety affects that of yourself and others. If in doubt on any point, get professional advice.

● If in spite of following these precautions, you are unfortunate enough to injure yourself, seek medical attention as soon as possible.

Frame and engine numbers

The frame serial number is stamped into the right side of the steering head and also appears on the identification plate attached to the right side of the frame. The engine number is stamped into the right upper side of the crankcase, directly above the clutch unit. Both of these numbers should be recorded and kept in a safe place so they can be furnished to law enforcement officials in the event of a theft.

The frame serial number, engine serial number and carburetor identification number should also be kept in a handy place (such as with your driver's license) so they are always available when purchasing or ordering parts for your machine.

The procedures in this manual identify the bikes by model code for UK models and production year for US models. The model code (eg CBR900RR-**S**) or production year is printed on the color code label, which is stuck to the top of the frame, next to the fuel tank rear mounting.

The model code or production year can also be determined from the engine and frame serial numbers as follows:

Model	Initial engine number	Initial frame number
UK CBR900RR-N (1992)	SC28E-2000064 to 2001053	SC28-2000043 to 2009388
UK CBR900RR-P (1993)	SC28E-2105040 to 2115746	SC28-2100006 to 2108740
UK CBR900RR-R (1994)	SC28E-2250388 on	SC28-2250391 on
UK CBR900RR-S (1995)	SC28E-2350001 on	SC28-2350001 on
UK CBR900RR-T (1996)	SC33E-2000001 on	SC33A-TM000001 on
UK CBR900RR-V (1997)	SC33E-2100001 on	SC33A-VM100001 on
UK CBR900RR-W (1998)	SC33E-2200001 on	SC33A*-WM200001 on
UK CBR900RR-X (1999)	SC33E-3300001 on	SC33A*-XM300001 on
US CBR900RR 1993 - California	SC28E-2100012 to 2100692	SC281*PM100004 to PM101026
US CBR900RR 1993 - except California	SC28E-2100007 to 2105828	SC280*PM100002 to PM104964
US CBR900RR 1994 - California	SC28E-2200001 to 2204138	SC281*RM200001 to RM200683
US CBR900RR 1994 - except California	SC28E-2200001 to 2204092	SC280*RM200001 to RM203322
US CBR900RR 1995 - California	SC28E-2300001 on	SC281*SM300001 on
US CBR900RR 1995 - except California	SC28E-2300001 on	SC280*SM300001 on
US CBR900RR 1996 - California	SC33E-2000001 on	SC331*TM300001 on
US CBR900RR 1996 - except California	SC33E-2000001 on	SC330*TM300001 on
US CBR900RR 1997 - California	SC33E-2100001 on	SC331*VM000001 on
US CBR900RR 1997 - except California	SC33E-2100001 on	SC330*VM000001 on
US CBR900RR 1998 - California	SC33E-2200001 on	SC331*-WM200001 on
US CBR900RR 1998 - except California	SC33E-2200001 on	SC330*-WM200001 on
US CBR900RR 1999 - California	SC33E-2300001 on	SC331*-XM300001 on
US CBR900RR 1999 - except California	SC33E-2300001 on	SC330*-XM300001 on

Buying spare parts

Once you have found all the identification numbers, record them for reference when buying parts. Since the manufacturers change specifications, parts and vendors (companies that manufacture various components on the machine), providing the ID numbers is the only way to be reasonably sure that you are buying the correct parts.

Whenever possible, take the worn part to the dealer so direct comparison with the new component can be made. Along the trail from the manufacturer to the parts shelf, there are numerous places that the part can end up with the wrong number or be listed incorrectly.

The two places to purchase new parts for your motorcycle - the accessory store and the franchised dealer - differ in the type of parts they carry. While dealers can obtain virtually every part for your motorcycle, the accessory dealer is usually limited to normal high wear items such as shock absorbers, tune-up parts, various engine gaskets, cables, chains, brake parts, etc. Rarely will an accessory outlet have major suspension components, cylinders, transmission gears, or cases.

Used parts can be obtained for roughly half the price of new ones, but you can't always be sure of what you're getting. Once again, take your worn part to the wrecking yard (breaker) for direct comparison.

Whether buying new, used or rebuilt parts, the best course is to deal directly with someone who specializes in parts for your particular make.

Color code label is stuck to the top of the frame, near the fuel tank rear mounting

The engine number is stamped on the right side of the crankcase

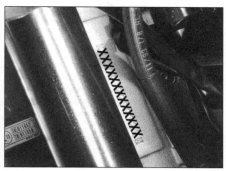

The frame number is stamped on the right side of the steering head

1 Engine/transmission oil level

Before you start:

✔ Take the motorcycle on a short run to allow it to reach normal operating temperature. *Caution: Do not run the engine in an enclosed space such as a garage or workshop.*

✔ Stop the engine and support the motorcycle in an upright position, using an auxiliary stand if required. Allow it to stand undisturbed for a few minutes to allow the oil level to stabilise. Make sure the motorcycle is on level ground.

Bike care:

● If you have to add oil frequently, you should check whether you have any oil leaks. If there is no sign of oil leakage from the joints and gaskets the engine could be burning oil *(see Fault Finding).*

The correct oil

● Modern, high-revving engines place great demands on their oil. It is very important that the correct oil for your bike is used.
● Always top up with a good quality oil of the specified type and viscosity and do not overfill the engine.

Oil type	API grade SF or SG
Oil viscosity	SAE 10W40

US 1993 through 1995 models and UK N to S models

1 Unscrew the oil filler cap (arrow) from the right hand side crankcase cover. The dipstick is integral with the oil filler cap.

2 Wipe off all the oil from the dipstick, then insert the clean dipstick back into the engine, but do not screw it in.

3 Remove the dipstick and observe the level of the oil, which should be somewhere in between the upper and lower level marks (arrows).

4 If the level is below the lower mark, top up with the recommended grade and type of oil, to bring the level up to the upper mark on the dipstick. Do not overfill.

US 1996 through 1999 models and UK T to X models

1 Check the oil level at the inspection window in the bottom of the clutch cover. The oil level should lie between the upper and lower level marks (arrows).

2 The oil filler cap is located at the top of the clutch cover. Unscrew the cap to add oil.

3 Add the specified oil to bring the level to the upper level mark on the inspection window. Do not overfill.

2 Legal and safety checks

Safety:
● Check that the throttle grip rotates smoothly and snaps shut when released, in all steering positions.
● Check that the engine shuts off when the kill switch is operated.
● Check that sidestand return spring holds the stand securely up when retracted. The same applies to the centre stand.
● Check that the engine cuts out if the sidestand is lowered when the engine is running and in gear.
● Check for any loose cables and body parts.

Lighting and signalling:
● Take a minute to check that the headlight, taillight, brake light turn signals and gauges all work correctly.
● Check that the horn sounds when the switch is operated.
● A working speedometer, graduated in mph, is a statutory requirement in the UK.

Fuel:
● This may seem obvious, but check that you have enough fuel to complete your journey. If you notice signs of fuel leakage - rectify the cause immediately.
● Ensure you use the correct grade unleaded fuel - see Chapter 4 Specifications.

3 Brake fluid levels

⚠ **Warning: Brake hydraulic fluid can harm your eyes and damage painted surfaces, so use extreme caution when handling and pouring it and cover surrounding surfaces with rag. Do not use fluid that has been standing open for some time, as it absorbs moisture from the air which can cause a dangerous loss of braking effectiveness.**

Before you start:

✔ Support the motorcycle in an upright position, using an auxiliary stand if required, and turn the handlebars until the top of the front master cylinder is as level as possible. If necessary, tilt the motorcycle to make it level. The rear master cylinder reservoir is located below the seat on the right-hand side of the machine.

✔ Make sure you have the correct hydraulic fluid. DOT 4 is recommended.

Bike care:

● The fluid in the front and rear brake master cylinder reservoirs will drop slightly as the brake pads wear down.

● If any fluid reservoir requires repeated topping-up this is an indication of a hydraulic leak somewhere in the system, which should be investigated immediately.

● Check for signs of fluid leakage from the hydraulic hoses and components - if found, rectify immediately.

● Check the operation of both brakes before taking the machine on the road; if there is evidence of air in the system (spongy feel to lever or pedal), it must be bled as described in Chapter 7.

1 The front brake fluid level is visible through the reservoir body - it must be between the UPPER and LOWER level lines (arrows).

2 If the level is below the LOWER level line, remove the two reservoir cap screws and remove the cover, the diaphragm plate and the diaphragm.

3 Top up with new clean hydraulic fluid of the recommended type, until the level is above the lower mark. Take care to avoid spills (see **Warning** above).

4 Ensure that the diaphragm is correctly seated before installing the plate and cover.

5 The rear brake fluid level is visible through the reservoir body - it must be between the UPPER and LOWER level lines (arrows).

6 If the level is below the LOWER level line, remove the reservoir mounting bolt and swing the reservoir out from the frame. Remove all dust and dirt from the area around the cap.

7 Unscrew the reservoir cap and remove the diaphragm plate and diaphragm. Top up with new clean hydraulic fluid of the recommended type, until the level is above the lower mark. Take care to avoid spills (see **Warning** above).

8 Ensure that the diaphragm is correctly seated before installing the plate and cap. Tighten the cap securely, then bolt the reservoir back into position.

4 Suspension, steering and final drive

Suspension and Steering:

● Check that the front and rear suspension operates smoothly without binding.

● Check that the suspension is adjusted as required.
● Check that the steering moves smoothly from lock-to-lock.

Final drive:

● Check that the drive chain slack isn't excessive.
● If the chain looks dry, lubricate it (see Chapter 1).

5 Coolant level

> **Warning: DO NOT remove the radiator pressure cap to add coolant. Topping up is done via the coolant reservoir tank filler. DO NOT leave open containers of coolant about, as it is poisonous.**

Before you start:

✔ Make sure you have a supply of coolant available (a mixture of 50% distilled water and 50% corrosion inhibited ethylene glycol anti-freeze is needed).

✔ Support the motorcycle in an upright position, using an auxiliary stand if required, whilst checking the level. Make sure the motorcycle is on level ground.

✔ Always check the coolant level when the engine is at normal working temperature. Take the motorcycle on a short run to allow it to reach normal temperature.
Caution: Do not run the engine in an enclosed space such as a garage or workshop.

Bike care:

● Use only the specified coolant mixture. It is important that anti-freeze is used in the system all year round, and not just in the winter. Do not top the system up using only water, as the system will become too diluted.

● Do not overfill the reservoir tank. If the coolant is significantly above the UPPER level line at any time, the surplus should be siphoned or drained off to prevent the possibility of it being expelled out of the overflow hose.

● If the coolant level falls steadily, check the system for leaks (see Chapter 1). If no leaks are found and the level continues to fall, it is recommended that the machine is taken to a Honda dealer for a pressure test.

1 The coolant reservoir is located below the tank on the right-hand side of the machine. The coolant UPPER and LOWER level markings are visible on the back of the reservoir (arrows).

2 If the coolant level is not in between the UPPER and LOWER markings, remove the filler cap and top the level up with the recommended coolant mixture.

6 Tires

The correct pressures:

● The tires must be checked when **cold**, not immediately after riding. Note that low tire pressures may cause the tire to slip on the rim or come off. High tire pressures will cause abnormal tread wear and unsafe handling.

● Use an accurate pressure gauge.

● Proper air pressure will increase tire life and provide maximum stability and ride comfort.

Tire care:

● Check the tires carefully for cuts, tears, embedded nails or other sharp objects and excessive wear. Operation of the motorcycle with excessively worn tires is extremely hazardous, as traction and handling are directly affected.

● Check the condition of the tire valve and ensure the dust cap is in place.

● Pick out any stones or nails which may have become embedded in the tire tread. If left, they will eventually penetrate through the casing and cause a puncture.

● If tire damage is apparent, or unexplained loss of pressure is experienced, seek the advice of a tire fitting specialist without delay.

Tire tread depth:

● At the time of writing UK law requires that tread depth must be at least 1 mm over 3/4 of the tread breadth all the way around the tire, with no bald patches. Many riders, however, consider 2 mm tread depth minimum to be a safer limit. Honda recommend a minimum of 1.5 mm on the front and 2 mm on the rear.

● Many tires now incorporate wear indicators in the tread. Identify the triangular pointer or TWI marking on the tire sidewall to locate the indicator bar and replace the tire if the tread has worn down to the bar.

Loading	Front	Rear
Rider only	36 psi (2.27 Bar)	42 psi (2.27 Bar)
Rider and passenger	36 psi (2.27 Bar)	42 psi (2.83 Bar)

1 Check the tire pressures when the tires are **cold** and keep them properly inflated.

2 Measure tread depth at the centre of the tire using a tread depth gauge.

3 Use the pointer (arrowed) on the sidewall to locate the tread wear indicator bars.

Chapter 1
Routine maintenance and servicing

Contents

Degrees of difficulty

| **Easy,** suitable for novice with little experience | | **Fairly easy,** suitable for beginner with some experience | | **Fairly difficult,** suitable for competent DIY mechanic | | **Difficult,** suitable for experienced DIY mechanic | | **Very difficult,** suitable for expert DIY or professional | |

Specifications

Engine

Spark plugs
  Type .... NGK CR9EH-9 or ND U27FER-9
  Electrode gap .... 0.8 to 0.9 mm (0.031 to 0.035 in)
Valve clearances (COLD engine)
  Intake .... 0.13 to 0.19 mm (0.005 to 0.007 in)
  Exhaust
    US 1993 through 1997 models and UK N to V models .... 0.19 to 0.25 mm (0.007 to 0.010 in)
    US 1998 and 1999 models and UK W and X models .... 0.22 to 0.28 mm (0.009 to 0.011 in)
Engine idle speed:
  US 1996 through 1999 California models .... 1200 ± 100 rpm
  All other models .... 1100 ± 100 rpm
Cylinder compression
  US 1993 through 1997 models and UK N to V models .... 171 psi (11.8 bar)
  US 1998 and 1999 models and UK W and X models .... 185 psi (12.7 bar)
Carburetor synchronization
  Maximum vacuum difference between any two cylinders........ 20 mm (0.8 in) Hg
Cylinder numbering (from left side to right side of the bike) 1-2-3-4
Firing order 1-2-4-3

Miscellaneous

Brake pad minimum thickness . . . . See text
Freeplay adjustments
    Throttle grip . . . . 2 to 6 mm (0.08 to 0.24 in)
    Clutch lever . . . . 10 to 20 mm (0.4 to 0.8 in)
    Drive chain
        US 1993 through 1995 models and UK N to S models . . . . 25 to 35 mm (1.0 to 1.4 in)
        US 1996 through 1999 models and UK T to X models . . . . 30 to 40 mm (1.2 to 1.6 in)
Minimum tire tread depth* . . . . see "Daily (pre-ride) checks"
Tire pressures (cold) . . . . see "Daily (pre-ride) checks"

Torque settings

	Nm	ft-lbs
Crankshaft cap	18	13
Engine oil pan drain bolt		
US 1993 through 1995 models and UK N to S models	36	26
US 1996 through 1999 models and UK T to X models	29	22
Oil filter (see text)	10	7
Spark plugs	12	9
Rear wheel axle nut	93	69
Steering stem adjuster nut (see Text)		
US 1993 through 1995 models and UK N to S models	31	22
US 1996 through 1999 models and UK T to X models	25	18
Steering stem nut	103	76
Upper triple clamp bolts		
US 1993 through 1997 models and UK N to V models	23	17
US 1998 and 1999 models and UK W and X models	22	16

Recommended lubricants and fluids

Engine/transmission oil
    Type . . . . API grade SF or SG
    Viscosity . . . . SAE 10W40
    Capacity (US 1993 and 1994 models and UK N to R models)
        Oil change only . . . . 3.1 liters (3.3 US qt, 5.5 Imp pts)
        With filter change . . . . 3.2 liters (3.4 US qt, 5.7 Imp pts)
        After engine rebuild . . . . 4.0 liters (4.2 US qt, 7.0 Imp pts)
    Capacity (US 1995 through 1999 models and UK S to X models)
        Oil change only . . . . 3.5 liters (3.7 US qt, 6.2 Imp pts)
        With filter change . . . . 3.6 liters (3.8 US qt, 6.3 Imp pts)
        After engine rebuild . . . . 4.4 liters (4.7 US qt, 7.7 Imp pts)
Coolant
    Mixture type . . . . 50% distilled water, 50% corrosion inhibited ethylene glycol antifreeze
    Capacity
      Radiator and engine
        US 1993 through 1995 models and UK N to S models . . . . 2.80 lit (3.00 US qt, 5.00 Imp pt)
        US 1996 and 1997 models and UK T and V models . . . . 2.77 lit (2.93 US qt, 4.88 Imp pt)
        US 1998 and 1999 models and UK W and X models . . . . 2.64 lit (2.79 US qt, 4.64 Imp pt)
      Coolant reservoir
        US 1993 through 1997 models and UK N to V models . . . . 0.45 lit (0.48 US qt, 0.80 Imp pt)
        US 1998 and 1999 models and UK W and X models . . . . 0.35 lit (0.30 US qt, 0.62 Imp pt)
Brake fluid . . . . DOT 4

Miscellaneous

Drive chain . . . . SAE 80 to 90W gear oil
Steering head bearings . . . . Lithium-based multi-purpose grease
Swingarm pivot bearings . . . . Lithium-based multi-purpose grease
Suspension linkage bearings . . . . Lithium-based multi-purpose grease
Shock absorber mounting bearings . . . . Lithium-based multi-purpose grease
Bearing seal lips . . . . Lithium-based multi-purpose grease
Gearchange lever/clutch lever/rear brake pedal pivots . . . . Lithium-based multi-purpose grease
Front brake lever pivot and piston tip . . . . Silicone grease
Cables . . . . 10W40 motor oil
Side stand pivot . . . . Molybdenum disulfide grease
Throttle grip . . . . Multi-purpose grease or dry film lubricant

Note: *Always perform the Daily (pre-ride) checks at every maintenance interval (in addition to the procedures listed). The intervals listed below are the intervals recommended by the manufacturer for each particular operation during the model years covered in this manual. Your owner's manual may have different intervals for your model.*

Daily (pre-ride)

See *'Daily (pre-ride) checks'* at the beginning of this manual.

After the initial 600 miles (1000 km)

Note: *This check is usually performed by a Honda dealer after the first 600 miles (1,000 km) from new. Thereafter, maintenance is carried out according to the following intervals of the schedule.*

Every 500 miles (800 km)

☐ Check, adjust and lubricate the drive chain - US 1996 and 1997 models (Section 1)

Every 600 miles (1000 km)

☐ Check, adjust and lubricate the drive chain - all except US 1996 and 1997 models (Section 1)

Every 4000 miles (6000 km) or 6 months (whichever comes sooner)

☐ Check and adjust the idle speed (Section 2)
☐ Check the brake pads (Section 3)
☐ Check and adjust the clutch (Section 4)
☐ Check the spark plug gaps - US models (Section 5)
☐ Lubricate the clutch/gearshift/brake lever/brake pedal/side stand pivots and the throttle/choke/clutch cables (Section 6)

Every 8000 miles (12,000 km) or 12 months (whichever comes sooner)

Carry out all the items under the 4000 mile (6000 km) check, plus the following
☐ Replace the engine oil and filter (Section 7)
☐ Check the fuel system and hoses (Section 8)
☐ Check the battery terminals (Section 9)
☐ Check and adjust the throttle and choke cables (Section 10)
☐ Check the spark plug gaps - UK models (Section 11)
☐ Replace the spark plugs - US models (Section 12)
☐ Check/adjust the carburetor synchronization (Section 13)
☐ Check the condition of the PAIR system hoses - California models only (Section 14)
☐ Check the cooling system (Section 15)
☐ Check the brake system and brake light switch operation (Section 16)
☐ Check and adjust the headlight aim (Section 17)

☐ Check the sidestand (Section 18)
☐ Check the suspension (Section 19)
☐ Check and adjust the steering head bearings (Section 20)
☐ Check the tightness of all nuts, bolts and fasteners (Section 21)
☐ Check the condition of the wheels and tires (Section 22)
☐ Check the drive chain slider for wear (Section 23)
☐ Check the condition of the exhaust system (Section 24)

Every 12,000 miles (18,000 km) or 18 months (whichever comes first)

Carry out all the items under the 4000 mile (6000 km) check, plus the following
☐ Replace the air filter element (Section 25)
☐ Check the EVAP system hoses - California models only (Section 26)
☐ Change the brake fluid (Section 27)

Every 16,000 miles (24,000 km) or two years (whichever comes sooner)

Carry out all the items under the 8000 mile (12000 km) check, plus the following
☐ Check and adjust the valve clearances (Section 28)
☐ Replace the spark plugs - UK models (Section 29)

Every 24,000 miles (36,000 km) or three years (whichever comes sooner)

Carry out all the items under the 12000 mile (18000 km) and 8000 mile (12000 km) checks, plus the following
☐ Replace the coolant (Section 30)

Non-scheduled maintenance

☐ Check the cylinder compression (Section 31)
☐ Check the wheel bearings (Section 32)
☐ Re-grease the steering head bearings (Section 33)
☐ Re-grease the swingarm and suspension linkage bearings (Section 34)
☐ Replace the brake master cylinder and caliper seals (Section 35)
☐ Replace the brake hoses (Section 36)
☐ Change the front fork oil (Section 37)
☐ Check the engine oil pressure (Section 38)

1

Component locations - left-hand side

1	Clutch cable adjuster	4	Air filter	7	Drive chain	10	Coolant drain plug
2	Spark plugs and valves	5	Battery	8	Fuel tap	11	Oil filter
3	Idle speed adjuster	6	Drive chain adjuster	9	Oil drain plug	12	Front brake caliper

Component locations - right-hand side

1 Rear brake fluid reservoir	5 Front brake fluid reservoir	9 Timing mark inspection cap	12 Rear brake light switch
2 Coolant reservoir	6 Fuse box	10 Clutch cable adjuster	13 Drive chain adjuster
3 Carburetors	7 Fork seals	11 Oil filler cap	14 Rear brake caliper
4 Radiator pressure cap	8 Front brake caliper		

Introduction

1 This Chapter is designed to help the home mechanic maintain his/her motorcycle for safety, economy, long life and peak performance.

2 Deciding where to start or plug into the routine maintenance schedule depends on several factors. If the warranty period on your motorcycle has just expired, and if it has been maintained according to the warranty standards, you may want to pick up routine maintenance as it coincides with the next mileage or calendar interval. If you have owned the machine for some time but have never performed any maintenance on it, then you may want to start at the nearest interval and include some additional procedures to ensure that nothing important is overlooked. If you have just had a major engine overhaul, then you may want to start the maintenance routine from the beginning. If you have a used machine and have no knowledge of its history or maintenance record, you may desire to combine all the checks into one large service initially and then settle into the maintenance schedule prescribed.

3 Before beginning any maintenance or repair, the machine should be cleaned thoroughly, especially around the oil filter, spark plugs, valve cover, side panels, carburettors, etc. Cleaning will help ensure that dirt does not contaminate the engine and will allow you to detect wear and damage that could otherwise easily go unnoticed.

4 Certain maintenance information is sometimes printed on decals attached to the motorcycle. If the information on the decals differs from that included here, use the information on the decal.

Every 600 miles (1000 km)

Note: *This interval is reduced to 500 miles (800 km) on 1996 and 1997 US models*

1 Drive chain and sprockets - check, adjustment and lubrication

Check

1 A neglected drive chain won't last long and can quickly damage the sprockets. Routine chain adjustment and lubrication isn't difficult and will ensure maximum chain and sprocket life.

2 To check the chain, place the bike on its side stand and shift the transmission into neutral. Make sure the ignition switch is OFF.

3 Push up on the bottom run of the chain and measure the slack midway between the two sprockets, then compare your measurements to the value listed in this Chapter's Specifications **(see illustration)**. Since the chain will rarely wear evenly, roll the bike forwards so that another section of chain can be checked; do this several times to check the entire length of chain. In some cases where lubrication has been neglected, corrosion and galling may cause the links to bind and kink, which effectively shortens the chain's length. If the chain is tight between the sprockets, rusty or kinked, it's time to replace it with a new one. If you find a tight area, mark it with felt pen or paint, and repeat the measurement after the bike has been ridden. If the chain's still tight in the same area, it may be damaged or worn. Because a tight or kinked chain can damage the transmission countershaft bearing, it's a good idea to replace it.

Caution: If the machine is ridden with more than 50 mm (2 inches) of slack in the drive chain, the chain will contact the frame and swingarm, causing severe damage.

4 Check the entire length of the chain for damaged rollers, loose links and pins and replace if damage is found. **Note:** *Never install a new chain on old sprockets, and never use the old chain if you install new sprockets - replace the chain and sprockets as a set.*

5 Remove the engine sprocket cover (see Chapter 6). Check the teeth on the engine sprocket and the rear wheel sprocket for wear **(see illustration)**.

6 Inspect the drive chain slider on the swingarm for excessive wear and replace if worn down to the wear indicator arrow (see Chapter 6).

Adjustment

US 1993 through 1995 models and UK N to S models

7 Rotate the rear wheel until the chain is positioned with the tightest point at the center of its bottom run.

8 Slacken the rear axle nut **(see illustration)**.

9 Back off the locknut and turn the adjusting bolts on both sides of the swingarm until the proper chain tension is obtained (get the adjuster on the chain side close, then set the adjuster on the opposite side) **(see illustration)**.

1.3 Measuring drive chain slack

1.5 Check the sprockets in the areas indicated to see if they are worn excessively

1.8 Slacken off rear axle nut

1.9a Slacken each adjuster locknut (A) and rotate adjuster bolt (B) to adjust chain tension

1.9b Check the front edge of the adjuster block in relation to the alignment scale (A) and the chain wear indicator decal (B)

1.14 Chain adjuster bolt (A). Check the index marks (B) and the chain wear indicator decal (C) on the adjuster in relation to the mark on the swingarm (D)

Be sure to turn the adjusting bolts evenly to keep the rear wheel in alignment; the front edge of the chain adjuster block can be aligned with the graduated scale to ensure this **(see illustration)**. Having completed the adjustment, check the relationship of the front edge of the chain adjuster block with the wear decal on the swingarm ends; if it aligns with the red REPLACE CHAIN zone, the drive chain has stretched excessively and must be replaced.

10 Tighten the axle nut to the specified torque setting.

11 With the axle nut tightened, tighten the chain adjuster locknuts securely.

US 1996 through 1999 models and UK T to X models

12 Rotate the rear wheel until the chain is positioned with the tightest point at the center of its bottom run.

13 Slacken the rear axle nut.

14 Turn the adjusting bolts on both sides of the swingarm until the proper chain tension is obtained (get the adjuster on the chain side close, then set the adjuster on the opposite side) **(see illustration)**. Turn the bolts clockwise to tighten the chain. Be sure to turn the adjusting bolts evenly to keep the rear wheel in alignment; the index marks on the top edge of the chain adjuster can be aligned with the index mark on the swingarm to ensure this. Having completed the adjustment, check the relationship of the wear indicator label on the adjuster with the index

mark on the swingarm ends; if the index mark aligns with the red REPLACE CHAIN zone, the drive chain has stretched excessively and must be replaced.

15 Tighten the axle nut to the specified torque setting.

16 With the axle nut tightened, tighten the chain adjuster bolts lightly.

Lubrication

Note: If the chain is extremely dirty, it should be removed and cleaned before it's lubricated (see Chapter 6).

17 For routine lubrication, the best time to lubricate the chain is after the motorcycle has been ridden. When the chain is warm, the lubricant will penetrate the joints between the side plates better than when cold. **Note:** Honda specifies SAE 80 to SAE 90W gear oil only; do not use chain lube, which may contain solvents that could damage the O-rings.

18 Apply the oil to the area where the side plates overlap - not the middle of the rollers. After applying the lubricant, let it soak in a few minutes before wiping off any excess.

> **HAYNES HiNT** *Apply oil to the top of the lower chain run, so centrifugal force will work the oil into the chain when the bike is moving*

Every 4000 miles (6000 km) or 6 months

2 Idle speed - check and adjustment

1 The idle speed should be checked and adjusted before and after the carburetors are synchronized and when it is obviously too high or too low. Before adjusting the idle speed, make sure the valve clearances and spark plug

gaps are correct. Also, turn the handlebars back-and-forth and see if the idle speed changes as this is done. If it does, the throttle cables may not be adjusted correctly, or may be worn out. This is a dangerous condition that can cause loss of control of the bike. Be sure to correct this problem before proceeding.

2 The engine should be at normal operating temperature, which is usually reached after 10 to 15 minutes of stop and go riding. Place the

motorcycle on its side stand and make sure the transmission is in neutral.

3 Turn the idle speed knob, which is located in a wire guide which extends from the middle fairing section bracket on the left side, until the idle speed listed in this Chapter's Specifications is obtained **(see illustration)**.

4 Snap the throttle open and shut a few times, then recheck the idle speed. If necessary, repeat the adjustment procedure.

5 If a smooth, steady idle can't be achieved, the fuel/air mixture may be incorrect. Refer to Chapter 4 for additional carburetor information.

3 Brake pads - wear check

Front brake (US 1993 through 1997 models and UK N to V models)

1 Pry the pad inspection cover from the back of each caliper **(see illustration)**. View the friction material thickness on each pad; if

2.3 Engine idle speed is adjusted using idle knob (arrow)

3.1a Pry the pad inspection cover from the back of the front calipers . . .

3.1b ... to view the amount of pad material remaining

3.1c Replace the pads when or before the friction material has worn down level with the bottom of the groove(s) (arrow) - note non-original equipment pad shown

3.3 Rear brake pad wear indicator groove details

1 Caliper   2 Pads   3 Wear limit
4 Minimum thickness groove

worn down so that the grooves are no longer visible, i.e. so that friction material remaining is level with the base of the grooves, both pads in each front caliper must be renewed immediately **(see illustrations)**. Clip the inspection cover back into place so that its tabs top and bottom engage the cutouts in the caliper body.

2 If in doubt about the amount of pad material remaining or the pad condition, remove the pads for detailed inspection (see Chapter 7).

Front brake (US 1998 and 1999 models and UK W and X models) and all rear brake calipers

3 View the pads from the rear underside of the caliper. If either pad has worn down to, or

4.3a Clutch cable freeplay is measured at lever ball end

beyond the groove in the friction material, both pads must be replaced as a set **(see illustration)**.

4 If in doubt about the amount of pad material remaining or the pad condition, remove the pads for detailed inspection (see Chapter 7).

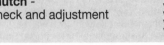

4 Clutch -
check and adjustment

1 Check that the clutch cable operates smoothly and easily.
2 If the clutch lever operation is heavy or stiff, remove the cable as described in Chapter 2 and lubricate it as described in Section 15. Install the lubricated cable, making sure it takes the smoothest possible route.
3 With the cable operating smoothly, it is necessary to check that the clutch lever is correctly adjusted. Clutch cable freeplay is measured in terms of travel at the ball end of the lever, and should be as given in this Chapter's Specifications **(see illustration)**. If adjustment is required, slacken the handlebar end adjuster lockwheel on the lever mounting bracket **(see illustration)**. Reposition the adjuster as required and securely tighten the lockwheel.
4 If there is insufficient range in the handlebar

adjuster it will be necessary to adjust the freeplay at the lower adjuster on the crankcase **(see illustration)**. Screw the upper adjuster fully inwards and slacken the locknut on the lower adjuster. Rotate the adjuster nut until the required freeplay is obtained at the handlebar lever, then securely tighten the lower adjuster locknut. If necessary, fine adjustments can then be made using the handlebar adjuster.

5 Spark plug gaps - check and adjustment (US models)

1 This motorcycle is equipped with spark plugs that have 10 mm threads and a 16 mm wrench hex. Make sure your spark plug socket is the correct size before attempting to remove the plugs, a suitable one is supplied in the motorcycle's toolkit.
2 Remove the fairing middle sections (see Chapter 8).
3 Remove the fuel tank and air filter housing (see Chapter 4).
4 Remove the ignition HT coils (see Chapter 5).
5 Release the rubber dust cover from the tabs of the air deflector, then remove the two bolts which retain the air deflector to the frame **(see illustrations)**. Maneuver the air

1

4.3b A small amount of cable adjustment can be made at the upper adjuster on the handlebar lever (arrow)

4.4 Clutch cable lower adjuster is located in bracket on clutch cover

5.5a Free the rubber dust cover from the air deflector tabs (arrows) ...

5.5b . . . remove the two retaining bolts . . .

5.5c . . . and maneuver the air deflector out of the frame

deflector out from under the frame cross-member **(see illustration)**.

6 Pull the spark plug caps off the spark plugs and using a deep socket type wrench, unscrew them from the cylinder head **(see illustrations)**. Lay the plugs out in relation to their cylinder number; if any plug shows up a problem it will then be easy to identify the troublesome cylinder.

7 Inspect the electrodes for wear. Both the center and side electrodes should have square edges and the side electrode should be of uniform thickness. Look for excessive deposits and evidence of a cracked or chipped insulator around the center electrode. Compare your spark plugs to the color spark plug reading chart at the end of the manual.

Check the threads, the washer and the ceramic insulator body for cracks and other damage.

8 If the electrodes are not excessively worn, and if the deposits can be easily removed with a wire brush, the plugs can be regapped and re-used (if no cracks or chips are visible in the insulator). If in doubt concerning the condition of the plugs, replace them with new ones, as the expense is minimal.

9 Cleaning spark plugs by sandblasting is permitted, provided you clean the plugs with a high flash-point solvent afterwards.

10 Before installing new plugs, make sure they are the correct type and heat range. Check the gap between the electrodes, as they are not preset. For best results, use a

wire-type gauge rather than a flat (feeler) gauge to check the gap. If the gap must be adjusted, bend the side electrode only and be very careful not to chip or crack the insulator nose **(see illustrations)**. Make sure the washer is in place before installing each plug.

11 Since the cylinder head is made of aluminum, which is soft and easily damaged, thread the plugs into the heads by hand. Since the plugs are recessed, slip a short length of hose over the end of the plug to use as a tool to thread it into place. The hose will grip the plug well enough to turn it, but will start to slip if the plug begins to cross-thread in the hole - this will prevent damaged threads and the resultant repair costs.

12 Once the plugs are finger-tight, the job can be finished with a socket. If a torque wrench is available, tighten the spark plugs to the specified torque listed in this Chapter's Specifications. If you do not have a torque wrench, tighten the plugs finger-tight (until the washers bottom on the cylinder head) then use a wrench to tighten them an additional 1/4 turn. Regardless of the method used, do not over-tighten them.

13 Reconnect the spark plug caps and reinstall all disturbed components.

6 Lubrication - general

1 Since the controls, cables and various other components of a motorcycle are exposed to the elements, they should be lubricated periodically to ensure safe and trouble-free operation.

2 The footpegs, clutch and brake lever, brake pedal, gearshift lever linkage (where applicable) and side stand pivots should be lubricated frequently. In order for the lubricant to be applied where it will do the most good, the component should be disassembled. However, if chain and cable lubricant is being used, it can be applied to the pivot joint gaps and will usually work its way into the areas where friction occurs. If motor oil or light

5.6a Pull the spark plug caps out of the valve cover . . .

5.6b . . . and unscrew the plugs using a long extension passed down through the frame, or the tool contained in the bike's toolkit

5.10a A wire type gauge is recommended to measure spark plug electrode gap

5.10b Using a feeler gauge to measure spark plug electrode gap

5.10c Electrode gap is adjusted by bending the side electrode

grease is being used, apply it sparingly as it may attract dirt (which could cause the controls to bind or wear at an accelerated rate). **Note:** *One of the best lubricants for the control lever pivots is a dry-film lubricant (available from many sources by different names).*

3 To lubricate the cables, disconnect the relevant cable at its upper end, then lubricate the cable with a pressure lube adapter **(see illustration)**. See Chapter 4 for the choke and throttle cable removal procedures, and Chapter 2 for clutch cable removal details.

4 The speedometer cable on US 1993 and 1994 models, and UK CBR900RR-N and RR-P, should be removed from its housing and lubricated with motor oil or cable lubricant. Do not lubricate the upper few inches of the cable as the lubricant may travel up into the speedometer head.

6.3 Lubricating a cable with a pressure lube adapter (make sure the tool seats around the inner cable)

Every 8000 miles (12,000 km) or 12 months

7 Engine oil/filter - change

1 Consistent routine oil and filter changes are the single most important maintenance procedure you can perform on a motorcycle. The oil not only lubricates the internal parts of the engine, transmission and clutch, but it also acts as a coolant, a cleaner, a sealant, and a protectant. Because of these demands, the oil takes a terrific amount of abuse and should be replaced often with new oil of the recommended grade and type. Saving a little money on the difference in cost between a good oil and a cheap oil won't pay off if the engine is damaged.

2 Before changing the oil and filter, warm up the engine so the oil will drain easily. Be careful when draining the oil, as the exhaust pipes, the engine, and the oil itself can cause severe burns.

3 Put the motorcycle on its side stand and position a clean drain pan below the engine. Unscrew the oil filler cap to vent the crankcase and act as a reminder that there is no oil in the engine. Refer to Chapter 8 and remove the fairing lower section.

4 Next, remove the drain plug from the oil pan and allow the oil to drain into the pan **(see illustration)**. Discard the sealing washer on the drain plug; it should be replaced whenever the plug is removed.

5 When the engine oil has drained, reposition another drain pan under the oil filter on the front of the engine. Slacken the oil filter using a strap wrench or the Honda service tool (Pt. No. 07HAA-PJ70100) **(see illustration)**. Unscrew the filter from the oil cooler unit and empty its contents into the drain pan. If additional maintenance is planned for this time period, check or service another component while the oil is allowed to drain completely.

> ⚠ **Warning: Take great care not to burn your hands on the exhaust system.**

6 Clean the filter thread and housing on the engine with solvent or clean shop towels. Wipe any remaining oil off the filter sealing area of the oil cooler unit.

7 Slip a new sealing washer over the drain plug **(see illustration)**. Fit the plug to the oil pan and tighten it to the specified torque setting. Avoid overtightening, as damage to the oil pan will result.

8 Apply a smear of clean oil to the sealing ring of the new filter and screw it into position on the engine **(see illustration)**. Tighten the filter firmly by hand. If access to the special Honda service tool can be gained (see Step 5), the filter can be tightened to the specified torque setting.

9 Before refilling the engine, check the old oil carefully. If the oil was drained into a clean pan, small pieces of metal or other material can be easily detected. If the oil is very metallic colored, then the engine is experiencing wear from break-in (new engine) or from insufficient lubrication. If there are flakes or chips of metal in the oil, then something is drastically wrong internally and the engine will have to be disassembled for inspection and repair.

10 If there are pieces of fiber-like material in the oil, the clutch is experiencing excessive wear and should be checked.

11 If inspection of the oil turns up nothing unusual, refill the crankcase to the proper level with the recommended type and amount of oil and install the filler cap. Start the engine and let it run for two or three minutes. Shut it off, wait a few minutes, then check the oil level. If necessary, add more oil to bring the level up to the upper mark (see Section 3). Check around the drain plug and filter for leaks.

7.4 Engine oil drain plug location

7.5 Use a strap wrench to slacken off the oil filter if the Honda tool is not available

7.7 Always use a new sealing washer on the oil drain plug

7.8 Apply oil to the filter sealing ring before installation

1

8.5a Fuel tank gauze filter can be withdrawn for cleaning

8.5b Always use a new O-ring between the tank and fuel tap to prevent leaks

8.6 Fuel filter is fitted in pipe between tank and pump; arrow on filter body must point in direction of fuel flow

12 The old oil drained from the engine cannot be re-used and should be disposed of properly. Check with your local refuse disposal company, disposal facility or environmental agency to see whether they will accept the used oil for recycling. Don't pour used oil into drains or onto the ground.

 Check the old oil carefully - if it is very metallic coloured, then the engine is experiencing wear from break-in (new engine) or from insufficient lubrication. If there are flakes or chips of metal in the oil, then something is drastically wrong internally and the engine will have to be disassembled for inspection and repair. If there are pieces of fibre-like material in the oil, the clutch is experiencing excessive wear and should be checked.

 8 Fuel system - checks and filter cleaning/replacement

⚠️ *Warning: Gasoline (petrol) is extremely flammable, so take extra precautions when you work on any part of the fuel system. Don't smoke or allow open flames or bare light bulbs near the work area, and don't work in a garage where a natural gas-type appliance (such as a water heater or clothes dryer) is present. If you spill any fuel on your skin, rinse it off immediately with soap and water. When you perform any kind of work on the fuel system, wear safety glasses and have a fire extinguisher suitable for a Class B type fire (flammable liquids) on hand.*

Checks

1 Remove the fuel tank (see Chapter 4) and check the breather hose (not California models), the overflow hose and the vacuum hose (US 1996 through 1999 models and UK T to X models only) for signs of damage and

deterioration. Check all the fuel hoses for signs of leakage. Replace any hoses which are cracked or deteriorated.

2 If the carburetor gaskets are leaking, the carburetors should be disassembled and rebuilt by referring to Chapter 4.

3 If the fuel tap is leaking, tightening the retaining nut may help but if leakage persists, the tap should be disassembled and repaired or replaced with a new one. On US 1996 through 1999 models and UK T to X models, check that the diaphragm cover screws are tight. To check the operation of the diaphragm, disconnect the vacuum hose from its union on the intake manifold. Turn the fuel tap ON and apply a suction or vacuum to the hose. Fuel should flow from the tap. If it doesn't, or the flow is restricted, remove the tap and replace the diaphragm (see Chapter 4).

4 On models so equipped, check that there is no fuel leakage from the fuel pump.

Filter cleaning/replacement

5 The fuel filter, which is attached to the fuel tap, may become clogged and should be removed and cleaned periodically. In order to clean the filter, the fuel tank must be drained and the fuel tap removed as described in Chapter 4. Slip the filter out of the fuel tank and clean it thoroughly; if severely blocked or torn, replace the filter with a new one **(see illustration)**. Install a new O-ring on the fuel tap pipe, followed by the filter and install the

9.1 Battery terminals must be clean, free of corrosion and the leads securely fastened

fuel tap as described in Chapter 4 **(see illustration)**.

6 On US 1993 through 1995 models and UK N to S models, an in-line fuel filter is fitted in the fuel pipe from the tap to the fuel pump **(see illustration)**. Remove the fuel tank (see Chapter 4). Have a rag handy to soak up any residual fuel and disconnect the pipes from the filter. Slip the filter out of its bracket and install the new filter so that its arrow points in the direction of fuel flow (i.e. towards the pump). Secure the pipes to the filter with the retaining clips. Install the fuel tank (see Chapter 4), turn the tap ON and check that there are no fuel leaks.

9 Battery - check

1 All models covered in this manual are fitted with a sealed battery, and therefore require no maintenance. **Note:** *Do not attempt to remove the battery caps to check the electrolyte level or battery specific gravity. Removal will damage the caps, resulting in electrolyte leakage and battery damage.* All that should be done is to check that its terminals are clean and tight and that the casing is not damaged or leaking **(see illustration)**. See Chapter 9 for further details

2 If the machine is not in regular use, disconnect the battery and give it a refresher charge every month to six weeks, as described in Chapter 9.

10 Throttle and choke operation/grip freeplay - check and adjustment

Throttle cables

1 Make sure the throttle grip rotates easily from fully closed to fully open with the front wheel turned at various angles. The grip should return automatically from fully open to fully closed when released.

2 If the throttle sticks, this is probably due to a cable fault. Remove the cables as described

10.3 Throttle cable freeplay is measured in terms of twistgrip rotation at the grip flange (arrow)

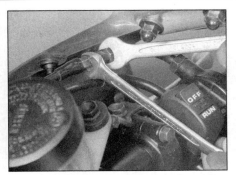

10.4 Take up throttle cable freeplay at the upper adjuster . . .

10.5 . . . or at the lower adjuster on the throttle pulley (arrow)

in Chapter 4 and lubricate them as described in Section 15. Install each cable, routing them so they take the smoothest route possible. If this fails to improve the operation of the throttle, the cables must be replaced. Note that in very rare cases the fault could lie in the carburetors rather than the cables, necessitating the removal of the carburetors and inspection of the throttle linkage (see Chapter 4).

3 With the throttle operating smoothly, check for a small amount of freeplay at the grip **(see illustration)**. The amount of freeplay in the throttle cables, measured in terms of twistgrip rotation, should be as given in this Chapter's Specifications. If adjustment is necessary, adjust idle speed first (see Section 17).

4 Slacken the locknut on the cable upper adjuster and rotate the adjuster until the correct amount of freeplay is obtained, then tighten the locknut **(see illustration)**. If it is not possible to obtain the correct freeplay with the upper adjuster, it will also be necessary to make adjustment at the lower adjuster, situated on the carburetors.

5 To gain access to the lower adjuster remove the fuel tank and air filter housing as described in Chapter 4 **(see illustration)**. Screw the upper cable adjuster in to obtain the maximum possible freeplay, then slacken the lower adjuster locknut and set the cable freeplay using first the lower adjuster and then, if necessary, the upper adjuster. Once the freeplay is correct tighten the locknuts securely.

6 Check that the throttle twistgrip operates smoothly and snaps shut quickly when released.

> ⚠ **Warning: Turn the handlebars all the way through their travel with the engine idling. Idle speed should not change. If it does, the cables may be routed incorrectly. Correct this condition before riding the bike (see Chapter 4).**

Choke cable

7 Remove the fuel tank and air filter housing as described in Chapter 4. Operate the choke knob whilst observing the movement of the carburetor choke mechanism on the right side of the carburetor assembly. The mechanism should extend smoothly when the knob is pulled, and return home fully when the knob is returned.

8 If the choke mechanism does not operate smoothly this is probably due to a cable fault. Remove the cable as described in Chapter 4 and lubricate it as described in Section 15. Install the cable, routing it so it takes the smoothest route possible. If this fails to improve the operation of the choke, the cable must be replaced. Note that in very rare cases the fault could lie in the carburetors rather than the cable, necessitating the removal of the carburetors and inspection of the choke plungers as described in Chapter 4.

9 With the choke mechanism operating smoothly check for a small amount of freeplay at the base of the choke knob **(see illustration)**. There is no specific setting for freeplay, but a

small amount should exist to ensure that the choke mechanism is fully off. On later models no adjustment of the cable is possible (the outer cable end fitting clips in position) but on early models the cable can be adjusted by slackening the clamping screw and repositioning the outer cable in the clamp **(see illustration)**. Once the cable is correctly positioned, securely tighten the clamping screw.

10 Once the choke mechanism is know to operating correctly, install the air filter housing and fuel tank as described in Chapter 4.

---

11 Spark plug gaps - check and adjustment (UK models)

See Section 5 "Spark plug gaps - check and adjustment (US models)" under the 4000 mile (6000 km) or 6 months heading for details

12 Spark plugs - replacement (US models)

See Section 5 "Spark plug gaps - check and adjustment (US models)" under the 4000 mile (6000 km) or 6 months heading for details

13 Carburetor synchronization - check and adjustment

> ⚠ **Warning: Gasoline (petrol) is extremely flammable, so take extra precautions when you work on any part of the fuel system. Don't smoke or allow open flames or bare light bulbs near the work area, and don't work in a garage where a natural gas-type appliance (such as a water heater or clothes dryer) is present. If you spill any fuel on your skin, rinse it off immediately with soap and water. When you perform any kind of work on the fuel system, wear safety glasses and have a fire extinguisher suitable for a Class B type fire (flammable liquids) on hand.**

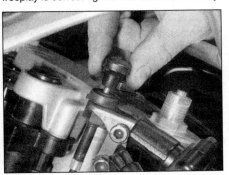

10.9a A small amount of freeplay should be felt at the choke knob

10.9b On early models, the choke cable can be adjusted by slackening the clamping screw (arrow) and repositioning the outer cable

1

13.9a Remove rubber cap (arrow) from vacuum take-off tube on No. 1 cylinder intake manifold - US 1993 through 1995 models (except California models) and UK N to S models

13.9b Carburetor synchronization equipment connections - US 1993 through 1995 models (except California models) and UK N to S models

13.15 Carburetor synchronization screws (arrows) - cylinder numbers circled (air filter housing removed for clarity)

Warning: Take great care not to burn your hand on the hot engine unit when accessing the gauge take-off points on the intake manifolds.

1 Carburetor synchronization is simply the process of adjusting the carburetors so they pass the same amount of fuel/air mixture to each cylinder. This is done by measuring the vacuum produced in each cylinder. Carburetors that are out of synchronization will result in decreased fuel mileage, increased engine temperature, less than ideal throttle response and higher vibration levels.

2 To properly synchronize the carburetors, you will need some sort of vacuum gauge set-up, preferably with a gauge for each cylinder, or a mercury manometer, which is a calibrated tube arrangement that utilizes columns of mercury to indicate engine vacuum. Adaptors will be required to screw into the intake ports holes - see Step 9 or 10.

3 A manometer can be purchased from a motorcycle dealer or accessory shop and should have the necessary rubber hoses supplied with it for hooking into the vacuum hose fittings/adaptors.

4 A vacuum gauge setup can also be purchased from a dealer or fabricated from commonly available hardware and automotive vacuum gauges.

5 The manometer is the more reliable and accurate instrument, and for that reason is preferred over the vacuum gauge setup; however, since the mercury used in the manometer is a liquid, and extremely toxic, extra precautions must be taken during use and storage of the instrument.

6 Because of the nature of the synchronization procedure and the need for special instruments, most owners leave the task to a dealer service department or a reputable motorcycle repair shop.

7 Start the engine and let it run until it reaches normal operating temperature, then shut it off.

8 Remove the fuel tank as described in Chapter 4, and the fairing middle sections as described in Chapter 8.

9 On US 1993 through 1995 (except California models) models and UK N to S

models, remove the vacuum take-off tube rubber cap from the No. 1 cylinder intake manifold **(see illustration)**. Grip the end of the cap only, otherwise the take-off tube may distort. Remove the vacuum take-off screws from the underside of the intake manifolds for cylinders 2, 3 and 4. Screw the gauge adaptors into the intake manifolds of cylinders 2, 3 and 4, then connect the gauge tubes to No. 1 cylinder take-off tube and the three adaptors **(see illustration)**. Make sure there are no leaks in the setup, as false readings will result.

10 On California 1993 through 1995 models, disconnect the EVAP tube from cylinder No. 1 intake manifold and the PAIR tube from cylinder No. 3 intake manifold. Remove the vacuum take-off screws from the underside of the intake manifolds of cylinders 2 and 4 and screw the gauge adaptors in their place. Connect the gauge tubes to the adaptors of cylinders 2 and 4 and the tube unions of cylinders 1 and 3. Make sure there are no leaks in the setup, as false readings will result.

11 On US 1996 through 1999 models and UK T to X models, remove the vacuum take-off screws from the underside of the intake manifolds for cylinders 1, 2 and 4 and screw the gauge adaptors in their place. Disconnect the fuel tap vacuum hose from cylinder 3 manifold. Connect the gauge tubes to No. 3 cylinder take-off tube and the three adaptors. Make sure there are no leaks in the setup, as false readings will result.

12 Arrange a temporary fuel supply, either by using a small temporary tank or by using extra long fuel pipes to the now remote fuel tank on a nearby bench. Note that if the fuel tank is used, a three-way union must be fitted to the No. 3 cylinder gauge tube so that the fuel tap vacuum hose can be incorporated into the system. Otherwise the diaphragm in the fuel tap will remain closed and no fuel will flow from the tap.

13 Start the engine and make sure the idle speed is correct. If it isn't, adjust it (see Section 17). If the gauges are fitted with damping adjustment, set this so that the needle flutter is just eliminated but so that

they can still respond to small changes in pressure.

14 The vacuum readings for all of the cylinders should be the same, or at least within the tolerance listed in this Chapter's Specifications. If the vacuum readings vary, adjust as necessary. Cylinder No. 3 is the base carburetor and the other carburetors should be balanced to it's setting.

15 The carburetors are adjusted by the three screws situated between each carburetor, in the throttle linkage **(see illustration)**. The screws are accessible from underneath the rear of the air filter housing. **Note:** Do not press down on the screws whilst adjusting them, otherwise a false reading will be obtained. When all the carburetors are synchronized, open and close the throttle quickly to settle the linkage, and recheck the gauge readings, readjusting if necessary.

16 When the adjustment is complete, recheck the vacuum readings and idle speed, then stop the engine. Remove the vacuum gauge or manometer. Unscrew the adaptors and fit the screws, tightening them securely. Install the rubber cap over No. 1 cylinder's take-off tube on US 1993 through 1995 models (except California models) and UK N to S models. On California 1993 through 1995 models, reconnect the EVAP tube to cylinder No. 1 intake manifold and the PAIR tube to cylinder No. 3 intake manifold. On US 1996 through 1999 models and UK T to X models, reconnect the fuel tap vacuum hose to cylinder No. 3 intake manifold.

17 Detach the temporary fuel supply and install the fuel tank and fairing sections.

14 Pulse secondary air injection (PAIR) and Evaporative emission control (EVAP) - check

1 These systems are installed on California models to conform to stringent state emission control standards. Both systems are explained in greater detail in Chapter 4.

2 To begin the inspection of the system, remove the fuel tank and fairing middle

15.8 Radiator pressure cap is accessed after removing upper fairing right inner panel

16.5 Rear brake switch knurled ring is accessed behind rider's footpeg bracket (arrow)

16.6 Ensure arrow and notch align on front brake lever span adjuster

sections (see Chapters 4 and 8). Refer to the hose routing diagram on the air filter housing cover and trace the hoses between the system components, looking for signs of cracking, perishing or other damage. Any such hoses must be replaced.

3 Check the EVAP canister, mounted behind the carburetors on the left side of the frame, for damage or fuel leakage.

15 Cooling system - check

> **Warning: The engine must be cool before beginning this procedure.**

1 Check the coolant level (see "Daily (pre-ride) checks").
2 Remove the left and right middle fairing sections as described in Chapter 8.
3 The entire cooling system should be checked for evidence of leakage. Examine each rubber coolant hose along its entire length, including those which link the oil cooler to the engine and water pump. Look for cracks, abrasions and other damage. Squeeze each hose at various points. They should feel firm, yet pliable, and return to their original shape when released. If they are dried out or hard, replace them with new ones.
4 Check for evidence of leaks at each cooling system joint. Tighten the hose clips carefully to prevent future leaks.
5 Check the radiator for leaks and other damage. Leaks in the radiator leave telltale scale deposits or coolant stains on the outside of the core below the leak. If leaks are noted, remove the radiator (see Chapter 3) and have it repaired at a radiator shop or replace it with a new one.
Caution: Do not use a liquid leak stopping compound to try to repair leaks.
6 Check the radiator fins for mud, dirt and insects, which may impede the flow of air through the radiator. If the fins are dirty, force water or low pressure compressed air through the fins from the backside. If the fins are bent or distorted, straighten them carefully with a screwdriver.

7 Remove the right inner panel from the upper fairing (see Chapter 8).
8 Remove the pressure cap by turning it counterclockwise (anti-clockwise) until it reaches a stop **(see illustration)**. If you hear a hissing sound (indicating there is still pressure in the system), wait until it stops. Now press down on the cap and continue turning the cap until it can be removed. Check the condition of the coolant in the system. If it is rust-colored or if accumulations of scale are visible, drain, flush and refill the system with new coolant (See Section 20). Check the cap seal for cracks and other damage. If in doubt about the pressure cap's condition, have it tested by a Honda dealer or replace it with a new one. Install the cap by turning it clockwise until it reaches the first stop then push down on the cap and continue turning until it can turn further.
9 Check the antifreeze content of the coolant with an antifreeze hydrometer. Sometimes coolant looks like it's in good condition, but might be too weak to offer adequate protection. If the hydrometer indicates a weak mixture, drain, flush and refill the system (see Section 20).
10 Start the engine and let it reach normal operating temperature, then check for leaks again. As the coolant temperature increases, the fan should come on automatically and the temperature should begin to drop. If it does not, refer to Chapter 3 and check the fan and fan circuit carefully.
11 If the coolant level is consistently low, and no evidence of leaks can be found, have the entire system pressure checked by a Honda dealer.
12 Periodically, check the drainage hole on the underside of the water pump cover (see Chapter 3). Leakage from this hole indicates failure of the pump's mechanical seal.

16 Brake system - general check

1 A routine general check of the brakes will ensure that any problems are discovered and remedied before the rider's safety is jeopardized.
2 Check the brake lever and pedal for loose

connections, excessive play, bends, and other damage. Replace any damaged parts with new ones (see Chapter 7).
3 Make sure all brake fasteners are tight. Check the brake pads for wear (see Section 5) and make sure the fluid level in the reservoirs is correct (see Section 3). Look for leaks at the hose connections and check for cracks in the hoses. If the lever or pedal is spongy, bleed the brakes as described in Chapter 7.
4 Make sure the brake light operates when the front brake lever is depressed. The front brake light switch is not adjustable. If it fails to operate properly, replace it with a new one (see Chapter 9).
5 Make sure the brake light is activated just before the rear brake pedal takes effect. If adjustment is necessary, hold the switch and turn the knurled adjusting ring on the switch body until the brake light is activated when required **(see illustration)**. If the switch doesn't operate the brake lights, check it as described in Chapter 9.
6 The front brake lever incorporates a span adjuster to cater for different hand sizes. Rotate the knurled wheel on the lever to adjust its position, noting that the arrow on the lever must align exactly with the notch of the knurled wheel **(see illustration)**.

17 Headlight aim - check and adjustment

Note: *An improperly adjusted headlight may cause problems for oncoming traffic or provide poor, unsafe illumination of the road ahead. Before adjusting the headlight aim, be sure to consult with local traffic laws and regulations. For UK readers, refer to MOT Test Checks in the Reference section of this manual.*

1 The headlight beam can adjusted both horizontally and vertically. Before making any adjustment, check that the tyre pressures are correct and the suspension is adjusted as required. Make any adjustments to the headlight aim with the machine on level ground, with the fuel tank half full and with an assistant sitting on the seat. If the bike is

17.2a Headlight aim adjusters are situated at the top outer corner of each unit . . .

17.2b . . . and between the headlight units at the bottom (later type headlight shown)

usually ridden with a passenger on the back, have a second assistant to do this.

2 Adjustment is made on the back on the headlight unit, using the adjusters at the top corners and those between the individual headlights at the bottom **(see illustrations)**.

3 On US 1993 through 1997 models and UK N to V models, horizontal adjustment is made by turning the upper adjusters in the top corners (rotate clockwise to move the beam to the right, anti-clockwise to move it to the left) and vertical adjustment is made by turning the lower adjusters situated between the headlights (rotate clockwise to raise the beam, anti-clockwise to lower it).

4 On US 1998 and 1999 models and UK W and X models, horizontal adjustment is made by turning the lower adjusters situated between the headlights (rotate clockwise to move the beam to the right, anti-clockwise to move it to the left) and vertical adjustment is made by turning the upper adjusters in the top corners (rotate clockwise to raise the beam, anti-clockwise to lower it).

5 Due to the heat build-up in the headlight assembly on US 1995 through 1999 models and UK R to X models (with plastic lens), vents are provided at several points in the back of the unit. Short rubber tubes fit over the vent holes and incorporate plastic mesh filters to prevent dust entering the headlight; check that these filters are not obstructed.

18 Sidestand - check

1 The sidestand return spring must be capable of retracting the stand fully and holding the stand retracted when the motorcycle is in use. If the spring is sagged or broken it must be replaced.

2 Lubricate the sidestand pivot regularly (see Section 6).

3 The sidestand switch prevents the motorcycle being started if the stand is extended. Check its operation by shifting the transmission into neutral, retracting the stand and starting the engine. Pull in the clutch lever and select a gear. Extend the sidestand. The engine should stop as the sidestand is extended. If the sidestand switch does not operate as described, check its circuit (see Chapter 9).

19 Suspension - checks

1 The suspension components must be maintained in top operating condition to ensure rider safety. Loose, worn or damaged suspension parts decrease the vehicle's stability and control.

Front suspension

2 While standing alongside the motorcycle, apply the front brake and push on the handlebars to compress the forks several times. See if they move up-and-down smoothly without binding. If binding is felt, the forks should be disassembled and inspected as described in Chapter 6.

3 Carefully inspect the area around the fork seals for any signs of fork oil leakage. If leakage is evident, the seals must be replaced as described in Chapter 6.

4 Although not specified as a maintenance item, the fork oil will degrade over a period of time and require renewal. This necessitates removal of the fork legs as described in Chapter 6.

5 Check the tightness of all suspension nuts and bolts to be sure none have worked loose.

Rear suspension

6 Inspect the rear shock for fluid leakage and tightness of its mountings. If leakage is found, the shock should be replaced.

7 Position the motorcycle on an auxiliary stand so that the rear wheel is off the ground **(see illustration 23.2)**. Grab the swingarm on each side, just ahead of the axle. Rock the swingarm from side to side - there should be no discernible movement at the rear. If there's a little movement or a slight clicking can be heard, make sure the swingarm pivot shaft locknut is tight. If the pivot nut is tight but movement is still noticeable, the swingarm pivot adjustment or bearings, or the suspension linkage bearings require attention (see Chapter 6).

8 Inspect the tightness of the rear suspension nuts and bolts.

20 Steering head bearings - freeplay check and adjustment

1 This motorcycle is equipped with caged ball type steering head bearings which can become dented, rough or loose during normal use of the machine. In extreme cases, worn or loose steering head bearings can cause steering wobble - a condition that is potentially dangerous.

Check

2 A auxiliary stand will be needed to hold the motorcycle securely upright and allow the front wheel to be raised off the ground **(see illustration)**.

3 Point the wheel straight-ahead and slowly move the handlebars from side-to-side. Dents or roughness in the bearing races will be felt and the bars will not move smoothly.

4 Next, grasp the wheel and try to move it forward and backward **(see illustration)**. Any looseness in the steering head bearings will be felt as front-to-rear movement of the fork legs. If play is felt in the bearings, adjust the steering head as follows.

20.2 Use of an auxiliary stand will enable the steering head bearings to be checked - ensure that the rear of the machine is weighted or tied down so that the front wheel is off the ground

20.4 Grasp the front wheel and try to pull it back and forth; if it moves, the steering head bearings are loose and in need of adjustment

20.5 Remove the fork clamp bolt (arrow) from each side of the top triple clamp

20.6 Remove the steering stem nut and lift off the top triple clamp

20.8 Bend down the lockwasher tabs to enable the locknut to be unscrewed

HAYNES HiNT *Freeplay in the fork due to worn bushes can be misinterpreted for steering head bearing play - do not confuse the two.*

Adjustment

5 Remove the front fork clamp bolts in the top triple clamp **(see illustration)**. The handlebar clamp bolts can remain in place.
6 Prise the plug out (where fitted) of the steering stem nut and remove the nut **(see illustration)**.
7 Gently ease the top triple clamp upwards off the fork tubes.
8 Prise the lockwasher tabs out of the slots in the locknut and adjuster nut **(see illustration)**. Unscrew the locknut using a C-spanner and discard the lockwasher; a new lockwasher must be used on reassembly.
9 Slacken the adjuster nut slightly until pressure is just released, then tighten it until all freeplay is removed, yet the steering is able to move freely **(see illustration)**. Note that Honda specify a torque setting for the adjuster nut - if this is applied, check afterwards that the steering is still able to move freely from side to side. The object is to set the adjuster nut so that the bearings are under a very light loading, just enough to remove any freeplay.
Caution: Take great care not to apply excessive pressure because this will cause premature failure of the bearings.
10 With the bearings correctly adjusted, fit a

new lockwasher over the steering stem **(see illustration)**. Bend down two opposite lock washer tabs (the shorter tabs on the washer) into the grooves of the adjuster nut.
11 Hold the adjuster nut to prevent it from moving, then install the locknut and tighten it finger-tight. Tighten the locknut approximately 90° more until its slots align with the remaining lockwasher tabs **(see illustration)**. Secure the locknut in position by bending up the lock washer tabs into its slots **(see illustration)**.
12 Fit the top triple clamp to the steering stem, then install the nut and tighten it and both the fork clamp bolts to their specified torque settings (see Chapter 6). Fit the plug (where fitted) into the stem nut.
13 Check the bearing adjustment as described above and re-adjust if necessary.

21 Nuts, bolts and fasteners - check

1 Since vibration of the machine tends to loosen fasteners, all nuts, bolts, screws, etc. should be periodically checked for proper tightness.
2 Pay particular attention to the following:
   Spark plugs
   Engine oil drain plug
   Gearshift lever
   Footpegs and side stand
   Engine mounting bolts
   Shock absorber mounting bolts

Handlebar and triple clamp bolts
Rear suspension linkage bolts
Front axle and clamp bolts
Rear axle nut
Exhaust system bolts/nuts
3 If a torque wrench is available, use it along with the torque specifications at the beginning of this, or other, Chapters.

22 Wheels/tires - general check

Wheels

1 The cast wheels used on this machine are

20.9 Use a C-spanner to adjust steering head bearing freeplay

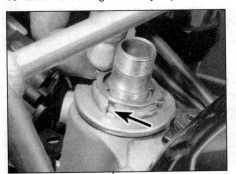

20.10 Always use a new lockwasher and bend its shorter tabs down into the adjuster nut slots (arrow)

20.11a Tighten the locknut . . .

20.11b . . . and bend the remaining lockwasher tabs up into the locknut slots

25.2a Remove its nine retaining screws . . .

25.2b . . . and lift off the air filter cover

25.3 Air filter element is simply lifted out of the housing

virtually maintenance free, but they should be kept clean and checked periodically for cracks and other damage. Never attempt to repair damaged cast wheels; they must be replaced with new ones.

2 Check the valve rubber for signs of damage or deterioration and have it replaced if necessary. Also, make sure the valve stem cap is in place and tight. If it is missing, install a new one made of metal or hard plastic.

Tires

3 Refer to the Daily (pre-ride) checks at the beginning of this Manual.

23 Drive chain slider - check

See Section 1 *"Drive chain and sprockets - check, adjustment and lubrication" under the 600 mile (1000 km) heading for details*

24 Exhaust system - check

1 Periodically check all of the exhaust system

joints for leaks and loose fasteners. The lower fairing section and middle sections will have to be removed to do this properly (see Chapter 8). If tightening the fasteners fails to stop any leaks, replace the gaskets with new ones (a procedure which requires disassembly of the system). Refer to Chapter 4 for further information.

2 The exhaust pipe flange nuts at the cylinder heads are especially prone to loosening, which could cause damage to the head. Check them frequently and keep them tight.

Every 12,000 miles (18,000 km) or 18 months

25 Air filter element - change

1 Remove the fuel tank (see Chapter 4).
2 Undo the nine retaining screws and remove the cover from the air filter housing **(see illustrations)**.
3 Lift out the air filter element **(see illustration)**.
4 Wipe out the housing with a clean rag, particularly the drain tray at the forward end into which the sediment from crankcase vapors collects.
5 Fit the new element to the housing, making sure it is the correct way up. Install the cover and securely tighten its retaining screws.
6 Install the fuel tank (see Chapter 4).

26 Evaporative emission control system (EVAP) (California models only) - check

See Section 14 *"Pulse secondary air injection (PAIR) system and Evaporative emission control system (EVAP) (California models only) - check" under the 8000 mile (12,000 km) or 12 month heading for details.*

27 Brake fluid change

1 The brake fluid should be replaced at the prescribed interval or whenever a master cylinder or caliper overhaul is carried out. Refer to the brake bleeding section in Chapter 7, noting that all old fluid must be pumped from the fluid reservoir and hydraulic line before filling with new fluid.

> **HAYNES HINT** *Old brake fluid is invariably much darker in color than new fluid, making it easy to see when all old fluid has been expelled from the system.*

Every 16,000 miles (24,000 km) or two years

28 Valve clearances - check and adjustment

1 The engine must be completely cool for this maintenance procedure, so let the machine sit overnight before beginning.

2 Remove the valve cover (see Chapter 2).
3 Refer to Chapter 2 *"Cam chain tensioner - removal and installation"* and retract the tensioner plunger; there is no need to remove the tensioner.
4 Remove the fairing lower section (see Chapter 8). Unscrew the center cap to reveal the bolt head on the right end of the

crankshaft. Using a socket wrench on this bolt, rotate the engine clockwise so that the line next to the T mark on the ignition rotor aligns exactly with the notch in the cover **(see illustrations)**. Check that the IN and EX marks on the camshaft sprockets are pointing outwards (in the 9 o'clock and 3 o'clock positions respectively); if they face each other,

28.4a Remove the center cap from the crankshaft right end cover and rotate the crankshaft using a socket and extension bar

28.4b Position the crankshaft so that the line next to the T mark is aligned with the notch (arrow) in the cover . . .

28.4c . . . and the IN and EX marks (arrows) on the camshaft sprockets are level with the cylinder head surface

turn the crankshaft 360° and realign the T mark **(see illustration)**.

5 Draw the valve positions on a piece of paper, numbering both the intake and exhaust valves from 1 to 8, from the left end of the engine.

6 With the engine in this position, the intake valves of cylinders 1 and 3 can be checked. Insert a feeler gauge of the correct thickness (see Specifications) between each cam lobe and follower and check that it is a firm sliding fit **(see illustration)**. If it is not, use the feeler gauges to obtain the exact clearance.

7 Rotate the crankshaft clockwise half a turn (180°) so that the single scribed line on the ignition rotor is in the 12 o'clock position **(see illustration)**. The exhaust valves of cylinders 2

and 4 can now be checked. **Note:** *The clearance is different for the exhaust valves.*

8 Turn the crankshaft clockwise half a turn (180°) and realign the line next to the T mark with the notch. In this position check the intake valve clearances for cylinders 2 and 4.

9 Finally, turn the crankshaft a further half turn (180°) clockwise and position the single scribed line in the 12 o'clock position. Check the exhaust valve clearances on cylinders 1 and 3.

10 If any of the clearances need to be adjusted the relevant camshaft(s) must be removed as described in Chapter 2.

11 With the camshaft removed, using a magnet, lift the follower on the valve to be adjusted out of the cylinder head and remove the shim. Note that the shim is likely to stick to the inside of the follower so take great care not to lose it as the follower is removed. If more than one follower and shim is to be removed, make sure they are not interchanged.

12 The shim size should be stamped on its face, however, it is recommended that the shim is measured to check that it has not worn **(see illustrations)**. The size marking is in the form of a three figure number, e.g. 180 indicating that the shim is 1.800 mm thick. Where the number does not equal a shim thickness, it should be rounded up or down, e.g. 182 or 183 both indicate that the shim is 1.825 mm thick. Shims are available in 0.025

mm increments from 1.200 to 2.800 mm. The new shim thickness required can then be calculated as follows. **Note:** *Always aim to get the clearance at the mid-point of the specified range.*

13 If the valve clearance was less than specified, subtract the measured clearance from the specified clearance then deduct the result from the original shim thickness. For example:

Sample calculation - intake valve clearance too small

> Clearance measured (A) - 0.08 mm
> Specified clearance (B) - 0.16 mm (0.13 to 0.19 mm)
> Difference (B - A) - 0.08 mm
> Shim thickness fitted - 2.475 mm
> Correct shim thickness required - 2.475 - 0.08 = 2.395 mm

14 If the valve clearance was greater then specified, subtract the specified clearance from the measured clearance, and add the result to the thickness of the original shim. For example:

Sample calculation (early engine) - exhaust valve clearance too large

> Clearance measured (A) - 0.35 mm
> Specified clearance (B) - 0.22 mm (0.19 to 0.25 mm)
> Difference (A - B) - 0.13 mm
> Shim thickness fitted - 1.975 mm
> Correct shim thickness required - 1.975 + 0.13 = 2.105 mm

1

28.6 Measuring a valve clearance

28.7 Rotate the crankshaft through 180° so that the index line (arrow) on the ignition rotor is vertical

28.12a Shim thickness is indicated by three numbers stamped on its surface; in the example shown 205 indicates that the shim is 2.050 mm thick

28.12b Measuring shim thickness

15 Obtain the correct thickness shims from your Honda dealer.

16 Install the shim in position on top of the relevant valve, making sure it is correctly seated in the valve spring retainer.

17 Lubricate the followers with engine oil and insert them in their respective positions in the cylinder head, making sure each one squarely enters its bore.

18 Install the camshaft(s) as described in Chapter 2.

19 Rotate the crankshaft a few times, to settle all disturbed components, and recheck all valve clearances as described above. If necessary, repeat the adjustment procedure.

20 Release the stopper key from the cam chain tensioner. Install a new sealing washer on the tension bolt and tighten the bolt securely.

21 Install the valve cover as described in Chapter 2.

22 Apply a smear of oil to the crankshaft cap O-ring and tighten the cap to the specified torque setting.

23 Install all the remaining components in a reverse of the removal sequence.

29 Spark plugs - replacement (UK models)

See Section 5 "Spark plug gaps - check and adjustment (US models)" under the 4000 mile (6000 km) or 6 months heading for details

Every 24,000 miles (36,000 km) or three years

30 Cooling system - draining, flushing and refilling

Warning: Allow the engine to cool completely before performing this maintenance operation. Also, don't allow antifreeze to come into contact with your skin or the painted surfaces of the motorcycle. Rinse off spills immediately with plenty of water. Antifreeze is highly toxic if ingested. Never leave antifreeze lying around in an open container or in puddles on the floor; children and pets are attracted by its sweet smell and may drink it. Check with local authorities (councils) about disposing of antifreeze. Many communities have collection centers which will see that antifreeze is disposed of safely. Antifreeze is also combustible, so don't store it near open flames.

Draining

1 Remove the fairing lower section and right inner panel from the upper fairing (see Chapter 8).

2 Position a suitable container beneath the water pump, then remove the drain bolt and sealing washer from the pump cover **(see illustration)**.

3 Remove the pressure cap by turning it counterclockwise (anti-clockwise) until it reaches a stop. If you hear a hissing sound (indicating there is still pressure in the system),

wait until it stops. Now press down on the cap and continue turning the cap until it can be removed. As the cap is removed, the flow of coolant will increase - be prepared for this.

4 Drain the coolant reservoir. Refer to Chapter 3 for reservoir removal procedure. Wash out the reservoir with fresh water.

Flushing

5 Flush the system with clean tap water by inserting a garden hose in the radiator filler neck. Allow the water to run through the system until it is clear and flows cleanly out of the drain hole. If the radiator is extremely corroded, remove it by referring to Chapter 3 and have it cleaned at a radiator shop.

6 Clean the drain hole then install the drain bolt and sealing washer.

7 Fill the cooling system with clean water mixed with a flushing compound. Make sure the flushing compound is compatible with aluminum components, and follow the manufacturer's instructions carefully.

8 Start the engine and allow it reach normal operating temperature. Let it run for about ten minutes.

9 Stop the engine. Let it cool for a while, then cover the pressure cap with a heavy shop towel and turn it counterclockwise (anti-clockwise) to the first stop, releasing any pressure that may be present in the system. Once the hissing stops, push down on the cap and remove it completely.

10 Drain the system once again.

11 Fill the system with clean water and repeat the procedure in Steps 8 through 10.

Refilling

13 Fit a new sealing washer to the drain bolt and tighten it securely **(see illustration)**.

14 Fill the system with the proper coolant mixture (see this Chapter's Specifications) **(see illustration)**. Note: *Pour the coolant in slowly to minimise the amount of air entering the system.*

15 When the system is full (all the way up to the top of the radiator filler neck), install the pressure cap. Also top up the coolant reservoir to the UPPER level mark.

16 Start the engine and allow it to idle for 2 to 3 minutes. Flick the throttle twistgrip part open 3 or 4 times, so that the engine speed rises to approximately 4000 - 5000 rpm, then stop the engine. Any air trapped in the system should have bled back to the radiator filler neck via the small-bore air bleed hoses.

17 Let the engine cool then remove the pressure cap as described in Step 9. Check that the coolant level is still up to the radiator filler neck. If it's low, add the specified mixture until it reaches the top of the filler neck. Reinstall the cap.

18 Check the coolant level in the reservoir and top up if necessary.

19 Check the system for leaks. If all is well, install the fairing panels (Chapter 8).

20 Do not dispose of the old coolant by pouring it down the drain. Instead pour it into a heavy plastic container, cap it tightly and take it into an authorized disposal site or service station - see **Warning** at the beginning of this Section.

30.2 Remove drain bolt in water pump cover to allow cooling system to drain

30.13 Use a new sealing washer on coolant drain bolt

30.14 A funnel and hose arrangement is recommended for filling the cooling system

Non-scheduled maintenance

31 Cylinder compression - check

1 A compression test will provide useful information about an engine's condition, and if performed regularly, can give warning of trouble before any other symptoms become apparent.
2 Refer to the procedure under the *Fault Finding Equipment* heading in the Reference section of this manual. The cylinder compression figure is given in the Specifications at the beginning of this Chapter.

32 Wheel bearings - check

1 Place the motorcycle on its centre stand, or support it using an auxiliary stand, and check for any play in the bearings by pushing and pulling the wheel against the hub. Also rotate the wheel and check that it rotates smoothly. If any play is detectable in the hub, or if the wheel does not rotate smoothly (and this is not due to brake drag), the wheel bearings must be removed and inspected for wear or damage (see Chapter 7).

33 Steering head bearings - re-greasing

1 Over a period of time the grease will harden or be washed out of the bearings by incorrect use of jet washes.
2 Disassemble the steering head for re-greasing of the bearings. Refer to Chapter 6 for details.

34 Swingarm and suspension linkage bearings - re-greasing

1 Over a period of time the grease will harden or dirt will penetrate the bearing due to failed dust seals.
2 The swingarm is not equipped with grease nipples. Remove the swingarm as described in Chapter 6 for greasing of the bearings.

35 Brake caliper and master cylinder - seal replacement

1 Brake piston fluid and dust seals will deteriorate with age and must be replaced with new ones.
2 Refer to Chapter 7 and dismantle the components for seal replacement.

36 Brake hose - replacement

1 The flexible brake hoses will deteriorate with age and must be replaced with new ones.
2 Refer to Chapter 7 and disconnect the brake hoses from the master cylinders and calipers. The hoses should be replaced regardless of their condition. Always replace the banjo union sealing washers with new ones.

37 Front fork oil - change

1 The front fork oil will deteriorate with age and must be replaced.
2 Referring to Chapter 6, remove the forks (Section 6) and replace the fork oil (Section 7, Steps 1 to 7, and 25 to 30). There is no need to dismantle the forks completely.

38 Engine oil pressure - check

1 The oil pressure can be checked to ensure that the lubrication system is functioning correctly. Refer to Chapter 2 for details.

1

Notes

Chapter 2
Engine, clutch and transmission

Contents

Degrees of difficulty

Easy, suitable for novice with little experience	**Fairly easy,** suitable for beginner with some experience	**Fairly difficult,** suitable for competent DIY mechanic	**Difficult,** suitable for experienced DIY mechanic	**Very difficult,** suitable for expert DIY or professional

Specifications

General
Capacity
  US 1993 through 1995 models and UK N to S models . . . . 893 cc
  US 1996 through 1999 models and UK T to X models . . . . 919 cc
Bore
  US 1993 through 1995 models and UK N to S models . . . . 70 mm (2.76 in)
  US 1996 through 1999 models and UK T to X models . . . . 71 mm (2.80 in)
Stroke . . . . 58 mm (2.28 in)
Compression ratio
  US 1993 through 1995 models and UK N to S models 11.0:1
  US 1996 through 1999 models and UK T to X models 11.1:1

Camshafts
Intake cam lobe height
  California models
    Standard . . . . 34.940 to 35.180 mm (1.3756 to 1.3850 in)
    Service limit . . . . 34.91 mm (1.374 in)
  All other models
    Standard . . . . 36.040 to 36.280 mm (1.4189 to 1.4283 in)
    Service limit . . . . 36.01 mm (1.418 in)

Camshafts (continued)

Exhaust cam lobe height
  California models
    Standard. .... 35.100 to 35.340 mm (1.3819 to 1.3913 in)
    Service limit. .... 35.07 mm (1.381 in)
  All other models
    Standard .... 35.800 to 36.040 mm (1.4094 to 1.4189 in)
    Service limit .... 35.77 mm (1.408 in)
Camshaft bearing oil clearance
  Standard .... 0.020 to 0.062 mm (0.0008 to 0.0024 in)
  Service limit .... 0.1 mm (0.004 in)
Camshaft runout .... Less than 0.05 mm (0.002 in)
Camshaft follower OD
  Standard .... 25.978 to 25.993 mm (1.0228 to 1.0233 in)
  Service limit .... 25.97 mm (1.022 in)

Cylinder head

Maximum warpage .... 0.10 mm (0.004 in)
Cylinder head follower bore ID
  Standard .... 26.010 to 26.026 mm (1.0240 to 1.0246 in)
  Service limit .... 26.040 mm (1.0252 in)

Valves, guides and springs

Intake valve stem OD
  Standard .... 4.475 to 4.490 mm (0.1762 to 0.1768 in)
  Service limit .... 4.465 mm (0.1758 in)
Exhaust valve stem OD
  Standard .... 4.465 to 4.480 mm (0.1758 to 0.1764 in)
  Service limit .... 4.455 mm (0.1754 in)
Valve guide ID - intake and exhaust
  Standard .... 4.500 to 4.512 mm (0.1772 to 0.1776 in)
  Service limit .... 4.540 mm (0.1787 in)
Valve stem-to-guide clearance
  Intake .... 0.010 to 0.037 mm (0.0004 to 0.0015 in)
  Exhaust. .... 0.020 to 0.047 mm (0.0008 to 0.0019 in)
Valve seat width
  Standard .... 0.9 to 1.1 mm (0.035 to 0.043 in)
  Service limit .... 1.5 mm (0.06 in)
Inner valve spring free length
  Standard .... 35.77 mm (1.408 in)
  Service limit .... 34.07 mm (1.341 in)
Outer valve spring free length
  Standard .... 39.69 mm (1.563 in)
  Service limit .... 37.79 mm (1.488 in)

Clutch

Friction plate thickness
  US 1996 and 1997 models, UK T and V models
    Standard .... 2.62 to 2.78 mm (0.103 to 0.109 in)
    Service limit .... 2.30 mm (0.09 in)
  All other models
    Standard .... 2.92 to 3.08 mm (0.115 to 0.121 in)
    Service limit .... 2.60 mm (0.102 in)
Plain plate maximum warpage .... 0.3 mm (0.012 in)
Clutch spring free length
  US 1993 through 1995 models and UK N to S models
    Standard .... 45.5 mm (1.79 in)
    Service limit .... 43.6 mm (1.72 in)
  US 1996 and 1997 models and UK T and V models
    Standard .... 50.2 mm (1.98 in)
    Service limit .... 49.2 mm (1.93 in)
  US 1998 and 1999 models and UK W and X models
    Standard .... 48.8 mm (1.92 in)
    Service limit .... 47.0 mm (1.85 in)
Clutch outer drum guide bush OD
  Standard .... 34.975 to 34.991 mm (1.3770 to 1.3776 in)
  Service limit .... 34.965 mm (1.3766 in)
Clutch outer drum guide bush ID
  Standard .... 24.9935 to 25.0065 mm (0.98399 to 0.98451 in)
  Service limit .... 25.016 mm (0.9849 in)
Mainshaft OD at clutch guide bush contact point
  Standard .... 24.980 to 24.993 mm (0.9835 to 0.9840 in)
  Service limit .... 24.96 mm (0.983 in)

Lubrication system

Oil pressure . . . . 71 psi (4.9 Bars) at 6000 rpm/80°C (176°F)
Oil pump rotor tip-to-outer rotor clearance
  Standard . . . . 0.15 to 0.22 mm (0.006 to 0.009 in)
  Service limit . . . . 0.20 mm (0.008 in)
Oil pump outer rotor-to-body clearance
  Standard . . . . 0.15 to 0.22 mm (0.006 to 0.009 in)
  Service limit . . . . 0.35 mm (0.014 in)
Oil pump rotor endfloat
  Standard . . . . 0.02 to 0.07 mm (0.001 to 0.003 in)
  Service limit . . . . 0.10 mm (0.004 in)

Starter clutch

Driven gear OD
  Standard . . . . 51.699 to 51.718 mm (2.0354 to 2.0361 in)
  Service limit . . . . 51.684 mm (2.0348 in)

Shift drum and forks

Shift fork end thickness
  Standard . . . . 5.93 to 6.00 mm (0.233 to 0.236 in)
  Service limit . . . . 5.90 mm (0.232 in)
Shift fork bore ID
  Standard . . . . 12.000 to 12.021 mm (0.4724 to 0.4733 in)
  Service limit . . . . 12.030 mm (0.4736 in)
Shift fork shaft OD
  Standard . . . . 11.957 to 11.968 mm (0.4707 to 0.4712 in)
  Service limit . . . . 11.95 mm (0.470 in)

Cylinder block

Cylinder bore ID
  US 1993 through 1995 models and UK N to S models
    Standard . . . . 70.000 to 70.015 mm (2.7559 to 2.7565 in)
    Service limit . . . . 70.10 mm (2.760 in)
  US 1996 through 1999 models and UK T to X models
    Standard . . . . 71.000 to 71.015 mm (2.7953 to 2.7963 in)
    Service limit . . . . 71.10 mm (2.795 in)
Maximum ovality (out-of-round) . . . . 0.10 mm (0.004 in)
Maximum taper . . . . 0.10 mm (0.004 in)
Cylinder-to-piston clearance . . . . 0.015 to 0.050 mm (0.0006 to 0.0020 in)
Maximum gasket face warpage . . . . 0.05 mm (0.002 in)

Pistons

Piston OD (measured 15 mm (0.6 in) up from base of skirt)
  US 1993 through 1995 models and UK N to S models
    Standard . . . . 69.965 to 69.985 mm (2.7545 to 2.7553 in)
    Service limit . . . . 69.90 mm (2.752 in)
  US 1996 through 1999 models and UK T to X models
    Standard . . . . 70.965 to 70.985 mm (2.7939 to 2.7947 in)
    Service limit . . . . 70.90 mm (2.791 in)
Piston pin bore ID
  Standard . . . . 17.002 to 17.008 mm (0.6694 to 0.6696 in)
  Service limit . . . . 17.03 mm (0.670 in)
Piston pin OD
  US 1995 model, UK R and S models
    Standard . . . . 16.994 to 17.000 mm (0.6691 to 0.6693 in)
    Service limit . . . . 16.98 mm (0.669 in)
  All other models
    Standard . . . . 16.993 to 17.000 mm (0.6690 to 0.6693 in)
    Service limit . . . . 16.98 mm (0.669 in)
Piston-to-piston pin clearance
  US 1995 model, UK R and S models . . . . 0.002 to 0.014 mm (0.0001 to 0.0006 in)
  All other models . . . . 0.002 to 0.015 mm (0.0001 to 0.0006 in)
Connecting rod to piston pin clearance
  US 1995 model, UK R and S models . . . . 0.016 to 0.040 mm (0.0006 to 0.0016 in)
  All other models . . . . 0.016 to 0.041 mm (0.0006 to 0.0016 in)

2

Piston rings

Top ring-to-groove clearance
  US 1993 through 1995 models and UK N to S models
    Standard .... 0.030 to 0.065 mm (0.0012 to 0.0026 in)
    Service limit .... 0.08 mm (0.0031 in)
  US 1996 through 1999 models and UK T to X models
    Standard .... 0.015 to 0.050 mm (0.0006 to 0.0020 in)
    Service limit .... 0.07 mm (0.0028 in)
Top ring end gap
  US 1993 through 1995 models and UK N to S models
    Standard .... 0.20 to 0.35 mm (0.008 to 0.014 in)
    Service limit .... 0.5 mm (0.02 in)
  US 1996 through 1999 models and UK T to X models
    Standard .... 0.28 to 0.38 mm (0.011 to 0.015 in)
    Service limit .... 0.5 mm (0.02 in)
Second ring-to-groove clearance
  Standard .... 0.015 to 0.045 mm (0.0006 to 0.0018 in)
  Service limit .... 0.07 mm (0.003 in)
Second ring end gap
  Standard .... 0.40 to 0.55 mm (0.016 to 0.022 in)
  Service limit .... 0.7 mm (0.03 in)
Oil control ring side rail end gap
  US 1993 through 1995 models and UK N to S models
    Standard .... 0.2 to 0.8 mm (0.01 to 0.03 in)
    Service limit .... 1.0 mm (0.039 in)
  US 1996 through 1999 models and UK T to X models
    Standard .... 0.2 to 0.7 mm (0.01 to 0.03 in)
    Service limit .... 0.9 mm (0.035 in)

Connecting rods and bearings

Connecting rod side clearance
  Standard .... 0.05 to 0.20 mm (0.002 to 0.008 in)
  Service limit .... 0.3 mm (0.012 in)
Connecting rod piston pin bore ID
  Standard .... 17.016 to 17.034 mm (0.6699 to 0.6706 in)
  Service limit .... 17.04 mm (0.671 in)
Connecting rod crankpin bore ID
  Size group 1 .... 39.000 to 39.006 mm (1.5354 to 1.5357 in)
  Size group 2 .... 39.006 to 39.012 mm (1.5357 to 1.5359 in)
  Size group 3 .... 39.012 to 39.018 mm (1.5359 to 1.5361 in)
Crankshaft crankpin OD
  US 1993 through 1995 models and UK N to S models
    Size group A .... 35.994 to 36.000 mm (1.4171 to 1.4173 in)
    Size group B .... 35.988 to 35.994 mm (1.4168 to 1.4171 in)
    Size group C .... 35.982 to 35.988 mm (1.4166 to 1.4168 in)
  US 1996 through 1999 models and UK T to X models
    Size group A .... 36.497 to 36.503 mm (1.4369 to 1.4371 in)
    Size group B .... 36.491 to 36.497 mm (1.4367 to 1.4369 in)
    Size group C .... 36.485 to 36.491 mm (1.4364 to 1.4367 in)
Connecting rod bearing oil clearance
  Standard .... 0.030 to 0.052 mm (0.0012 to 0.0020 in)
  Service limit .... 0.06 mm (0.002 in)

Crankshaft and main bearings

Maximum crankshaft runout
  US 1993 through 1995 models and UK N to S models .... 0.05 mm (0.002 in)
  US 1996 through 1999 models and UK T to X models .... 0.30 mm (0.012 in)
Crankcase main bearing bore ID
  Size group A .... 37.000 to 37.006 mm (1.4566 to 1.4569 in)
  Size group B .... 37.006 to 37.012 mm (1.4569 to 1.4572 in)
  Size group C .... 37.012 to 37.018 mm (1.4572 to 1.4574 in)
Crankshaft journal OD
  Size group 1 .... 34.000 to 34.006 mm (1.3386 to 1.3388 in)
  Size group 2 .... 33.994 to 34.000 mm (1.3383 to 1.3386 in)
  Size group 3 .... 33.988 to 33.994 mm (1.3381 to 1.3383 in)
Main bearing oil clearance
  Standard .... 0.017 to 0.035 mm (0.0007 to 0.0014 in)
  Service limit (all models) .... 0.04 mm (0.002 in)

Transmission shafts

Ratios	US 1993 through 1995 models and UK N to S models	US 1996 and 1997 models and UK T and V models	US 1998 and 1999 models and UK W and X models
1st	2.769 to 1 (36/13T)	2.727 to 1 (30/11T)	2.769 to 1 (36/13T)
2nd	2.000 to 1 (32/16T)	1.933 to 1 (29/15T)	2.000 to 1 (26/13T)
3rd	1.579 to 1 (30/19T)	1.600 to 1 (24/15T)	1.600 to 1 (24/15T)
4th	1.400 to 1 (28/20T)	1.400 to 1 (28/20T)	1.368 to 1 (26/19T)
5th	1.250 to 1 (25/20T)	1.263 to 1 (24/19T)	1.227 to 1 (27/22T)
6th	1.174 to 1 (27/23T)	1.167 to 1 (21/18T)	1.130 to 1 (26/23T)

Gear ID
  Mainshaft 5th and 6th gears
    Standard . . . . 28.000 to 28.021 mm (1.1024 to 1.1032 in)
    Service limit . . . . 28.04 mm (1.104 in)
  Countershaft 1st gear
    Standard . . . . 24.000 to 24.021 mm (0.9449 to 0.9457 in)
    Service limit . . . . 24.04 mm (0.946 in)
  Countershaft 2nd, 3rd and 4th gears
    Standard . . . . 31.000 to 31.025 mm (1.2205 to 1.2215 in)
    Service limit . . . . 31.04 mm (1.222 in)

Gear bushing OD
  Mainshaft 5th and 6th gears
    Standard . . . . 27.959 to 27.980 mm (1.1007 to 1.1016 in)
    Service limit . . . . 27.94 mm (1.100 in)
  Countershaft 2nd gear
    Standard . . . . 30.955 to 30.980 mm (1.2187 to 1.2197 in)
    Service limit . . . . 30.93 mm (1.218 in)
  Countershaft 3rd and 4th gears
    Standard . . . . 30.950 to 30.975 mm (1.2187 to 1.2197 in)
    Service limit . . . . 30.93 mm (1.218 in)

Gear bushing ID
  Mainshaft 5th gear
    Standard . . . . 24.985 to 25.006 mm (0.9837 to 0.9845 in)
    Service limit . . . . 25.02 mm (0.985 in)
  Countershaft 2nd gear
    Standard . . . . 27.985 to 28.006 mm (1.1018 to 1.1026 in)
    Service limit . . . . 28.02 mm (1.103 in)

Gear-to-bushing clearance
  Mainshaft 5th and 6th gear
    Standard . . . . 0.020 to 0.062 mm (0.0008 to 0.0024 in)
    Service limit . . . . 0.10 mm (0.004 in)
  Countershaft 2nd gear
    Standard . . . . 0.020 to 0.070 mm (0.0008 to 0.0028 in)
    Service limit . . . . 0.11 mm (0.004 in)
  Countershaft 3rd and 4th gear
    Standard . . . . 0.025 to 0.075 mm (0.0008 to 0.0030 in)
    Service limit . . . . 0.11 mm (.004 in)

Mainshaft OD at 5th gear bushing point
    Standard . . . . 24.967 to 24.980 mm (0.9830 to 0.9835 in)
    Service limit . . . . 24.96 mm (0.983 in)

Mainshaft OD at clutch outer guide
    Standard . . . . 24.980 to 24.993 mm (0.9835 to 0.9840 in)
    Service limit . . . . 24.96 mm (0.982 in)

Countershaft OD at 2nd gear bushing point
    Standard . . . . 27.967 to 27.980 mm (1.1011 to 1.1016 in)
    Service limit . . . . 27.96 mm (1.101 in)

Shaft-to-bushing clearance
  Mainshaft 5th gear
    Standard . . . . 0.005 to 0.039 mm (0.0002 to 0.0015 in)
    Service limit . . . . 0.08 mm (0.003 in)
  Countershaft 2nd gear
    Standard . . . . 0.005 to 0.039 mm (0.0002 to 0.0015 in)
    Service limit . . . . 0.08 mm (0.003 in)

2

Torque settings

	Nm	ft-lbs
Engine mountings		
Rear upper mounting nut	39	28
Rear upper mounting bracket bolts	27	20
Rear lower mounting nut	39	28
Rear lower mounting adjuster	11	8
Rear lower mounting adjuster locknut	54	39
Left side front mounting bolts	39	28
Right side front mounting bolt	44	32
Engine sprocket bolt	54	39
Valve cover bolts	10	7
Valve cover breather plate bolts	12	9
Cam chain tensioner bolts	12	9
Camshaft holder bolts	12	9
Camshaft sprocket bolts	20	14
Cylinder head bolts (see text)	48	35
Clutch center nut	130	94
Clutch cover bolts	12	9
Oil pump sprocket bolt	15	11
Oil cooler center bolt	64	46
Gearshift drum cam bolt	23	17
Gearshift shaft return spring anchor post	22	16
Starter clutch bolts	16	12
Alternator rotor bolt	103	74
Alternator stator bolts	12	9
Crankshaft end cover bolts	12	9
Crankshaft cap	18	13
Pulse generator rotor bolt	59	43
Oil pressure switch	12	9
Neutral switch	12	9
Crankcase bolts		
6 mm bolts	12	9
8 mm bolts	25	18
9 mm bolts	35	26
10 mm bolt	39	28
Connecting rod bearing cap nuts	34	25

1 General information

The engine/transmission unit is of water-cooled four-cylinder in-line design, fitted transversely across the frame. The sixteen valves are operated by double overhead camshafts, chain driven off the right end of the crankshaft. The engine/transmission unit is constructed in aluminum alloy with the crankcase being divided horizontally. The crankcase incorporates a wet sump, pressure fed lubrication system, and houses a chain driven dual rotor oil pump.

The alternator is situated on the left end of the crankshaft with the starter clutch being built into the rear of the alternator rotor. The water pump is mounted on the left side of the crankcase and is driven off the oil pump shaft.

The clutch is of the wet multi-plate type and is gear driven off the crankshaft. The transmission is of the six-speed constant mesh type. Final drive to the rear wheel is by chain and sprockets.

2 Operations possible with the engine in the frame

The components and assemblies listed below can be removed without having to remove the engine/transmission assembly from the frame. If however, a number of areas require attention at the same time, removal of the engine is recommended.

Valve cover
Cam chain tensioner
Camshafts
Cam chain, sprockets and guides
Cylinder head
Starter motor
Starter motor clutch
Alternator
Clutch assembly
Gearshift mechanism external components
Oil pan, oil pump and relief valves
Shift drum and forks - not advised due to poor access

3 Operations requiring engine removal

It is necessary to remove the engine/transmission assembly from the frame and separate the crankcase halves to gain access to the following components.

Transmission shafts
Crankshaft and bearings
Piston/connecting rod assemblies and bearings
Shift drum and forks (see Section 2)

4 Major engine repair - general note

1 It is not always easy to determine when or if an engine should be completely overhauled, as a number of factors must be considered.

2 High mileage is not necessarily an indication that an overhaul is needed, while low mileage, on the other hand, does not preclude the need for an overhaul. Frequency of servicing is probably the single most important consideration. An engine that has regular and frequent oil and filter changes, as well as other required maintenance, will most likely give many miles of reliable service. Conversely, a neglected engine, or one which has not been broken in properly, may require an overhaul very early in its life.

3 Exhaust smoke and excessive oil consumption are both indications that piston rings and/or valve guides are in need of attention, although make sure that the fault is not due to oil leakage. Refer to Chapter 1 and perform a cylinder compression check to determine for certain the nature and extent of the work required.

4 If the engine is making obvious knocking or rumbling noises, the connecting rod and/or main bearings are probably at fault.

5 Loss of power, rough running, excessive valve train noise and high fuel consumption rates may also point to the need for an overhaul, especially if they are all present at the same time. If a complete tune-up does not remedy the situation, major mechanical work is the only solution.

6 An engine overhaul generally involves restoring the internal parts to the specifications of a new engine. During an overhaul the piston rings are replaced and the cylinder walls are bored and/or honed. If a rebore is done, then new pistons will also be required. The main and connecting rod bearings are usually replaced during a major overhaul. Generally the valve seats are serviced as well, since they are usually in less than perfect condition at this point. While the engine is being overhauled, other components such as the carburetors and the starter motor can also be rebuilt. The end result should be a like new engine that will give as many trouble-free miles as the original.

7 Before beginning the engine overhaul, read through the related procedures to familiarize yourself with the scope and requirements of the job. Overhauling an engine is not all that difficult, but it is time consuming. Plan on the motorcycle being tied up for a minimum of two weeks. Check on the availability of parts and make sure that any necessary special tools, equipment and supplies are obtained in advance.

8 Most work can be done with typical shop hand tools, although a number of precision measuring tools are required for inspecting parts to determine if they must be replaced. Often a dealer service department or motorcycle repair shop will handle the inspection of parts and offer advice concerning reconditioning and replacement. As a general rule, time is the primary cost of an overhaul so it does not pay to install worn or substandard parts.

9 As a final note, to ensure maximum life and minimum trouble from a rebuilt engine, everything must be assembled with care in a spotlessly clean environment.

5 Engine - removal and installation

Note: *Engine removal and installation should be carried out with the aid of an assistant; personal injury or damage could occur if the engine falls or is dropped. An hydraulic floor-type jack should be used to support and lower the engine to the floor if possible (they can be rented at low cost).*

Removal

1 Since no center stand is fitted, the machine must be supported in an upright position using an auxiliary stand so it can't be accidentally knocked over while the engine is removed **(see illustration 23.2 in Chapter 1)**. Work can also be made easier by raising the machine to a suitable working height on a hydraulic ramp or a suitable platform.

2 Remove the fairing lower section and both middle sections (see Chapter 8). Additionally, to avoid damage to the inner middle panels which extend rearwards towards the frame, its is advised that they also be removed as described in Chapter 8.

3 If the engine is dirty, particularly around its mountings, wash it thoroughly before starting any major dismantling work. This will make work much easier and rule out the possibility of caked on lumps of dirt falling into some vital component.

4 Remove the fuel tank as described in Chapter 4.

5 Drain the engine oil and coolant as described in Chapter 1.

6 Remove the radiator and its mounting bracket as described in Chapter 3.

7 Remove the rider's seat (see Chapter 8). Disconnect both battery cables from the battery.

⚠️ **Warning: Always disconnect the battery negative lead first and reconnect it last.**

8 Remove the exhaust system as described in Chapter 4.

9 Remove the air filter housing and carburetors as described in Chapter 4 and plug the intake manifold joints with clean shop towels.

10 Disconnect the spark plug caps from the plugs and pull the HT leads up through the dust cover.

11 Disconnect the clutch inner cable from the release lever as described in Section 15.

12 Peel back the rubber cover then undo the nut and disconnect the lead from the starter motor, freeing it from the wire clamp. Screw the nut back onto the starter motor terminal for safe-keeping. Remove the forward mounting bolt from the starter motor to free the earth lead; insert the bolt back into the crankcase for safe-keeping.

13 Trace the wiring back from the alternator (three yellow wires) and side stand switch (green, yellow/black and green/white wires) and disconnect the connectors where they join the harness under the seat **(see illustration)**. Disconnect the three-pin wire connector on the inside of the frame right top rail; this contains the neutral, oil pressure and coolant temperature sender wires **(see illustration)**. Trace the wiring up from the pulse generator (yellow and yellow/white wires) and disconnect it where it joins the main wire harness **(see illustration 4.2 in Chapter 5)**. Work back along the wiring, releasing it from any relevant retaining clips so that it is free to be removed with the engine unit.

14 Remove the clamp bolt and disconnect the gearshift lever or linkage crank (as applicable) from the engine. Note the alignment of, and any existing alignment

5.13a Disconnect the alternator wiring (A) and side stand switch wiring (B) under the seat

5.13b Neutral, oil pressure and temperature sender wires share the same three-pin connector

2

5.14 Check for alignment punch marks (arrow) before removing gearshift lever or linkage crank from its shaft

marks between, the shaft and the lever or crank, and make your own marks if none are visible **(see illustration).**

5.17a Release the clamp and disconnect the air bleed hose from the rear of the cylinder head

5.17b Slacken the clamp and disconnect the radiator top hose from the thermostat housing (early model shown)

5.18b ... and front left ...

5.15a Disconnect electronic speedometer wiring at three-pin connector inside frame ...

15 On later models with an electronically-driven speedometer, trace the wiring back from the drive unit/sensor and disconnect its wiring connector. On US 1995 through 1997 models and UK R to V models, undo the two bolts and remove the drive unit from the sprocket cover.
16 Remove the drive sprocket cover, chain guide plate and drive sprocket as described in Chapter 6.
17 Release the retaining clips or hose clamps

5.17c Coolant hose detail on engine left side – US 1993 through 1997 models and UK N to V models

1 *Water pump-to-coolant union hose*
2 *Radiator bottom hose*
3 *Air bleed hose*
4 *Oil cooler-to-water pump hose*

5.18c ... then at the frame right ...

5.15b On US 1995 through 1997 models and UK R to V models, undo the two bolts and remove the drive unit from the sprocket cover

and disconnect the cooling system air bleed hose from the rear of the cylinder head and the radiator top hose from the thermostat housing **(see illustrations).** The coolant hoses on the left-hand side of the engine can be left in place, although removal will be necessary if a complete engine overhaul is planned **(see illustration).**
18 To prevent them being distorted as the engine is manhandled out of the frame, remove the fairing mounting brackets from the engine (front) and frame (rear) **(see illustrations).**
19 Position a jack and block of wood beneath the engine and raise the jack so that it is supporting the weight of the engine/transmission unit **(see illustration 5.24).**
20 Remove the nut from the rear lower engine mounting bolt on the right side of the

5.18a Remove the fairing mounting brackets at the engine front right ...

5.18d ... and frame left sides

5.20 Engine rear lower mounting bolt nut

5.21 Engine front mounting bolt on right side

5.22 Engine front mounting bolts on left side

frame and withdraw the mounting bolt from the left side (see illustration). Note that an adjuster and locknut are located on the right side of this mounting point. Its purpose is to take up play in the engine's lower mounting so that no stress is placed on the frame. Engine removal was found to be possible without disturbing the adjuster position, but if not, slacken off the locknut and back off the adjuster a few turns.

21 Check that the jack is supporting the weight of the engine (see Step 20) and remove the front right engine mounting bolt, retrieving its spacer from between the frame and engine (see illustration).

22 Remove the two front left engine mounting bolts (see illustration).

23 Remove the nut from the rear upper engine mounting bolt on the right side of the frame and withdraw the bolt from the left (see illustration). Retrieve the short collar from the right side, the two small dampers positioned on each side of the engine and the long center collar between the engine lugs (see illustrations). Damping rubbers are located in the engine lugs (see illustration).

24 Have an assistant steady the engine as it is lowered on the jack until it is clear of the frame lugs, then move it to one side (see illustration). Lift the engine unit off the jack and lower it carefully on to the work surface, taking not to break the long fins cast onto the bottom of the oil pan. These fins are there specifically for the engine to stand on and keep it in an upright position.

⚠ **Warning: The engine unit is heavy and may cause injury if it falls.**

25 The rear upper engine mounting brackets can be removed if desired; each is retained by two bolts (see illustration).

5.23a Engine rear upper mounting bolt is removed from the left side

5.23b As it is withdrawn, retrieve the short collar . . .

5.23c . . . the small dampers . . .

5.23d . . . and the long center collar

5.23e Slip the damping rubbers out of the engine mounting lugs

5.24 With the engine supported on a jack, carefully lower it out of the frame

5.25 Engine rear upper mounting brackets are retained to inside of the frame by two bolts

2

Installation

26 Prior to installation check the condition of the damping rubbers located in the crankcase at the rear upper mounting point and the dampers fitted on each side of this mounting point (see Step 23). If damaged or deteriorated in any way, replace them with new ones.

27 If the rear upper mounting brackets were removed, install them at this stage and tighten their bolts to the specified torque setting.

28 With the aid of an assistant place the engine unit on top of the jack and block of wood and carefully raise it into position in the frame.

29 Locate the center spacer between the damping rubbers in the engine lugs. Position a damper between the left mounting bracket and the engine, and slide the rear upper mounting bolt partway in. Position the short spacer and second damper between the right mounting bracket and engine and push the bolt fully into position. Thread the nut onto the bolt.

30 Slip the spacer between the engine and frame right front mounting point and thread the right front mounting bolt into the engine unit. **Note:** *Don't mix this bolt with those on the left side - it should be 47 mm long.*

31 Install the front left mounting bolts, both 40 mm long.

32 Install the rear lower engine mounting bolt from the left side. At this point tighten the rear upper mounting bolt nut and all three front mounting bolts to their specified torque settings. If the adjuster on the rear lower mounting bolt was disturbed on removal, it must be tightened to the specified torque, then held steady while the locknut is tightened to its specified torque (Honda produce a special crowsfoot type wrench (Pt. No. 07HMA-MR70200) to enable the locknut to be secured to the correct torque). Finally, tighten the lower engine mounting bolt nut to the specified torque setting.

33 The remainder of the installation procedure is a direct reversal of the removal sequence, noting the following points.

a) *Tighten all nuts and bolts to the specified torque settings (where given).*

b) *Install the engine sprocket so that its marked side (i.e. 16T) faces outwards.*

c) *Align the marks noted or made on removal between the gearshift lever or linkage crank and the gearshift shaft.*

d) *Make sure all wiring is correctly routed and retained by all the relevant clips and ties.*

e) *Adjust the drive chain as described in Chapter 1.*

f) *Fill the engine oil and cooling systems as described in Chapter 1.*

g) *Prior to installing the fairing, start the engine and check for signs of coolant/oil leakage.*

6 Engine disassembly and reassembly - general information

Disassembly

1 Before disassembling the engine, the external surfaces of the unit should be thoroughly cleaned and degreased. This will prevent contamination of the engine internals, and will also make working a lot easier and cleaner. A high flash-point solvent, such as kerosene (paraffin) can be used, or better still, a proprietary engine degreaser. Use old paintbrushes and toothbrushes to work the solvent into the various recesses of the engine casings. Take care to exclude solvent or water from the electrical components and intake and exhaust ports.

 Warning: The use of gasoline (petrol) as a cleaning agent should be avoided because of the risk of fire.

2 When clean and dry, arrange the unit on the workbench, leaving suitable clear area for working. Gather a selection of small containers and plastic bags so that parts can be grouped together in an easily identifiable manner. Some paper and a pen should be on hand to permit notes to be made and labels attached where necessary. A supply of clean shop towels is also required.

3 Before commencing work, read through the appropriate section so that some idea of the necessary procedure can be gained. When removing various engine components it should be noted that great force is seldom required, unless specified. In many cases, a component's reluctance to be removed is indicative of an incorrect approach or removal method. If in any doubt, re-check with the text.

4 When disassembling the engine, keep "mated" parts together (including gears, cylinders, pistons, valves, etc. that have been in contact with each other during engine operation). These "mated" parts must be reused or replaced as an assembly.

5 Engine/transmission disassembly should be done in the following general order with reference to the appropriate Sections.

> Remove the camshafts
> Remove cam chain, lower sprocket and guides
> Remove the cylinder head
> Remove the clutch
> Remove the oil pump
> Remove the external shift mechanism
> Remove the alternator
> Remove the starter motor (see Chapter 9)
> Remove the water pump (See Chapter 3)
> Remove the oil pan
> Separate the crankcase halves
> Remove the connecting rod/piston assemblies
> Remove the crankshaft
> Remove the transmission shafts/gears
> Remove the shift cam/forks

Reassembly

6 Reassembly is accomplished by reversing the general disassembly sequence.

7 Valve cover - removal and installation

Note: *The valve cover can be removed with the engine in the frame. If the engine has been removed, ignore the steps which do not apply.*

Removal

1 Remove the fairing middle sections as described in Chapter 8.

2 Remove the fuel tank and air filter housing (see Chapter 4).

3 Remove the ignition HT coils (see Chapter 5).

4 Release the rubber dust cover from the tabs of the air deflector, then remove the two bolts which retain the air deflector to the frame. Maneuver the air deflector out from under the frame cross-member **(see illustrations 14.5a through 14.5c in Chapter 1)**.

5 Disconnect the spark plug caps from the plugs and position them clear of the cover.

6 Remove the radiator as described in Chapter 3; this will allow access for the valve cover to be withdrawn forwards out of the frame.

7 Slacken and remove the six cover bolts along with their sealing washers.

8 Lift the valve cover away from the head and maneuver it out of the frame.

9 Examine the rubber seal for signs of damage or deterioration and replace if it is cracked or brittle. Also check the cover bolt seals for signs of damage and replace if necessary. The crankcase breather plate can be unbolted from inside the valve cover if required.

Installation

10 If the breather plate was removed, apply a drop of non-permanent thread locking compound to the bolt threads and tighten them to the specified torque setting.

11 If a new seal is being fitted, note that it must be stuck into the cover groove using a

7.11a Apply adhesive to valve cover groove . . .

7.11b ... when tacky press the new cover seal into place

7.12 Smear sealant on the half circle cutouts in the cylinder head (arrows) before installing the valve cover

7.13 Sealing washer UP markings must face upwards

7.14a Install the valve cover bolts ...

7.14b ... and tighten those next to the triangular markings first (arrow)

7.15 Attach the breather hose to the valve cover and secure with the spring clip

suitable adhesive. Apply the adhesive to the cover groove, and when tacky, stick the seal in place **(see illustrations)**.

12 Apply a smear of sealant (not adhesive) to the half circle cutouts in the cylinder head, and carefully install the cover on the cylinder head **(see illustration)**.

13 Fit the sealing washers to the valve cover making sure the "UP" mark on each one is facing upwards **(see illustration)**.

14 Install the six cover retaining bolts and tighten them to the specified torque setting, noting that those next to the triangular markings on the cover rear outer bolt holes should be tightened first **(see illustrations)**.

15 The remainder of installation is the reverse of removal. If the breather hose was detached

from the valve cover, push it on the union and secure with the spring clip **(see illustration)**.

8 Cam chain tensioner -
removal and installation

Removal

1 Remove the fairing right middle section as described in Chapter 8. Unbolt the fairing support bracket from the frame **(see illustration 5.18c)**.

2 Unscrew the bolt and sealing washer from the end of the cam chain tensioner. If the Honda locking key or a home-made

equivalent is available, insert it in the end of the tensioner so that it engages the slotted plunger and rotate the plunger fully clockwise, then push the key into the end of the tensioner body to hold it in this position **(see illustrations)**. Remove the two bolts to free the tensioner from the engine.

3 If the locking key is not available, use a small flat-bladed screwdriver to rotate the plunger fully clockwise and hold it in this position whilst the tensioner body bolts are removed **(see illustration)**. The plunger will spring back out once the screwdriver is removed, but can be easily reset on installation.

4 Discard the gasket; a new one must be used on installation. Do not dismantle the tensioner.

8.2a A copy of Honda's tensioner locking key can be made from a piece of 1 mm mild steel

8.2b Locking key in position and tensioner plunger shown retracted. Tensioner mounting bolts arrowed

8.3 Tensioner plunger can be retracted using a small flat-bladed screwdriver as shown

8.5 Install a new gasket at the tensioner-to-cylinder block joint

Installation

5 Ensure the tensioner and cylinder block surfaces are clean and dry and fit a new gasket to the tensioner **(see illustration)**.

6 If the locking key described above is available, insert it in the tensioner body and rotate the plunger fully clockwise to retract it into the body, then push the key shoulders into the end of the body to lock it. Install the tensioner on the engine and tighten its bolts to the specified torque setting. Remove the key and install the tensioner end bolt with a new sealing washer.

7 If the key is not available, rotate the plunger fully clockwise with a flat-bladed screwdriver

9.4 Align the line next to the T mark on the ignition rotor with the notch (arrow) in the cover

9.5b . . . to free the cam chain upper guide

8.7 Use a new sealing washer on the tensioner end bolt

and hold it in this position whilst the tensioner bolts are installed and fully tightened to the specified torque setting. Install the tensioner end bolt with a new sealing washer **(see illustration)**.

8 Install the fairing support bracket and fairing panel as described in Chapter 8.

---

9 Camshafts and followers - removal, inspection and installation

Note: *This procedure can be carried out with the engine in the frame.*

9.5a Remove the three bolts (arrows) . . .

9.6 Take great care not to drop the bolts down into the engine unit when unscrewing the camshaft sprocket bolts

Removal

1 Remove the valve cover as described in Section 7.

2 Remove the fairing lower section as described in Chapter 8.

3 Remove the cam chain tensioner as described in Section 8.

4 Unscrew the inspection cap from the crankshaft right end cover and rotate the crankshaft bolt clockwise until the line next to the T mark on the ignition rotor aligns with the notch cut in the cover **(see illustration)**. The valves for cylinder No. 1 should all be closed; if not, rotate the crankshaft 360° and realign the T mark with the notch.

5 Remove the three bolts which secure the cam chain upper guide and remove the guide **(see illustrations)**.

6 Unscrew the two visible camshaft sprocket retaining bolts **(see illustration)**. **Note:** *Take care not to drop the bolts down into the engine unit as they are removed. If a bolt is dropped, it must be recovered before the engine can be started - drain the engine oil and remove the right crankshaft end cover to recover the bolt.*

7 Rotate the crankshaft clockwise until the remaining two camshaft bolts are accessible, then remove them. Reposition the crankshaft as described in Step 4, then slip the sprockets off the camshaft ends and disengage them from the cam chain **(see illustration)**. **Note:** *Use a felt-tipped marker pen, label the sprockets IN and EX to aid installation - they are otherwise identical.*

8 In a **reverse** of the numbered sequence stamped on the intake camshaft holder, slacken all bolts evenly, a little at a time so that the holder is released without danger of distortion. Retrieve the two dowels if they are loose. Carry out the same procedure to remove the exhaust camshaft holder. Lift each camshaft from the cylinder head.

9 Obtain a container which is divided into sixteen compartments, and label each compartment with the number of its corresponding valve in the cylinder head. Pick each follower out of the cylinder head (using a magnet if necessary) and store it in its

9.7 Disengage each camshaft sprocket from the chain and remove them from the engine

9.9 Lift each cam follower out of its bore

9.10 Check the lobes for wear - here's a good example of damage which will require replacement (or repair) of the camshaft

9.12 Measure the height of the camshaft lobes with a micrometer

corresponding compartment in the container (see illustration). Note that the shim is likely to stick to the inside of the follower so take great care not to lose it as the follower is removed. Remove the shims and store each one with its respective follower.

Inspection

Note: *Before replacing the camshafts or the cylinder head and camshaft holders because of damage, check with local machine shops specializing in motorcycle engineering work. In the case of the camshafts, it may be possible for cam lobes to be welded, reground and hardened, at a cost far lower than that of a new camshaft. If the bearing surfaces in the cylinder head are damaged, it may be possible for them to be bored out to accept bearing inserts. Due to the cost of a new cylinder head it is recommended that all options be explored before condemning it as trash!*

10 Inspect the cam bearing surfaces of the head and the holders. Look for score marks, deep scratches and evidence of spalling (a pitted appearance). Check the camshaft lobes for heat discoloration (blue appearance), score marks, chipped areas, flat spots and spalling (see illustration).

11 Camshaft runout can be checked by supporting each end of the camshaft on V-blocks, and measuring any runout using a dial gauge. If the runout exceeds the specified limit the camshaft must be replaced.

12 Measure the height of each lobe with a micrometer (see illustration) and compare

the results to the lobe height service limit listed in this Chapter's Specifications. If damage is noted or wear is excessive, the camshaft must be replaced.

13 The camshaft bearing oil clearance should then be checked using a product known as Plastigage.

14 Clean the camshafts, the bearing surfaces in the cylinder head and the holders with a clean, lint-free cloth, then lay the camshafts in place in the cylinder head.

15 Cut strips of Plastigage and lay one piece on each bearing journal, parallel with the camshaft centerline. Make sure the camshaft holder dowels are installed and fit the holders in their proper positions. Ensuring the camshafts are not rotated at all, tighten the holder retaining bolts evenly, a little at a time, working in the tightening sequence stamped on the holder, until the specified torque setting is reached.

16 Now unscrew the bolts in a reverse of the tightening sequence and carefully lift off the holders, again making sure the camshafts are not rotated.

17 To determine the oil clearance, compare the crushed Plastigage (at its widest point) on each journal to the scale printed on the Plastigage container.

18 Compare the results to this Chapter's Specifications. If the oil clearance is greater than specified, the camshaft and/or cylinder head and camshaft holder bearing surfaces are worn.

19 Except in cases of oil starvation, the cam chain wears very little. If the cam chain has stretched excessively, which makes it difficult to maintain proper tension, replace it with a new one (see Section 10).

20 Check the sprockets for wear, cracks and other damage, replacing them if necessary. If the sprockets are worn, the cam chain is also worn, and also the sprocket on the crankshaft. If wear this severe is apparent the cam chain and all sprockets should be replaced.

21 Check the upper cam chain guide for wear or damage. If it is worn or damaged, the cam chain may be worn out. Refer to Section 10 for cam chain replacement information.

Installation

22 Fit each shim to the top of its correct valve making sure it is correctly seated in the valve spring retainer (see illustration). Note: *It is most important that the shims are returned to their original valves otherwise the valve clearances will be inaccurate.*

23 Install the followers in their respective positions in the cylinder head, making sure each one squarely enters its bore. Lubricate the followers with clean engine oil (see illustration).

24 Position the crankshaft as described in Step 4.

25 Apply a smear of clean engine oil to the cylinder head camshaft bearing surfaces.

26 Lay the intake camshaft in position on the cylinder head so that its No. 1 cylinder lobes point away from the followers (see illustration).

2

9.22 Make sure the shim (arrow) is correctly seated in the valve spring retainer

9.23 Lubricate the followers with clean engine oil prior to installing the camshafts

9.26a Installing the intake camshaft

9.26b Camshafts are marked IN and EX for identification

9.28a Installing the intake camshaft holder; note the dowels (arrows)

9.28b Cam holders are also marked IN and EX for identification

Note: *Ensure that the camshafts are fitted correctly; the intake camshaft is marked "IN" and the exhaust camshaft is marked "EX"* **(see illustration)**.

27 Apply a smear of clean engine oil to the camshaft bearing journals and camshaft holder bearing surfaces.

28 Make sure the locating dowels are in position and install the intake camshaft holder on the head **(see illustration)**. **Note:** *Ensure the holders are fitted correctly, the intake holder is marked "IN" and the exhaust holder "EX"* **(see illustration)**.

29 Screw in the camshaft holder bolts (noting that the longer bolts fit into the outer holes) by hand only until all bolts are contacting the holders. Do not install the No. 10 bolts in the

9.35 Ensure EX marking (arrow) is level with head surface and pointing outwards when installing exhaust cam sprocket on camshaft

tightening sequence yet; these will be installed after fitting the cam chain upper guide.

30 Work in the numerical sequence marked on the top of the holder and tighten its bolts by half a turn at a time to gradually draw the holder into position. Whilst tightening the bolts make sure that the holder is being pulled squarely down onto the cylinder head and is not sticking on the dowels.

Caution: If the bolts are carelessly tightened and the camshaft holder is not drawn squarely onto the head, it is likely to break. If this happens the complete cylinder head assembly must be replaced; the holders are matched to the cylinder head and cannot be replaced separately.

31 Once the camshaft holder is in contact with the head, go around in the specified sequence and tighten the bolts to the specified torque setting.

32 Repeat steps 26 through 31 to install the exhaust camshaft.

34 Make sure the crankshaft is still positioned as described in Step 4.

35 Keeping the front run of the cam chain tight, locate the exhaust sprocket with the cam chain so that its EX mark is level with the upper surface of the cylinder head and pointing outwards **(see illustration)**. Locate the sprocket on the end of the exhaust camshaft.

36 Engage the intake sprocket with the cam chain so that its IN mark is level with the upper surface of the cylinder head and

pointing outwards. Locate the sprocket on the end of the intake camshaft.

37 Remove all traces of old locking compound from the camshaft sprocket bolts using a wire brush.

38 Apply a drop of non-permanent locking compound to the threads of each bolt **(see illustration)**. Fit one bolt to each visible camshaft sprocket hole, tightening them lightly only at this stage.

39 Watch the cam sprockets carefully to make sure the chain doesn't jump a tooth, and using a suitable socket, rotate the crankshaft clockwise until it is possible to insert the two remaining sprocket bolts. Apply a drop of non-permanent locking compound to the threads of the bolts, then screw them into position and tighten to the specified torque setting.

40 Rotate the crankshaft clockwise until the other sprocket bolts are accessible then tighten them to the specified torque setting.

41 Position the cam chain upper guide on the camshaft holders. Press the side of the guide toward the cam sprockets whilst its retaining bolts are tightened **(see illustration)**. The No. 10 cam holder bolts should be tightened to the specified torque setting.

42 Install the cam chain tensioner (see Section 8).

43 Align the T mark on the crankshaft rotor with the index mark on the cover (see Step 4) and check that both the sprocket timing marks are correctly aligned with the cylinder head upper surface **(see illustration)**. If the

9.38 Apply a drop of non-permanent thread locking compound to sprocket bolts

9.41 Cam chain upper guide installation

9.43 Sprocket timing marks (arrows) must align with head surface

10.2a Slacken and remove the nut and sealing washer (arrow) . . .

10.2b . . . and lift the tensioner blade out of the cylinder head

10.4 Slip the tensioner stud through the hole in the cylinder head

marks aren't lined up, disengage the sprocket(s) from the chain and adjust their position.

44 Rotate the crankshaft a few times, to settle all disturbed components, and check all valve clearances as described in Chapter 1, making adjustments as necessary.

45 Lubricate all bearing surfaces with clean engine oil and fit the valve cover as described in Section 7.

46 Install any components removed to improve access.

10 Cam chain and tensioner/guide blades - removal and installation

Note: *The cam chain and blades can be removed with the engine in the frame.*

Cam chain tensioner blade (rear)
Removal

1 Remove the intake camshaft sprocket as described in Section 9.

2 Slacken and remove the nut and sealing washer securing the guide to the cylinder head and lift the guide out of position **(see illustrations)**.

3 Check the tensioner blade for deep grooves, cracking and other obvious damage, replacing it if necessary.

Installation

4 Installation is the reverse of removal using a new sealing washer **(see illustration)**.

Cam chain guide blade (front)
Removal

5 Remove the exhaust camshaft as described in Section 9.

6 Drain the engine oil as described in Chapter 1.

7 Trace the wiring from the ignition pulse generator coil up to its two-pin connector along the top right side of the frame and disconnect it. Free the wiring from any ties.

8 Remove the eight crankshaft end cover retaining bolts and withdraw the cover squarely from the engine unit **(see illustration)**. Remove the gasket and recover the two dowels if they are loose.

9 Slacken and remove the pulse generator rotor retaining bolt and washer **(see illustration)**. To prevent the crankshaft

rotating, remove the left crankshaft end cover as described in Section 21 and retain the alternator rotor using a large open-ended wrench on the rotor flats **(see illustration 21.6)**. Alternatively, if the engine is still in the frame, the engine can be locked through the transmission by selecting top gear and applying the rear brake hard.

10 Slide off the pulse generator rotor.

11 Remove the bolt from the cam chain guide blade and allow the blade to drop down to the bottom of the casing **(see illustration)**.

12 Use paint or a suitable marker pen to mark the outside edge of the crankshaft cam chain sprocket **(see illustration)**. This mark can then be used to make sure the sprocket is installed the correct way around. Disengage the chain from the sprocket and withdraw the sprocket from the crankshaft **(see illustration)**.

10.8 Crankshaft right end cover is retained by eight bolts (arrows)

10.9 Remove the pulse generator retaining bolt and washer

10.11 Remove the cam chain guide blade bolt and allow the blade to drop to the bottom of the casing

10.12a Make an identification mark on the sprocket using paint or a marker pen . . .

10.12b . . . then slip the sprocket off the crankshaft

10.13 Withdraw the guide blade from the crankcase

10.20 Tighten the pulse generator rotor bolt to the specified torque setting

13 Withdraw the guide blade from the engine **(see illustration)**.
14 Check the guide blade for deep grooves, cracking and other obvious damage, replacing it if necessary.

Installation

15 Remove all traces of gasket from the crankcase and cover mating surfaces. Make sure the oil gallery plug is in position in the crankcase.
16 Lubricate the pivot bush with engine oil and insert it into the guide, making sure the bush shoulder is on the inside of the guide blade (between the guide blade and crankcase) **(see illustration)**.
17 Insert the guide blade into the engine, but don't install its bolt at this stage.

10.22 Apply sealant 10 to 15 mm each side of the crankcase half joint

A Crankshaft right end cover mating surface
B Clutch cover mating surface

10.16 Fit the pivot bush to the guide blade so that its collar will be positioned between the guide blade and crankcase

18 Slide the sprocket on the crankshaft using the mark made on removal to ensure it is installed the correct way around. Engage the chain on the sprocket, then bring the guide blade up into position and tighten its bolt securely **(see illustration)**.
19 Align the pulse generator rotor splines with those of the crankshaft and slide on the rotor. **Note:** *Make sure the rotor timing marks are facing outwards.*
20 Tighten the rotor bolt to the specified torque setting whilst preventing crankshaft rotation using the method employed on removal **(see illustration)**.
21 Install the exhaust camshaft sprocket and check the valve timing (see Section 9).
22 Apply sealant across the crankcase half joints **(see illustration)**. Apply a smear of sealant to the cover wiring grommet. Install the locating dowels and fit a new gasket to the crankcase.
23 Fit the cover to the engine noting that a drop of non-permanent thread locking compound should be applied to the two bolts which go in the holes marked with the cast triangles **(see illustration)**. Tighten the cover bolts to the specified torque setting.
24 Make sure the wiring is correctly routed up to the two-pin connector and reconnect it. Secure the wiring in position with all the necessary ties.
25 Fill the engine with the correct type and amount of oil as described in Chapter 1.

10.23 Apply thread-lock to the bolts next to the triangular markings (arrows)

10.18 Install the guide blade bolt and tighten it securely

Cam chain

Removal

26 Remove the camshaft sprockets and tensioner/guide blades as described above.
27 Drop the chain down and remove it from the end of the crankshaft.

Inspection

28 Check the cam chain for binding and obvious damage, and inspect the sprocket for damage such as chipped or missing teeth. If either of these conditions are visible, or if the chain appears to be stretched, both the cam chain and sprockets (crankshaft and both camshaft sprockets) should be replaced as a set.

Installation

29 Feed the cam chain over the boss on the intake cam holder and down into the tunnel **(see illustration)**. Hang the chain over the camshafts and locate it over the crankshaft.
30 Install the tensioner/guide blades and camshaft sprockets as described above.

---

11 Cylinder head -
removal and installation

Caution: The engine must be completely cool before beginning this procedure or the cylinder head may become warped.
Note: *This procedure can be performed with the engine in the frame. If the engine has*

10.29 Slip the cam chain over the intake cam holder boss and into the cam chain tunnel

11.6 Disconnect the air bleed hose from its union on the rear of the cylinder head

11.9 Two external cylinder head bolts are located on the right side

11.12 Lifting the cylinder head off the block

11.15 Prior to installing the head, lubricate the bores with clean engine oil

already been removed, ignore the preliminary steps which don't apply.

Removal

1 Remove the exhaust system as described in Chapter 4.

2 Remove the carburetors as described in Chapter 4.

3 On California models, remove the pulse secondary air injection system (PAIR) control valve as described in Chapter 4 and disconnect the EVAP hose and PAIR hose from intake manifold Nos. 1 and 3 (4 on 1996 model) respectively.

4 Remove the camshafts and followers as described in Section 9.

5 Slacken and remove the nut and sealing washer securing the cam chain tensioner blade to the cylinder head and lift out the blade **(see illustrations 10.2a and 10.2b)**.

6 On US 1993 through 1997 models and UK N to V models, disconnect the air bleed hose from the rear of the cylinder head **(see illustration)** and the air bleed hose and the radiator top hose from the thermostat housing **(see illustrations 5.17a and b)**. Also disconnect the wiring connector from the coolant temperature sender on the thermostat housing.

7 On US 1998 and 1999 models and UK W and X models, disconnect the thermostat housing hose and the air bleed hose from the outlet on the rear of the cylinder head and disconnect the wiring connector from the coolant temperature sender unit. Undo the bolt securing the thermostat housing bracket

to the cylinder head and recover the collar from the bracket mounting.

8 Remove the upper of the two front left engine mounting bolts **(see illustration 5.22)**.

9 Unscrew the two external cylinder head bolts from the right end of the head **(see illustration)**.

10 Working from the outside to the inside in a criss-cross pattern, slacken the ten cylinder head bolts by half a turn at a time. Once all pressure is released from the bolts, fully unscrew them and remove along with their washers.

11 Tap around the joint faces of the cylinder head with a soft-faced mallet to free the head. Don't attempt to free the head by inserting a screwdriver between the head and cylinder block - you'll damage the sealing surfaces.

12 Lift the head off the block, and remove it from the engine **(see illustration)**. Pass a piece of wire or a screwdriver through the cam chain to prevent it falling down into its tunnel.

13 Remove the old head gasket and discard it. If loose, remove the cylinder head locating dowels from the cylinder block and store them with the head for safe-keeping.

14 Check the cylinder head gasket and the mating surfaces on the cylinder head and block for signs of leakage, which could indicate warpage. Check the flatness of the head as described in Section 13.

Installation

15 Ensure both cylinder head and block mating surfaces are clean and fit the locating dowels to the block (if removed). Apply a

smear of engine oil to the surface of each cylinder bore **(see illustration)**.

16 Fit the new head gasket over the locating dowels **(see illustration)**.

17 Carefully lower the cylinder head onto the block whilst feeding the cam chain up through the head. Pass a screwdriver or piece of wire through the chain to prevent it falling back into the engine **(see illustration)**.

18 Apply a drop of clean engine oil to the threads and undersides of the cylinder head bolts **(see illustration)**.

19 Fit the cylinder head bolts and washers and tighten them all by hand.

20 Working from the inside to the outside in a criss-cross pattern, tighten the cylinder head bolts to approximately half the specified torque setting given in the Specifications. Then go around in the same sequence and

2

11.16 Ensure the locating dowels (arrows) are in position and fit the new head gasket

11.17 Pass a suitable tool through the cam chain to prevent it falling back into the engine

11.18 Apply a smear of oil to the threads and underside of the heads of the cylinder head bolts

11.20 Tighten the head bolts to the specified torque as described in the text

tighten the bolts to the full specified torque setting **(see illustration)**.

21 Install the two bolts to the right end of the cylinder head and tighten them securely.

22 Install the engine mounting bolt to the engine left side and tighten it to the specified torque setting.

23 Connect the coolant and air bleed hoses to their unions and secure with the clamp/clips. On US 1998 and 1999 models and UK W and X models, fit the collar to the thermostat housing bracket and secure the bracket to the rear of the cylinder head with the retaining bolt.

24 Connect the wiring connector to the coolant temperature sender.

25 Lower the cam chain tensioner blade into position, fit a new sealing washer and securely tighten its retaining nut.

26 Install the camshafts and followers as described in Section 9.

27 Fit the exhaust system, carburetors and, on California models, the PAIR and EVAP components.

13.3 Cylinder head and valve components

1 Follower	8 Exhaust valve
2 Shim	9 Valve guide seal
3 Keepers (collets)	10 Outer spring seat
4 Spring retainer	11 Inner spring seat
5 Outer valve spring	12 Valve guide
6 Inner valve spring	13 Spark plug
7 Intake valve	

28 Fill the cooling system as described in Chapter 1.

12 Valves/valve seats/valve guides - servicing

1 Because of the complex nature of this job and the special tools and equipment required, servicing of the valves, the valve seats and the valve guides (commonly known as a valve job) is best left to a professional.

2 The home mechanic can, however, remove and disassemble the head, do the initial cleaning and inspection, then reassemble and deliver the head to a dealer service department or properly equipped motorcycle repair shop for the actual valve servicing. Refer to Section 13 for those procedures.

3 The dealer service department will remove the valves and springs, recondition or replace the valves and valve seats, replace the valve guides, check and replace the valve springs, spring retainers and keepers (collets) (as necessary), replace the valve seals with new ones and reassemble the valve components.

4 After the valve job has been performed, the head will be in like-new condition. When the head is returned, be sure to clean it again very thoroughly before installation on the engine to remove any metal particles or abrasive grit that may still be present from the valve service operations. Use compressed air, if available, to blow out all the holes and passages.

13 Cylinder head and valves - disassembly, inspection and reassembly

1 As mentioned in the previous Section, valve servicing and valve guide replacement should be left to a dealer service department or motorcycle repair shop. However, disassembly, cleaning and inspection of the valves and related components can be done (if the necessary special tools are available) by the home mechanic. This way no expense is incurred if the inspection reveals that service work is not required at this time.

2 To properly disassemble the valve

13.7a Follower bore protector can be made from an old 35 mm film container . . .

components without the risk of damaging them, a valve spring compressor is absolutely necessary. This special tool can usually be rented, but if it's not available, have a dealer service department or motorcycle repair shop handle the entire process of disassembly, inspection, service or repair (if required) and reassembly of the valves.

Disassembly

3 Remove the followers and their shims if you haven't already done so (see Section 9). Store the components in such a way that they can be returned to their original locations without getting mixed up **(see illustration)**.

4 Before the valves are removed, scrape away any traces of gasket material from the head gasket sealing surface. Work slowly and do not nick or gouge the soft aluminum of the head. Gasket removing solvents, which work very well, are available at most motorcycle shops and auto parts stores.

5 Carefully scrape all carbon deposits out of the combustion chamber area. A hand held wire brush or a piece of fine emery cloth can be used once the majority of deposits have been scraped away. Do not use a wire brush mounted in a drill motor, or one with extremely stiff bristles, as the head material is soft and may be eroded away or scratched by the wire brush.

6 Before proceeding, arrange to label and store the valves along with their related components so they can be kept separate and reinstalled in the same valve guides they are removed from (labelled plastic bags work well for this).

7 To prevent damage to the follower bore from the valve spring compressor, you are advised to protect the bore surface. A plastic container from a photographic 35 mm film works well since it fits between the valve spring and follower bore. Cut the container away as shown and slip it into place **(see illustrations)**.

8 Compress the valve spring on the first valve with a spring compressor, then remove the keepers (collets) from the valve groove. **Note:** *Take great care not to mark the cylinder head follower bore with the spring compressor.* Do not compress the springs any more than is absolutely necessary. Carefully release the valve spring

13.7b . . . and inserted into the follower bore as shown

13.8a Take the valve out of the combustion chamber, but don't force it if it's stuck . . .

13.8b . . . check the area around the keeper (collet) groove for burrs and remove any that you find

1 Burrs (remove)   2 Valve stem

13.11 Check that each drain hole is clear (arrow)

13.16 Measuring valve seat width

compressor and remove the springs and the valve from the head **(see illustration)**. If the valve binds in the guide (won't pull through), push it back into the head and deburr the area around the keeper (collet) groove with a very fine file or whetstone **(see illustration)**.

9 Repeat the procedure for the remaining valves. Remember to keep the parts for each valve together so they can be reinstalled in the same location.

10 Once the valves have been removed and labelled, pull off the valve stem seals with pliers and discard them (the old seals should never be reused), then remove the spring seats.

11 Next, clean the cylinder head with solvent and dry it thoroughly. Compressed air will speed the drying process and ensure that all holes and recessed areas are clean. Check that the drain hole under the exhaust ports is clear; its purpose is to drain off any water which might collect in the spark plug channels **(see illustration)**.

12 Clean all of the valve springs, keepers (collets), retainers and spring seats with solvent and dry them thoroughly. Do the parts from one valve at a time so that no mixing of parts between valves occurs.

13 Scrape off any deposits that may have formed on the valve, then use a motorized wire brush to remove deposits from the valve heads and stems. Again, make sure the valves do not get mixed up.

Inspection

14 Inspect the head very carefully for cracks and other damage. If cracks are found, a new head will be required. Check the cam bearing surfaces for wear and evidence of seizure. Check the camshafts and followers for wear as well (see Section 9).

15 Using a precision straightedge and a feeler gauge, check the head gasket mating surface for warpage. Lay the straightedge lengthways, across the head and diagonally (corner-to-corner), intersecting the head stud holes, and try to slip a feeler gauge under it, on either side of each combustion chamber. The gauge should be the same thickness as the cylinder head warp limit listed in this Chapter's Specifications. If the feeler gauge can be inserted between the head and the straightedge, the head is warped and must either be machined or, if warpage is excessive, replaced with a new one.

16 Examine the valve seats in each of the combustion chambers. If they are pitted, cracked or burned, the head will require valve service that's beyond the scope of the home mechanic. Measure the valve seat width and compare it to this Chapter's Specifications **(see illustration)**. If it exceeds the service limit, or if it varies around its circumference, valve service work is required.

17 Clean the valve guides to remove any carbon build-up, then measure the inside

diameters of the guides (at both ends and the center of the guide) with a small hole gauge and micrometer **(see illustrations)**. Record the measurements for future reference. These measurements, along with the valve stem diameter measurements, will enable you to compute the valve stem-to-guide clearance. This clearance, when compared to the Specifications, will be one factor that will determine the extent of the valve service work required. The guides are measured at the ends and at the center to determine if they are worn in a bell-mouth pattern (more wear at the ends). If they are, guide replacement is an absolute must.

18 Carefully inspect each valve face for cracks, pits and burned spots. Check the valve stem and the keeper (collet) groove area for cracks **(see illustration)**. Rotate the valve

13.17a Insert a small hole gauge into the valve guide and expand it so there's a slight drag when it's pulled out

13.17b Measure the small hole gauge with a micrometer

13.18 Check the valve face (A), stem (B) and keeper/collet groove (C) for signs of damage or wear

13.19 Measure the valve stem diameter with a micrometer

13.20a Measure the free length of the valve springs

13.20b Check the valve springs for squareness

and check for any obvious indication that it is bent. Check the end of the stem for pitting and excessive wear. The presence of any of the above conditions indicates the need for valve servicing.

19 Measure the valve stem diameter **(see illustration)**. By subtracting the stem diameter from the valve guide diameter, the valve stem-to-guide clearance is obtained. If the stem-to-guide clearance is greater than listed in this Chapter's Specifications, the guides and valves will have to be replaced with new ones.

20 Check the end of each valve spring for wear and pitting. Measure the free length and compare it to this Chapter's Specifications **(see illustration)**. Any springs that are shorter

13.24 Apply lapping compound very sparingly, in small dabs, to the valve face only

than specified have sagged and should not be reused. Stand the spring on a flat surface and check it for squareness **(see illustration)**.

21 Check the spring retainers and keepers (collets) for obvious wear and cracks. Any questionable parts should not be reused, as extensive damage will occur in the event of failure during engine operation.

22 If the inspection indicates that no service work is required, the valve components can be reinstalled in the head.

Reassembly

23 Before installing the valves in the head, they should be lapped to ensure a positive seal between the valves and seats. This procedure requires coarse and fine valve lapping compound (available at auto parts stores) and a valve lapping tool. If a lapping tool is not available, a piece of rubber or plastic hose can be slipped over the valve stem (after the valve has been installed in the guide) and used to turn the valve.

24 Apply a small amount of coarse lapping compound to the valve face, then slip the valve into the guide **(see illustration)**. **Note:** *Make sure the valve is installed in the correct guide and be careful not to get any lapping compound on the valve stem.*

25 Attach the lapping tool (or hose) to the valve and rotate the tool between the palms of your hands. Use a back-and-forth motion rather than a circular motion. Lift the valve off the seat and turn it at regular intervals to

distribute the lapping compound properly. Continue the lapping procedure until the valve face and seat contact area is of uniform width and unbroken around the entire circumference of the valve face and seat **(see illustrations)**.

26 Carefully remove the valve from the guide and wipe off all traces of lapping compound. Use solvent to clean the valve and wipe the seat area thoroughly with a solvent soaked cloth.

27 Repeat the procedure with fine valve lapping compound, then repeat the entire procedure for the remaining valves.

28 Lay the spring seats in place in the cylinder head, then install new valve stem seals on each of the guides. Use an appropriate size deep socket to push the seals into place until they are properly seated. Don't twist or cock them, or they will not seal properly against the valve stems. Also, don't remove them again or they will be damaged.

29 Coat the valve stems with clean engine oil, then install one of them into its guide. Next, install the springs and retainer, compress the springs and install the keepers (collets). **Note:** *Install the springs with the tightly wound coils at the bottom, next to the spring seat* **(see illustration)**. When compressing the springs with the valve spring compressor, depress them only as far as is absolutely necessary to slip the keepers (collets) into place. **Note:** *Use the protector described in Step 7 to avoid damaging the*

13.25a After lapping, the valve face should exhibit a uniform, unbroken contact pattern (arrow) . . .

13.25b . . . and the seat should be the specified width (arrow) with a smooth, unbroken appearance

13.29a Install the valve springs with their tightly wound coils downward (against the cylinder head)

13.29b A small dab of grease will help hold the keepers (collets) in place on the valve while the valve spring is released

14.4 Remove the ten clutch cover retaining bolts (arrows) noting that the longer bolts are fitted in holes A

14.5 Withdraw the clutch cover

cylinder head follower bore with the spring compressor. Apply a small amount of grease to the keepers (collets) to help hold them in place as the pressure is released from the springs **(see illustrations)**. Make certain that the keepers (collets) are securely locked in their retaining grooves.

30 Support the cylinder head on blocks so the valves can't contact the workbench top, then very gently tap each of the valve stems with a soft-faced hammer. This will help seat the keepers (collets) in their grooves.

 Check for proper sealing of the valves by pouring a small amount of solvent into each of the valve ports. If the solvent leaks past any valve(s) into the combustion chamber area the valve grinding operation should be repeated.

14 Clutch - removal, inspection and installation

Note: *This procedure can be performed with the engine in the frame. If the engine has already been removed, ignore the preliminary steps which don't apply.*

Removal

1 Remove the fairing right middle section and lower section as described in Chapter 8.

14.7 Slacken the clutch spring bolts evenly and in a criss-cross pattern

2 Drain the engine oil as described in Chapter 1.

3 Disconnect the clutch cable from the release lever as described in Section 15.

4 Working in a criss-cross pattern, evenly slacken the ten clutch cover retaining bolts **(see illustration)**. Three of the cover bolts are longer than the others; take note of their location as a guide to installation.

5 Lift the cover away from the engine, being prepared to catch any residual oil which may be released as the cover is removed **(see illustration)**.

6 Remove the gasket and discard it. Note the two locating dowels fitted to the crankcase and remove these for safe-keeping if they are loose.

7 Working in a criss-cross pattern, gradually

slacken the clutch spring retaining bolts until spring pressure is released **(see illustration)**. Unscrew the bolts, then remove the clutch pressure plate complete with release bearing and pushrod.

8 Lift out the clutch plates, followed by the anti-judder spring and its seat **(see illustration)**. Unless the plates are to be replaced, keep them in order to aid installation.

9 Relieve the staking on the clutch nut using a hammer and suitable pointed-nose chisel, taking care not to damage the mainshaft end.

10 The clutch center must be prevented from rotating while the center nut is slackened. The Honda service tool (Pt. No. 07724-0050001 for US 1993 through 1995 models and UK N to S models, and Pt. No. 07724- 0050002 for US

2

14.8 Clutch detail

1 Bolts	7 Lock washer	13 Clutch center
2 Springs	8 Friction plates	14 Thrust washer
3 Pressure plate	9 Plain plates	15 Outer drum
4 Release bearing	10 Inner friction plate	16 Needle roller bearing
5 Pushrod	11 Anti-judder spring	17 Guide bush
6 Clutch nut	12 Spring seat	

14.14 Measuring friction plate thickness

14.20 Release bearing is a press fit in pressure plate

14.21 Measuring clutch spring free length

1996 through 1999 models and UK T to X models) or a home-made copy can be used to clamp the center splines and outer drum slots **(see Tool Tip)**. Alternatively, if the engine is still in the frame, lock the clutch through the transmission, by selecting top gear and applying the rear brake hard whilst the nut is slackened.

A clutch centre holding tool can be easily made using two strips of steel, bent over at the ends and bolted together in the middle.

11 Remove the nut and discard it; a new one must be used on installation.
12 Remove the washer; its outer face should be marked "OUT".
13 Withdraw the clutch center followed by the large thrust washer, outer drum and its guide bush.

Inspection

14 After an extended period of service the clutch friction plates will wear and promote clutch slip. Measure the thickness of each friction plate using a vernier caliper **(see illustration)**. If any plate has worn to or beyond the service limit given in the Specifications, the friction plates must be replaced as a set.
15 The plain plates should not show any signs of excess heating (blueing). Check for warpage using a flat surface and feeler gauges. If any plate exceeds the maximum

permissible amount of warpage, or shows signs of blueing, all plain plates must be replaced as a set.
16 Inspect the clutch assembly for burrs and indentations on the edges of the protruding tangs of the friction plates and/or slots in the edge of the outer drum with which they engage. Similarly check for wear between the inner tongues of the plain plates and the slots in the clutch center. Wear of this nature will cause clutch drag and slow disengagement during gear changes, since the plates will snag when the pressure plate is lifted. With care a small amount of wear can be corrected by dressing with a fine file, but if this is excessive the worn components can be replaced.
17 Also inspect the anti-judder spring and seat for signs of wear or distortion and replace if necessary.
18 Inspect the mainshaft, guide bush and outer drum bearing surfaces for signs of wear and damage. If access to the necessary measuring equipment can be gained, the condition of the above components can be judged by direct measurement. If any component shows signs of wear or damage, or has worn beyond its service limit given in the Specifications, it must be replaced.
19 Inspect the outer drum needle roller bearing for signs of wear or damage. If replacement is necessary, the task should be entrusted to a Honda dealer. The bearing is a press fit in the drum and a hydraulic press

and suitable spacers will be required to remove the original bearing and install the new one.
20 Check the clutch release bearing for wear. Ensure that the inner race of the bearing spins freely without any sign of notchiness. Push the bearing out of the pressure plate if replacement is required **(see illustration)**.
21 Measure the free length of each clutch spring **(see illustration)**. If any one has settled to less than the service limit, the clutch springs must be replaced as a set.

Installation

22 Remove all traces of gasket from the crankcase and clutch cover surfaces.
23 Lubricate the guide bush with engine oil and slide it on the mainshaft so that its slotted end is facing outwards **(see illustration)**. Lubricate the outer drum needle roller bearing and install it over the mainshaft **(see illustration)**. To enable the outer drum to mesh with the crankshaft gear it will be necessary to align the teeth of the main clutch outer drum gear which those of the sprung slim gear behind it; this can be done with a flat-bladed screwdriver as the outer drum is pushed fully on the mainshaft. Note that the slots on the back of the outer drum must engage the dogs on the oil pump drive gear - check that the dogs are engaged by rotating the outer drum; the oil pump sprocket should turn as it is rotated.
24 Install the large thrust washer on the

14.23a Install the guide bush making sure its slotted end is facing outwards

14.23b Install the outer drum over the mainshaft

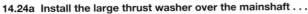

14.24a Install the large thrust washer over the mainshaft . . .

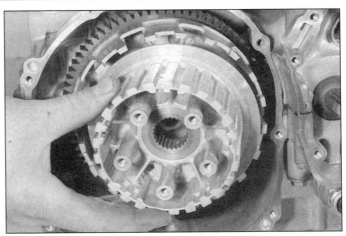

14.24b . . . followed by the clutch center

mainshaft, followed by the clutch center **(see illustrations)**.

25 Install the lock washer with its "OUT" marking facing outwards, followed by a **new** clutch nut **(see illustrations)**.

26 Using the method employed on removal (see Step 10), hold the clutch steady and tighten the clutch nut to the specified torque setting **(see illustration)**. Rotate the mainshaft so that its slot is uppermost, then stake the shoulder of the clutch nut into the slot to lock it in position **(see illustration)**.

27 Fit the spring seat to the clutch center followed by the anti-judder spring **(see illustration)**. **Note:** *The anti-judder spring must be fitted with its convex side facing the spring seat (see illustration).*

28 Install the inner friction plate in the outer

14.25a The lockwasher must be installed so that its OUT marking faces outwards

14.25b Always fit a new clutch nut

14.26a Using the holding tool, tighten the clutch nut to the specified torque setting . . .

14.26b . . . and stake its shoulder into the shaft groove

14.27a Install the spring seat and anti-judder spring

14.27b Correct fitting of anti-judder spring

1 Clutch center   3 Spring seat
2 Inner friction plate   4 Anti-judder spring

14.28 Install the inner friction plate first (it has a narrower friction surface and larger inside diameter than the others)

14.29a Fit the plain and friction plates alternately . . .

14.29b . . . noting that the tangs of the last friction plate locate in the shallow slots of the outer drum (arrows)

drum (see illustration). This plate can be identified by its larger inside diameter which allows it to locate over the anti-judder spring and seat. Note: If new clutch plates are being installed, apply a coating of oil to their surfaces to prevent seizure.

29 Install a plain plate followed by one of the ordinary friction plates then alternately install the remaining plain and friction plates noting that the tangs of the last friction plate fit into the shallow slots in the outer drum (see illustrations). Note: On US 1998 and 1999 models and UK W and X models, the outer friction plate is slightly different to the others, it can be identified by the size of its friction material pads in comparison to the other plates (see illustration).

30 Install the pressure plate, complete with release bearing and pushrod (see illustrations). Secure the pressure plate with the springs and headed bolts, tightening them evenly in a diagonal sequence (see illustration).

31 Apply sealant across the crankcase half joints (see illustration 10.22). Install the two dowels in the cover and fit a new gasket over them (see illustration). Offer up the clutch cover and seat it fully onto the crankcase. Install the cover bolts, making sure the longer bolts are fitted in the correct holes (see

14.29c Correct arrangement of clutch friction plates on US 1998 and 1999 models and UK W and X models

A Outer friction plate   B Ordinary friction plates   C Inner friction plate

14.30a Install the pushrod in the pressure plate . . .

14.30b . . . and insert the pressure plate over the clutch center posts

14.30c Install the springs, washers and bolts

14.31 Install a new gasket over the cover dowels (arrows)

illustration 14.4) and that the cable bracket is secured. Tighten the bolts evenly in a diagonal sequence to the specified torque setting.

32 Reconnect the clutch cable end to the release lever as described in Section 15 and carry out adjustment as described in Chapter 1.

33 Refill the engine with the specified quantity and type of oil (see Chapter 1).

34 Install the fairing sections (see Chapter 8).

15 Clutch cable and release lever - removal and installation

Clutch cable

Removal

1 Remove the right middle fairing section (see Chapter 8).

2 Back off the cable lower adjuster to allow the cable end to be disconnected from the release lever **(see illustration)**. Free the adjuster from its bracket on the clutch cover **(see illustration)**.

3 Align the slots of the knurled adjuster and lockring at the lever end of the cable and detach the cable from the underside of the clutch lever.

4 Take note of its routing as the old cable is removed from the bike.

Installation

5 Install the new cable making sure it is correctly routed and retained by all necessary clips.

6 Adjust the cable as described in Chapter 1 then install the fairing section as described in Chapter 8.

Clutch release lever

Removal

7 Remove the clutch cover as described in Steps 1 through 6 of Section 14.

8 Disconnect the return spring arm from the cover stop and pull the release lever out of the cover.

9 Inspect the two needle roller bearings and oil seal set in the clutch cover; these components can remain in position unless they require replacement.

Installation

10 Prior to installation of the release lever, apply engine oil to the bearings and a smear of grease to the oil seal lip.

11 Install the return spring and washer on the release lever and slide it into the clutch cover. Hook the short arm of the return spring around the lever and tension the longer end of the spring so that it rests against the stop on the cover **(see illustration)**.

15.2a Fully back off the cable lower adjuster to allow the cable nipple to be disconnected . . .

15.2b . . . then withdraw the cable and its adjuster from the bracket

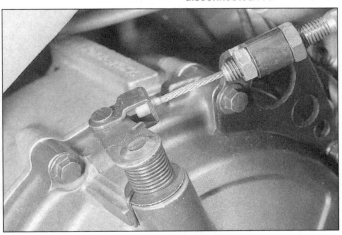

15.11 Correct installation of clutch release lever spring

2

16.4 Slacken the oil pan bolts evenly in a criss-cross pattern

16.10a Oil pump strainer seal is installed with flange facing the strainer (arrow)

16.10b Tab on strainer must engage slot in crankcase (arrow)

16 Oil pan - removal and installation

Note: *The oil pan can be removed with the engine in the frame. If work is being carried out with the engine removed ignore the preliminary steps.*

Removal

1 Remove the fairing lower section as described in Chapter 8.

2 Remove the complete exhaust system as described in Chapter 4.

3 Drain the engine oil as described in Chapter 1.

4 Working in a criss-cross pattern, gradually loosen the oil pan retaining bolts **(see illustration)**.

5 Remove the eighteen retaining bolts and lower the oil pan away from the crankcase. If the engine is in the frame, note that as the oil pan is removed, the oil pump pick-up strainer and oil pressure relief valve may fall out of the bottom of the crankcase.

6 Recover the gasket and discard it.

7 If they were not released when the oil pan was removed, remove the oil pump pick-up strainer and the oil pressure relief valve from the base of the crankcase. Remove the seal from the pick-up and the O-ring from the pressure relief valve and discard them.

8 Clean the pick-up strainer mesh in solvent. Check it for clogging or splitting and replace if necessary.

Installation

9 Remove all traces of gasket from the oil pan and crankcase mating surfaces.

10 Fit a new seal to the oil pump pick-up strainer making sure its flange is facing the strainer **(see illustration)**. Fit the strainer to the base of the crankcase aligning its tab with the slot in the crankcase **(see illustration)**.

11 Fit a new O-ring to the oil pressure relief valve groove. Apply a smear of oil to the O-ring and ease the relief valve into position in the base of the crankcase **(see illustration)**.

12 Position a new gasket on the oil pan and fit the pan to the engine **(see illustrations)**. If the engine is in the frame, use a smear of grease on the gasket to hold it in place as the oil pan is installed.

13 Make sure the gasket is correctly positioned then insert the retaining bolts and tighten them by hand.

14 Working in a criss-cross pattern, securely tighten all the oil pan retaining bolts.

15 Install the exhaust system as described in Chapter 4.

16 Fill the engine with the correct type and quantity of oil as described in Chapter 1. Start the engine and check for leaks.

17 If all is well, fit the fairing lower section as described in Chapter 8.

16.11 Oil pressure relief valve is a press fit in crankcase

17 Oil pump - pressure check, removal, inspection and installation

Note: *The oil pump can be removed with the engine in the frame.*

Pressure check

1 To check the oil pressure, a suitable gauge and adapter piece (which screws into the oil pressure switch thread) will be needed.

2 Warm the engine up to normal operating temperature then stop it.

3 Peel back the rubber dust cover and disconnect the wire from the oil pressure switch **(see illustration)**.

4 Unscrew the switch and swiftly screw the

16.12a Always use a new gasket . . .

16.12b . . . when installing the oil pan

17.3 Oil pressure wire is a screw fit in end of switch

17.11 Insert a screwdriver or similar item through the oil pump sprocket hole to prevent rotation as the bolt is slackened

17.13a Undo the three bolts (arrows) . . .

17.13b . . . and remove the oil pump

adapter into the crankcase threads. Connect the gauge to the adapter.

5 Start the engine and increase the engine speed to 6000 rpm whilst watching the gauge reading. The oil pressure should be similar to that given in the Specifications at the start of this Chapter.

6 If the pressure is significantly lower than the standard, either the relief valve is stuck open, the oil pump is faulty, the oil pump pick-up strainer is blocked or there is other engine damage. Begin diagnosis by checking the oil pump pick-up strainer and relief valve (see Sections 16 and 18), then the oil pump. If those items check out okay, chances are the bearing oil clearances are excessive and the engine needs to be overhauled.

7 If the pressure is too high, the relief valve is stuck closed. To check it, see Section 18.

8 Stop the engine and unscrew the gauge and adapter from the crankcase.

9 Having applied a smear of sealant to its threads, install the oil pressure switch and tighten it securely. Reconnect its wire terminal and fit the dust cover over the switch.

Removal

10 Remove the clutch as described in Section 14.

11 Slacken and remove the oil pump sprocket retaining bolt whilst preventing the sprocket turning by inserting a screwdriver through one of the sprocket holes (see illustration).

12 Slide the drive sprocket off the mainshaft and remove the drive sprocket, chain and pump sprocket as an assembly. Remove the guide bush from the center of the drive sprocket.

13 Undo the three bolts and remove the oil pump from the crankcase (see illustrations).

Inspection

14 Wash the oil pump in solvent, then dry it off (see illustration).

15 Remove the pump cover screw (see illustration).

16 Lift off the cover and recover the locating dowel (see illustration).

17 Remove the thrust washer from the pump driveshaft.

18 Slide out the driveshaft, noting which way around it is fitted, and remove the drive pin.

19 Remove the inner and outer rotors from the pump body.

20 Check the pump body and rotors for scoring and wear. If any damage or uneven or excessive wear is evident, replace the pump (individual parts aren't available). If you are rebuilding the engine, it's a good idea to install a new oil pump.

21 Install the rotors in the pump body and measure the clearance between the outer rotor and body with a feeler gauge (see illustration). Compare it to the value listed in this Chapter's Specifications. If it's excessive, replace the pump.

22 Measure the clearance between the inner

1 Cover screw
2 Dowel
3 Cover
4 Thrust washer
5 Drive pin
6 Driveshaft
7 Inner rotor
8 Outer rotor
9 Body

PUNCH MARK

H.28100

17.14 Exploded view of the oil pump

17.15 Undo the screw . . .

17.16 . . . and slide off the pump cover

17.21 Measuring outer rotor-to-body clearance

2

17.22 Measuring rotor tip clearance

17.23 Measuring rotor endfloat

17.26 Install the outer rotor, making sure the punch mark (arrow) is facing away from the body

rotor tip and the outer rotor tip **(see illustration)**. Again, replace the pump if the clearance is excessive.

23 Lay a straightedge across the rotors and pump body and measure the rotor endfloat (gap between the rotors and pump body) with a feeler gauge **(see illustration)**. If it's outside the limits listed in this Chapter's Specifications, replace the pump.

24 Inspect the pump drive chain and sprockets for wear and damage and replace if necessary. If replacement is necessary note that both sprockets and the chain should be replaced as a set.

25 If the pump is good make sure all components are clean and lubricate them with clean engine oil. Reassemble the pump as follows.

26 Fit the outer rotor making sure its punch

mark is facing away from the pump body **(see illustration)**.

27 Install the inner rotor making sure its drive pin slot is facing away from the pump body **(see illustration)**.

28 Insert the driveshaft, making sure it is fitted the correct way around and insert the drive pin **(see illustration)**. Slide the driveshaft into position so that the drive pin is engaged in its slot in the inner rotor **(see illustration)**.

29 Fit the thrust washer to the driveshaft **(see illustration)**.

30 Fit the locating dowel then install the pump cover and securely tighten the retaining screw.

Installation

31 Lubricate the pump rotors with clean

engine oil and check that the pump driveshaft rotates freely.

32 Install the pump in the crankcase making sure its driveshaft end is correctly aligned with the slot in the end of the water pump shaft.

33 Fit the pump bolts and tighten them securely.

34 Engage both the drive sprocket and pump sprocket with the chain noting that the "OUT" mark on the pump sprocket must be positioned so that it will be facing away from the pump when the chain is installed.

35 Fit the guide bush on the mainshaft **(see illustration)**. Install the chain and sprocket assembly over the mainshaft guide bush and pump driveshaft and check the sprocket is fitted the correct way around **(see illustration)**.

17.27 Install the inner rotor with its slot facing away from the body

17.28a Insert the driveshaft and drive pin . . .

17.28b . . . making sure the pin is correctly located in the inner rotor slot (arrow)

17.29 Do not omit the thrust washer from between the rotor and cover

17.35a Slide the guide bush on the mainshaft . . .

17.35b . . . and install the oil pump chain and sprocket assembly. Make sure the pump sprocket OUT mark (arrow) is facing outwards

17.36 Apply thread-lock to the threads of the oil pump sprocket retaining bolt prior to installation

19.4 Disconnect the water pump hose from the side of the oil cooler . . .

19.5 . . . and the coolant union hose (A) from the top of the oil cooler; oil cooler retaining bolt (B)

36 Clean the sprocket bolt and apply a few drops of a suitable locking compound to its threads **(see illustration)**.

37 Fit the sprocket bolt and tighten it to the specified torque. Prevent the sprocket from rotating by inserting a screwdriver through one of the sprocket holes **(see illustration 17.11)**.

38 Install the clutch as described in Section 14.

18 Oil pressure relief valve - removal, inspection and installation

Note: The pressure relief valve can be removed with the engine in the frame.

Removal

1 Remove the oil pan and pressure relief valve as described in Section 16.

Inspection

2 Push the plunger into the relief valve body and check for free movement. If the valve operation is sticky it must be replaced (individual parts are not available).

Installation

3 Install the pressure relief valve and oil pan as described in Section 16.

19 Oil cooler - removal and installation

Note: The oil cooler can be removed with the engine in the frame. If work is being carried out with the engine removed ignore the preliminary steps.

Removal

1 Remove the fairing lower section and both middle sections as described in Chapter 8.

2 Drain the engine oil as described in Chapter 1 and remove the oil filter. **Note:** *If the filter is damaged or disfigured on removal it must be replaced.*

3 Drain the coolant as described in Chapter 1.

4 Slacken their clamps and disconnect the two coolant hoses from the oil cooler body **(see illustration)**.

5 Undo the bolt and withdraw the oil cooler from the front of the crankcase **(see illustration)**. Recover the large O-ring.

Installation

6 Install a new O-ring in the oil cooler groove and smear it with engine oil **(see illustration)**.

7 Apply a few drops of non-permanent thread locking agent to the threads of the oil cooler bolt, position the oil cooler on the crankcase so that its slot engages the lug on the

crankcase, and tighten the oil cooler bolt to the specified torque setting **(see illustrations)**.

8 Reconnect the coolant hoses and secure them with the clamps.

9 Apply a smear of engine oil to the oil filter O-ring and screw it onto the oil cooler bolt. If the Honda tool is available, it can be secured to a torque setting (see Chapter 1).

10 Refill the engine with oil and the cooling system with coolant as described in Chapter 1. Start the engine and check that there are no leaks from the oil cooler.

11 Install the fairing sections as described in Chapter 8.

20 Gearshift mechanism - removal, inspection and installation

Note: The gearshift mechanism components can be removed with the engine in the frame. If work is being carried out with the engine removed ignore the preliminary steps.

Removal

1 Remove the clutch as described in Section 14.

2 Undo the clamp bolt and disconnect the gearshift lever or linkage crank (as applicable) from the engine. Note the alignment of, and any existing alignment marks between, the

2

19.6 Fit a new O-ring in the groove on the oil cooler body

19.7a Apply thread-lock to the oil cooler bolt threads and align the slot with the crankcase lug (arrow)

19.7b Tighten the oil cooler bolt to the specified torque setting

1 Right shift fork
2 Center shift fork
3 Left shift fork
4 Shift drum
5 Shift drum cam
6 Shift fork shaft
7 Stopper arm
8 Spring
9 Gearshift shaft
10 Return spring
11 Spring anchor post
12 Retaining plate
13 Bolt
14 Washer
15 Thrust washer
16 Bearing
17 Snap-ring
18 Bolt
19 Locating pin
20 Bolt
21 Washer (early models only)

20.3 Gearshift mechanism components

shaft and the lever or crank, and make your own marks if none are visible **(see illustration 5.14)**.

3 Withdraw the gearshift shaft from the right side of the crankcase and recover the thrust washer from the shaft **(see illustration)**.

4 Unscrew the stopper arm bolt and remove the stopper arm, washer and spring, noting their correct fitted positions.

5 Unscrew the shift drum cam bolt and remove the cam **(see illustration)**. Remove the locating pin from the shift drum and store

it with the cam for safe-keeping **(see illustration)**.

Inspection

6 Inspect the gearshift shaft return spring anchor post. If it's worn or damaged, replace it. If it's loose, unscrew it, apply a few drops of thread locking compound to the threads, reinstall the post and tighten it to the specified torque setting.

7 Check the gearshift shaft for straightness and damage to the splines. If the shaft is bent,

you can attempt to straighten it, but if the splines are damaged it will have to be replaced.

8 Inspect the gearshift shaft return spring, and selector pawl and spring for damage. The return spring can be replaced individually but if the selector pawl or spring are damaged the complete shaft must be replaced. To replace the return spring, remove the snap-ring and washer (US 1993 and 1994 models, UK N and P models), then slide off the spring. Fit the new spring, making sure it is the correct way around and thus correctly engaged with the shaft, install the washer (where fitted) and secure it in position with the snap-ring **(see illustrations)**. Note that the snap-ring should be fitted with its chamfered edge facing the return spring and must be correctly located in the shaft groove.

9 Check the condition of the stopper lever and spring. Replace the stopper lever if it's worn where it contacts the shift cam. Replace the spring if it's distorted.

10 Inspect the pins on the end of the shift cam. If they're worn or damaged, replace the cam.

11 Check the condition of the oil seal in the crankcase. If it has been leaking, pry it out (on US 1996 through 1999 models and UK T to X models first undo the bolt and remove the seal retainer plate) **(see illustration)**. It's a good idea to replace it in any case, since gaining access to it requires a fair amount of work. Install a new seal with its spring-side facing inwards. It should be possible to install the seal with thumb pressure, but if necessary, drive it in with a socket the same diameter as the seal's outer edge **(see illustration)**.

20.5a Unscrew the bolt then remove the shift cam . . .

20.5b . . . and withdraw the locating pin

20.8a Slide the return spring along the gearshift shaft . . .

20.8b . . . and engage it with the tab (arrow). Secure it in position with the snap-ring

20.11a Prise out the gearshift shaft oil seal with a screwdriver . . .

20.11b . . . and press the new seal into position with a suitable socket

20.13 Install the shift cam making sure its hole is correctly engaged with the locating pin (arrow)

20.14 Apply thread-lock to the shift cam bolt threads before installing it

20.15a Fit the stopper arm, washer and spring to the bolt . . .

20.15b . . . and screw the assembly into position in the crankcase, making sure the stopper arm is correctly engaged with the cam's neutral detent as shown

20.16 Slide the thrust washer (arrow) on the gearshift shaft . . .

20.18 . . . and install the shaft in the crankcase making sure the spring engages correctly with the anchor post (arrow) - components are shown in neutral position

Installation

12 Fit the locating pin to the shift drum.
13 Fit the shift cam to the drum, aligning its hole with the locating pin **(see illustration)**.
14 Clean the shift cam bolt and apply a drop of non-permanent thread locking compound to its threads **(see illustration)**. Install the bolt and tighten it to the specified torque setting.
15 Fit the stopper arm, washer and spring to the stopper arm bolt, noting that the spring should be positioned to hold the stopper arm against the cam **(see illustration)**. Screw the stopper arm bolt into the crankcase. Using a screwdriver, lift the arm and position it on the shift cam. With the arm correctly positioned, securely tighten the bolt **(see illustration)**.
16 Slide the thrust washer on the gearshift shaft **(see illustration)**.
17 Apply a smear of grease to the lip of the gearshift shaft oil seal and wrap the splines of the gearshift shaft with electrical tape, so the splines don't damage the seal as the shaft is installed.
18 Slide the gearshift shaft into the crankcase **(see illustration)**. Make sure the return spring is correctly located over its anchor post and the selector pawls are aligned with the pins on the shift cam. Remove the tape.
19 Align the marks noted or made on removal between the gearshift lever or linkage

crank and the gearshift shaft, then locate the gearshift lever/linkage crank on the shaft splines **(see illustration 5.14)**. Fit the clamp bolt and tighten it securely.
20 Check the operation of the external shift mechanism then install the clutch as described in Section 14.

21 Alternator -
removal and installation

Note: *To remove the alternator rotor the special Honda rotor puller, Part Number 07733-0020001, or a pattern equivalent will be required. Do not attempt to remove the rotor using any other method. The alternator rotor can be removed with the engine in the frame. If work is being carried out with the engine removed, ignore the preliminary steps.*

Removal

1 Remove the fairing lower section, left middle section and rider's seat as described in Chapter 8.
2 Drain the engine oil as described in Chapter 1.
3 Trace the wiring back from the left crankshaft end cover to the three-pin connector under the seat which contains the yellow alternator wires **(see illustration**

5.13a). Disconnect the alternator wiring connector and free the wiring from the clips on the inside of the frame and fuel pump bracket.
4 Unscrew the nine cover retaining bolts and withdraw the cover squarely from the engine unit **(see illustration)**. **Note:** *Due to the magnetic pull of the rotor, the cover may prove difficult to remove. Do not pry the cover away with a screwdriver as the mating surfaces will be damaged.*
5 Remove the cover locating dowel from the crankcase and discard the gasket.
6 Slacken and remove the rotor retaining bolt and washer whilst holding the rotor to prevent it turning. The rotor can be retained using a

21.4 Crankshaft left end cover is retained by nine bolts

2

21.6 Retain the rotor with a large open-ended wrench and loosen the retaining bolt

21.7 Use the special Honda puller to release the alternator rotor

21.8 Pick the Woodruff key out of the crankshaft

21.13 Oil the threads and underside of the rotor bolt head prior to installation

21.14a Apply sealant 10 to 15 mm each side of the crankcase half joint when installing the end cover

21.14b Smear sealant over the wiring grommet face

large open-ended wrench on the rotor flats **(see illustration)**. Alternatively, if the engine is still in the frame, the engine can be locked through the transmission by selecting top gear and applying the rear brake hard.
7 Screw the rotor puller tool into the center of the rotor and tighten it securely **(see illustration)**. Sharply tap on the end of puller tool to release the rotor's grip on the tapered crankshaft end. Remove the rotor.
8 Recover the Woodruff key from the crankshaft and store it safely inside the alternator rotor **(see illustration)**.
9 Refer to Chapter 9 for details of alternator stator coil removal.

Installation

10 Degrease the rotor and crankshaft tapers and remove any metal particles of swarf from the rotor magnet. Remove all traces of gasket from the cover and crankcase mating surfaces.
11 Install the Woodruff key in the crankshaft taper.
12 Align the slot in the rotor taper with the Woodruff key and gently push the rotor on the crankshaft making sure the starter gear teeth are correctly meshed. Gently tap the rotor center with a soft-faced hammer to seat it on the crankshaft taper.
13 Oil the rotor bolt threads and underside if its flanged head. Install the washer on the bolt and tighten it to the specified torque setting

whilst holding the rotor using the method employed on removal **(see illustration)**.
14 Apply sealant to the crankcase half joints **(see illustration)**. Apply a smear of sealant to the crankshaft left end cover wiring grommet **(see illustration)**.
15 Install the locating dowel in the end cover and fit a new gasket over it **(see illustration)**.
16 Install the end cover on the crankcase and tighten its bolts evenly in a criss-cross pattern to the specified torque setting.
17 Make sure the wiring is correctly routed up to the three-pin connector and secure it with the ties.
18 Fill the engine with the correct type and amount of oil as described in Chapter 1.

21.15 Install a new gasket over the dowel (arrow)

19 Install the seat and fairing sections as described in Chapter 8.

22 Starter motor clutch - removal, inspection and installation

Note: *The starter motor clutch can be removed with the engine in the frame.*

Removal

1 Remove the alternator rotor as described in Section 21.
2 Remove the starter driven gear from the rear of the rotor **(see illustration)**.

22.2 Remove the starter driven gear from the rear of the alternator rotor

22.3 Withdraw its shaft and remove the starter idler gear from the engine

22.5a Inspect the starter clutch rollers . . .

22.5b . . . and the driven gear surface for signs of wear or damage - replace damaged components

3 Slide the idle gear shaft out of the crankcase and remove the idler gear **(see illustration)**.

Inspection

4 Inspect the starter idler gear and driven gear teeth and replace them as a pair if any teeth are chipped or missing. Check the idler shaft and gear bearing surfaces for signs of wear or damage, and replace if necessary.
5 Inspect the starter clutch rollers and driven gear contact surfaces for signs of wear and scoring **(see illustrations)**. The starter clutch rollers should be unmarked with no signs of wear such as pitting or flat spots. The degree of wear on the driven gear can be assessed by measuring the outside diameter of its boss and comparing it to the service limit given in the Specifications.
6 Inspect the crankshaft needle roller bearing and driven gear contact surfaces for wear or scoring. The bearing can be drawn off the crankshaft using a suitable puller. Install the new bearing, using a suitable tubular drift or a press.
Caution: When removing the bearing, take great care not to damage the surface of the main bearing journal. Worn main bearing shells can be used to protect the journal.
7 To replace the starter clutch roller assembly, clamp the rotor in a vise equipped with soft jaws then undo the six bolts and

remove the clutch from the back off the rotor **(see illustration)**.
8 Clean the starter clutch bolts and apply a drop of non-permanent thread locking compound to their threads **(see illustration)**.
9 Lubricate the starter clutch rollers with new engine oil and position on the rear of the rotor, install the bolts and tighten them to the specified torque setting **(see illustration)**.

Installation

10 Insert the idler gear shaft into the crankcase.
11 Apply a smear of clean engine oil to the shaft and slide on the idler gear.
12 Fit the driven gear to the rear of the alternator rotor, turning it counterclockwise (anti-clockwise) to help it engage with the starter clutch rollers.
13 Fit the alternator rotor as described in Section 21.

---

23 Shift drum and forks - removal, inspection and installation

Note: *The shift drum and forks can be removed with the engine in the frame via the oil pan aperture. However, if a complete overhaul is being carried out the shift drum and forks may be left in position until after the crankcase halves have been separated.*

Removal

1 Remove the oil pan as described in Section 16.
2 Remove the gearshift mechanism components as described in Section 20.
3 Unscrew the bolts securing the shift drum bearing retaining plates to the crankcase and remove both plates, noting which way around they are fitted.
4 Withdraw the shift fork shaft slowly and remove the shift forks from the crankcase as they are released from the end of the shaft. When all three shift forks have been removed, fully withdraw the shaft from the crankcase.
5 Remove the bearing and withdraw the shift drum from the crankcase.

Inspection

6 The shift forks and shaft should be closely inspected to ensure that they are not badly damaged or worn.
7 Measure the width of both fork ends and the internal diameter of the shaft bore. If either fork end or the shaft bore has worn beyond its service limit the shift fork(s) must be replaced.
8 The shift fork shaft can be checked for trueness by rolling it along a flat surface. A bent shaft will cause difficulty in selecting gears and make the gearshift action heavy. Measure the diameter of the shaft at the points where it is in contact with the shift forks. If the shaft is bent or has worn beyond

2

22.7 Starter clutch is retained by six bolts (arrows)

22.8 Apply thread-lock to the starter clutch retaining bolts prior to installation . . .

22.9 . . . and tighten them to the specified torque setting

23.11 Fit the bearing to the shift drum . . .

23.12 . . . and insert the drum and bearing into the crankcase

23.13 Locate the shift fork shaft in the crankcase

23.14 Each shift fork is marked with a letter to identify its correct fitted position (arrows)

23.15a Making sure all shift forks are fitted with their markings facing the right, install the right fork . . .

its service limit at any point it must be replaced.

9 Inspect the shift drum grooves and selector fork guide pins for signs of wear or damage. If either component shows signs of wear or damage the shift fork(s) and drum must be replaced.

10 Check that the shift drum bearing rotates freely and has no sign of freeplay between its inner and outer race. Replace the bearing if necessary.

Installation

11 Fit the bearing to the shift drum **(see illustration)**.

12 Lubricate the bearing and shift drum

grooves with clean engine oil and insert the shift drum and bearing into position in the crankcase **(see illustration)**.

13 Apply a smear of engine oil to the shift fork shaft and slide the shaft partially into the crankcase **(see illustration)**.

14 The shift forks can be identified by the letter cast on each one; L denotes the left fork, C the center, and R the right **(see illustration)**. Note: *All shift forks must be installed in the crankcase so that the letter on each one faces towards the right side of the casing (clutch).*

15 Locate the right fork with its grooves in the gear and shift drum and slide in the shift fork shaft until it engages with the fork. Repeat the process for the center and left fork

and push the shaft fully home, making sure each fork is positioned as described in Step 14 **(see illustrations)**.

16 Clean the shift drum bearing plate bolts and apply a drop of non-permanent locking compound to their threads.

17 Fit the bearing retaining plates making sure the "OUT" marks are facing outwards (away from the crankcase) **(see illustration)**. Clean the threads of the retaining plate bolts and apply a drop of non-permanent locking compound to them. Install the bolts and tighten them securely.

18 Install the gearshift mechanism components as described in Section 20.

19 Install the oil pan as described in Section 16.

24 Crankcase -
separation and reassembly

Separation

1 To examine and repair or replace the crankshaft, pistons and connecting rods, bearings and transmission components, the crankcase must be split into two parts.

2 To enable the crankcases to be split the engine must be removed from the frame (see Section 5) and the following components first

23.17 Fit the bearing retaining plates with the OUT mark facing outwards making sure each is correctly engaged with the crankcase peg (arrow)

23.15b . . . followed by the center fork . . .

23.15c . . . and finally the left fork

24.5 Crankcase upper half bolts

1 6 mm bolts   2 8 mm bolts

24.6 Crankcase lower half bolts

1 6 mm bolts   2 10 mm bolt   3 9 mm bolts

24.9 Remove the three dowels if they are loose

removed with reference to the relevant Sections.

a) *Camshafts and followers*
b) *Cam chain and blades*
c) *Cylinder head*
d) *Clutch*
e) *Oil pan*
f) *Oil pump*
g) *Gearshift mechanism components*
h) *Alternator rotor*

Note: *If the crankcase halves are being separated just to examine the transmission shafts or crankshaft then there is no need to remove the cylinder head.*

3 If a complete engine overhaul is planned, also remove the starter motor (see Chapter 9), the starter clutch idler gear (see Section 22), the oil galley plug **(see illustration 24.27)**, the water pump and coolant union (see Chapter 3), the oil cooler (see Section 19) and the neutral switch (see Chapter 9).

4 With all the relevant components removed proceed as follows.

5 With the crankcase the right way up, slacken and remove the four 6 mm and two 8 mm bolts from the top of the crankcase **(see illustration)**. **Note:** *As each bolt is removed, store it in its relative position in a cardboard template of the crankcase halves. This will ensure all bolts are installed in the correct location on reassembly.* Discard the sealing

washers fitted to five of the bolts; new ones must be fitted on reassembly.

6 Turn the crankcase upside down. Working around the crankcase, unscrew the fourteen 6 mm lower crankcase bolts **(see illustration)**. **Note:** *As each bolt is removed, store it in its relative position in a cardboard template of the crankcase halves. This will ensure all bolts are installed in the correct location on reassembly.* Unscrew the single 10 mm bolt from the left rear corner of the crankcase.

7 Working in a criss-cross pattern, starting from the outside and working inwards, gradually slacken the ten 9 mm lower crankcase bolts **(see illustration 24.6)**. Once all the bolts are loose, unscrew and remove them along with their sealing washers, where fitted.

8 Carefully lift the lower crankcase half, leaving the crankshaft and transmission shafts in the upper half of the crankcase. As the upper half is lifted away take care not to dislodge or lose any main bearing inserts. **Note:** *If it won't come easily away, make sure all fasteners have been removed. Don't pry against the crankcase mating surfaces or they will leak; initial separation can be achieved by tapping gently with a soft-faced mallet.*

9 Remove the three locating dowels from the upper crankcase half **(see illustration)**.

10 Remove the two oil jets from the upper crankcase half noting which way around they

are fitted. **Note:** *The jets differ in profile - take note of their exact location.*

Reassembly

11 Install the crankshaft and transmission shafts in the upper crankcase as described in Sections 29 and 30.

12 Remove all traces of sealant from the crankcase mating surfaces, being careful not to let any fall into the case as this is done.

13 Check that all components are installed and that they can rotate smoothly and easily.

14 Lubricate the transmission shafts and crankshaft with clean engine oil then use a rag soaked in high flash-point solvent to wipe over the gasket surfaces of both halves to remove all traces of oil.

15 Make sure the oil jet holes are clear. Fit both jets to the upper crankcase half **(see illustration)**.

16 Install the three locating dowels in the upper crankcase half **(see illustration 24.15)**.

17 Apply a small amount of suitable sealant to the mating surface of the upper crankcase half **(see illustration)**.

Caution: Don't apply an excessive amount of sealant, as it will ooze out when the case halves are assembled and may obstruct oil passages and prevent the bearings from seating.

18 Check the position of the shift cam, shift forks and transmission shafts - make sure they're in the neutral position (i.e. the mainshaft and countershaft rotate independently of each other).

19 Make sure that the main bearing inserts are in position and carefully lower the lower crankcase half onto the upper half. The shift forks must engage with their respective slots in the transmission gears as the halves are joined.

20 Check that the lower crankcase half is correctly seated and that all shafts are free to rotate. **Note:** *If the casings are not correctly seated, remove the lower crankcase half and investigate the problem. Do not attempt to pull them together using the crankcase bolts as the casing will crack and be ruined.*

21 Clean the threads of the ten 9 mm lower crankcase bolts thoroughly, then apply engine oil to their threads and undersides of their

2

24.15 Crankcase dowels (1) and oil jets (2)

24.17 Apply sealant to the shaded areas of the upper crankcase half

heads. Where fitted, install new sealing washers on the bolts and insert them in their original locations **(see illustration)**.

22 Starting from the center and working outwards in a criss-cross pattern, tighten all the bolts to approximately half the specified torque. Go around a second time in the same sequence and tighten them to the full torque setting given in the Specifications at the start of this Chapter.

23 Fit the single 10 mm crankcase bolt and tighten it to the specified torque setting.

24 Fit the fourteen 6 mm bolts in their original locations and tighten them to the specified torque setting.

25 Turn the crankcase over so that it is upright and install the two 8 mm upper crankcase bolts with new sealing washers; tighten them to the specified torque. Install new sealing washers on the three 6 mm bolt which locate in the holes marked with the triangles **(see illustration 24.5)**, then install all four 6 mm bolts and tighten them to the specified torque setting.

26 With all crankcase fasteners tightened, check that the crankshaft and transmission shafts rotate smoothly and easily. If there are any signs of undue stiffness or of any other problem, the fault must be rectified before proceeding further.

27 Fit a new O-ring to the oil gallery plug. Apply a smear of oil to the O-ring to ease installation and insert the plug into position in the crankcase **(see illustration)**.

28 Install all other removed assemblies in the reverse of the sequence given in Steps 3 and 2.

25 Crankcase - inspection and servicing

1 After the crankcases have been separated and the crankshaft and transmission components have been removed, the crankcases should be cleaned thoroughly with new solvent and dried with compressed air.

Cylinder bores

Note: *Don't attempt to separate the liners from the cylinder block.*

2 Check the cylinder walls carefully for scratches and score marks.

3 Using the appropriate precision measuring tools, check each cylinder's diameter. Measure near the top, center and bottom of the cylinder bore, parallel to the crankshaft axis. Next, measure each cylinder's diameter at the same three locations across the crankshaft axis. Compare the results to this Chapter's Specifications. If the cylinder bores are tapered, out-of-round, worn beyond the specified limits, or badly scuffed or scored, have them rebored and honed by a dealer service department or a motorcycle repair

24.21 Lubricate the threads and underside of the heads of the 9 mm lower crankcase bolts prior to installation

shop. If a rebore is done, oversize pistons and rings will be required as well (see Section 27).

4 As an alternative, if the precision measuring tools are not available, a dealer service department or motorcycle repair shop will make the measurements and offer advice concerning servicing of the cylinders.

5 If they are in reasonably good condition and not worn to the outside of the limits, and if the piston-to-cylinder clearances can be maintained properly (see Section 27), then the cylinders do not have to be rebored; honing is all that is necessary.

6 To perform the honing operation you will need the proper size flexible hone with fine stones, or a "bottle brush" type hone, plenty of light oil or honing oil, some shop towels and an electric drill motor. Hold the upper crankcase half in a vise (cushioned with soft jaws or wood blocks) when performing the honing operation. Mount the hone in the drill motor, compress the stones and slip the hone into the top of the cylinder. Lubricate the cylinder thoroughly, turn on the drill and move the hone up and down in the cylinder at a pace which will produce a fine crosshatch pattern on the cylinder wall with the crosshatch lines intersecting at approximately a 60° angle. Be sure to use plenty of lubricant and do not take off any more material than is absolutely necessary to produce the desired effect. Do not withdraw the hone from the cylinder while it is running. Instead, shut off the drill and continue moving the hone up and down in the cylinder until it comes to a complete stop, then compress the stones and withdraw the hone. Wipe the oil out of the cylinder and repeat the procedure on the other cylinders. Remember, do not remove too much material from the cylinder wall. If you do not have the tools, or do not desire to perform the honing operation, a dealer service department or motorcycle repair shop will generally do it for a reasonable fee.

7 Next, the cylinders must be thoroughly washed with warm soapy water to remove all traces of the abrasive grit produced during the honing operation. Be sure to run a brush through the bolt holes and flush them with running water. After rinsing, dry the cylinders

24.27 Fit a new O-ring (arrow) to the oil galley plug and install it in the right end of the crankcase

thoroughly and apply a coat of light, rust-preventative oil to all machined surfaces.

Crankcase castings

8 Remove any oil passage plugs that haven't already been removed. All oil passages should be blown out with compressed air.

9 All traces of old gasket sealant should be removed from the mating surfaces. Minor damage to the surfaces can be cleaned up with a fine sharpening stone or grindstone. *Caution: Be very careful not to nick or gouge the crankcase mating surfaces or leaks will result. Check both crankcase halves very carefully for cracks and other damage.*

10 Small cracks or holes in aluminum castings may be repaired with an epoxy resin adhesive as a temporary measure. Permanent repairs can only be effected by argon-arc welding, and only a specialist in this process is in a position to advise on the economy or practical aspect of such a repair. If any damage is found that can't be repaired, replace the crankcase halves as a set.

11 Damaged threads can be economically reclaimed by using a diamond section wire insert, of the Helicoil type, which is easily fitted after drilling and re-tapping the affected thread. Most motorcycle dealers and small engineering firms offer a service of this kind.

12 Sheared studs or screws can usually be removed with screw extractors, which consist of a tapered, left thread screws of very hard steel. These are inserted into a pre-drilled hole in the stud, and usually succeed in dislodging the most stubborn stud or screw. If a problem arises which seems beyond your scope, it is worth consulting a professional engineering firm before condemning an otherwise sound casing. Many of these firms advertise regularly in the motorcycle press.

26 Main and connecting rod bearings - general note

1 Even though main and connecting rod bearings are generally replaced with new ones during the engine overhaul, the old bearings should be retained for close examination as they may reveal valuable information about the condition of the engine.

2 Bearing failure occurs mainly because of lack of lubrication, the presence of dirt or other foreign particles, overloading the engine and/or corrosion. Regardless of the cause of bearing failure, it must be corrected before the engine is reassembled to prevent it from happening again.

3 When examining the bearings, remove the main bearings from the case halves and the rod bearings from the connecting rods and caps and lay them out on a clean surface in the same general position as their location on the crankshaft journals. This will enable you to match any noted bearing problems with the corresponding crankshaft journal.

4 Dirt and other foreign particles get into the engine in a variety of ways. It may be left in the engine during assembly or it may pass through filters or breathers. It may get into the oil and from there into the bearings. Metal chips from machining operations and normal engine wear are often present. Abrasives are sometimes left in engine components after reconditioning operations such as cylinder honing, especially when parts are not thoroughly cleaned using the proper cleaning methods. Whatever the source, these foreign objects often end up imbedded in the soft bearing material and are easily recognized. Large particles will not imbed in the bearing and will score or gouge the bearing and journal. The best prevention for this cause of bearing failure is to clean all parts thoroughly and keep everything spotlessly clean during engine reassembly. Frequent and regular oil and filter changes are also recommended.

5 Lack of lubrication or lubrication breakdown has a number of interrelated causes. Excessive heat (which thins the oil), overloading (which squeezes the oil from the bearing face) and oil leakage or throw off from excessive bearing clearances, worn oil pump or high engine speeds all contribute to lubrication breakdown. Blocked oil passages will also starve a bearing and destroy it. When lack of lubrication is the cause of bearing failure, the bearing material is wiped or extruded from the steel backing of the bearing. Temperatures may increase to the point where the steel backing and the journal turn blue from overheating.

6 Riding habits can have a definite effect on bearing life. Full throttle low speed operation, or lugging (labouring) the engine, puts very high loads on bearings, which tend to squeeze out the oil film. These loads cause the bearings to flex, which produces fine cracks in the bearing face (fatigue failure). Eventually the bearing material will loosen in pieces and tear away from the steel backing. Short trip riding leads to corrosion of bearings, as insufficient engine heat is produced to drive off the condensed water and corrosive gases produced. These products collect in the engine oil, forming acid and sludge. As the oil is carried to the engine bearings, the acid attacks and corrodes the bearing material.

7 Incorrect bearing installation during engine assembly will lead to bearing failure as well. Tight fitting bearings which leave insufficient bearing oil clearances result in oil starvation. Dirt or foreign particles trapped behind a bearing insert result in high spots on the bearing which lead to failure.

8 To avoid bearing problems, clean all parts thoroughly before reassembly, double check all bearing clearance measurements and lubricate the new bearings with clean engine oil during installation.

27 Piston/connecting rod assemblies - removal, inspection and installation

Removal

1 Separate the crankcase halves as described in Section 24. Before removing the piston/connecting rods from the crankshaft measure the side clearance of each rod with a feeler gauge. If the clearance on any rod is greater than the service limit listed in this Chapter's Specifications, that rod will have to be replaced with a new one.

2 Using a center punch or paint, mark the relevant cylinder number on each connecting rod and bearing cap (No. 1 cylinder on left end).

3 Unscrew the bearing cap nuts and withdraw the cap, complete with the lower bearing insert, from each of the four connecting rods **(see illustration)**. Push the connecting rods up and off their crankpins, then remove the upper bearing insert. Keep the cap, nuts and (if they are to be reused) the bearing inserts together in their correct sequence.

4 Remove the ridge of carbon from the top of each cylinder bore. If there is a pronounced wear ridge on the top of each bore, remove with a ridge reamer.

5 Push each piston/connecting rod assembly up and remove it from the top of the bore making sure the connecting rod does not mark the cylinder bore walls.

Caution: Do not try to remove the piston/connecting rod from the bottom of the cylinder bore. The piston will not pass the crankcase main bearing webs. If the piston is pulled right to the bottom of the bore the oil control ring will expand and lock the piston in position. If this happens it is likely the ring will be broken.

6 Immediately install the relevant bearing cap, inserts and nuts on each piston/connecting rod assembly so that they are all kept together as a matched set.

7 Using a sharp scriber, scratch the number of each piston into its crown (or use a suitable marker pen if the piston is clean enough).

8 Support the first piston and, using a small screwdriver or scriber, carefully pry out a snap-ring from the piston groove **(see illustration)**.

9 Push the piston pin out from the opposite end to free the piston from the rod. You may have to deburr the area around the groove to enable the pin to slide out (use a triangular file for this procedure). If the pin is tight, use a piston pin puller (see *Maintenance techniques, tools and working facilities*) or tap it out using a suitable hammer and punch, taking care not to damage the piston. Repeat the procedure for the other pistons.

> **HAYNES HINT** *If a piston pin is a tight fit in the bosses, soak a rag in boiling water then wring it out and wrap it around the piston - this will expand the alloy piston sufficiently to release its grip on the pin.*

27.3 On removal make sure the bearing insert stays in the cap

27.8 Using a scriber to pry out a piston pin snap-ring

2

27.11 Remove the piston rings with a ring removal and installation tool

27.18 Measuring piston ring-to-groove clearance

27.19 Measuring piston diameter

Inspection

Pistons

10 Before the inspection process can be carried out, the pistons must be cleaned and the old piston rings removed.

11 Using a piston ring removal and installation tool, carefully remove the rings from the pistons (see illustration). Do not nick or gouge the pistons in the process.

12 Scrape all traces of carbon from the tops of the pistons. A hand-held wire brush or a piece of fine emery cloth can be used once most of the deposits have been scraped away. Do not, under any circumstances, use a wire brush mounted in a drill motor to remove deposits from the pistons; the piston material is soft and will be eroded away by the wire brush.

13 Use a piston ring groove cleaning tool to remove any carbon deposits from the ring grooves. If a tool is not available, a piece broken off an old ring will do the job. Be very careful to remove only the carbon deposits. Do not remove any metal and do not nick or gouge the sides of the ring grooves.

14 Once the deposits have been removed, clean the pistons with solvent and dry them thoroughly. Make sure the oil return holes below the oil ring grooves are clear.

15 If the pistons are not damaged or worn excessively and if the cylinders are not to be rebored, new pistons will not be necessary. Normal piston wear appears as even, vertical wear on the thrust surfaces of the piston and slight looseness of the top ring in its groove. New piston rings, on the other hand, should always be used when an engine is rebuilt.

16 Carefully inspect each piston for cracks around the skirt, at the pin bosses and at the ring lands.

17 Look for scoring and scuffing on the thrust faces of the skirt, holes in the piston crown and burned areas at the edge of the crown. If the skirt is scored or scuffed, the engine may have been suffering from overheating and/or abnormal combustion, which caused excessively high operating temperatures. The oil pump and oil cooler should be checked thoroughly. A hole in the piston crown, an extreme to be sure, is an

indication that abnormal combustion (pre-ignition) was occurring. Burned areas at the edge of the piston crown are usually evidence of spark knock (detonation). If any of the above problems exist, the causes must be corrected or the damage will occur again.

18 Measure the piston ring-to-groove clearance by laying a new piston ring in the ring groove and slipping a feeler gauge in beside it (see illustration). Check the clearance at three or four locations around the groove. Be sure to use the correct ring for each groove; they are different. If the clearance is greater than the service limit, new pistons will have to be used when the engine is reassembled.

19 Calculate the piston-to-bore clearance by measuring the bore (see Section 25) and the piston diameter. Make sure that the pistons and cylinders are correctly matched. Measure the piston across the skirt on the thrust faces at a 90° angle to the piston pin, 15 mm (0.6 inch) up from the bottom of the skirt (see illustration). Subtract the piston diameter from the bore diameter to obtain the clearance. If it is greater than specified, the cylinders will have to be rebored and new oversized pistons and rings installed.

20 Apply clean engine oil to the pin, insert it into the piston and check for freeplay by rocking the pin back-and-forth (see illustration). If the pin is loose, new pistons and pins must be installed. If the necessary measuring equipment is available measure the pin diameter and piston pin bore and

check the readings obtained do not exceed the limits given in this Chapter's Specifications. Replace components that are worn beyond the specified limit.

21 If the pistons are to be replaced, ensure the correct size of piston is ordered. As well as standard pistons, Honda produce two oversizes (+0.50 mm and +1.0 mm) for US 1993 through 1997 models and UK N to V models, and one oversize (+0.25 mm) for US 1998 and 1999 and UK W and X models. **Note:** *Oversize pistons have their relevant size stamped on top of the piston crown, eg a 0.50 mm piston will be marked 0.50.*

22 Install the rings on the pistons as described in Section 28.

Connecting rods

23 Check the connecting rods for cracks and other obvious damage Lubricate the piston pin for each rod, install it in its original rod and check for play (see illustration). If it wobbles, replace the connecting rod and/or the pin. If the necessary measuring equipment is available measure the pin diameter and connecting rod bore and check the readings obtained do not exceed the limits given in this Chapter's Specifications. Replace components that are worn beyond the specified limit.

24 Refer to Section 26 and examine the connecting rod bearing inserts If they are scored, badly scuffed or appear to have been seized, new bearings must be installed. Always replace the bearings in the connecting

27.20 Slip the pin into the piston and try to wiggle it back-and-forth; if it's loose, replace the piston and pin

27.23 Slip the piston pin into the rod and rock it back-and-forth to check for looseness

27.27 The color code is painted on the side of the bearing

27.28 Crankshaft crankpin journal identification marks (A) and main bearing journal identification marks (B)

rods as a set. If they are badly damaged, check the corresponding crankpin. Evidence of extreme heat, such as discoloration, indicates that lubrication failure has occurred. Be sure to thoroughly check the oil pump and pressure relief valve as well as all oil holes and passages before reassembling the engine.

25 Have the rods checked for twist and bending at a dealer service department or other motorcycle repair shop.

26 If a connecting rod is to replaced, it is essential that the new rod is of the correct weight group to minimise vibration. The weight is indicated by a letter stamped on the big-end cap of each rod. This letter together with the connecting rod size mark (see Step 29) should be quoted when purchasing new connecting rod(s). *Note: Honda state that the maximum difference between any two connecting rods in the engine must be only one weight group.*

Bearing selection

27 The connecting rod bearing running clearance is controlled in production by selecting one of five grades of bearing insert. The grades are indicated by a color-coding marked on the edge of each insert **(see illustration)**. In order, from the thickest to the thinnest, the insert grades are: Blue, Black, Brown, Green and Yellow. New bearing inserts are selected as follows using the crankpin and connecting rod size markings.

28 The standard crankpin journal diameter is divided into three size groups to allow for manufacturing tolerances. The size group of each crankpin can be determined by the letters which are stamped on the left end crank web **(see illustration)**. *Note: Ignore the numbers as these refer to the main bearing journals.* On the web will be an L followed by four letters, made up of the letters A, B and C, for example L ABAB. The letters indicate the diameter of each crankpin, starting with the left crankpin (No. 1 cylinder) and finishing with the right crankpin (no. 4 cylinder). If the equipment is available, these marks can be checked by direct measurement.

29 The connecting rods are also divided into three size groups to allow for manufacturing tolerances. The size group is in the form of

numbers (either 1, 2 or 3) **(see illustration)**. *Note: Ignore the letter as this indicates the weight group of the connecting rod.* If the equipment is available, these marks can be checked by direct measurement.

30 Match the relevant connecting rod code with its crankshaft code and select a new set of bearing inserts using the following table.

Connecting rod mark	Crankshaft mark	Insert color
1	A	Yellow
1	B	Green
1	C	Brown
2	A	Green
2	B	Brown
2	C	Black
3	A	Brown
3	B	Black
3	C	Blue

Oil clearance check

31 Whether new bearing inserts are being fitted or the original ones are being re-used, the connecting rod bearing oil clearance should be checked prior to reassembly.

32 Clean the backs of the bearing inserts and the bearing locations in both the connecting rod and bearing cap.

33 Press the bearing inserts into their locations, ensuring that the tab on each insert engages in the notch in the connecting rod/bearing cap. Make sure the bearings are fitted in the correct locations and take care not to touch any insert's bearing surface with your fingers.

27.29 Connecting rod bearing diameter number and weight group letter

34 There are two possible ways of checking the oil clearance, the first method is by direct measurement (see Steps 35 and 38) and the second by the use of a product known as Plastigauge (see Steps 36 to 38).

35 If the first method is to be used, fit the bearing cap to the connecting rod, with the bearing inserts in place. Make sure the cap is fitted the correct way around so the connecting rod and bearing cap weight/size markings are correctly aligned. Tighten the cap retaining nuts to the specified torque and measure the internal diameter of each assembled pair of bearing inserts. If the diameter of each corresponding crankpin journal is measured and then subtracted from the bearing internal diameter, the result will be the connecting rod bearing oil clearance.

36 If the second method is to be used, cut several lengths of the appropriate size Plastigauge (they should be slightly shorter than the width of the crankpin). Place a strand of Plastigauge on each (cleaned) crankpin journal and fit the (clean) piston/connecting rod assemblies, inserts and bearing caps. Make sure the cap is fitted the correct way around so the connecting rod and bearing cap weight/size markings are correctly aligned and tighten the bearing cap nuts to the specified torque wrench setting whilst ensuring that the connecting rod does not rotate. Take care not to disturb the Plastigauge. Slacken the bearing cap nuts and remove the connecting rod assemblies, again taking great care not to rotate the crankshaft.

37 Compare the width of the crushed Plastigauge on each crankpin to the scale printed on the Plastigauge envelope to obtain the connecting rod bearing oil clearance **(see illustration)**.

38 If the clearance is not within the specified limits, the bearing inserts may be the wrong grade (or excessively worn if the original inserts are being reused). Before deciding that different grade inserts are needed, make sure that no dirt or oil was trapped between the bearing inserts and the connecting rod or bearing cap when the clearance was measured. If the clearance is excessive, even with new inserts (of the correct size), the

27.37 Place the Plastigauge scale next to the flattened Plastigauge to measure the bearing clearance

2

27.41 When coupling the rod and piston make sure the piston IN mark is on the same side as the rod oilway (arrows)

27.42 Make sure both piston pin snap-rings are securely seated in the piston grooves

27.44 Install the bearings making sure each insert tab (arrow) is correctly engaged in its slot

crankpin is worn and the crankshaft should be replaced.

39 On completion carefully scrape away all traces of the Plastigauge material from the crankpin and bearing inserts using a fingernail or other object which is unlikely to score the inserts.

Installation

Note: *On US 1996 through 1999 models and UK T to X models, the standard pistons for cylinder Nos. 1 and 4 are different to those fitted to cylinder Nos. 2 and 3 pistons; Nos. 2 and 3 are marked with a B in the center of the top of the piston crown. Never install Nos. 2 and 3 pistons in cylinder Nos. 1 or 4 or vice versa.*

40 Check that each piston has one new snap-ring fitted to it and insert the piston pin from the opposite side. If it is a tight fit, the piston should be warmed first. If the original pistons/connecting rods are being installed, use the marks made on disassembly to ensure each piston is fitted to its correct connecting rod.

41 Lubricate the piston pin and connecting rod bores with clean engine oil and fit each piston to its respective connecting rod making sure that the IN mark on the crown of the piston is on the same side as the connecting rod oilway **(see illustration)**.

42 Push the piston pin through both piston bosses and the connecting rod bore. If necessary the pin can be tapped carefully into position, using a hammer and suitable drift, whilst supporting the connecting rod and piston. Secure each piston pin in position with

a second new snap-ring, making sure it is correctly seated in the piston groove **(see illustration)**.

43 Clean the backs of the bearing inserts and the bearing recesses in both the connecting rod and bearing cap. If new inserts are being fitted, ensure that all traces of the protective grease are cleaned off using kerosene (paraffin). Wipe dry the inserts and connecting rods with a lint-free cloth.

44 Press the bearing inserts into their locations. Make sure the tab on each insert engages in the notch in the connecting rod or bearing cap **(see illustration)**. Make sure the bearings are fitted in the correct locations and take care not to touch any insert's bearing surface with your fingers.

45 Lubricate the cylinder bores, the pistons and piston rings then lay out each piston/connecting rod assembly in its respective position.

46 Starting with assembly No. 1, position the top and second ring end gaps so they are 180° apart then position the oil control ring side rails so that their end gaps are 180° apart.

47 With the piston rings correctly positioned, clamp them in position with a piston ring compressor **(see illustration)**.

48 Insert the piston/connecting rod assembly into the top of its bore, taking care not to allow the connecting rod to mark the bore **(see illustration)**. Make sure the IN mark on the piston crown is on the intake side of the bore and push the piston into the bore until the piston crown is flush with the top of the bore.

49 Ensure that the connecting rod bearing insert is still correctly installed. Taking care not to mark the cylinder bores, liberally lubricate the crankpin and both bearing inserts, then pull the piston/connecting rod assembly down its bore and onto the crankpin.

50 Fit the bearing cap and insert to the connecting rod. Make sure the cap is fitted the correct way around so the connecting rod and bearing cap weight/size markings are correctly aligned **(see illustration 27.29)**.

51 Apply a smear of clean engine oil the threads and underside of the bearing cap nuts. Fit the nuts to the connecting rod and tighten them evenly, in two or three stages, to the specified torque setting **(see illustrations)**.

52 Check that the crankshaft is free to rotate easily, then install the three remaining assemblies in the same way.

27.47 Clamp the piston rings in position with a ring compressor . . .

27.48 . . . and insert the piston/connecting rod assembly, making sure each piston IN mark (arrow) is on the intake side of the bore

27.51a Lubricate the threads and heads of the connecting rod bearing cap nuts . . .

27.51b . . . and tighten the nuts to the specified torque as described in text

28.3 Measuring piston ring end gap

28.5 If the end gap is too small, clamp a file in a vise and file the ring ends (from outside in only) to enlarge the gap slightly

28.9a Installing the oil expander ring - make sure the ends don't overlap

28 Piston rings - installation

1 Before installing the new piston rings, the ring end gaps must be checked.

2 Lay out the pistons and the new ring sets so the rings will be matched with the same piston and cylinder during the end gap measurement procedure and engine assembly.

3 Insert the top ring into the top of the first cylinder and square it up with the cylinder walls by pushing it in with the top of the piston. The ring should be about 25 mm below the top edge of the cylinder. To measure the end gap, slip a feeler gauge between the ends of the ring and compare the measurement to the Specifications **(see illustration)**.

4 If the gap is larger or smaller than specified, double check to make sure that you have the correct rings before proceeding.

5 If the gap is too small, it must be enlarged or the ring ends may come in contact with each other during engine operation, which can cause serious damage. The end gap can be increased by filing the ring ends very carefully with a fine file. When performing this operation, file only from the outside in **(see illustration)**.

6 Excess end gap is not critical unless it is greater than 1 mm. Again, double check to make sure you have the correct rings for your engine.

7 Repeat the procedure for each ring that will be installed in the first cylinder and for each ring in the remaining cylinders. Remember to keep the rings, pistons and cylinders matched up.

8 Once the ring end gaps have been checked/corrected, the rings can be installed on the pistons.

9 The oil control ring (lowest on the piston) is installed first. It is composed of three separate components. Slip the expander into the groove, then install the upper side rail. Do not use a piston ring installation tool on the oil ring side rails as they may be damaged. Instead, place one end of the side rail into the groove between the expander and the ring land. Hold it firmly in place and slide a finger around the piston while pushing the rail into the groove. Next, install the lower side rail in the same manner **(see illustrations)**.

10 After the three oil ring components have been installed, check to make sure that both the upper and lower side rails can be turned smoothly in the ring groove.

11 Install the second (middle) ring next. **Note:** *The second ring and top rings are slightly different in profile.* To avoid breaking

the ring, use a piston ring installation tool and make sure that the identification mark (the letters RN or T) is facing up **(see illustration)**. Fit the ring into the middle groove on the piston. Do not expand the ring any more than is necessary to slide it into place.

12 Finally, install the top ring in the same manner. Make sure the identifying mark (the letter R or T) is facing up.

13 Repeat the procedure for the remaining pistons and rings.

29 Crankshaft and main bearings - removal, inspection and installation

Removal

1 Separate the crankcase halves as described in Section 24.

2 Remove the piston/connecting rod assemblies as described in Section 27. **Note:** *If no work is to be carried out on the piston/connecting rod assemblies there is no need to remove them from the bores. The cylinder head can be left in position although the connecting rod bearing caps should be removed (see Section 27, Steps 1 through 3) and the pistons pushed up to the top of the bores so that the connecting rod ends are positioned clear of the crankshaft.*

3 Lift the crankshaft out of the upper crankcase half, taking care not to dislodge the bearing inserts **(see illustration)**.

28.9b Installing an oil ring side rail - don't use a ring installation tool to do this

28.11 Piston ring profiles

1   *Top ring*
2   *Second (middle) ring*
3   *Oil ring*
4   *Identification mark location*

29.3 Lifting the crankshaft out of position

2

4 The main bearing inserts can be removed from the crankcase halves by pushing their centers to the side, then lifting them out. Keep the bearing inserts in order.

Inspection

5 Clean the crankshaft with solvent, using a rifle-cleaning brush to scrub out the oil passages. If available, blow the crank dry with compressed air. Inspect the starter clutch needle roller bearing as described in Section 22 **(see illustration)**.

6 Refer to Section 26 and examine the main bearing inserts. If they are scored, badly scuffed or appear to have been seized, new bearings must be installed. Always replace the main bearings as a set. If they are badly damaged, check the corresponding crankshaft journal. Evidence of extreme heat, such as discoloration, indicates that lubrication failure has occurred. Be sure to thoroughly check the oil pump and pressure relief valve as well as all oil holes and passages before reassembling the engine.

7 The crankshaft journals should be given a close visual examination, paying particular attention where damaged bearing inserts have been discovered. If the journals are scored or pitted in any way a new crankshaft will be required. Note that undersizes are not available, precluding the option of re-grinding the crankshaft.

8 Set the crankshaft on V-blocks and check the runout with a dial indicator touching the center main bearing journal, comparing your findings with this Chapter's Specifications. If the runout exceeds the limit, replace the crank.

9 On US 1996 through 1999 models and UK T to X models, a sprung type primary drive sub-gear is mounted on the end of the crankshaft outside the primary drive main gear. Before dismantling the assembly, make a note of the positions of the springs in the sub-gear (there are six spring holes and three springs) so that they are correctly positioned on installation. Remove the snap-ring and the friction spring which sits behind it, then draw the sub-gear off the end of the crankshaft. Discard the snap-ring as a new one must be used. Remove the collar and springs. Check

29.5 Inspect the starter clutch needle roller bearing for signs of wear or damage

the gear teeth and springs for signs of wear or damage. Apply a smear of molybdenum disulfide oil (a mixture of molybdenum disulfide grease and oil in equal quantities) to the contact surfaces between the collar, the sub-gear and the main gear. Slide the collar onto the crankshaft with its grooved side facing in, then install the sub-gear, aligning the small hole with that in the main gear **(see illustration)**. Install the friction spring, followed by a new snap-ring, making sure the larger end tab faces the right (as you look at it) and the chamfered side faces in. Do not re-use the old snap-ring, and use only the specified type. Position the open end of the snap-ring so that it is at right-angles to the cutouts in the snap-ring groove in the crankshaft **(see illustration)**. Fit each spring into its hole, making sure they are positioned as noted on removal.

Bearing selection

10 The main bearing running clearance is controlled in production by selecting one of five grades of bearing insert. The grades are indicated by a color-coding marked on the edge of each insert **(see illustration 27.27)**. In order, from the thickest to the thinnest, the insert grades are: Black, Brown, Green, Yellow and Pink. New bearing inserts are selected as follows using the crankshaft journal and crankcase main bearing bore size markings.

11 The standard crankshaft journal diameter is divided into three size groups to allow for

manufacturing tolerances. The size group of each journal can be determined by the numbers which are stamped on the left end crank web **(see illustration 27.28)**. **Note:** *Ignore the letters as these refer to the crankpin journals.* On the web will be an L followed by five numbers, made up of the numbers 1, 2 and 3, for example L 12121. The numbers indicate the diameter of each crankshaft journal, starting with the left journal and finishing with the right journal. If the equipment is available, these marks can be checked by direct measurement.

12 The crankcase main bearing bore diameters are divided into three size groups to allow for manufacturing tolerances. The size group of each main bearing bore can be determined using the five letters stamped on the left end of the upper crankcase half **(see illustration)**. These will be made up of the letters A, B or C. The first letter indicates the diameter of the left journal, and the last the diameter of the right journal. If the equipment is available, these marks can be checked by direct measurement.

13 Match the relevant crankcase code with its crankshaft code and select a new set of bearing inserts using the following table.

Crankshaft mark	Crankcase mark	Insert color
1	A	Pink
1	B	Yellow
1	C	Green
2	A	Yellow
2	B	Green
2	C	Brown
3	A	Green
3	B	Brown
3	C	Black

Oil clearance check

14 Whether new bearing inserts are being fitted or the original ones are being re-used, the main bearing oil clearance should be checked prior to reassembly.

15 Clean the backs of the bearing inserts and the bearing locations in both crankcase halves.

16 Press the bearing inserts into their locations, ensuring that the tab on each insert engages in the notch in the crankcase. Make

29.9a Align the small holes between the main gear and the sub-gear as shown

29.9b Snap-ring end (A), cutouts (B), springs (C)

29.12 Crankcase main bearing bore diameter marks (arrow) are stamped on the left end of the upper crankcase half

29.27 Install the main bearing inserts making sure each insert tab (arrow) is correctly engaged in the crankcase slot

29.28 Lubricate all bearing inserts with clean engine oil prior to installing the crankshaft

sure the bearings are fitted in the correct locations and take care not to touch any insert's bearing surface with your fingers.

17 There are two possible ways of checking the oil clearance, the first method is by direct measurement (see Step 17 and 23) and the second by the use of a product known as Plastigauge (see Steps 18 to 23).

18 If the first method is to be used, with the main bearing inserts in position, carefully lower the lower crankcase half onto the upper half. Make sure that the shift forks (if fitted) engage with their respective slots in the transmission gears as the halves are joined. Check that the lower crankcase half is correctly seated. **Note:** *Do not tighten the crankcase bolts if the casing is not correctly seated.* Install the ten 9 mm lower crankcase bolts in their original locations and, starting from the center and working outwards in a criss-cross pattern, tighten them to the specified torque setting. Measure the internal diameter of each assembled pair of bearing inserts. If the diameter of each corresponding crankshaft journal is measured and then subtracted from the bearing internal diameter, the result will be the connecting rod bearing oil clearance.

19 If the second method is to be used, ensure the main bearing inserts are correctly fitted and that the inserts and crankshaft are clean and dry. Lay the crankshaft in position in the upper crankcase.

20 Cut several lengths of the appropriate size Plastigauge (they should be slightly shorter

than the width of the crankshaft journal). Place a strand of Plastigauge on each (cleaned) crankshaft journal.

21 Carefully install the lower crankcase half onto the upper half. Make sure that the shift forks (if fitted) engage with their respective slots in the transmission gears as the halves are joined. Check that the lower crankcase half is correctly seated. **Note:** *Do not tighten the crankcase bolts if the casing is not correctly seated.* Install the ten 9 mm lower crankcase bolts in their original locations and, starting from the center and working outwards in a criss-cross pattern, tighten them to the specified torque setting. Make sure that the crankshaft is not rotated as the bolts are tightened.

22 Slacken and remove the crankcase bolts, working in a criss-cross pattern from the outside in, then carefully lift off the lower crankcase half, making sure the Plastigauge is not disturbed.

23 Compare the width of the crushed Plastigauge on each crankshaft journal to the scale printed on the Plastigauge envelope to obtain the main bearing oil clearance **(see illustration 27.37)**.

24 If the clearance is not within the specified limits, the bearing inserts may be the wrong grade (or excessively worn if the original inserts are being reused). Before deciding that different grade inserts are needed, make sure that no dirt or oil was trapped between the bearing inserts and the crankcase halves when the clearance was measured. If the

clearance is excessive, even with new inserts (of the correct size), the crankshaft journal is worn and the crankshaft should be replaced.

25 On completion carefully scrape away all traces of the Plastigauge material from the crankshaft journal and bearing inserts; use a fingernail or other object which is unlikely to score the inserts.

Installation

26 Clean the backs of the bearing inserts and the bearing recesses in both crankcase halves. If new inserts are being fitted, ensure that all traces of the protective grease are cleaned off using kerosene (paraffin). Wipe dry the inserts and crankcase halves with a lint-free cloth.

27 Press the bearing inserts into their locations. Make sure the tab on each insert engages in the notch in the casing **(see illustration)**. Make sure the bearings are fitted in the correct locations and take care not to touch any insert's bearing surface with your fingers.

28 Lubricate the bearing inserts in the upper crankcase with clean engine oil **(see illustration)**.

29 Lower the crankshaft into position in the upper crankcase.

30 Fit the piston/connecting rod assemblies to the crankshaft as described in Section 27 if they were disconnected.

31 Reassemble the crankcase halves as described in Section 24.

30 Transmission shafts - removal and installation

Removal

1 Separate the crankcase halves as described in Section 24.

2 Unscrew the mainshaft bearing retaining plate bolts and remove the plate from the right side of the upper crankcase half, noting which way around it is fitted **(see illustration)**.

3 Lift the countershaft and mainshaft out of the crankcase **(see illustrations)**. Do not lose the end plate from the right end of the countershaft.

2

30.2 Undo the two bolts and remove the bearing retaining plate . . .

30.3a . . . then lift the countershaft . . .

30.3b . . . and mainshaft out of the crankcase

30.4a Recover the countershaft bearing half ring . . .

30.4b . . . and dowel pin from the upper crankcase half

4 Recover the countershaft bearing half ring and dowel pin from the upper crankcase half and store them with the transmission shafts for safe-keeping **(see illustrations)**.

5 Remove the oil seal from the end of the countershaft and discard it, a new one must be used on installation.

6 If necessary, the transmission shafts can be disassembled and inspected for wear or damage as described in Section 31.

Installation

7 Install the countershaft bearing half ring and dowel pin in the upper crankcase.

8 Slide a new oil seal on the end of the countershaft making sure it is fitted with its sealing lip (spring side) facing inwards **(see illustration)**.

9 Lower the mainshaft into position in the upper crankcase. Make sure the locating pin in the mainshaft bearing outer race is correctly located in the groove in the crankcase.

10 Lower the countershaft into position in the crankcase half. Make sure the oil seal lip, bearing pin and groove on the left end of the shaft are correctly engaged with the crankcase slots and bearing half ring, and the hole in the needle bearing race on the right

30.8 Fit a new oil seal to the countershaft making sure its sealing lip is facing inwards

end of the shaft is correctly engaged with the dowel pin **(see illustrations)**.

11 Make sure both transmission shafts are correctly seated.

Caution: If the mainshaft bearing locating pin and/or countershaft half ring or dowel pin are not correctly engaged, the crankcase halves will not seat correctly.

12 Clean the mainshaft bearing plate bolts and apply a few drops of non-permanent locking compound to their threads.

30.10a Lower the countershaft into position making sure the oil seal lip and bearing pin (arrows) . . .

13 Fit the bearing retaining plate to the crankcase making sure its OUTSIDE mark is facing outwards (away from the crankcase). Install the retaining bolts and tighten them securely **(see illustration)**.

14 Position the gears in the neutral position and check the shafts are free to rotate easily before proceeding further.

15 Reassembly the crankcase halves as described in Section 24.

30.10b . . . and the bearing race and dowel pin are correctly aligned

30.13 Ensure the mainshaft bearing retaining plate is fitted with its OUT SIDE mark facing outwards

1	Needle roller bearing	4	Lock washer
2	Thrust washer	5	Special splined washer
3	2nd gear	6	6th gear
		7	6th gear bushing
		8	Splined thrust washer
		9	Snap-ring
		10	3rd/4th gear
		11	Snap-ring
		12	Splined thrust washer
		13	5th gear
		14	5th gear bushing
		15	Thrust washer
		16	Mainshaft
		17	Bearing

31.2 Mainshaft components

31 Transmission shafts - disassembly, inspection and reassembly

1 Remove the shafts from the casing as described in Section 30. Always disassemble the transmission shafts separately to avoid mixing up the components.

 HAYNES HINT *When disassembling the transmission shafts, place the parts on a long rod or thread a wire through them to keep them in order and facing the proper direction.*

Mainshaft

Disassembly

2 Slide off the needle roller bearing and thrust washer from the left end of the shaft **(see illustration)**.
3 Slide off the 2nd gear.
4 Disengage the lock washer from the special splined washer and slide both off the mainshaft.
5 Remove the 6th gear followed by its splined bushing and thrust washer.
6 Remove the snap-ring using a suitable pair of snap-ring pliers.
7 Remove the 3rd/4th gear, noting which way around it is fitted.
8 Remove the second snap-ring.
9 Slide off the splined thrust washer followed by the 5th gear, 5th gear bushing and thrust washer.

Inspection

10 Wash all of the components in clean solvent and dry them off.
11 Check the gear teeth for cracking and

other obvious damage. Check the gear bushings and the surface in the inner diameter of each gear for scoring or heat discoloration. If the gear or bushing is damaged, replace it.
12 Inspect the dogs and the dog holes in the gears for excessive wear. Replace the paired gears as a set if necessary.
13 The shafts is unlikely to sustain damage unless the engine has seized, placing an unusually high loading on the transmission, or the machine has covered a very high mileage. Check the surface of the shaft, especially where a pinion turns on it, and replace the

shaft if it has scored or picked up. Inspect the threads of the shafts and check them for trueness by setting them up in V-blocks and measuring any runout with a dial gauge. Damage of any kind can only be cured by replacement.
14 Measure the internal diameter of all gears which run on bushings and the external diameter of the bushings which they run on. If either component has worn to beyond its service limit it must be replaced. Using the above measurements calculate the gear to bushing clearance, if this exceeds the specified limit replace the relevant gear and bushing as a pair.
15 Check that the outer race of the bearing fitted to the end of the shaft rotates freely and has no sign of freeplay between its inner and outer races. If the bearing requires replacement, a bearing puller will be required to extract the bearing from its shaft. Note the position of the locating groove in the outer race of the bearing prior to removing it and ensure that the new bearing is fitted with the groove in the same position. Pull the bearing off of the shaft and fit the new bearing using a hammer and tubular drift which bears only on the inner race of the bearing.

Reassembly

16 During reassembly, always use new snap-rings. Lubricate the components with engine oil before assembling them. **Note:** *If the thrust washers and snap-rings are examined closely it will be seen that they are chamfered on one side. During reassembly it is crucial that each thrust washer and snap-ring is fitted so its chamfer is on the correct side* **(see illustration)**.

2

31.16 Correct fitted orientation of mainshaft snap-rings and thrust washers

1	Needle roller bearing	7	6th gear bushing	13	5th gear
2	Thrust washer	8	Splined thrust washer	14	5th gear bushing
3	2nd gear	9	Snap-ring	15	Thrust washer
4	Lock washer	10	3rd/4th gear	16	Mainshaft
5	Special splined washer	11	Snap-ring	17	Bearing
6	6th gear	12	Splined thrust washer		

31.17 Slide on the thrust washer . . .

31.18a . . . followed by the 5th gear bushing

31.18b Fit the 5th gear with its dogs facing as shown . . .

17 Slide on the thrust washer making sure its chamfered edge is facing away from the integral 1st gear **(see illustration)**.

18 Slide on the 5th gear bushing then fit the 5th gear with its dogs facing towards the left end of the shaft. Fit the splined thrust washer with its chamfered edge facing the 5th gear **(see illustrations)**.

19 Secure the 5th gear components in position with a new snap-ring making sure its chamfered edge is facing the thrust washer **(see illustration)**. Check the snap-ring is correctly located in the mainshaft groove.

20 Install the 3rd/4th gear with its larger 4th gear facing the 5th gear. Engage the gear on the shaft splines ensuring that its oil holes are correctly aligned with the shaft oilways **(see illustration)**.

21 Fit a second new snap-ring to the shaft with its chamfered edge facing away from the 3rd/4th gear pinion. Make sure the snap-ring is correctly located in the shaft groove **(see illustration)**.

22 Slide on the splined thrust washer with its chamfered edge facing away from the snap-ring **(see illustration)**.

23 Align the 6th gear splined bushing oil holes with the shaft oilways and slide it along the shaft. Fit the 6th gear so that its dogs are facing the 3rd/4th gear **(see illustrations)**.

24 Slide the special splined washer along until it abuts the 6th gear, followed by the lock washer. Rotate the splined washer until its

31.18c . . . then fit the splined thrust washer

31.20 Align the gear oil hole with the mainshaft oilway when installing the 3rd/4th gear. Gear must be fitted with the larger 4th gear facing the 5th gear

31.19 Secure 5th gear components in position with a snap-ring making sure it is correctly seated in the mainshaft groove

31.21 Fit a second snap-ring to the next groove . . .

31.22 . . . then slide on a splined thrust washer

31.23a Fit the 6th gear splined bushing, aligning its oil holes with the shaft oilways . . .

31.23b . . . and fit the 6th gear with its dogs facing the 3rd/4th gear

31.24a Slide on the special splined washer . . .

31.24b . . . then fit the lock washer engaging its tabs with the splined washer slots (arrows)

31.25a Fit the 2nd gear . . .

31.25b . . . followed by the thrust washer . . .

31.26 . . . then install the needle roller bearing

Countershaft

Disassembly

27 Remove the end plate from the right end of the countershaft and slide off the needle roller bearing **(see illustration)**.
28 Remove the thrust washer followed by the 1st gear, needle roller bearing and second thrust washer.
29 Remove the 5th gear noting which way around it is fitted.
30 Remove the snap-ring with a suitable pair of snap-ring pliers.
31 Slide off the splined washer followed by the 4th gear and splined bushing.
32 Disengage the lock washer from the special splined washer and slide both off the countershaft.
33 Remove the 3rd gear along with its splined bushing and thrust washer.
34 Remove the second snap-ring and slide off the 6th gear.
35 Remove the third snap-ring and slide off the splined thrust washer followed by the 2nd gear and 2nd gear bushing.

Inspection

36 Refer to Steps 10 through 15.

Reassembly

37 During reassembly, always use new snap-rings. Lubricate the components with engine oil before assembling them. **Note:** *If the thrust washers and snap-rings are examined closely it will be seen that they are chamfered on one side. During reassembly it is crucial that each thrust washer and snap-ring is fitted so its chamfer is on the correct side* **(see illustration)**.
38 Slide on the 2nd gear bushing and install the 2nd gear so that its plain surface abuts the countershaft bearing. Fit the splined thrust washer with its chamfered edge facing the 2nd gear and secure the 2nd gear components in position with a new snap-ring. Fit the snap-ring with its chamfered edge facing the thrust washer and make sure it is correctly located in the countershaft groove **(see illustrations)**.
39 Fit the 6th gear to the shaft so that its shift fork groove is facing away from the 2nd gear. Align the gear oil holes with the shaft oilways

cutouts align with the lock washer tabs, then engage the lock washer with the splined washer to lock it in position **(see illustrations)**.
25 Fit the 2nd gear followed by the thrust washer, making sure the thrust washer chamfered edge faces the gear **(see illustrations)**.
26 Liberally oil the needle bearing and install it on the end of the shaft **(see illustration)**.

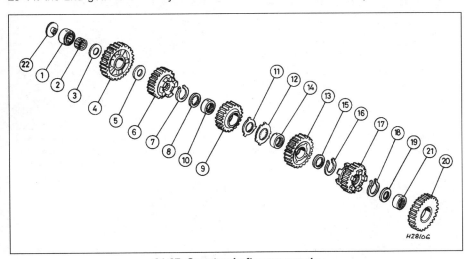

31.27 Countershaft components

1 Needle roller bearing	*8 Splined thrust washer*	*16 Snap-ring*
2 1st gear needle roller bearing	*9 4th gear*	*17 6th gear*
3 Thrust washer	*10 4th gear bushing*	*18 Snap-ring*
4 1st gear	*11 Lock washer*	*19 Splined thrust washer*
5 Thrust washer	*12 Special splined washer*	*20 2nd gear*
6 5th gear	*13 3rd gear*	*21 2nd gear bushing*
7 Snap-ring	*14 3rd gear bushing*	*22 End plate*
	15 Splined thrust washer	

31.37 Correct fitted orientation of countershaft snap-rings and thrust washers

1 Needle roller bearing
2 1st gear needle roller bearing
3 Thrust washer
4 1st gear
5 Thrust washer
6 5th gear
7 Snap-ring

8 Splined thrust washer
9 4th gear
10 4th gear bushing
11 Lock washer
12 Special splined washer
13 3rd gear
14 3rd gear bushing
15 Splined thrust washer

16 Snap-ring
17 6th gear
18 Snap-ring
19 Splined thrust washer
20 2nd gear
21 2nd gear bushing
22 Countershaft

31.38a Fit the 2nd gear bushing . . .

and slide the gear on the shaft **(see illustration)**.
40 Fit a second new snap-ring with its chamfered edge facing away from the 6th gear. Ensure the snap-ring is correctly located in the shaft groove **(see illustration)**.
41 Slide on the splined thrust washer with its

chamfered edge facing away from the snap-ring **(see illustration)**.
42 Align the 3rd gear splined bushing oil holes with the shaft oilways and slide it along the shaft. Fit the 3rd gear so that its dog holes are facing the 6th gear **(see illustrations)**.

31.38b . . . and install the 2nd gear with its plain surface facing the bearing

31.38c Slide on a splined thrust washer . . .

31.38d . . . and secure the 2nd gear components in position with a snap-ring

31.39 Slide on the 6th gear as shown making sure its oil holes are correctly aligned with the shaft oilways (arrows)

31.40 Fit a second snap-ring to the countershaft . . .

31.41 . . . and slide on a splined thrust washer

31.42a Fit the 3rd gear bushing, aligning its oil holes with the shaft oilways . . .

31.42b ... and install the 3rd gear with its dog holes facing the 6th gear

31.43 Fit the special splined washer and lock washer engaging the lock washer tabs with the splined washer cutouts (arrows)

31.44a Slide on the 4th gear bushing, aligning its oil holes with the shaft oilways ...

31.44b ... and fit the 4th gear with its dog holes facing away from the 3rd gear

31.44c Slide on a splined thrust washer ...

43 Slide the special splined washer along until it abuts the 3rd gear, followed by the lock washer. Rotate the splined washer until its cutouts align with the lock washer tabs then engage the lock washer with the splined washer to lock it in position (see illustration).
44 Align the 4th gear splined bushing oil holes with the shaft oilways and slide it along the shaft. Fit the 4th gear so that its dog holes are facing away from the 3rd gear, then slide on the splined thrust washer with its chamfered edge facing the 4th gear (see illustrations).
45 Secure the 4th gear components in position with a new snap-ring. Fit the snap-ring with its chamfered edge facing the thrust washer and make sure it is correctly located in the countershaft groove (see illustration).
46 Fit the 5th gear to the shaft so that its shift fork groove is facing the 4th gear (see illustration). Align the gear oil holes with the shaft oilways and slide the gear on the shaft.
47 Fit the thrust washer to the countershaft with its chamfered edge facing away from the 5th gear then install the 1st gear needle roller bearing (see illustrations).
48 Liberally lubricate the bearing, then fit the 1st gear so that its dog holes are facing the 5th gear and slide on the second thrust washer (see illustrations). The chamfered edge of the thrust washer should face the 1st gear.

31.45 ... and secure it in position with another snap-ring

31.46 Fit the 5th gear as shown

31.47a Install the thrust washer ...

31.47b ... followed by the 1st gear needle roller bearing ...

31.48a ... then fit the 1st gear with its dog holes facing the 5th gear

2

49 Lubricate the needle roller bearing assembly and fit it to the end of the countershaft. Fit the end plate to the bearing **(see illustration)**.

32 Initial start-up after overhaul

1 Make sure the engine oil and coolant levels are correct (see Chapter 1), then remove the spark plugs from the engine. Place the engine kill switch in the OFF position.
2 Turn on the ignition switch and crank the engine over with the starter until the oil pressure indicator light goes off (which indicates that oil pressure exists). Reinstall the spark plugs, connect the HT leads and turn the kill switch to RUN.
3 Make sure there is fuel in the tank, then turn the fuel tap to the ON position and operate the choke.
4 Start the engine and allow it to run at a moderately fast idle until it reaches operating temperature.

 Warning: If the oil pressure indicator light doesn't go off, or it comes on while the engine is running, stop the engine immediately.

5 Check carefully for oil leaks and make sure the transmission and controls, especially the brakes, function properly before road testing the machine. Refer to Section 33 for the recommended break-in procedure.
6 Upon completion of the road test, and after the engine has cooled down completely,

31.48b Slide on another thrust washer . . .

recheck the valve clearances and check the engine oil and coolant levels (see Chapter 1).

33 Recommended break-in procedure

1 Treat the machine gently for the first few miles to make sure oil has circulated throughout the engine and any new parts installed have started to seat.
2 Even greater care is necessary if the engine has been rebored or a new crankshaft has been installed. In the case of a rebore, the engine will have to be broken in as if the machine were new. This means greater use of the transmission and a restraining hand on the throttle until at least 500 miles (800 km) have been covered. There's no point in keeping to any set speed limit - the main idea is to keep from lugging (labouring) the engine and to gradually increase performance until the 500

31.49 . . . then fit the needle roller bearing and end plate

mile (800 km) mark is reached. These recommendations can be lessened to an extent when only a new crankshaft is installed. Experience is the best guide, since it's easy to tell when an engine is running freely. The following recommendations, which Honda provide for new motorcycles, can be used as a guide.
a) *0 to 600 miles (0 to 1000 km): Keep engine speed below 5,000 rpm. Vary the engine speed and don't use full throttle.*
b) *600 to 1000 miles (1,000 to 1,600 km): Keep engine speed below 7,000 rpm. Rev the engine freely through the gears, but don't use full throttle for prolonged periods.*
c) *After 1000 miles (1,600 km): Full throttle can be used. Don't exceed maximum recommended engine speed (redline).*
3 If a lubrication failure is suspected, stop the engine immediately and try to find the cause. If an engine is run without oil, even for a short period of time, severe damage will occur.

Chapter 3
Cooling system

Contents

Degrees of difficulty

Easy, suitable for novice with little experience	**Fairly easy,** suitable for beginner with some experience	**Fairly difficult,** suitable for competent DIY mechanic	**Difficult,** suitable for experienced DIY mechanic	**Very difficult,** suitable for expert DIY or professional

Specifications

Coolant

Mixture type . . . . 50% distilled water, 50% corrosion inhibited ethylene glycol antifreeze

Capacity

  Radiator and engine

    US 1993 through 1995 models and UK N to S models . . . . 2.80 lit (3.00 US qt, 5.00 Imp pt)

    US 1996 and 1997 models and UK T and V models . . . . 2.77 lit (2.93 US qt, 4.88 Imp pt)

    US 1998 and 1999 models and UK W and X models . . . . 2.64 lit (2.79 US qt, 4.64 Imp pt)

  Coolant reservoir

    US 1993 through 1997 models and UK N to V models . . . . 0.45 lit (0.48 US qt, 0.80 Imp pt)

    US 1998 and 1999 models and UK W and X models . . . . 0.35 lit (0.30 US qt, 0.62 Imp pt)

Radiator

Cap valve opening pressure

  US 1993 through 1995 models and UK N to S models . . . . 16 to 20 psi (1.1 to 1.4 Bar)

  US 1996 through 1999 models and UK T to X models . . . . 16 psi (1.1 Bar)

Cooling fan switch

  Switches on . . . . 98 to 102°C (208 to 216° F)

  Switches off . . . . 93 to 97°C (199 to 207° F)

Thermostat

Opening temperature . . . . 80 to 84°C (176 to 183°F)

Fully open . . . . 95°C (203°F)

Minimum valve lift . . . . 8 mm (0.32 in) @ 95°C (203°F)

Coolant temperature sender

Resistance

  US 1993 through 1997 models and UK N to V models

    At 80°C (176°F) . . . . 45 to 60 ohms

    At 120°C (248°F) . . . . 10 to 20 ohms

  US 1998 and 1999 models and UK W and X models

    At 80°C (176°F) . . . . 2500 to 3100 ohms

    At 120°C (248°F) . . . . 600 to 750 ohms

Torque settings

	Nm	ft-lbs
Cooling fan thermostatic switch	18	13
Cooling fan nut	2.5	1.8
Temperature gauge sender unit	10	7
Water pump mounting and cover bolts	13	9

3

1 General information

The cooling system uses a water/antifreeze coolant to carry away excess energy in the form of heat. The cylinders are surrounded by a water jacket from which the heated coolant is circulated by thermo-syphonic action in conjunction with a water pump, driven off the oil pump. The hot coolant passes upwards to the thermostat and through to the radiator. The coolant then flows across the radiator core, where it is cooled by the passing air, down to the water pump and back up to the engine where the cycle is repeated. An air bleed hose is fitted between the cylinder head and radiator filler neck.

A thermostat is fitted in the system to prevent the coolant flowing through the radiator when the engine is cold, therefore accelerating the speed at which the engine reaches normal operating temperature. A thermostatically-controlled cooling fan is also fitted to aid cooling in extreme conditions.

The cooling system is used to cool the engine oil. A short hose connects the coolant union on the front of the cylinder block to the oil cooler unit. Coolant circulates around the oil cooler body and is then routed back to the water pump via a rubber hose.

The complete cooling system is partially sealed and pressurised, the pressure being controlled by a valve contained in the spring-loaded radiator cap. By pressurising the coolant the boiling point is raised, preventing premature boiling in adverse conditions. The overflow pipe from the system is connected to a reservoir into which excess coolant is expelled under pressure. The discharged coolant automatically returns to the radiator when the engine cools.

 Warning: Do not remove the pressure cap from the radiator when the engine is hot. Scalding hot coolant and steam may be blown out under pressure, which could cause serious injury. To gain access to the pressure cap, remove the right lower fairing panel (see Chapter 8), then remove the fuse access panel from the upper fairing and the upper fairing right mounting screw; ease the edge of the fairing away from the fuel tank so that the cap can be reached between the fairing and tank. When the engine has cooled, place a thick rag, like a towel over the radiator cap; slowly rotate the cap counterclockwise (anti-clockwise) to the first stop. This procedure allows any residual pressure to escape. When the steam has stopped escaping, press down on the cap while turning it counterclockwise (anti-clockwise) and remove it.

 Warning: Do not allow antifreeze to come in contact with your skin or painted surfaces of the motorcycle. Rinse off any spills immediately with plenty of water. Antifreeze is highly toxic if ingested. Never leave antifreeze lying around in an open container or in puddles on the floor; children and pets are attracted by its sweet smell and may drink it. Check with the local authorities about disposing of used antifreeze. Many communities will have collection centers which will see that antifreeze is disposed of safely.

2 Radiator cap - check

If problems such as overheating or loss of coolant occur, check the entire system as described in Chapter 1. The radiator cap opening pressure should be checked by a Honda dealer or service station equipped with the special tester required to do the job. If the cap is defective, replace it with a new one.

3 Coolant reservoir - removal and installation

Removal

1 Remove the fuel tank as described in Chapter 4.
2 On US 1993 through 1995 models and UK N to S models, remove the fuel pump as described in Chapter 9. Remove the bolt which retains the fuel pump mounting bracket to the frame, leaving the bracket attached to the reservoir tank.
3 Free the hoses from the fuel filter mounting bracket slots and unbolt the bracket from the frame.
4 Maneuver the coolant reservoir out of the top of the frame. As the overflow hose becomes accessible, disconnect it and drain the coolant into a suitable container (see illustration).

3.5 Coolant reservoir hook locates in frame hole (A) and tab in slot (B)

3.4 Have a container ready to catch the coolant as the overflow hose is removed

Installation

5 Installation is the reverse of the removal sequence noting the following.
a) Engage the hook at the base of the tank with the hole in the frame, and the tab with the slot in the frame (see illustration).
b) On completion refill the cooling system as described in Chapter 1.

4 Cooling fan and thermostatic switch - check and replacement

Check

1 If the engine is overheating and the cooling fan isn't coming on, first check the cooling fan switch fuse. If the fuse is blown, check the fan circuit for a short to ground/earth (see the wiring diagrams at the end of this book).
2 If the fuse is sound, remove the fairing left middle section (see Chapter 8) and disconnect the wire from the fan switch fitted to the left side of the radiator (see illustration). Turn the ignition switch ON and ground (earth) the fan switch wire. As the wire is grounded (earthed) the fan should come on. If it does, the fan switch is defective and must be replaced.
3 If the fan does not come on, the fault lies in either the cooling fan motor or relevant wiring. The wiring can be tested as described in Chapter 9.

4.2 Disconnect wire from fan switch

4.4 Fan motor two-pin wire connector is clamped behind the radiator

4.6 Remove the three bolts (arrows) to separate the fan assembly from the radiator; note the ground (earth) lead location

4.7 Fan blade is retained by a single nut (arrow)

4 To test the cooling fan motor, separate the two-pin connector behind the radiator **(see illustration)**. Using a 12 volt battery and two jumper wires, connect the battery across the connector terminals on the fan motor side of the connector. Once connected the fan should operate. If this is not the case the fan motor is faulty and must be replaced.

Replacement

Fan motor

Warning: The engine must be completely cool before carrying out this procedure.

5 Remove the radiator as described in Section 7.

6 Unscrew the three bolts to separate the fan assembly from the radiator, noting the correct position of the fan motor ground (earth) lead **(see illustration)**.

7 Unscrew the retaining nut and remove the fan blade from the motor **(see illustration)**.

8 Release the clip and free the wiring from the back of the fan motor shroud.

9 Unscrew the three nuts and separate the fan motor from the shroud **(see illustration 4.7)**.

10 Installation is the reverse of removal. On fitting the fan blade ensure its slot is correctly aligned with the motor shaft and tighten its nut to the specified torque setting. Make sure the motor ground (earth) lead is correctly positioned and that the wiring is secured by the clip.

11 Install the radiator as described in Section 7.

Thermostatic fan switch

Warning: The engine must be completely cool before carrying out this procedure.

12 Remove the fairing left side middle section as described in Chapter 8.

13 Disconnect the wiring connector from the switch **(see illustration 4.2)**.

14 Unscrew the switch from the left side of the radiator and recover the O-ring. Plug the radiator opening to minimise coolant loss.

15 Fit a new O-ring to the switch and apply a smear of sealant to the switch threads.

16 Remove the plug and quickly install the

new switch, tightening it to the specified torque setting.

17 Connect the wiring connector to the switch and install the fairing section.

18 Check the coolant level and top up as described in Chapter 1.

---

5 Coolant temperature gauge and sender unit - check and replacement

Check

1 The circuit consists of the sender unit mounted in the right end of the cylinder head and the gauge assembly mounted in the instrument panel. If the system malfunctions check first that the battery is fully charged and that the fuse labelled METER, TAIL, HORN is in good condition.

2 If the gauge is not working, first remove the fuel tank (see Chapter 4) to gain access to the sender unit. Turn the ignition switch ON and disconnect the wire from the temperature sender unit **(see illustration)**. Ground (earth) the sender unit wire on the engine. When the wire is grounded (earthed) the needle should swing immediately over to the H on the gauge (US 1993 through 1997 and UK N to V models) or the gauge should read 132°C/270°F (US 1998 and 1999 models and UK W and X models). If the gauge performs as described, the sender unit is proven defective and must be replaced.

5.2 Disconnecting the temperature gauge sender unit wire

Caution: Do not ground (earth) the wire for any longer than is necessary to take the reading, or the gauge may be damaged.

3 If the gauge operation is still faulty, the fault lies in the wiring or the gauge itself. Remove the instrument cluster as described in Chapter 9 and check the relevant wiring connectors. If all appears to be well, the gauge is defective and must be replaced.

4 If the gauge is thought to be giving a false reading, remove the sender unit as described in Steps 7 to 12 below and check it as follows. Fill a small heatproof container with oil and place it on a stove. Using an ohmmeter, connect the positive (+) probe of the meter to the terminal on the sender, and the negative (-) probe to the sender body. Support the sender in the oil so just the sensing portion and threads are submerged and the base of the sender is at least 40 mm (1.5 in) above the bottom of the container. Place a thermometer capable of reading temperatures in excess of 120°C (248°F) in the oil so that its bulb is close to the sender. **Note:** *Ensure the sender and thermometer are not in contact with the container.*

5 Heat the oil, stirring it gently, and take the resistance readings of the sender at 80°C (176°F) and 120°C (248°F). If the readings obtained differ by more than 10% from those given in the specifications the sender is faulty and should be replaced.

3

Warning: This must be done very carefully to avoid the risk of personal injury.

Replacement

Temperature gauge sender unit

Warning: The engine must be completely cool before carrying out this procedure.

6 Remove the fuel tank as described in Chapter 4.

7 Disconnect the wiring connector from the switch **(see illustration 5.2)**.

8 Unscrew the sender unit from the cylinder head. Plug the head opening to minimise coolant loss.

9 Apply a smear of sealant to the switch threads.

10 Remove the plug and quickly install the

6.5 Disconnect the air bleed pipe from its union on the thermostat housing

6.6 Thermostat housing is retained by two bolts

6.8 Slacken the clip and disconnect the cylinder head coolant hose from the thermostat housing

new sender unit, tightening it to the specified torque setting.

11 Connect the wiring connector to the sender unit and install the fuel tank as described in Chapter 4.

12 Check the coolant level and top up as described in Chapter 1.

Temperature gauge

13 See Chapter 9.

6 Thermostat - removal, check and installation

Removal

> ⚠ **Warning: The engine must be completely cool before carrying out this procedure.**

1 The thermostat is automatic in operation and should give many years service without requiring attention. In the event of a failure, the valve will probably jam open, in which case the engine will take much longer than normal to warm up. Conversely, if the valve jams shut, the coolant will be unable to circulate and the engine will overheat. Neither condition is acceptable, and the fault must be investigated promptly.

2 Partially drain the cooling system to prevent the escape of coolant when the thermostat housing is removed (see Chapter 1).

3 Remove the fairing right middle section as described in Chapter 8.

4 Remove the fuel tank as described in Chapter 4.

US 1993 through 1997 models and UK N to V models

5 Release its spring clip and pull the small air bleed hose off its union on the thermostat housing **(see illustration)**.

6 Unscrew the two bolts and remove the thermostat housing; the large coolant hose can remain attached to the housing **(see illustration)**. Recover the housing O-ring.

7 Remove the thermostat from the cylinder head.

US 1998 and 1999 models and UK W and X models

8 Slacken the clip and disconnect the cylinder head coolant hose from the thermostat housing **(see illustration)**.

9 To improve access, remove the bolt securing the thermostat housing bracket to the cylinder head and recover the collar from the bracket mounting **(see illustration)**.

10 Unscrew the bolts and free the thermostat housing and mounting bracket from the cover **(see illustration)**. Remove the thermostat from the housing and recover the housing cover O-ring.

Check

11 Examine the thermostat visually before carrying out the test. If it remains in the open

position at room temperature, it should be replaced.

12 Suspend the thermostat by a piece of wire in a container of cold water. Place a thermometer in the water so that the bulb is close to the thermostat **(see illustration)**. Heat the water, noting the temperature when the thermostat opens and how much valve lift it has when it is fully open, and compare the results with those given in the Specifications. If the readings obtained differ from those given, the thermostat is faulty and must be replaced.

> ⚠ **Warning: This must be done very carefully to avoid the risk of personal injury.**

13 In the event of thermostat failure, as an emergency measure only, it can be removed and the machine used without it. **Note:** *Take care when starting the engine from cold as it will take much longer than usual to warm up. Ensure that a new unit is installed as soon as possible.*

Installation

US 1993 through 1997 models and UK N to V models

14 Fit the thermostat to the cylinder head noting that its small bypass hole must be positioned at the top **(see illustration)**.

15 Fit a new O-ring to the housing cover and install the cover **(see illustration)**. Securely tighten the cover retaining bolts.

16 Reconnect the air bleed hose and secure with its retaining clip.

17 Refill the cooling system as described in Chapter 1.

18 Install the fuel tank as described in Chapter 4.

6.9 Unscrew the bolt (arrow) securing the thermostat housing bracket to the cylinder head and recover the collar

6.10 Unscrew the bolts (arrows) and free the thermostat housing from the mounting bracket and cover

6.12 Thermostat opening check

6.14 Ensure thermostat bypass hole is positioned at the top on installation

6.15 Use a new O-ring in the thermostat housing groove

7.3a Disconnect the air bleed hose and the overflow hose (arrow) from the radiator

7.3b Disconnect the main radiator top hose . . .

7.3c . . . and bottom hose

7.5 Radiator is retained to mounting bracket by a bolt and collar

19 Fit the fairing middle section as described in Chapter 8.

US 1998 and 1999 models and UK W and X models

20 Fit a new O-ring to the thermostat housing cover groove.

21 Fit the thermostat to the housing making sure its small bypass hole is at the top.

22 Assemble the thermostat housing, cover and mounting bracket and install the cover bolts, tightening them securely.

23 Fit the collar to the thermostat housing bracket and secure the bracket to the rear of the cylinder head with the retaining bolt.

24 Reconnect the cylinder head hose and securely tighten its clip.

25 Refit the fuel tank as described in Chapter 4.

26 Refill the cooling system as described in Chapter 1.

27 Refit the fairing middle section as described in Chapter 8.

7 Radiator -
removal and installation

Removal

> **Warning: The engine must be completely cool before carrying out this procedure.**

1 Remove both middle fairing sections as described in Chapter 8.

2 Drain the cooling system as described in Chapter 1.

3 Release their retaining clips and disconnect

the overflow hose and air bleed hose from the top rear of the radiator **(see illustration)**. Slacken their clamps and pull the main coolant hoses off their unions at the top and bottom of the radiator **(see illustrations)**.

4 Disconnect the fan wiring connector behind the radiator **(see illustration 4.4)**.

5 Remove the radiator lower mounting bolt and collar **(see illustration)**.

6 Remove the radiator top mounting bolt and collar from the left side, then move the radiator to the right to disengage it from its mounting peg **(see illustrations)**.

7 Check the radiator mounting rubbers for signs of damage or deterioration and replace if necessary.

8 The radiator mounting bracket can be detached from the cylinder block by removing its two bolts **(see illustration)**.

3

7.6a Radiator top mounting is by a bolt and collar (arrow) on the left side . . .

7.6b . . . and by a peg on right side

7.8 Radiator mounting bracket is retained by two bolts

7.9 Radiator and fan detail

1 Grille	5 Mounting rubbers	9 Bottom hose	13 Fan blade
2 Radiator	6 Mounting bracket	10 Air bleed hose	14 Fan motor
3 Mounting bolts	7 Pressure cap	11 Overflow hose	15 Fan shroud
4 Collars	8 Top hose	12 Reservoir tank	16 Thermostatic fan switch

Installation

9 Installation is the reverse of the removal sequence noting the following **(see illustration)**.

a) *Locate the radiator on its mounting peg, fit the collar to each mounting bolt and securely tighten the mounting bolts.*

b) *The main wire harness must fit between the two raised plastic tangs on the radiator grille right side, next to the pressure cap.*

c) *Make sure that the fan wiring is correctly connected.*

d) *Ensure the coolant hoses are securely retained by their clips.*

e) *On completion refill the cooling system as described in Chapter 1.*

8.2 Leakage from the drainage hole (arrow) on the underside of the pump indicates mechanical seal failure

8 Water pump - check, removal and installation

Check

1 Visually check the area around the water pump for signs of leakage; if necessary remove the fairing lower section for improved access (see Chapter 8).

2 To prevent leakage of water or oil from the cooling system to the lubrication system and vice versa, two seals are fitted on the pump shaft. On the underside of the pump body there is also a drainage hole. If either seal fails, this hole should allow the coolant or oil to escape and prevent the oil and coolant mixing **(see illustration)**.

3 The seal on the water pump side is of the mechanical type which bears on the rear face of

8.6a Disconnect the air bleed hose . . .

the impeller. The second seal, which is mounted behind the mechanical seal is of the normal feathered lip type. However, neither seal is available as a separate item as the pump is a sealed unit. Therefore, if on inspection the drainage hole shows signs of leakage, the pump must be removed and replaced.

Removal

 Warning: The engine must be completely cool before carrying out this procedure.

4 Remove fairing lower section as described in Chapter 8.

5 Drain the cooling system as described in Chapter 1.

6 Release the retaining clips and disconnect the air bleed and/or bypass hose(s) (as applicable) and the oil cooler hose from the water pump cover **(see illustrations)**.

8.6b . . . and oil cooler hose from the water pump cover

8.7a Slacken the main coolant hose clamps . . .

8.7b . . . and pull them off their unions on the pump cover and body

8.8 Remove the two mounting bolts and withdraw the water pump - the remaining two bolts (arrows) retain the pump cover to the body

8.11a Align the water pump impeller shaft slot with the oil pump shaft projection (arrows) . . .

8.11b . . . and insert the pump in the crankcase. Do not forget to replace the pump O-ring (arrow)

7 Slacken their retaining clamps and pull the main coolant hoses off their unions on the water pump body and cover **(see illustrations)**.

8 Unscrew the two mounting bolts and withdraw the water pump from the engine unit **(see illustration)**. Recover the O-ring from the water pump body.

9 Undo the remaining bolts and lift off the pump cover. Recover the sealing ring.

10 Wiggle the water pump impeller back-and-forth and in-and-out. If there is excessive movement the pump must be replaced.

Installation

11 Fit a new O-ring to the rear of the pump body and install the pump, aligning the slot in the impeller shaft with the projection on the oil pump shaft **(see illustrations)**.

12 Fit a new O-ring to the pump body and fit the cover to the pump body **(see illustrations)**.

13 Install the cover retaining bolts and the pump mounting bolts and tighten them to the specified torque setting.

14 Reconnect the coolant hoses to the pump and cover, making sure each one is securely retained by its clip or clamp.

15 Refill the cooling system as described in Chapter 1.

16 Install the fairing lower section as described in Chapter 8.

3

8.12a Fit a new O-ring to the pump body groove . . .

8.12b . . . before installing the pump cover

9.5 Ensure that screw-type hose clamps are positioned correctly on the union; avoid overtightening otherwise the union could distort

9.8 Disconnect the water pump hose and oil cooler hose from the coolant union

9.9 Coolant union is retained by two bolts

9 Coolant hoses and union - removal and installation

Coolant hoses

Removal

 Warning: The engine must be completely cool before carrying out this procedure.

1 Before removing a hose, drain the coolant as described in Chapter 1.

2 Use a screwdriver to slacken the hose clamps, then slide them back along the hose and clear of the union spigot.

3 Many of the smaller-bore hoses are secured by spring clips which can be expanded by squeezing their ears together with pliers. If a hose proves stubborn, release it by rotating it on its union before working it off. If all else fails, cut the hose with a sharp knife then slit it at each union so that it can be peeled off in two pieces. Whilst this is expensive it is preferable to buying a new radiator.

Caution: The radiator unions are fragile. Do not use excessive force when attempting to remove the hoses.

Installation

4 Slide the clips onto the hose and then work it on to its respective union.

> **HAYNES HINT** *If the hose is difficult to push on its union, it can be softened by soaking it in very hot water, or alternatively a little soapy water can be used as a lubricant.*

5 Rotate the hose on its unions to settle it in position before sliding the clamps into place and tightening them securely **(see illustration)**.

Coolant union

Removal

 Warning: The engine must be completely cool before carrying out this procedure.

6 Remove the fairing lower section as described in Chapter 8.

7 Drain the cooling system as described in Chapter 1.

8 Slacken their clamps and disconnect the water pump hose and oil cooler hose from the coolant union **(see illustration)**.

9 Remove its two mounting bolts to free the

9.10 Fit a new O-ring to the coolant union groove

union from the cylinder block **(see illustration)**. Recover the O-ring.

Installation

10 Ensure both mating faces are clean and install a new O-ring in the coolant union groove **(see illustration)**.

11 Install the two bolts and tighten them securely.

12 Reconnect the coolant hoses and secure with their clamps.

13 Refill the cooling system as described in Chapter 1.

14 Install the fairing lower section as described in Chapter 8.

Chapter 4
Fuel and exhaust systems

Contents

Degrees of difficulty

Easy, suitable for novice with little experience	**Fairly easy,** suitable for beginner with some experience	**Fairly difficult,** suitable for competent DIY mechanic	**Difficult,** suitable for experienced DIY mechanic	**Very difficult,** suitable for expert DIY or professional

Specifications

Fuel
Grade . . . . Unleaded or leaded (according to local regulations), minimum 91
octane (research method)

Fuel tank capacity . . . . 18 lit (4.8 US gal, 4.0 Imp gal)
Fuel tank reserve capacity
  US 1993 through 1995 models and UK N to S models . . . . 3.8 lit (1.0 US gal, 0.8 Imp gal)
  US 1996 through 1999 models and UK T to X models . . . . 3.5 lit (0.92 US gal, 0.77 Imp gal)

Carburetors
Type . . . . Keihin CV 38 mm
Identification code
  California models
    1993 through 1995 models VP81A
    1996 and 1997 models VP89A
    1998 and 1999 models VP8DA
  US models (except California models)
    1993 through 1995 models VP84A
    1996 and 1997 models VP88B
    1998 and 1999 models VP8CP
  UK models
    N to S models VP80B
    T and V models VP88A
    W and X models VP8CA

4

Jet sizes

Main jet
  US 1993 through 1997 models and UK N to
  V models 115
  US 1998 and 1999 models and UK W
  and X models 120
Pilot jet 40
Pilot screw - initial setting (turns out)
  California models
    1993 through 1995 models 2 3/4
    1996 and 1997 models 3
    1998 and 1999 models 2
  US models (except California)
    1993 through 1995 models 2 1/2
    1996 and 1997 models 3
    1998 and 1999 models 1 5/8
  UK models
    N to V models 3
    W and X models 2

Carburetor adjustments

Float height (all models) . . . . 13.7 mm (0.54 in)
Idle speed . . . . See Chapter 1

Torque settings

	Nm	ft-lbs
Carburetor joining bolts		
5 mm nut	5	3.6
6 mm nut	10	7
Exhaust system		
Front pipe nuts	12	9
Exhaust pipe and muffler (silencer) nuts	26	19

---

1 General information and precautions

General information

The fuel system consists of the fuel tank, the fuel tap and filter, the fuel pump (US 1993 through 1995 models and UK N to S models), the carburetors and the connecting lines, hoses and control cables. US 1996 through 1999 models and UK T to X models use a vacuum operated tap, whilst all other models use a conventional tap in conjunction with the fuel pump.

The carburetors used on the CBR900RR are four 38 mm Keihin CV carburetors. For cold starting, an enrichment circuit is actuated by a cable and the choke knob on the top triple clamp. US 1996 through 1999 models and UK T to X models have a throttle sensor mounted on the carburettors and connected to the ignition control module.

Air is drawn into the carburetors from a moulded plastic air filter housing containing a pleated paper type element.

The exhaust system is a four-into-one design.

Many of the fuel system service procedures are considered routine maintenance items and for that reason are included in Chapter 1.

Precautions

Warning: Gasoline (petrol) is extremely flammable, so take extra precautions when you work on any part of the fuel system. Don't smoke or allow open flames or bare light bulbs near the work area, and don't work in a garage where a natural gas-type appliance (such as a water heater or clothes dryer) is present. If you spill any fuel on your skin, rinse it off immediately with soap and water. When you perform any kind of work on the fuel system, wear safety glasses and have a fire extinguisher suitable for a class B type fire (flammable liquids) on hand.

Always perform service procedures in a well-ventilated area to prevent a build-up of fumes.

Never work in a building containing a gas appliance with a pilot light, or any other form of naked flame. Ensure that there are no naked light bulbs or any sources of flame or sparks nearby.

Do not smoke (or allow anyone else to smoke) while in the vicinity of gasoline (petrol) or of components containing it. Remember the possible presence of vapor from these sources and move well clear before smoking.

Check all electrical equipment belonging to the house, garage or workshop where work is being undertaken (see the Safety first! section of this manual). Remember that certain electrical appliances such as drill, cutters etc. create sparks in the normal course of operation and must not be used near gasoline (petrol) or any component containing it. Again, remember the possible presence of fumes before using electrical equipment.

Always mop up any spilt fuel and safely dispose of the shop towel or rag used.

Any stored fuel that is drained off during servicing work, must be kept in sealed containers that are suitable for holding gasoline (petrol), and clearly marked as such; the containers themselves should be kept in a safe place. Note that this last point applies equally to the fuel tank, if it is removed from the machine; also remember to keep its cap closed at all times.

Note that the fuel system consists of the fuel tank, with its cap and related hoses, the fuel pump and filters. On US California models, this includes the Evaporative Emission Control (EVAP) System components.

Read the Safety first! section of this manual carefully before starting work.

Owners of machines used in the US, particularly California, should note that their machines must comply at all times with Federal or State legislation governing the permissible levels of noise and of pollutants such as unburnt hydrocarbons, carbon monoxide etc. that can be emitted by those machines. All vehicles offered for sale must comply with legislation in force at the date of manufacture and must not subsequently be altered in any way which will affect their emission of noise or of pollutants.

In practice, this means that adjustments may not be made to any part of the fuel, ignition or exhaust systems by anyone who is not authorized or mechanically qualified to do so, or who does not have the tools, equipment and data necessary to properly carry out the task. Also if any part of these systems is to be replaced it must be replaced

2.3a Remove the front mounting bolt(s) (one on US 1993 through 1995 models and UK N to S models, two on all others). . .

2.3b . . . and the rear mounting bolt

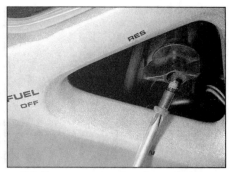

2.4 Remove screw to release fuel tap control knob

with only genuine Honda components or by components which are approved under the relevant legislation. The machine must never be used with any part of these systems removed, modified or damaged.

2 Fuel tank and tap -
removal and installation

Warning: Refer to the precautions given in Section 1 before starting work.

Fuel tank removal

1 Set the bike on its side stand.
2 Remove the rider's seat as described in Chapter 8.
3 Unscrew the fuel tank front and rear mounting bolts together with their washers **(see illustrations)**.
4 Ensure the fuel tap is turned OFF. Using a cross-head screwdriver passed down through the center of the tap knob, unscrew the retaining screw and withdraw the knob **(see illustration)**.
5 Lift the tank up at the rear to access the hoses on the tank underside. Release their spring clips and free the large-diameter overflow hose and small-diameter breather hose from their unions **(see illustration)**. Release the spring clip and disconnect the fuel hose from its union on the tap **(see illustration)**. On US 1996 through 1999 models and UK T to X models, also

disconnect the vacuum hose from its union on the tap.
6 Lift the fuel tank away from the machine.
7 Inspect the tank mounting rubbers for signs of damage or deterioration and replace if necessary.

Fuel tank installation

8 Lower the fuel tank into position, making sure the mounting rubbers remain in place, and reconnect the breather and overflow hoses to their unions on the tank underside; secure the hoses with their clips. Fit the fuel hose, and on US 1996 through 1999 models and UK T to X models the vacuum hose, to the tap and secure them with their clips.
9 Ensure that the collars are installed under the mounting rubbers and install the mounting bolts, tightening them securely **(see illustration)**.
10 Align the square hole of the tap knob with the corresponding square on the tap and secure it with the screw **(see illustration)**.
11 Install the rider's seat as described in Chapter 8.
12 Turn the fuel tap ON and check that there is no sign of fuel leakage.

Fuel tap removal
US 1996 through 1999 models and UK T to X models

13 Remove the fuel tank as described above. Connect a drain hose to the fuel tap stub and insert its end in a container suitable for storing gasoline (petrol). Connect a suitable hose to the vacuum hose union. Turn the fuel tap to

2.5a Disconnect breather (A) and drain (B) hoses from tank underside . . .

RES, then apply a suction or vacuum to the vacuum hose and allow the tank to fully drain.
14 Unscrew the tap gland nut and withdraw the tap, O-ring and filter from the tank.
15 Clean the gauze filter to remove all traces of dirt and fuel sediment. If it is holed or torn replace it with a new one.
16 To replace the diaphragm, unscrew the four screws and remove the diaphragm cover and spring. The diaphragm can be checked for cracks or splits by holding it up to the light. If it is suspected of being faulty (see Chapter 1) it must be replaced.

US 1993 through 1995 models and UK N to S models

17 Remove the fuel tank as described above. Connect a drain hose to the fuel tap stub and insert its end in a container suitable for storing gasoline (petrol). Turn the fuel tap to RES and allow the tank to fully drain.

2.5b . . . and disconnect fuel hose from fuel tap (non-vacuum tap shown)

2.9 Tank mounting collars fit underneath mounting rubbers

2.10 Tap control knob end locates over square on the tap body

2.18a Unscrew gland nut to free fuel tap from the tank

2.18b Note the O-ring between the tap and tank (arrow)

18 Unscrew the tap gland nut and withdraw the tap, O-ring and filter from the tank **(see illustrations)**.
19 Clean the gauze filter to remove all traces of dirt and fuel sediment. If it is holed or torn replace it with a new one.
20 Note that the tap is a sealed unit - if it fails, a new tap must be fitted.

Fuel tap installation

21 Installation is a reverse of the removal procedure, noting that a new O-ring should be used at the tap joint.

3 Fuel tank -
cleaning and repair

1 All repairs to the fuel tank should be carried out by a professional who has experience in this critical and potentially dangerous work. Even after cleaning and flushing of the fuel system, explosive fumes can remain and ignite during repair of the tank.
2 If the fuel tank is removed from the vehicle, it should not be placed in an area where sparks or open flames could ignite the fumes coming out of the tank. Be especially careful inside garages where a natural gas-type appliance is located, because the pilot light could cause an explosion.

4 Idle fuel/air mixture
adjustment - general information

1 Due to the increased emphasis on controlling motorcycle exhaust emissions, certain governmental regulations have been formulated which directly affect the carburation of this machine. In order to comply with the regulations, the carburetors on some models have a plastic limiter cap stuck onto the end of the pilot screw (which controls the idle fuel/air mixture) on each carburetor, so they can't be tampered with. These should only be removed in the event of a complete carburetor overhaul, and even then the screws should be returned to their original settings. The pilot screws on other models are

accessible, but the use of an exhaust gas analyzer is the only accurate way to adjust the idle fuel/air mixture and be sure the machine doesn't exceed the emissions regulations.
2 If the engine runs extremely rough at idle or continually stalls, and if a carburetor overhaul does not cure the problem, take the motorcycle to a Honda dealer or other repair shop equipped with an exhaust gas analyzer. They will be able to properly adjust the idle fuel/air mixture to achieve a smooth idle and restore low speed performance.

5 Carburetor overhaul -
general information

1 Poor engine performance, hesitation, hard starting, stalling, flooding and backfiring are all signs that major carburetor maintenance may be required.
2 Keep in mind that many so-called carburetor problems are really not carburetor problems at all, but mechanical problems within the engine or ignition system malfunctions. Try to establish for certain that the carburetors are in need of maintenance before beginning a major overhaul.
3 Check the fuel filter, the fuel lines, the tank breather hose (except California models), the intake manifold joint clamps, the fuel pump (US 1993 through 1995 models and UK N to S models), the air filter element, the cylinder compression, the spark plugs and carburetor synchronization before assuming that a

6.2 Slip the idle speed screw out of its wire holder

carburetor overhaul is required.
4 Most carburetor problems are caused by dirt particles, varnish and other deposits which build up in and block the fuel and air passages. Also, in time, gaskets and O-rings shrink or deteriorate and cause fuel and air leaks which lead to poor performance.
5 When the carburetor is overhauled, it is generally disassembled completely and the parts are cleaned thoroughly with a carburetor cleaning solvent and dried with filtered, unlubricated compressed air. The fuel and air passages are also blown through with compressed air to force out any dirt that may have been loosened but not removed by the solvent. Once the cleaning process is complete, the carburetor is reassembled using new gaskets and O-rings.
6 Before disassembling the carburetors, make sure you have a carburetor rebuild kit (which will include all necessary O-rings and other parts), some carburetor cleaner, a supply of rags, some means of blowing out the carburetor passages and a clean place to work. It is recommended that only one carburetor be overhauled at a time to avoid mixing up parts.

6 Carburetors -
removal and installation

⚠️ **Warning: Refer to the precautions given in Section 1 before starting work**

Removal

1 Remove the air filter housing as described in Section 12.
2 Remove both middle fairing sections (see Chapter 8). Free the idle speed screw from its wire holder on the on the left fairing bracket **(see illustration)**.
3 On California models, disconnect the relevant emission (EVAP) system hoses from the carburetors noting the correct fitted position of each hose. On US 1996 through 1999 models and UK T to X models, disconnect the throttle sensor wiring at its connector.
4 Free the fuel hose from the T-piece at the rear of the carburetors **(see illustration)**.

6.4a Release its clip and disconnect the fuel hose from the T-piece

6.4b Free the carburetor vent hose from its wire guide

6.5a Slacken the choke cable clamp screw to free the outer cable . . .

6.5b . . . and disconnect the inner cable from the choke linkage shaft

Release the vent hose (all models except California) from the wire guide on the right side of the frame **(see illustration)**.

5 Slacken the choke outer cable clamp screw and detach the inner cable from the choke linkage shaft **(see illustrations)**.

6 Slacken the four retaining clamps securing the carburetor intake rubbers to the cylinder head **(see illustration)**.

7 Ease the carburetors off the cylinder head stubs and tilt the assembly so gain access to the throttle cam **(see illustration)**. Slacken off the adjusters on the throttle cable bracket to create slack in the cables, then hook each cable out of the slot in the cam **(see illustrations)**. **Note:** *Keep the carburetors the right way up to prevent fuel spillage from the float chambers and the possibility of the piston diaphragms being damaged.*

8 With the carburetors removed, place a suitable container below their float chambers then slacken the drain screws and drain all the fuel from the carburetors. Once all the fuel has been drained, tighten all the drain screws securely. **Caution: Honda advise against resting the carburetors on the air funnels.**

Installation

9 Installation is the reverse of removal making sure the carburetor intake rubbers are fully

6.6 Slacken all four intake manifold joint clamps

engaged with the cylinder head and their retaining clips are securely tightened. Prior to installing the air filter housing, adjust the throttle and choke cables as described in Chapter 1.

---

7 Carburetors - disassembly, cleaning and inspection 🔧

⚠ **Warning: Refer to the precautions given in Section 1 before proceeding.**

6.7a Ease the carburetors rearwards, off the cylinder head

Caution: On US 1996 through 1999 models and UK T to X models, Honda advise against removing the throttle sensor from the carburetors unless necessary (i.e., for cleaning the carburetor bodies).

Disassembly

1 Remove the carburetors from the machine as described in the previous Section. **Note:** *Do not separate the carburetors unless absolutely necessary; each carburetor can be dismantled sufficiently for all normal cleaning and adjustments while in place on the mounting brackets. Dismantle the carburetors*

4

6.7b Slacken the throttle cable adjusters to provide enough slack in the cables . . .

6.7c . . . to slip their inner cables out of the throttle cam

7.2a Undo the three screws and remove the top cover . . .

7.2b . . . then recover the spring from the piston

7.1 Carburetor detail

1 Top cover screw	10 Float chamber screw	18 Pilot jet
2 Top cover	11 Float chamber	19 Pilot screw
3 Spring	12 Seal	20 Spring
4 Piston and diaphragm	13 Float pivot pin	21 Washer
5 Needle holder	14 Float	22 O-ring
6 O-ring	15 Needle valve	23 Choke plunger nut
7 Spring	16 Main jet	24 Spring
8 Needle	17 Needle jet	25 Choke plunger
9 Sealing washer		

separately to avoid interchanging parts. Note that it is necessary to separate the carburetors to remove the choke plungers **(see illustration)**.

2 Slacken and remove the top cover retaining screws. Lift off the cover and remove the spring from inside the piston **(see illustrations)**.

3 Carefully peel the diaphragm away from its sealing groove in the carburetor and withdraw the diaphragm and piston assembly **(see illustration)**.

Caution: Do not use a sharp instrument to displace the diaphragm as it is easily damaged.

4 To remove the needle from the piston, screw a 4 mm bolt into the thread in the centre of the needle holder (one of the top cover retaining screws will do), then use a pair of pliers to pull the needle holder out of the piston **(see illustration)**. Recover the O-ring and spring, then tip the needle and sealing washer out of the piston.

5 Remove the retaining screws and remove the float chamber from the base of the carburetor **(see illustration)**. Recover the rubber seal.

7.3 Withdrawing the diaphragm and piston assembly. Take care not to damage the diaphragm

7.4 Screw one of the cover bolts into the needle holder and pull the holder out from the piston

7.5 Float chamber is retained by three screws

7.6 Withdraw the pivot pin and remove the float and needle valve from the carburetor

7.7a Unscrew the main jet with a close-fitting screwdriver . . .

7.7b . . . and remove it from the end of the needle jet

6 Withdraw the float pivot pin, using a pair of pointed-nose pliers, and remove the float and needle valve assembly **(see illustration)**.

7 Unscrew the main jet from the base of the needle jet **(see illustrations)**.

8 Unscrew the needle jet from the carburetor **(see illustrations)**.

9 Unscrew the pilot jet, situated next to the needle jet, from the carburetor **(see illustration)**.

10 Remove the plastic limiter cap (where fitted) from the pilot screw which is screwed into the base of the carburetor. The cap will be cemented in place and can be removed using a pair of pliers.

11 The pilot screw can be removed from the carburettor, but note that its setting will be disturbed (see Haynes Hint). Unscrew and remove the pilot screw along with its spring, washer and O-ring **(see illustration)**. Discard the O-ring as a new one must be used.

HAYNES HINT *To record the pilot screw's current setting, turn the screw in until it seats lightly, counting the number of turns necessary to achieve this, then fully unscrew it. On installation, the screw is simply backed out the number of turns you've recorded.*

12 If the air funnels require removal, release the four screws and lift the holders and air funnels free **(see illustration)**. Recover the O-rings.

13 If the carburetors have been separated,

unscrew the valve nut and remove the choke plunger and spring from the carburetor.

Cleaning

Caution: Use only a petroleum based solvent for carburetor cleaning. Don't use caustic cleaners. On US 1996 through 1999 models and UK T to X models , remove the throttle sensor before cleaning the carburetor bodies (see Chapter 5).

14 Submerge the metal components in the solvent for approximately thirty minutes (or longer, if the directions recommend it).

15 After the carburetor has soaked long enough for the cleaner to loosen and dissolve most of the varnish and other deposits, use a brush to remove the stubborn deposits. Rinse it again, then dry it with compressed air. Blow out all of the fuel and air passages in the main and upper body.

7.8a Unscrew the needle jet . . .

Caution: Never clean the jets or passages with a piece of wire or a drill bit, as they will be enlarged, causing the fuel and air metering rates to be upset.

16 Use a jet of compressed air directed in the fuel inlet valve needle seat to clear the gauze fuel filter inside the carburetor body.

Inspection

17 Check the operation of the choke plunger. If it doesn't move smoothly, replace it, along with its spring. Inspect the needle on the end of the choke plunger and replace the plunger if it's worn or bent.

18 Check the tapered portion of the pilot screw for wear or damage. Replace the pilot screw if necessary **(see illustration)**.

19 Check the carburetor body, float chamber and top cover for cracks, distorted sealing surfaces and other damage. If any defects are

7.8b . . . and remove it from the carburetor

4

7.9 Pilot jet is also a screw fit in the carburetor

7.12 Air funnel holders are retained by four screws

7.18 Pilot screw components. Ensure the tapered portion of the screw is not bent or damaged

7.20 Check the piston diaphragm for signs of splitting and replace if necessary

found, replace the faulty component, although replacement of the entire carburetor will probably be necessary (check with your parts supplier for the availability of separate components).

20 Check the diaphragm for splits, holes and general deterioration. Holding it up to a light will help to reveal problems of this nature **(see illustration)**.

21 Insert the diaphragm piston in the carburetor body and check that it moves up-and-down smoothly. Check the surface of the piston for wear. If it's worn excessively or doesn't move smoothly in the bore, replace the carburetor.

22 Check the jet needle for straightness by rolling it on a flat surface (such as a piece of glass). Replace it if it's bent or if the tip is worn.

23 Check the tip of the float needle valve. If it has grooves or scratches in it, it must be replaced. Push in on the rod in the other end of the needle, then release it - if it doesn't spring back, replace the needle valve. If the needle valve seat is damaged the carburettor assembly must be replaced; it is not possible to replace the seat individually.

24 Check the float chamber gasket and replace it if it's damaged.

25 Operate the throttle shaft to make sure the throttle butterfly valve opens and closes smoothly. If it doesn't, replace the carburetor.

26 Check the floats for damage. This will usually be apparent by the presence of fuel inside one of the floats. If the floats are damaged, they must be replaced.

8 Carburetors - separation and joining

⚠️ *Warning: Refer to the precautions given in Section 1 before proceeding*

Separation

1 The carburetors do not need to be separated for normal overhaul. If you need to separate them (to replace a carburetor body, for example), refer to the following procedure **(see illustration)**.

8.1 Carburetor linkage components

1 Idle speed screw
2 Joining bolt and nuts - 6 mm
3 Joining bolt and nuts - 5 mm
4 Joining bolt dowel - 6 mm
5 Joining bolt dowel - 5 mm
6 Fuel hoses and unions
7 Breather hose and unions
8 Air vent hose and unions
9 Throttle linkage springs
10 Synchronization screws
11 Choke linkage shaft

2 Remove the carburetors from the machine as described in Section 6. Mark the body of each carburetor with its cylinder number to ensure that it is positioned correctly on reassembly.

3 To prevent damage to the air funnels, it is advised that they are removed. Remove the four screws and lift the holders and air funnels off the carburetors. Recover the O-rings.

4 Release the spring clips and pull the fuel hose off of the unions between carburetor Nos. 1 and 2 and carburetor Nos. 3 and 4. On all models except California, disconnect the air vent hoses from the unions between carburetor Nos. 1 and 2 and carburetor Nos. 3 and 4.

5 Unhook the choke linkage return spring and washer from between Nos. 1 and 2 carburetors. Undo the two screws and washers securing the linkage shaft to the top

8.5a Remove the choke linkage return spring and washer (arrow) . . .

8.5b . . . then undo the two retaining screws . . .

8.5c . . . and recover the washers

8.5d Lift off the choke linkage shaft . . .

8.5e . . . and recover the spacers from underneath it

of the carburetors then lift off the linkage shaft and recover the spacers from underneath the shaft **(see illustrations)**.

6 Make a note of how the throttle linkage spring and No. 2 carburetor synchronization spring are arranged to ensure that they are fitted correctly on reassembly.

7 Evenly unscrew the two retaining nuts from the No. 1 carburetor end **(see illustration)**. Withdraw the two joining bolts from the other end of the carburetors.

8 Carefully separate carburetor Nos. 2 and 3, leaving Nos. 1 and 2, and Nos. 3 and 4 still joined. Retrieve the synchronization springs, the two dowels and the breather hose T-piece as they are separated.

9 Separate carburetors 1 and 2 by gently pulling them apart. Retrieve the throttle linkage spring, synchronization springs, both dowels, air vent T-piece, fuel T-piece and breather joint. Carry out the same procedure to separate carburetor Nos. 3 and 4.

Joining

10 Assembly is the reverse of the disassembly procedure, noting the following.

a) *Use new O-rings on all the T-piece unions* **(see illustration)**.

b) *The carburetor joining bolts are different diameter; the front bolt is 6 mm and must have the choke cable clamp fitted to its right end, whereas the rear bolt is 5 mm diameter. Similarly, the dowels between*

8.7 Unscrew the carburetor retaining nuts (arrows)

each carburetor are sized accordingly. Tighten the nuts evenly to the specified torque setting, ensuring correct alignment. No more than 3 mm of thread should extend from the outer face of any nut **(see illustration)**.

c) *If the intake manifold joints were removed, ensure that the edge with the CARB faces the carburetor and align the groove with the carburetor lug.*

d) *Check the operation of both the choke and throttle linkages ensuring that both operate smoothly and return quickly under spring pressure before installing the carburetors on the machine.*

e) *Check carburetor synchronization (see Chapter 1).*

8.10a On reassembly renew all O-rings (arrows) on the unions

9 Carburetors - reassembly and float height check

Note: *When reassembling the carburetors, be sure to use the new O-rings, gaskets and other parts supplied in the rebuild kit. Do not overtighten the carburetor jets and screws as they are easily damaged.*

1 Install the choke plunger in its bore, followed by its spring and nut. Tighten the nut securely and install the cap.

2 Install the pilot screw (if removed) along with its spring, washer and O-ring, turning it in until it seats lightly **(see illustration)**. Now, turn the screw out the number of turns previously recorded. Where fitted, install a

4

8.10b Ensure that the joining bolt threads do not extend more than 3 mm from the face of the nut

9.2 Assemble the pilot screw components on the screw and install the screw as described in text

9.6 Make sure that the needle valve is correctly slotted into the float

9.7 Measuring the float height

9.8 Make sure the rubber seal is correctly located in its groove before installing the float chamber on the carburetor

new limiter cap on the screw, applying a little bonding agent to hold it in position.

3 Screw the needle jet into position in the carburetor.

4 Screw the main jet into the end of the needle jet. **Note:** *On US 1996 through 1999 models and UK T to X models, the main jets fitted to Nos. 2 and 3 carburetors are different to those fitted to Nos. 1 and 4 carburetors. Nos. 2 and 3 main jets can be identified by the punch mark at the end of the jet size marking (No. 1 and 4 main jets have no punch mark). Ensure the correct type of main jet is installed in each carburetor.*

5 Screw the pilot jet into position.

6 Hook the needle valve over the float, then install the float and secure it with the pivot pin **(see illustration)**.

7 To check the float height, hold the carburetor so the float hangs down, then tilt it back until

the needle valve is just seated, but not so far that the needle's spring-loaded tip is compressed. Measure the distance between the gasket face and the bottom of the float with an accurate ruler **(see illustration)**. The correct setting should be as given in the Specifications Section. The float height is not adjustable; if it is incorrect the float must be replaced. Repeat the procedure for all carburetors.

8 With the float height checked, fit a new rubber seal to the float chamber and install the chamber on the carburetor **(see illustration)**.

9 Fit the washer to the jet needle and insert the needle into the piston **(see illustration)**. Position a new O-ring in the groove of the needle jet holder and fit the spring inside the holder **(see illustration)**. Insert the needle holder into the center of the piston and press

it into position until the O-ring is heard to click into the groove in the base of the piston.

10 Insert the piston assembly into the carburetor body and lightly push it down, ensuring the needle is correctly aligned with the needle jet. Press the diaphragm outer edge into its groove, ensuring the diaphragm tongue is correctly seated in the cutout on the carburetor **(see illustration)**. Check the diaphragm is not creased, and that the piston moves smoothly up and down the bore.

11 Insert the spring and fit the top cover to the carburetor **(see illustration)**.

12 If the air funnels where removed, install the O-ring in the carburetor groove **(see illustration)**. Insert the air funnel into the holder and rotate it so that its tabs are locked in place **(see illustration)**. Align the cutout in the air funnel with the carburetor lugs and

9.9a Insert the jet needle and sealing washer into the piston . . .

9.9b . . . and fit the needle holder and spring. Make sure the O-ring (arrow) is correctly positioned

9.10 Insert the piston and locate the diaphragm in the carburetor groove

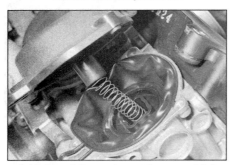

9.11 Install the spring and cover whilst making sure the diaphragm remains correctly seated

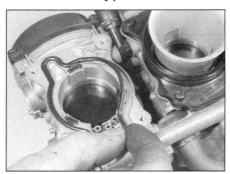

9.12a Install the O-ring in the carburetor groove

9.12b Insert the air funnel in its holder and rotate it so that it tabs are locked in place

9.12c Align the cutout in the air funnel with the carburetor lug (arrow)

10.3a Release the two screws to free the throttle grip housing cover . . .

10.3b . . . and access the throttle cables

install it; tighten the four screws securely **(see illustration)**.

13 On US 1996 and 1997 models and UK CBR900RR-T and RR-V, install the throttle sensor, if removed (See Chapter 5).

10 Throttle cables -
removal and installation

Warning: Refer to the precautions given in Section 1 before proceeding

Removal

1 Remove the air filter housing as described in Section 12.
2 Slacken the throttle cable locknuts then free each outer cable from its mounting bracket and detach the inner cables from the throttle cam **(see illustrations 6.7b and 6.7c)**. If necessary to improve access to throttle cam, slacken the four retaining clips securing the carburetor intake rubbers to the cylinder head and disengage the carburetors from the cylinder head **(see illustration 6.7a)**. Keep the carburetors upright to prevent fuel spillage.
3 US 1996 through 1999 models and UK T to X models, remove the two handlebar switch/throttle pulley housing screws from the underside of the switch and separate the halves. On all other models, remove the two throttle pulley housing screws and separate the halves **(see illustration)**. Hook the cable ends out of the pulley and unscrew the cable elbows from the rear of the housing **(see illustration)**. Mark each cable to ensure it is connected correctly on installation.
4 Remove the cables from the machine noting the correct routing of each cable.

Installation

5 Install the cables making sure they are correctly routed. The cables must not interfere with any other component and should not be kinked or bent sharply.
6 Screw the cables into the throttle pulley housing, making sure they are correctly connected. Lubricate the end of each cable with multi-purpose grease and attach the

cables to the pulley. Assemble the housing, aligning its locating pin with the hole in the handlebar. Install the retaining screws, and tighten them securely.
7 Lubricate the end of each cable with multi-purpose grease and attach them to the carburetor throttle cam.
8 Make sure the cables are correctly connected and locate the outer cable adjusters in the mounting bracket.
9 Where necessary, fit the carburetors to cylinder head and securely tighten the intake rubber clips.
10 Adjust the cables as described in Chapter 1. Turn the handlebars back and forth to make sure the cables don't cause the steering to bind.
11 Install the air filter housing as described in Section 12.
12 Start the engine and check that the idle speed does not rise as the handlebars are turned. If it does, correct the problem before riding the motorcycle.

11 Choke cable -
removal and installation

Removal

1 Remove the air filter housing as described in Section 12.
2 On early models, slacken the screw and free the choke outer cable from its retaining clamp and detach the inner cable from the carburetor linkage **(see illustrations 6.5a and 6.5b)**. On later models, unclip the choke outer cable end fitting from its bracket then detach the inner cable from the carburetor linkage.
3 Peel the rubber cover up to reveal the knurled ring under the choke knob. Unscrew the ring and the nut beneath the bracket, then slip the cable out of the bracket slot **(see illustration)**.
4 Remove the cable from the machine noting its correct routing.

Installation

5 Install the cable making sure it is correctly

routed. The cable must not interfere with any other component and should not be kinked or bent sharply.
6 Slip the cable into the bracket on the triple clamp, aligning its flat with that on the bracket. Secure with the nut and knurled ring. Fit the rubber cover back into place.
7 Lubricate the cable end with multi-purpose grease and attach it to the choke linkage.
8 On early models, locate the outer cable in the retaining clamp and adjust the cable as described in Chapter 1. On later models, clip the outer cable end fitting into the bracket then check the operation of the choke linkage as described in Chapter 1.
9 Install the air filter housing as described in Section 12.

12 Air filter housing and
carburetor breather filter -
removal and installation

Air filter housing

Removal

1 Remove the air filter element as described in Chapter 1.

4

11.3 The choke cable can be slipped out of its bracket after releasing the knurled ring and nut

12.2 Air filter housing is retained by a single bolt to ignition HT coil bracket

12.3 Disconnect the crankcase breather hose from the base of the housing

12.4a Slacken the two joint clamp screws on each side (arrows) . . .

2 Undo the bolt which secures the filter housing base in position **(see illustration)**.

3 Free the crankcase breather pipe from the front right corner of the housing **(see illustration)**. On California models only, disconnect the pulse secondary air injection (PAIR) system hose from the rear of the housing.

4 Slacken all four carburetor joint clamp screws and ease the housing off the air funnels **(see illustration)**. Disconnect the carburetor breather pipe from the filter on the base of the air filter housing **(see illustration)**.

Installation

5 Installation is the reverse of removal, noting

12.4b . . . and lift the housing off the carburetors to enable the carburetor breather hose to be disconnected from its filter (arrow)

that the air filter housing has a guide for the main wire harness.

Carburetor breather filter

Removal

6 Remove the fuel tank as described in Section 2 of this Chapter.

7 Unclip the cover to free the filter from the base of its chamber on the air filter housing **(see illustration)**. If the filter is excessively dirty it must be replaced with a new one.

Installation

8 Install the filter and clip the cover back into place.

9 Install the fuel tank as described in Section 2 of this Chapter.

12.7 Carburetor breather cover unclips for access to filter

13 Exhaust system -
removal and installation

Muffler (silencer)

Removal

1 Slacken and remove the muffler mounting nut and bolt and recover the washer and collar from the rubber mounting **(see illustration)**.

2 Loosen the muffler clamp bolts, then release the muffler from the exhaust front pipe using a twisting motion **(see illustration)**. Remove the muffler and recover the sealing ring.

Installation

3 Fit a new sealing ring to the front pipe **(see illustration)**.

4 Ensure the collar is in place in the mounting rubber (inserted with its flange on the inside), then install the muffler so that its mounting is on the inside of the footpeg bracket. Install the bolt, washers and nut and tighten to the specified torque setting. Tighten the three muffler clamp bolts securely.

Complete system

Removal

5 Remove the fairing lower section and both middle sections as described in Chapter 8.

13.1 Muffler (silencer) bolts to pillion footpeg bracket

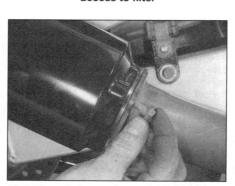

13.2 Three bolts retain muffler (silencer) to exhaust pipe

13.3 Use a new gasket at the muffler-to-exhaust pipe joint

13.7a Remove the eight joint nuts . . .

13.7b . . . and slide the joint plates off the cylinder head studs

6 Drain the cooling system (see Chapter 1) and remove the radiator (see Chapter 3).

7 Remove the eight nuts and slip the joint plates off the cylinder head studs **(see illustrations)**.

8 Slacken and remove the muffler mounting nut and bolt and recover the washer and collar from the rubber mounting **(see illustration 13.1)**.

9 Slacken and remove the nut and bolt securing the exhaust system to the base of the frame, taking exact note of the washer and collar positions in the rubber mounting **(see illustration)**. Remove the exhaust assembly from the bike and recover the gaskets from the cylinder head ports.

Installation

10 Inspect the mounting rubbers for signs of damage and replace if necessary.

11 Fit the collar to the exhaust front pipe mounting rubber so that its flange is on the outside. Insert the collar into the muffler mounting rubber so that its flange is on the inside.

12 Position a new gasket in each of the cylinder head ports **(see illustration)**.

13 Install the exhaust front pipe assembly,

aligning the pipes with the cylinder head ports, and fit the mounting bolt, washers and nut to the frame mounting.

14 Slide the joint plates onto the studs and fit the nuts. Tighten the exhaust front pipe nuts to the specified torque setting.

15 Securely tighten the frame mounting bolt nut to the specified torque setting.

16 Insert the muffler mounting bolt, washers and nut and tighten to the specified torque setting.

17 Install the radiator (see Chapter 3) and fill the cooling system (see Chapter 1).

18 Install the fairing sections as described in Chapter 8.

14 Pulse secondary air injection (PAIR) system - California models only

General information

1 On California models to reduce the amount of unburnt hydrocarbons released in the exhaust gases, a Pulse secondary air injection (PAIR) system is fitted **(see illustration 15.1)**.

The system consists of the pulse air control valve assembly, which is mounted on the front of the engine unit, and the air feed pipes which link the control valve to the cylinder head. The control valve is linked to the No. 3 intake manifold by a vacuum hose and to the air filter housing by an air suction hose.

2 When the engine is running, the depression present in the intake manifold acts on the vacuum diaphragm in the control valve and opens up the valve.

3 With the valve open, whenever there is a negative pulse in the exhaust system (i.e. on the overrun), filtered air is drawn from the air filter housing through the control valve and into the exhaust ports in the cylinder head. This fresh air promotes the burning of any excess fuel present in the exhaust gases, so reducing the amount of harmful hydrocarbons reduced into the atmosphere via the exhaust gases.

4 The control valve assembly is fitted with a pair of one-way check valves to prevent the exhaust gases passing through the control valve and into the air filter housing.

5 The system is not adjustable and can be tested only by a Honda dealer. Checks which

4

13.9 Remove the exhaust pipe-to-frame mounting bolt

13.12 Use new gaskets in the cylinder head ports

14.8 Pulse secondary air injection (PAIR) system components

1 Control valve   2 Control valve bracket   3 Air feed pipes   4 Gaskets   5 Hoses

can be performed by the owner are given in Chapter 1.

Removal

6 Remove the fairing middle sections as described in Chapter 8.

7 Release their retaining clips and disconnect the vacuum hose and air suction hose from the control valve.

8 Undo the three screws and washers securing the control valve to the front of the crankcase **(see illustration)**.

9 Unscrew the four nuts and release the air feed pipes from the front of the cylinder head.

10 Remove the control valve assembly, complete with pipes and hoses, from the front of the engine unit.

11 Recover the gaskets from the front of the cylinder head and discard them.

12 If necessary, unbolt the control valve mounting bracket from the front of the crankcase.

13 Inspect the pipes and hoses for signs of cracks and splits and replace damaged components.

Installation

14 Ensure the air feed pipe and cylinder head mating surfaces are clean and dry. Install the mounting bracket (where removed).

15 Fit a new gasket to each of the cylinder head unions, making sure each gasket is fitted the correct way around.

16 Install the control valve assembly locating the feed pipes on the cylinder head studs. Fit the air feed pipe nuts and control valve retaining screws and tighten them securely.

17 Connect the vacuum hose and air suction hose to the control valve and secure in position with the retaining clips.

18 Fit the fairing sections as described in Chapter 8.

15 Evaporative emission control (EVAP) system -
California models only

1 On all California models, an evaporative emission control (EVAP) system is fitted **(see illustration)**. This system prevents the escape of fuel vapors into the atmosphere and functions as follows.

2 When the engine is stopped, fuel vapor from the tank is directed into a charcoal canister where it is absorbed and stored whilst the motorcycle is standing. When the engine is started, inlet manifold depression opens the purge control valve diaphragm. The vapors which are stored in the canister are then drawn into the engine to be burned during the normal combustion process.

3 The system is not adjustable and can be tested only by a Honda dealer. Checks which can be performed by the owner are given in Chapter 1.

15.1 Evaporative emission control (EVAP) system and pulse secondary air injection (PAIR) system connections

1 Fuel tank
2 EVAP system charcoal canister
3 EVAP system purge control valve
4 EVAP system air vent control valve
5 Carburetors
6 Cylinder head
7 PAIR system control valve
8 Air filter housing

Chapter 5
Ignition system

Contents

Degrees of difficulty

| **Easy,** suitable for novice with little experience | | **Fairly easy,** suitable for beginner with some experience | | **Fairly difficult,** suitable for competent DIY mechanic | | **Difficult,** suitable for experienced DIY mechanic | | **Very difficult,** suitable for expert DIY or professional | |

Specifications

General information
Firing order	1-2-4-3
Cylinder identification	1-2-3-4 left to right
Spark plugs	See Chapter 1

Ignition timing
Initial	10°BTDC @ idle
Full advance	
US 1993 through 1995 models and UK R and S models	36° BTDC @ 4300 ± 100 rpm
UK N and P models	36° BTDC @ 6000 ± 100 rpm
US 1996 through 1999 models and UK T to X models	Not available

Pulse generator
Resistance	460 to 580 ohms @ 20°C (68°F)
Peak voltage	0.7 volts min

Ignition HT coils
Primary winding resistance	2.5 to 3.2 ohms @ 20°C (68°F)
Primary peak voltage	100 volts min
Secondary winding resistance	
With plug caps	21 to 27 K ohms @ 20°C (68°F)
Without plug caps	11 to 17 K ohms @ 20°C (68°F)

Torque settings
	Nm	ft-lbs
Crankshaft right end cover		
Retaining bolts	12	9
Center cap	18	13

5

1.1 Ignition circuit diagram

Bl	Black	G	Green	R	Red	Y	Yellow
Bl/Br	Black and brown	G/R	Green and red	R/Bl	Red and black	Y/Bl	Yellow and black
Bl/W	Black and white	G/W	Green and white	R/Y	Red and yellow	Y/G	Yellow and green
Bu/G	Blue and green	Lg	Light green	W/Y	White and yellow	Y/R	Yellow and red
Bu/Y	Blue and yellow	Lg/R	Light green and red				

1 General information

These models are fitted with a fully transistorized digital ignition system, which due to its lack of mechanical parts is totally maintenance free. The system comprises a rotor, pulse generator, control module and two ignition HT coils (see illustration). On US 1996 through 1999 models and UK T to X models, a throttle sensor is fitted to the carburettors and connected to the control module.

The raised triggers on the rotor, which is fitted to the right end of the crankshaft, magnetically operate the pulse generator as the crankshaft rotates. The pulse generator sends a signal to the ignition control module which then supplies the ignition HT coils with the power necessary to produce a spark at the plugs. Each coil supplies two spark plugs.

Cylinders 1 and 4 operate off one coil and cylinders 2 and 3 off the other. For any given

cylinder, the plug is fired twice for every engine cycle, but one of the sparks occurs during the exhaust stroke and therefore performs no useful function. This arrangement is usually known as a "spare spark" or "wasted spark" system.

Because of their nature, the individual ignition system components can be checked but not repaired. If ignition system troubles occur, and the faulty component can be isolated, the only cure for the problem is to replace the part with a new one. Keep in mind that most electrical parts, once purchased, can't be returned. To avoid unnecessary expense, make very sure the faulty component has been positively identified before buying a replacement part.

2 Ignition system - check

Caution: The energy levels in electronic systems can be very high. On no account should the ignition be switched on whilst the plugs or plug caps are being held.

Shocks from the HT circuit can be most unpleasant. Secondly, it is vital that the plugs are soundly grounded (earthed) when the system is checked for sparking. The ignition system components can be seriously damaged if the HT circuit becomes isolated.

1 As no means of adjustment is available, any failure of the system can be traced to failure of a system component or a simple wiring fault. Of the two possibilities, the latter is by far the most likely. In the event of failure, check the system in a logical fashion, as described below.

2 Disconnect the HT leads from No. 1 and No. 2 cylinder spark plugs and connect each lead to a spare spark plug. Lay each plug on the engine with the threads contacting the engine. If necessary, hold each spark plug with an insulated tool.

⚠ *Warning: Don't remove one of the spark plugs from the engine to perform this check - atomized fuel being pumped out of the open spark plug hole could ignite, causing severe injury!*

TOOL TIP

A simple spark gap testing tool can be made from a block of wood, a large alligator clip and two nails, one of which is fashioned so that a spark plug cap or bare HT lead end can be connected to its end. Make sure the gap between the two nail ends is the same as specified.

3 Having observed the above precautions, check that the kill switch is in the RUN position, turn the ignition switch to ON and turn the engine over on the starter motor. If the system is in good condition a regular, fat blue spark should be evident at each plug electrode. If the spark appears thin or yellowish, or is non-existent, further investigation will be necessary. Before proceeding further, turn the ignition off and remove the key as a safety measure.

4 The ignition system must be able to produce a spark which is capable of jumping a particular size gap. Whilst Honda do not specify the size of this gap, a healthy system should produce a spark capable of jumping at least 6 mm. A simple testing tool can be made to test the minimum gap across which the spark will jump **(see Tool Tip)**.

5 Connect one of the spark plug HT leads from one coil to the protruding electrode on the test tool, and clip the tool to a good earth on the engine or frame. Check that the kill switch is in the RUN position, turn the ignition switch ON and turn the engine over on the starter motor. If the system is in good condition a regular, fat blue spark should be seen to jump the gap between the nail ends.

Repeat the test for the other coil. If the test results are good the entire ignition system can be considered good. If the spark appears thin or yellowish, or is non-existent, further investigation will be necessary.

6 Ignition faults can be divided into two categories, namely those where the ignition system has failed completely, and those which are due to a partial failure. The likely faults are listed below, starting with the most probable source of failure. Work through the list systematically, referring to the subsequent sections for full details of the necessary checks and tests. **Note:** *Before checking the following items ensure that the battery is fully charged and that all fuses are in good condition.*

  a) *Loose, corroded or damaged wiring connections, broken or shorted wiring between any of the component parts of the ignition system (see Chapter 9).*
  b) *Faulty HT lead or spark plug cap, faulty spark plug, dirty, worn or corroded plug electrodes, or incorrect gap between electrodes.*
  c) *Faulty ignition switch or engine kill switch (see Chapter 9).*
  d) *Faulty neutral or side stand switch (see Chapter 9).*
  e) *Faulty pulse generator coils or damaged rotor.*
  f) *Faulty ignition HT coil(s).*
  g) *Faulty ignition control unit.*

7 If the above checks don't reveal the cause of the problem, have the ignition system tested by a Honda dealer. Honda produce a tester which can perform a complete diagnostic analysis of the ignition system.

3 Ignition HT coils - check, removal and installation

Check

1 In order to determine conclusively that the ignition HT coils are defective, they should be tested by a Honda dealer equipped with the special electrical tester required for this check.

2 However, the coils can be checked visually (for cracks and other damage) and the primary and secondary coil resistances can be measured with an ohmmeter. If the coils are undamaged, and if the resistances are as specified, they are probably capable of proper operation.

3 To gain access to the coils, remove the air filter housing as described in Chapter 4 **(see illustration)**.

4 Disconnect the primary circuit electrical connectors from the coil(s) and disconnect the HT leads from the plugs that are connected to the coil being checked. Gently pull the HT leads and plug caps through the dust/heat deflector sheet. Mark the locations of all wires before disconnecting them.

5 Set the meter to the ohms x 1 scale and measure the resistance between the low tension terminals **(see illustration)**. This will give a resistance reading of the primary windings and should be within the limits given in the Specifications.

6 To check the condition of the secondary windings, set the meter to the K ohm scale and connect the meter probes to the spark plug caps, noting the reading obtained **(see illustration)**. If this reading is not within the range shown in the Specifications, unscrew the plug caps from the HT leads then measure the resistance between the HT lead ends. If both values obtained differ greatly from those specified it is likely that the coil is defective. **Note:** *If only the first reading obtained is suspect, then the fault lies in the spark plug caps rather than the coil or its leads.*

7 Should any of the above checks not produce the expected result, the coil should be taken to a Honda dealer or auto-electrician for a more thorough check. If the coil is confirmed to be faulty, it must be replaced; the coil is a sealed unit and cannot therefore be repaired. Note that the HT leads can be unscrewed from the coils and replaced separately.

Removal

8 Remove the air filter housing as described in Chapter 4.

9 Disconnect the HT leads from the spark plugs that are connected to the coil(s) being

5

3.3 Ignition HT coils are mounted on frame cross-member

3.5 Measuring ignition HT coil primary winding resistance

3.6 Measuring ignition HT coil secondary winding resistance (plug caps connected)

3.10 Label the coil terminals or make written note of the wire connections before disconnecting primary circuit wires

3.11 Remove the two bolts to free the coil mounting bracket from the frame cross-member

4.2 Pulse generator wire connector is located on inside of the frame

removed. The cylinder number should be marked on the HT leads; if not, mark the locations of all leads before disconnecting them. Gently pull the HT leads and plug caps through the rubber dust cover.

10 Disconnect the primary circuit electrical connectors from the coils, having made note of their positions **(see illustration)**.

11 Remove the two bolts to release each coil from the frame cross-member **(see illustration)**. The coils can be separated from their mounting brackets by removing the throughbolts, washers and nuts.

Installation

12 Installation is the reverse of removal making sure the wiring connectors and HT leads are securely connected.

---

4 Pulse generator coil - check, removal and installation

Check

1 Remove the fuel tank as described in Chapter 4.

2 Trace the pulse generator wiring up from the crankshaft end cover to the black two-pin connector at the top of the frame **(see illustration)**. Disconnect the connector and

using a multimeter set to the ohms x 100 scale, measure the resistance between the white/yellow and yellow wires on the pulse generator side of the connector.

3 Compare the reading obtained with that given in the Specifications at the start of this Chapter. The pulse generator must be replaced if the reading obtained differs greatly from that given, particularly if the meter indicates a short circuit (no measurable resistance) or an open circuit (infinite, or very high resistance).

4 Should the above check not produce the expected result, first check that this is not due to a damaged or broken wire from the coil to the connector; pinched or broken wires can usually be repaired. In order to determine conclusively that the coil is defective, it should be tested by a Honda dealer equipped with the special electrical tester required for this check. If the coil is confirmed to be faulty, it must be replaced; the coil is a sealed unit and cannot therefore be repaired.

Removal

5 Remove the fuel tank as described in Chapter 4.

6 Remove the fairing lower section as described in Chapter 8.

7 Drain the engine oil as described in Chapter 1.

8 Trace the pulse generator wiring up from the crankshaft end cover to the black two-pin

connector at the top of the frame. Disconnect the connector and free the wiring from any relevant ties or clips.

9 Unscrew the cover retaining bolts and remove the cover squarely from the engine unit. Note the position of the oil gallery plug fitted behind the cover and make sure it stays in position in the crankcase.

10 Remove the cover locating dowels from the crankcase and discard the gasket.

11 Remove the bolts which secure the pulse generator to the cover and remove the generator **(see illustration)**.

12 Examine the rotor triggers for signs of damage such as chipped or missing teeth and replace if necessary (See Chapter 2, Section 10).

Installation

13 Fit the pulse generator to the cover and securely tighten its retaining bolts.

14 Remove all traces of old gasket from the crankcase and cover mating surfaces. Make sure the oil gallery plug is in position in the crankcase.

15 Install the locating dowels and fit a new gasket to the crankcase **(see illustrations)**.

16 Apply a smear of sealant to the right crankshaft end cover wiring grommet.

17 Fit the cover to the engine noting that the bolts located in the two holes next to the cam chain tensioner should have a drop of non-permanent thread locking compound applied

4.11 Pulse generator coil is retained by two bolts

4.15a Install the locating dowels (arrows) . . .

4.15b . . . and fit a new gasket to the crankcase. Ensure the oil gallery plug (arrow) is in position

to their threads **(see illustration)**. These holes are indicated by triangular marks cast in the cover **(see illustration)**. Tighten the cover bolts to the specified torque setting.

18 Route the wiring up to the wire harness and reconnect the two-pin connector. Secure the wiring in position with all the necessary clips and ties.

19 Fill the engine with the correct type and amount of oil as described in Chapter 1.

20 Install the fuel tank and fairing section as described in Chapters 4 and 8 respectively.

---

5 Ignition control module - removal, check and installation

Removal

1 Remove the seat (see Chapter 8).
2 Free the control module from its two retaining tabs **(see illustration)**.
3 Disconnect the wiring connector from the control module and remove it from the motorcycle **(see illustration)**.

Check

4 If the tests shown in the preceding Sections have failed to isolate the cause of an ignition fault, it is likely that the control module itself is faulty. No test details are available with which the unit can be tested; refer to a Honda dealer for advice.

Installation

5 Installation is the reverse of removal ensuring the wiring connector is securely connected.

---

6 Ignition timing - general information and check

General information

1 Since no provision exists for adjusting the ignition timing and since no component is

4.17a Fit the cover to the crankcase and install the bolts . . .

subject to mechanical wear, there is no need for regular checks; only if investigating a fault such as a loss of power or a misfire, should the ignition timing be checked.

2 The ignition timing can only be checked whilst the engine is running using a stroboscopic (timing) lamp. The inexpensive neon lamps should be adequate in theory, but in practice may produce a pulse of such low intensity that the timing mark remains indistinct. If possible, one of the more precise xenon tube lamps should be used, powered by an external source of the appropriate voltage. **Note:** *Do not use the machine's own battery as an incorrect reading may result from stray impulses within the machine's electrical system.*

Check

3 Warm the engine up to normal operating temperature then stop it.
4 Remove the fairing lower section and middle sections as described in Chapter 8.
5 Unscrew the center cap from the right crankshaft end cover to reveal the pulse generator rotor. Recover the cap O-ring.
6 The timing mark is stamped on the center

4.17b . . . noting that the two installed in the holes with the triangular marks (arrows) should have thread lock applied to them

of the rotor and is represented by a line of three punch marks next to the F mark. The static index mark, with which the three dots should align is a notch in the cover.
7 Connect the timing light to the No. 1 cylinder HT lead as described in the manufacturer's instructions.
8 Start the engine and aim the light at the inspection hole.
9 With the machine idling at the specified speed, the timing mark (three dots) should align with the cover notch **(see illustration)**.
10 Slowly increase the engine speed whilst observing the timing mark. Starting at approximately 1600 rpm, the timing mark should move counterclockwise (anticlockwise), increasing in relation to the engine speed.
11 As already stated, there is no means of adjustment of the ignition timing on these machines. If the ignition timing is incorrect one of the ignition system components is at fault, and the system must be tested as described in the preceding Sections of this Chapter.
12 When the check is complete, fit a new

 HAYNES HINT *Highlight the rotor timing mark with white paint to make it more visible under the stroboscopic light.*

5

5.2 Ignition control module is mounted on two tabs (arrows)

5.3 Release its tab and pull the wire connector free of the control module

6.9 Three dots on the rotor should align with the notch at idle if the ignition timing is correct (arrows)

6.12 On installation, fit a new O-ring (arrow) to the cover center cap

O-ring to the center cap and lubricate it with a smear of clean engine oil **(see illustration).** Install the cap and tighten it to the specified torque setting.

13 Install the fairing sections as described in Chapter 8.

7 Throttle sensor - US 1996 through 1999 models and UK T to X models,

Check

1 Remove the air filter housing (see Chapter 4).

2 The throttle sensor is mounted on the outside of the left-hand carburettor. In order to determine conclusively that the throttle sensor is defective, it should be tested by a Honda dealer equipped with the special electrical adapter required for this check.

3 However, the sensor can be checked visually (for cracks and other damage) and the wiring between the sensor and the ignition control module checked for continuity.

4 Trace the wiring to the 3-pin connector and disconnect it. Also disconnect the ignition control module wiring connector. Check the connectors for loose or corroded terminals.

5 Using a multimeter set to resistance or a continuity tester, check for continuity between the terminals of the sensor wiring connector and the corresponding terminals on the ignition control module connector. There should be continuity between each terminal. If not, this is probably due to a damaged or broken wire between the connectors; pinched or broken wires can usually be repaired.

6 If the sensor is suspected of being faulty, take it to a Honda dealer for testing. If it is confirmed to be faulty, it must be replaced; the sensor is a sealed unit and cannot therefore be repaired.

Replacement

7 Remove the carburetors (see Chapter 4).

8 The throttle sensor is mounted on the outside of the left-hand carburettor. Unscrew the sensor mounting screws and remove the sensor, noting how it fits.

9 Install the sensor, aligning the slot with the boss on the end of the throttle shaft, and tighten its screws securely.

10 Install the carburetors (see (Chapter 4).

Chapter 6
Frame, suspension and final drive

Contents

Degrees of difficulty

Easy, suitable for novice with little experience	**Fairly easy,** suitable for beginner with some experience	**Fairly difficult,** suitable for competent DIY mechanic	**Difficult,** suitable for experienced DIY mechanic	**Very difficult,** suitable for expert DIY or professional

Specifications

Front forks

Spring free length
  US 1993 and 1994 models and UK N and P models
    New . . . . 306.7 mm (12.07 in)
    Service limit . . . . 300.6 mm (11.83 in)
  US 1995 model and UK R and S models
    New . . . . 243.8 mm (9.60 in)
    Service limit . . . . 238.9 mm (9.41 in)
  US 1996 and 1997 models and UK T and V models
    New . . . . 248.2 mm (9.77 in)
    Service limit . . . . 243.2 mm (9.57 in)
  US 1998 and 1999 models and UK W and X models
    New . . . . 250.2 mm (9.85 in)
    Service limit . . . . 245.2 mm (9.65 in)
Oil capacity (per leg)
  US 1993 and 1994 models and UK N and P models . . . . 509 cc (17.2 US fl oz, 17.9 Imp fl oz)
  US 1995 model and UK R and S models . . . . 564 cc (19.1 US fl oz, 19.9 Imp fl oz)
  US 1996 and 1997 models and UK T and V models . . . . 561 ± 2.5 cc (19.0 ± 0.02 US fl oz, 19.7 ± 0.09 Imp fl oz)
  US 1998 and 1999 models and UK W and X models . . . . 540 ± 2.5 cc (18.3 ± 0.02 US fl oz, 19.7 ± 0.09 Imp fl oz)
Oil level
  US 1993 and 1994 models and UK N and P models . . . . 110 mm (4.3 in)*
  US 1995 model and UK R and S models . . . . 112 mm (4.4 in)*
  US 1996 through 1999 models and UK T to X models . . . . 114 ± 4 mm (4.5 ± 0.2 in)*
Oil level is measured from the top of the tube with the fork spring removed and the leg fully compressed
Fork oil type
  US models . . . . Pro Honda Suspension Fluid SS-8
  UK models . . . . SAE 10W fork oil

Rear shock absorber

Spring free length	**New**	**Service limit**
US 1993 through 1995 models and UK N to S models	163.5 mm (6.44 in)	160.2 mm (6.31 in)
US 1996 and 1997 models and UK T and V models	172.6 mm (6.80 in)	169.1 mm (6.66 in)
US 1998 and 1999 models and UK W and X models	167.7 mm (6.60 in)	164.3 mm (6.47 in)

6

Torque settings

	Nm	ft-lbs
Handlebar clamp bolt	23	17
Triple clamp pinch bolts		
US 1993 through 1997 models and UK N to V models		
Top triple clamp	23	17
Bottom triple clamp	50	36
US 1998 and 1999 models and UK W and X models		
Top triple clamp	22	16
Bottom triple clamp	27	20
Bottom triple clamp brake hose union assembly bolts	17	12
Front forks		
Top bolts	23	17
Damper rod Allen bolt	20	14
Steering stem adjuster nut (see Text)		
US 1993 through 1995 models and UK N to S models	31	22
US 1996 through 1999 models and UK T to X models	25	18
Steering stem top nut	105	76
Shock absorber mounting bolt nuts.	45	33
Rear suspension linkage pivot bolt nuts	45	33
Swingarm pivot adjusting bolt	15	11
Swingarm pivot locknut	65	47
Swingarm pivot nut	95	69
Front sprocket bolt	54	39
Rear sprocket nuts		
US 1993 through 1995 models and UK N to S models	88	64
US 1996 through 1999 models and UK T to X models	108	80

1 General information

The models covered in this manual use a diamond type twin-spar frame made of extruded aluminum, which uses the engine as a stressed member.

Front suspension is by a pair of Showa oil-damped, coil spring, telescopic forks with 45 mm stanchions and forged aluminum sliders.

Rear suspension is by Honda's "Pro-Link" system in which the swingarm acts on a Showa gas-charged, hydraulically-damped suspension unit via a two piece linkage.

The final drive uses an O-ring drive chain with a riveted master link. A rubber damper (often called a "cush drive") is installed between the rear wheel coupling and the wheel.

2 Frame - inspection and repair

1 The frame should not require attention unless accident damage has occurred. In most cases, frame replacement is the only satisfactory remedy for such damage. A few frame specialists have the jigs and other equipment necessary for straightening the frame to the required standard of accuracy, but even then there is no simple way of assessing to what extent the frame may have been over stressed.

2 After the machine has accumulated a lot of miles, the frame should be examined closely for signs of cracking or splitting at the welded joints. Loose engine mount bolts can cause ovaling or fracturing of the mounting tabs.

Minor damage can often be repaired by welding, depending on the extent and nature of the damage.

3 Remember that a frame which is out of alignment will cause handling problems. If misalignment is suspected as the result of an accident, it will be necessary to strip the machine completely so the frame can be thoroughly checked.

3 Footpegs and brackets - removal and installation

Rider's footpegs
Removal

1 Remove the cotter pin (split pin) and washer, then slide out the pivot pin and remove the footpeg from the bracket along with its return spring.

2 If necessary, undo the retaining screws and separate the rubber from the footpeg.

3.4 Remove the retaining bolt to release the gearshift lever and footpeg

Installation

3 Installation is the reverse of removal using a new cotter pin (split pin).

Rider's left footpeg bracket
Removal

4 Remove the pivot bolt securing the gearshift lever (models with gear linkage) and footpeg to the footpeg bracket and recover the washer from behind the lever **(see illustration)**.

5 Unscrew the two footpeg bracket mounting bolts and remove the bracket assembly from the frame **(see illustration)**.

Installation

6 Install the bracket and securely tighten its mounting bolts.

7 Apply a smear of grease to the bearing surface of the gearshift lever pivot and ensure that the washers are in place (models with gear linkage). Install the pivot bolt and tighten it securely.

Rider's right footpeg bracket
Removal

8 Remove the cotter pin (split pin) and the

3.5 Unscrew the two footpeg bracket mounting bolts

3.9 Unscrew the two step guard and master cylinder mounting bolts

clevis pin from the clevis joining the rear brake pedal to the rear brake master cylinder pushrod.

9 Unscrew the step guard and master cylinder mounting bolts. Remove the step guard and support the master cylinder so that no strain is put on the hoses **(see illustration)**.

10 Unhook the brake pedal return spring and the brake light switch return spring and keep them safe. Release the brake light switch from its holder on the footpeg bracket.

11· Unscrew the pivot bolt securing the brake pedal and footpeg to the footpeg bracket and recover the washer from behind the pedal.

12 Unscrew the two footpeg bracket mounting bolts and remove the bracket from the frame.

Installation

13 Install the bracket and securely tighten its mounting bolts.

14 Apply a smear of grease to the bearing surface of the brake pedal pivot. Position the washer behind the brake pedal then fit the pivot bolt, tightening it securely.

15 Install the rear brake light switch into its holder on the footpeg bracket, and hook up its return spring and the brake pedal return spring.

16 Install the rear brake master cylinder and the step guard on the footpeg bracket and tighten the mounting bolts securely.

17 Align the brake pedal with the master cylinder pushrod clevis and install the clevis pin. Fit a new cotter pin (split pin) to secure the clevis pin.

Passenger footpegs

Removal

18 Remove the cotter pin (split pin) and washer, then slide out the pivot pin and remove the footpeg from the bracket. As the footpeg is removed, recover the footpeg detent plate, spring and ball bearing, noting the correct fitted positions of each component.

Installation

19 Installation is the reverse of removal using a new cotter pin (split pin).

Left passenger footpeg bracket

Removal

20 Remove the left side cover (see Chapter 8, if necessary).

3.21 Passenger footpeg brackets are retained by two bolts (arrows)

21 Unscrew the footpeg bracket retaining bolts and remove the bracket from the motorcycle **(see illustration)**.

Installation

22 Installation is the reverse of removal.

Right passenger footpeg bracket

Removal

23 Remove the right side cover (see Chapter 8, if necessary).

24 Slacken and remove the mounting bolt securing the exhaust system muffler (silencer) to the footpeg bracket. Tie the muffler (silencer) to the frame to prevent strain on the exhaust system.

25 Unscrew the footpeg bracket retaining bolts and remove the bracket from the motorcycle.

Installation

26 Installation is the reverse of removal.

---

4 Side stand - maintenance

1 The side stand is attached to a bracket on the frame. An extension spring anchored to the bracket ensures that the stand is held in the retracted position. The side stand incorporates a rotary switch which cuts out the ignition if the side stand is down when the engine is running and in gear.

2 Make sure the pivot bolt is tight and the

5.5a Note the brackets linking the top triple clamp to the handlebars (arrow) . . .

extension spring is in good condition and not over-stretched. An accident is almost certain to occur if the stand extends while the machine is in motion. For check and replacement of the side stand switch see Chapter 9.

---

5 Handlebars - removal and installation

Right handlebar

Removal

1 On US 1996 through 1999 models and UK T to X models, refer to Chapter 9 (if necessary) and unscrew the two handlebar switch/throttle housing retaining screws and free the housing from the handlebar. Refer to Chapter 4 (if necessary) and release the throttle cables from the throttle grip. Position the switch/throttle housing away from the handlebar.

2 On all other models, refer to Chapter 9 (if necessary) and unscrew the two handlebar switch retaining screws and free the switch from the handlebar. Refer to Chapter 4 (if necessary) and unscrew the two throttle cable housing retaining screws and release the throttle cables from the throttle grip. Position the switch housing and the throttle housing away from the handlebar.

3 Disconnect the brake light switch wires from the master cylinder assembly. Unscrew the two master cylinder assembly clamp bolts and position the assembly clear of the handlebar, ensuring no strain is placed on the hydraulic hose. Keep the master cylinder reservoir upright to prevent possible fluid leakage.

4 Remove the steering stem nut cap, then unscrew the steering stem nut.

5 Unscrew the top triple clamp pinch bolts on each side, noting the position of the choke knob and the brackets between the triple clamp and the handlebars, then slide the triple clamp off the forks and position it away from the handelbars **(see illustrations)**.

6 Slacken the handlebar clamp pinch bolt and slide the handlebar off the fork.

6

5.5b . . . and the choke knob bracket on the left handlebar (arrow)

5.5c Slide the top triple clamp off the forks

5.10a Make sure the lug on the handlebar clamp fits into the slot in the top triple clamp (arrow)

5.10b Tighten the handlebar clamp pinch bolt to the specified torque setting

7 If necessary, unscrew the handlebar weight retaining screw, then remove the weight from the end of the handlebar and slide off the throttle twistgrip.

Installation

8 Where removed, apply a smear of grease to the throttle twistgrip and slide the grip on the handlebar. Apply locking compound to the handlebar weight retaining screw, then install the weight and securely tighten the screw.
9 Install the handlebar onto the fork, but do not yet tighten the clamp pinch bolt.
10 Install the top triple clamp on the forks and install the steering stem nut, tightening it to the torque setting specified at the beginning of the Chapter. Install the steering stem nut cap. Now position the handlebar so that the lug on the handlebar clamp fits into the slot in the underside of the triple clamp, and the bracket on the handlebar clamp aligns with the pinch bolt hole in the triple clamp. Tighten the handlebar clamp bolt to the specified torque setting (see illustrations).
11 Install the choke knob bracket to the left side of the triple clamp then tighten both triple clamp pinch bolts to the specified torque setting (see illustration).
12 Reconnect the throttle cables to the twistgrip as described in Chapter 4.
13 Install the handlebar switch as described in Chapter 9.
14 Install the master cylinder assembly,

making sure the "UP" mark on the clamp is upwards. Align the mating surfaces of the clamp with the punch mark on the handlebar, then tighten the upper clamp bolt first, followed by the lower (see illustration).
15 Reconnect the front brake light switch wiring.

Left handlebar
Removal

16 Disconnect the clutch switch wires from the clutch lever assembly. Free the handlebar switch as described in Chapter 9.
17 Unscrew the two clutch lever bracket mounting bolts, and position the lever assembly away from the handlebar.
18 Remove the steering stem nut cap, then unscrew the steering stem nut.
19 Unscrew the top triple clamp pinch bolts on each side, noting the position of the choke knob and the brackets between the triple clamp and the handlebars, then slide the triple clamp off the forks and position it away from the handlebars (see illustrations 5.5a, 5.5b and 5.5c).
20 Slacken the handlebar clamp pinch bolt and slide the handlebar off the fork.
21 If necessary, undo the retaining screw then remove the weight from the end of the handlebar and peel off the handlebar grip.

Installation

22 Where removed, apply a suitable adhesive to the inside of the handlebar grip

and slide it on the handlebar. Apply locking compound to the handlebar weight retaining screw then install the weight and securely tighten the screw.
23 Install the handlebar on the fork, but do not yet tighten the clamp pinch bolt.
24 Install the top triple clamp on the forks and install the steering stem nut, tightening it to the torque setting specified at the beginning of the Chapter. Install the steering stem nut cap. Now position the handlebar so that the lug on the handlebar clamp fits into the slot in the underside of the triple clamp (see illustration 5.10a), and the bracket on the handlebar clamp aligns with the pinch bolt hole in the triple clamp. Tighten the handlebar clamp bolt to the specified torque setting (see illustration 5.10b).
25 Install the choke knob bracket to the triple clamp then tighten both triple clamp pinch bolts to the specified torque setting (see illustration 5.11).
26 Install the handlebar switch as described in Chapter 9.
27 Install the clutch lever assembly, making sure the "UP" mark on the clamp is upwards. Align the mating surfaces of the clamp with the punch mark on the handlebar, then tighten the upper bolt first, followed by the lower.
28 Reconnect the clutch switch wiring.

6 Forks -
removal and installation

5.11 Tighten the top triple clamp pinch bolts to the specified torque setting

5.14 Align the mating surfaces of the master cylinder clamp with the punch mark on the handlebar (arrow)

Removal

1 Remove the front wheel as described in Chapter 7.
2 Remove the front fender/mudguard as described in Chapter 8, and pry off the fender/mudguard bracket from the top of the fork slider.
3 Slacken but do not remove the top triple clamp pinch bolts (see illustration 5.11). If the forks are to be disassembled, it is advisable to slacken the fork top bolts at this stage.

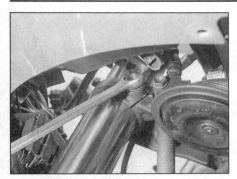

6.5 Slacken the bottom triple clamp pinch bolts

6.6 Remove the forks by twisting and pulling them down at the same time

6.7 Slide the forks into position through the bottom triple clamp

Slackening the fork pinch bolts in the top yoke before slackening the fork top bolt releases pressure on the top bolt. This makes it much easier to remove and helps to preserve the threads.

4 Slacken but do not remove both left and right handlebar clamp bolts **(see illustration 5.10b)**.

5 Slacken but do not remove the bottom triple clamp pinch bolts **(see illustration)**.

6 Remove the forks by twisting them and pulling them downwards **(see illustration)**. Once the forks are removed, make sure the right handlebar is supported so that the master cylinder reservoir is upright and no strain is placed on the hoses.

If the fork legs are seized in the triple clamps, spray the area with penetrating oil and allow time for it to soak in before trying again.

Installation

7 Remove all traces of corrosion from the fork tubes and the triple clamps and slide the fork legs back into place **(see illustration)**.

8 Position each leg so that the top surface on the fork tube aligns with the top surface of the top triple clamp, then tighten the top and

6.8 Align the top of the fork with the top surface of the top triple clamp

bottom triple clamp pinch bolts to the torque settings specified at the beginning of the Chapter **(see illustration)**.

9 Tighten both handlebar clamp pinch bolts to the specified torque setting.

10 If the fork legs have been dismantled, the fork tube top bolts should now be tightened to the specified torque setting.

11 Install the fender/mudguard bracket to the top of each fork slider, then install the front fender/mudguard as described in Chapter 8.

12 Install the front wheel as described in Chapter 7.

13 Adjust the fork settings as described in Section 12. Check the operation of the front

forks and brake before taking the machine out on the road.

7 Forks - disassembly, inspection and reassembly

Disassembly

1 Always dismantle the fork legs separately to avoid interchanging parts and thus causing an accelerated rate of wear. Store all components in separate, clearly marked containers **(see illustration)**.

1 Top bolt
2 O-ring
3 Slotted spring collar
4 Washer (later models only)
5 Spacer
6 Spring seat
7 Fork spring
8 Dust seal
9 Snap-ring
10 Damper rod Allen bolt
11 Allen bolt washer
12 Damper rod assembly
13 Fork tube
14 Damper rod seat
15 O-ring (later models only)
16 Oil seal
17 Washer
18 Top bush
19 Bottom bush
20 Fork slider

H30020

7.1 Exploded view of a front fork

6

7.5 Unscrew the fork top bolt whilst counter-holding the locknut

7.9 Pry the dust seal out of the fork lower leg using a flat-bladed screwdriver

7.10 Carefully remove the snap-ring

2 Before dismantling the fork, it is advised that the damper rod Allen bolt be slackened. Compress the fork leg so that the spring exerts pressure on the damper rod head, then have an assistant unscrew the damper rod bolt from the base of the fork leg.

3 If the fork top bolt was not slackened with the fork in situ, carefully clamp the fork tube in a vise, taking care not to overtighten or score its surface, then fully unscrew the preload adjuster as described in Section 12 and slacken the fork top bolt.

4 Unscrew the fork top bolt from the top of the fork tube.

5 Carefully clamp the fork slider in a vise and slide the fork tube down into the slider a little way (wrap a rag around the spring and the top of the tube to minimize oil spillage) while, with the aid of an assistant if necessary, keeping the damper rod and top cap fully extended. Counter-hold the locknut immediately below the top cap with a wrench, whilst the top bolt is unscrewed **(see illustration)**.

6 Remove the slotted spring collar by holding down the fork spring (keeping the damper rod fully extended) and slipping the collar out to the side. Keep the restraint on the fork spring and remove the washer (later models only), the spacer and the spring seat. Slowly release the spring until all pressure has been relieved, then withdraw the spring from the tube, noting which way up it fits.

 Warning: The fork spring may be exerting considerable pressure, making this a potentially

dangerous operation. Wipe off as much oil as possible to minimize the risk of your hands slipping on oily components and enlist the help of an assistant.

7 Invert the fork leg over a suitable container and pump the damper rod piston vigorously to expel as much fork oil as possible.

8 Remove the damper rod Allen bolt and its washer from the bottom of the slider, then withdraw the damper rod assembly from the fork.

9 Pry out the dust seal from the top of the slider to gain access to the oil seal retaining snap ring **(see illustration)**.

10 Carefully remove the snap ring whilst taking care not to scratch the surface of the tube **(see illustration)**.

11 To separate the tube from the slider it will be necessary to displace the top bush and oil seal. The bottom bush should not pass through the top bush, and this can be used to good effect. Push the tube gently inwards until it stops against the damper rod seat. Take care not to do this forcibly or the seat may be damaged. Then pull the tube sharply outwards until the bottom bush strikes the top bush. Repeat this operation until the top bush and seal are tapped out of the slider.

12 With the tube removed, slide off the oil seal and washer, noting which way up they fit. The top bush can then also be slid off its upper end.

Caution: Do not remove the bottom bush from the tube unless it is to be replaced.

13 Tip the damper rod seat out of the slider.

If necessary, on later models, unscrew the compression damping adjuster unit using a suitable wrench **(see illustration)**.

Inspection

14 Clean all parts in solvent and blow them dry with compressed air, if available. Check the fork tube and slider, the bushes and the damper rod assembly for score marks, scratches, flaking of the chrome and excessive or abnormal wear. Look for dents in the tubes and replace the tubes if any are found. Check the fork seal seat for nicks, gouges and scratches. If damage is evident, leaks will occur. If either bush is worn so badly that the copper base metal appears through the Teflon coating over more than 3/4 of the bush's surface area, that bush must be replaced. Always replace worn or defective parts with new ones.

15 Have the fork tube checked for runout at a dealer service department or other repair shop.

 Warning: If it is bent, it should not be straightened; replace it with a new one.

16 Measure the overall length of the spring and check it for cracks and other damage. Compare the length to the service length listed in this Chapter's Specifications. If it is defective or sagged, replace both fork springs with new ones. Never replace only one spring.

17 If it is necessary to replace the fork tube bottom bush, pry it apart at the slit and slide it off. Make sure the new one seats properly **(see illustration)**.

7.13 The compression damper unit can be removed if necessary using a suitable spanner

7.17 Pry the ends of the bottom bush apart with a screwdriver to remove it from the fork tube

7.18 Fit a new O-ring to the compression damping adjuster unit and install it in the fork slider

7.19 Slide the damper rod assembly into the fork tube

7.20 Fit a new washer to the damper rod assembly Allen bolt and apply thread-lock before installing it into the bottom of the fork slider

7.21a Lubricate the top bush and washer and slide them over the fork tube

Reassembly

18 If removed on later models, fit a new O-ring to the compression damping adjuster unit, then install it into the fork slider and tighten it securely **(see illustration)**.

19 Insert the damper rod assembly into the fork tube and slide it into place so that it projects fully from the bottom of the tube **(see illustration)**. Install a new O-ring onto the damper rod assembly seat (later models only), then install the seat on the bottom of the damper rod assembly.

20 Oil the fork tube and bottom bush and insert the assembly into position in the fork slider. Fit a new washer to the damper rod Allen bolt, then apply a drop of non-permanent locking compound to its threads and install the bolt into the bottom of the slider **(see illustration)**. Tighten the bolt to the specified torque setting. **Note:** *If the damper rod assembly turns inside the fork tube, preventing tightening of the Allen bolt, wait until the fork has been reassembled so that spring pressure holds the damper in place (see Step 29).*

21 Push the fork tube fully into the slider, then oil the top bush and slide it down over the tube. Press the bush squarely into its recess in the slider as far as possible by hand, then install the washer **(see illustration)**. It will be necessary to use the Honda service tool or to devise an alternative tubular drift to tap the bush fully into place. The best method is to use a length of tubing slightly larger in diameter than the fork tube, that will bear

squarely on the bush's washer, then tap the bush home using the tubing as a slide-hammer **(see illustration)**. Take care not to scratch the fork tube during this operation; it is best to make sure that the fork tube is pushed fully into the slider so that any accidental scratching is confined to the area above the oil seal.

22 When the bush is seated fully and squarely in its recess in the slider, so that the washer seats on the oil seal's recess (remove the washer to check, wipe the recess clean, then reinstall the washer), install the new oil seal. Note that the seal has two springs, one larger than the other. Smear the seal's lips with fork oil and slide it over the tube so that the larger spring faces down toward the slider **(see illustration)**.

23 Place a large plain washer against the oil

7.21b Use a piece of tubing as a drift to install the top bush in the slider

seal and drive it into place as described in Step 21 above until the snap-ring groove is just visible above the seal. Once the seal is correctly seated, remove the washer and fit the snap-ring, making sure it is correctly located in its groove **(see illustration)**.

24 Lubricate the lips of the dust seal then slide it down the fork tube and press it into position **(see illustration)**.

25 Slowly pour in the specified amount and grade of fork oil whilst pushing the damper rod piston up and down. Once the oil has been added, pump the fork tube in and out at least five times, and pump the damper rod piston at least another 10 times. This will ensure that the fork oil is evenly distributed. Fully insert both the tube and damper rod then check the fork oil level. Add or subtract fork oil until the oil is at the level specified in the Specifications Section of this Chapter **(see illustration)**.

7.22 Install the new oil seal making sure it is the right way up (see text)

7.23 Secure the seal in place with the snap-ring making sure it is properly located in its groove

7.24 Slide the dust seal into position in the slider

7.25 Fill the fork with the specified type and amount of fork oil then check the oil level with the fork held vertical

7.27a Install the fork spring making sure its tapered end (and tighter-pitched coils) faces downwards . . .

7.27b . . . then install the spring seat, spacer and washer (later models only)

7.28a Slide the slotted collar into position

26 Clamp the slider securely in a vice and fully extend the damper rod. Tie a piece of wire around the rod; the wire can then be used to hold the rod in the extended position whilst the slotted spring collar is installed.
27 Insert the fork spring, ensuring that its tapered end is at the bottom, followed by the spring seat, the spacer and the washer (later models only) **(see illustrations)**. Fit a new O-ring to the preload adjuster and the fork top bolt and lubricate them with a smear of fork oil.
28 With the aid of an assistant push down on the spring seat, compressing the fork spring, and slide the slotted spring collar into position. Screw the top bolt fully on the preload adjuster, counter-holding the locknut, then slowly release the fork spring, making sure the slotted collar is correctly seated against the base of the preload adjuster **(see illustrations)**.
29 Carefully screw the top bolt into the fork tube making sure it is not cross-threaded **(see illustration)**. **Note:** *The top bolt can be tightened to the specified torque setting at this stage if the tube is held between the padded jaws of a vise, but do not risk distorting the tube by doing so. A better method is to tighten the top bolt when the fork leg has been installed and is securely held in the triple clamps.* If the damper rod Allen bolt requires tightening (see Step 20), clamp the fork slider between the padded jaws of a vise and have an assistant compress the tube into

the slider so that maximum spring pressure is placed on the damper rod head - tighten the damper Allen bolt to the specified torque setting.

 TOOL TiP *Use a ratchet-type tool when installing the fork top bolt. This makes it unnecessary to remove the tool from the bolt whilst threading it in, making it easier to maintain a downward pressure on the spring.*

30 Install the forks as described in Section 6.

8 Steering stem - removal and installation

Caution: Although not strictly necessary, before removing the steering stem it is recommended that the fuel tank be removed. This will prevent accidental damage to the paintwork.

Removal

1 Remove the forks as described in Section 6 of this Chapter.
2 Unscrew the bolts securing the brake hose union assembly to the bottom triple clamp **(see illustration)**. Support the brake calipers so that no strain is placed on the hydraulic hose.

3 Disconnect the horn wires, then unscrew the horn mounting bolt and remove the horn.
4 Pry off the cap (where fitted) from the steering stem top nut. Remove the steering stem nut and lift off the top triple clamp.
5 Straighten the tabs of the steering stem adjuster nut lock washer, then using a suitable C-wrench, slacken and remove the adjuster nut locknut.
6 Remove the lock washer and discard it; a new one must be fitted on reassembly.
7 Support the bottom triple clamp and slacken the adjuster nut.
8 Remove the nut, dust seal, inner race and upper bearing from the top of the steering head.
9 Gently lower the bottom triple clamp and steering stem out of the frame. Remove the lower bearing from the steering stem.
10 Remove all traces of old grease from the bearings and races and check them for wear or damage as described in Section 9. **Note:** *Do not attempt to remove the outer races from the frame or the lower inner race and dust seal from the steering stem unless they are to be replaced.*

7.28b Screw the fork top bolt on the preload adjuster

7.29 Carefully screw the top bolt into the fork tube

8.2 Exploded view of steering stem and bearings

Installation

11 Smear a liberal quantity of grease on both inner and outer races and the steering stem. Work the grease well into both the upper and lower bearing races.

12 Fit the lower bearing on the steering stem.

13 Carefully lift the steering stem into position and fit the upper bearing and inner race.

14 Apply grease to the underside of the dust seal and fit it to the steering stem.

15 Apply clean engine oil to the threads of the adjuster nut and tighten it using hand pressure only.

16 To preload the bearings to the torque specified by the manufacturer (see Specifications at the beginning of the Chapter) it will be necessary to use the service tool, Pt. No. 07916-3710100 (US models), 07916-3710101 (UK models), which is a socket that fits the adjuster nut. Using the service tool, tighten the adjuster nut to the specified torque setting then turn the steering stem from lock to lock approximately 5 times to settle the bearings and races in position. After preloading the bearings, slacken the adjuster nut one full turn then tighten it again to the specified torque setting. **Note:** *It is important to check the feel of the steering afterwards as described below; if it is too tight readjust the bearings as described below.*

17 If the service tool is not available, tighten the adjuster nut hard using a conventional C-wrench to preload the bearings then adjust as follows.

18 Slacken the adjuster nut slightly until pressure is just released, then turn it slowly clockwise until resistance is just evident. The object is to set the adjuster nut so that the bearings are under a very light loading, just enough to remove any free play.

Caution: Take great care not to apply excessive pressure because this will cause premature failure of the bearings.

19 With the bearings correctly adjusted, fit a new lock washer to the adjuster nut. Bend down two opposite lock washer tabs (the shorter tabs on the washer) into the grooves of the adjuster nut.

20 Hold the adjuster nut to prevent it from moving, then install the locknut and tighten it finger-tight.

21 Again holding the adjuster nut, tighten the locknut approximately 90° more until its slots align with the remaining lock washer tabs. Secure the locknut in position by bending up the tabs into its slots.

22 Fit the top triple clamp to the steering stem and install the stem top nut.

23 Temporarily fit the fork legs, to align the triple clamps, then tighten the steering stem top nut to the specified torque setting. Fit the cap (where fitted).

24 Install the horn onto its mounting lug on the underside of the bottom triple clamp and tighten the retaining bolt securely, then fit the horn wires.

25 Fit the brake hose union assembly, and tighten the retaining bolts to the specified torque setting.

26 Install the fork legs as described in Section 6 of this Chapter.

27 Check that the steering head bearings are correctly adjusted as soon as the forks and front wheel are installed (see Chapter 1).

9 Steering head bearings - inspection and replacement

Inspection

1 Remove the steering stem as described in Section 8.

2 Remove all traces of old grease from the bearings and races and check them for wear or damage.

3 The ball bearing tracks of the races should be polished and free from indentations. Inspect the ball bearings for signs of wear, damage or discoloration, and examine the bearing retainer cage for signs of cracks or splits. If there are signs of wear on any of the above components both upper and lower bearing assemblies must be replaced as a set.

Replacement

4 The outer races are an interference fit in the steering head and can be tapped from position with a suitable drift. Tap firmly and evenly around each race to ensure that it is driven out squarely. It may prove advantageous to curve the end of the drift slightly to improve access.

5 Alternatively, the races can be removed using a slide-hammer type bearing extractor; these can often be hired from tool shops.

6 The new races can be pressed into the head using the drawbolt arrangement **(see illustration)**, or by using a large diameter tubular drift which bears only on the outer edge of the race. Ensure that the drawbolt

9.6 Drawbolt arrangement for fitting steering stem bearing outer races

1 *Long bolt or threaded bar*
2 *Thick washer*
3 *Guide for lower outer race*

washer or drift (as applicable) bears only on the outer edge of the race and does not contact the race bearing surface.

> **HAYNES HINT** *Installation of new head bearing races is made much easier if the races are left overnight in the freezer. This causes them to contract slightly, making them a looser fit.*

7 To remove the inner race from the steering stem, use two screwdrivers placed on opposite sides of the race to work it free.

8 With the inner race removed, lift off the dust seal. Inspect the seal for wear or damage and replace it if necessary.

9 Install the dust seal and slide on the new inner race. A length of tubing with an internal diameter slightly larger than the steering stem will be needed to tap the new race into position. Ensure that the drift bears only on the inner edge of the race and does not contact the bearing surface.

10 Install the steering stem as described in Section 8.

10 Rear shock absorber - removal and installation

Removal

1 In order to remove the shock absorber, it is necessary to support the bike securely in an upright position using an auxiliary stand or hoist. The bike must be supported so that the rear wheel is just resting on the ground (i.e. so that the bike's weight is off the rear suspension), but also so that the rear suspension will not drop, with the possible risk of personal injury, when the shock absorber mounting bolts are removed. If necessary, remove the fairing lower section as described in Chapter 8, and the exhaust system as described in Chapter 4.

2 Remove the rider's seat and open the pillion seat. Remove the side covers as described in Chapter 8.

3 Fully unscrew the retaining clip securing the shock absorber reservoir to the frame and slide off the clip **(see illustration)**.

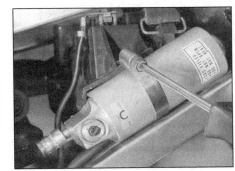

10.3 Unscrew the shock absorber reservoir clamp and release the reservoir

6

10.4 Unscrew the shock absorber lower mounting nut and remove the bolt

10.5 Unscrew the shock absorber upper mounting nut and remove the bolt

10.6 Examine the shock absorber lower mounting sleeve and bearings for wear

Caution: Do not attempt to separate the reservoir from the shock absorber.

4 Unscrew and remove the shock absorber lower mounting nut and bolt **(see illustration).**
5 Unscrew and remove the shock absorber upper mounting nut and bolt and maneuver the shock absorber and reservoir assembly out from the right side of the frame **(see illustration)**.
6 Withdraw the inner sleeve from the shock absorber lower mounting **(see illustration)**. Inspect the sleeve, bearing and dust seals for signs of wear and replace worn components as necessary. For bearing replacement, see Section 11.
7 All shock absorber components are available separately. However, disassembly requires the use of a suitable spring compressor. It is therefore recommended that the unit be taken to a Honda dealer who will have the necessary service tools to dismantle the unit.

Installation

8 Check that the mounting bolts are unworn, replacing them if necessary, and apply molybdenum disulfide grease to their shanks.
9 Install the shock absorber so that the rebound damping adjuster is on the left side of the bike.
10 Make sure the reservoir hose is correctly routed and insert both the shock absorber mounting bolts from the right side.

11 Fit the mounting bolt nuts and tighten them to the torque setting specified at the beginning of the Chapter.
12 Install the reservoir into its recess and securely tighten the retaining clip.
13 Install the side covers and rider's seat as described in Chapter 8.
14 Check the operation of the rear suspension and adjust the suspension settings as described in Section 12 before taking the bike on the road.

11 Rear suspension linkage - removal, inspection and installation

Removal

1 In order to remove the rear suspension linkage, it is necessary to support the bike securely in an upright position using an auxiliary stand or hoist. The bike must be supported so that the rear wheel is just resting on the ground (i.e. so that the bike's weight is off the rear suspension) but also so that the rear suspension will not drop, with the possible risk of personal injury, when the rear suspension linkage pivot bolts are removed. If necessary, remove the fairing lower section as described in Chapter 8, and the exhaust system as described in Chapter 4.
2 If not already done, remove the exhaust

system as described in Chapter 4. Alternatively, disconnect its rear mountings and support the exhaust system in such a way that no strain is placed on its front mountings.
3 Remove the exhaust mounting collar and rubber from the mounting lug **(see illustration)**.
4 Unscrew and remove the shock absorber lower mounting nut and bolt **(see illustration 10.4)**.
5 Unscrew and remove the nut and pivot bolt securing the shock link arm to the frame **(see illustration)**. Withdraw the bolt through the exhaust mounting lug.
6 Unscrew and remove the nut and pivot bolt securing the shock link arm to the shock link plates, and remove the arm **(see illustration)**.
7 Unscrew and remove the nut and pivot bolt securing the shock link plates to the swingarm. Note the "F" and the arrow on each plate indicating the forward facing edge.

Inspection

8 Withdraw the inner sleeves from both ends of the shock link arm and from the swingarm **(see illustrations)**.
9 Thoroughly clean all components, removing all traces of dirt, corrosion and grease.
10 Inspect all components closely, looking for obvious signs of wear such as heavy scoring, or for damage such as cracks or distortion.
11 Carefully lever out the dust seals, using a

11.3 Remove the collar and rubber (arrow) from the exhaust mounting lug

11.5 Unscrew the nut and remove the bolt securing the shock link arm to the frame

11.6 Unscrew the nut and remove the bolt securing the shock link arm to the shock link plates

11.8a Remove the inner sleeves from the shock link arm . . .

11.8b . . . and the swingarm

11.20a Offer up the shock link arm to the frame and the link plates to the shock absorber

flat-bladed screwdriver, and check them for signs of wear or damage; replace them if necessary.

12 Worn bearings can be drifted out of their bores, but note that removal will destroy them; new bearings should be obtained before work commences. The new bearings should be pressed or drawn into their bores rather than driven into position. In the absence of a press, a suitable drawbolt arrangement can be made up as described below.

13 It will be necessary to obtain a long bolt or a length of threaded rod from a local engineering works or some other supplier. The bolt or rod should be about one inch longer than the combined length of either link, and one bearing. Also required are suitable nuts and two large and robust washers having a larger outside diameter than the bearing housing. In the case of the threaded rod, fit one nut to one end of the rod and stake it in place for convenience.

14 Fit one of the washers over the bolt or rod so that it rests against the head, then pass the assembly through the relevant bore. Over the projecting end place the bearing, which should be greased to ease installation, followed by the remaining washer and nut.

15 Holding the bearing to ensure that it is kept square, slowly tighten the nut so that the bearing is drawn into its bore.

16 Once it is fully home, remove the drawbolt

arrangement and, if necessary, repeat the procedure to fit the other bearings. The dust seals can then be pressed into place.

17 Lubricate all the seals, needle roller bearings, inner sleeves and the pivot bolts with molybdenum disulfide grease. Insert the sleeves into the bearings.

Installation

18 If not already done, lubricate the seals, needle roller bearings, inner sleeves and the pivot bolts with molybdenum disulfide grease. When installing the linkage components, insert all the pivot bolts from the right side.

19 Install the shock link plates on the swingarm mount, making sure that the "F" mark and the arrow face forward.

20 Connect the shock link arm between the link plates and the frame, passing the frame mounting pivot bolt through the exhaust mounting lug, then connect the shock absorber to the link plates **(see illustrations)**. Tighten all the nuts to the torque setting specified at the beginning of the Chapter **(see illustration)**.

21 Install the exhaust mounting rubber and collar, then install the exhaust system as described in Chapter 4.

22 Install the fairing lower section as described in Chapter 8.

23 Check the operation of the rear suspension before taking the machine on the road.

12 Suspension - adjustments

Front forks

Caution: Always ensure that both front fork settings are the same. Uneven settings will upset the handling of the machine and could cause it to become unstable.

Spring preload

1 The front fork spring preload adjuster is located in the center of each fork top bolt and is adjusted using a suitable spanner **(see illustration)**.

2 The amount of preload is indicated by the number of grooves which are visible on the adjuster above the top surface of the top bolt hexagon. To set the preload to the standard amount, turn the adjuster until the third groove from the top aligns with the top surface of the hexagon.

3 To reduce the preload (i.e. soften the ride), rotate the adjuster counterclockwise (anti-clockwise).

4 To increase the preload (i.e. stiffen the ride), rotate the adjuster clockwise.

5 Always ensure both adjusters are set to the same position.

11.20b Note that the shock link arm front mounting bolt must pass through the exhaust mounting lug for access (shown with link arm removed for clarity)

11.20c Tighten all suspension linkage nuts to the specified torque setting

12.1 Adjust the front fork preload using a wrench - note preload setting grooves (arrow)

6

12.6 Adjust the front fork rebound damping using a flat-bladed screwdriver

12.13 Adjust the front fork compression damping using a flat-bladed screwdriver (later models only)

12.20 Adjust the rear shock absorber preload using a suitable C-wrench as supplied in the bike's toolkit

Rebound damping

6 The rebound damping adjuster is situated in the centre of the preload adjuster and is adjusted using a flat-bladed screwdriver **(see illustration)**.

7 On US 1993 through 1995 models and UK N to S models, damping positions are identified by counting the number of clicks emitted by the adjuster when it is turned. There are ten damping positions. On US 1996 through 1999 models and UK T to X models, there are no pre-set positions and the setting is identified by the number of turns out from the maximum setting.

8 The standard setting recommended by Honda is one turn (US 1996 through 1999 models and UK T to X models) or seven clicks (all other models) counterclockwise (anti-clockwise) from the maximum damping setting. In this position, the punch mark on the damping adjuster aligns with the reference mark on the preload adjuster body.

9 To establish the present setting, turn one of the adjusters fully clockwise whilst counting the number of clicks or turns, then rotate it back to its original position. Repeat the procedure on the other adjuster to ensure both are set in the same position.

10 To reduce the rebound damping, turn the adjuster counterclockwise (anti-clockwise) as denoted by the S arrow on the adjuster.

11 To increase the rebound damping, turn the adjuster clockwise as denoted by the H arrow on the adjuster.

12 Always ensure both adjusters are set to the same position.

Compression damping - US 1995 through 1999 models and UK R to X models

13 The compression damping adjuster is situated at the bottom of each fork slider and is adjusted using a flat-bladed screwdriver **(see illustration)**

14 On US 1995 models and UK R and S models, damping positions are identified by counting the number of clicks emitted by the adjuster when it is turned. The standard setting recommended by Honda is six clicks counterclockwise (anti-clockwise) from the maximum damping setting. In this position, the punch mark on the adjuster aligns with the reference mark on the damper unit.

15 On US 1996 through 1999 models and UK T to X models, there are no pre-set positions and the setting is identified by the number of turns out from the maximum setting. The standard setting recommended by Honda is one turn counterclockwise (anti-clockwise) from the maximum damping setting on US 1996 and 1997 models and UK T and V models, and one and a half turns out for all later models. In this position, the punch mark on the adjuster aligns with the reference mark on the damper unit.

16 To establish the present setting, rotate one of the adjusters fully clockwise whilst counting the number of clicks emitted, then rotate it back to its original position. Repeat the procedure on the other adjuster to ensure both are set in the same position.

17 To reduce the compression damping, turn

the adjuster counterclockwise (anti-clockwise) in the direction of the S arrow.

18 To increase the compression damping, turn the adjuster clockwise in the direction of the H arrow.

19 Always ensure both adjusters are set to the same position.

Rear shock absorber
Spring preload - all models

20 The rear shock absorber spring preload adjuster is in the form of a stepped collar fitted to the top of the shock absorber, and is adjusted by rotating the collar using a suitable C-wrench **(see illustration)**. One is supplied in the bike's toolkit.

21 The preload adjuster has seven numbered positions stamped on it, number 1 being the minimum (i.e. softest) setting and number seven the maximum (hardest) setting. Honda recommend position two as the standard setting on US 1993 through 1997 models and UK N to V models and position 3 on all later models. Align the number for the setting required with the adjuster lug on the shock absorber body.

Rebound damping

22 The rear suspension rebound damping adjuster is situated at the base of the shock absorber on its left side and is adjusted using a flat-bladed screwdriver **(see illustration)**.

23 The standard setting recommended by Honda is one turn counterclockwise (anti-clockwise) from the maximum damping setting. In this position, the punch mark on the adjuster aligns with the reference mark on the shock absorber.

24 To establish the current setting, turn the adjuster fully clockwise whilst counting the number of turns until it seats, then rotate it back to its original position. Reposition the adjuster by the required amount.

25 To reduce the rebound damping, turn the adjuster counterclockwise (anti-clockwise).

26 To increase the rebound damping, turn the adjuster clockwise.

Compression damping

27 The rear suspension compression damping adjuster is situated on the shock absorber reservoir, mounted on the left side of the bike, and is adjusted using a flat-bladed screwdriver **(see illustration)**.

12.22 Adjust the rear shock absorber rebound damping using a flat-bladed screwdriver

12.27 Adjust the rear shock absorber compression damping using a flat-bladed screwdriver

28 The standard setting recommended by Honda is one and a half turns counterclockwise (anti-clockwise) from the maximum setting on US 1993 through 1995 models and UK N to S models, and one turn counterclockwise on all later models. In this position, the punch mark on the adjuster aligns with the reference mark on the reservoir.

29 To establish the current setting, turn the adjuster fully clockwise whilst counting the number of turns until it seats, then rotate it back to its original position. Reposition the adjuster by the required amount.

30 To reduce the compression damping, turn the adjuster counterclockwise (anti-clockwise).

31 To increase the compression damping, turn the adjuster clockwise.

13 Swingarm bearings - check

1 Remove the rear wheel as described in Chapter 7, then remove the rear shock absorber as described in Section 10 of this Chapter.

2 Grasp the rear of the swingarm with one hand and place your other hand at the junction of the swingarm and the frame. Try to move the rear of the swingarm from side-to-side. Any wear (play) in the bearings should be

felt as movement between the swingarm and the frame at the front. The swingarm will actually be felt to move forward and backward at the front (not from side-to-side). If any play is noted, the bearings should be replaced (see Section 15).

3 Next, move the swingarm up and down through its full travel. It should move freely, without any binding or rough spots. If it does not move freely, refer to Section 14 for servicing procedures.

14 Swingarm - removal and installation

Removal

1 Unscrew the bolt securing the brake hose clamp to the swingarm.

2 Remove the rear brake caliper and its pads as described in Chapter 7. Do not separate the hose from the caliper. Support the caliper so that no strain is placed on the hose.

3 Remove the rear wheel as described in Chapter 7. If the swingarm is to be moved away from the bike for bearing replacement, remove the drive chain as described in Section 16.

4 Remove the rear brake caliper mounting bracket from its slot in the swingarm noting how it fits.

5 Remove the swingarm-mounted rear fender/mudguard as described in Chapter 8.

6 Maneuver the brake caliper out through the front of the swingarm, taking care not to twist the hose (see illustration). Once the caliper is free of the swingarm, support it so that no strain is placed on the hose.

7 Remove the rear shock absorber as described in Section 10.

8 Unscrew and remove the nut and pivot bolt securing the shock link plates to the swingarm.

9 Working on the left side of the bike, unscrew the swingarm pivot nut (see illustration).

10 Working on the right side of the bike, unscrew the swingarm pivot locknut. This requires the use of a Honda service tool, Pt No. 07908-4690002 for US 1993 through 1995 models and UK N to S models, and Pt No. 07908-4690003 for all later models, which is a special wrench that fits the locknut (see illustration). There is no alternative to the use of this tool; if you do not have access to it, the swingarm pivot locknut must be unscrewed and later tightened by a Honda dealer.

11 The swingarm pivot bolt fits into the head of the swingarm pivot adjusting bolt (actually a threaded sleeve). Using an Allen key, unscrew the swingarm pivot bolt which will unscrew the adjusting bolt (see illustration).

12 When the adjusting bolt is fully unscrewed, have an assistant support the swingarm, then withdraw the pivot bolt and the adjusting bolt and remove the swingarm.

13 Remove the front and rear drive chain guards and the chain slider from the swingarm if necessary.

14 Remove the collar from the left side of the swingarm. Inspect all components for wear or damage as described in Section 15.

Installation

15 If removed, install the front and rear drive chain guards and the chain slider. Apply a drop of non-permanent locking compound to the chain slider mounting screws.

16 Lubricate the dust seals, bearings, collar, center spacer and the pivot bolt with grease.

17 Fit the collar to the left side of the swingarm (see illustration).

14.6 Maneuver the rear brake caliper out through the front of the swingarm

14.9 Unscrew the swingarm pivot nut

14.10 This Honda service tool is essential for removing and installing the swingarm

14.11 Use an Allen key in the head of the swingarm pivot bolt to unscrew the adjusting bolt

14.17 Install the collar into the left side of the swingarm

6

14.18a Install the adjusting bolt into the swingarm and tighten as much as possible by hand . . .

14.18b . . . then insert the swingarm pivot bolt and engage it with the adjusting bolt . . .

18 Offer up the swingarm, and have an assistant hold it in place. Install the swingarm pivot adjusting bolt and tighten it as much as possible by hand. Then install the swingarm pivot bolt through the swingarm, and engage its flats with those of the adjusting bolt and tighten the adjusting bolt further by turning the pivot bolt using a suitable Allen key. Tighten the adjusting bolt in this way to the torque setting specified at the beginning of the Chapter **(see illustrations)**.

19 Check the movement of the swingarm.

20 Install the swingarm pivot locknut and tighten it as much as possible by hand.

14.18c . . . and tighten the adjusting bolt to the specified torque setting using an Allen key in the head of the pivot bolt

Tighten the locknut further using the service tool as described in Step 10, using an Allen key applied through its middle to prevent the swingarm pivot bolt and adjusting bolt from turning. Then, using a torque wrench applied to the hole in the arm of the service tool, tighten the locknut to the specified torque setting **(see illustrations)**. **Note:** *The specified torque setting takes into account the extra leverage provided by the service tool and cannot be duplicated without it.*

21 Install the swingarm pivot nut on the pivot bolt left end, and whilst preventing the pivot bolt from turning using the Allen key in its right end, tighten the nut to the specified torque setting **(see illustration)**. Recheck the movement of the swingarm in accordance with Section 13.

22 Install the shock link plates on the swingarm and tighten the nut to the specified torque setting.

23 Install the rear shock absorber as described in Section 10.

24 Maneuver the rear brake caliper through the front of the swingarm, install its pads and mount on the bracket as described in Chapter 7. Install the bracket into the slot in the swingarm.

25 Install the rear fender/mudguard as described in Chapter 8.

26 Install the rear wheel as described in

Chapter 7. If removed, install the drive chain as described in Section 16.

27 Install the brake hose clamp on the swingarm and tighten the bolt securely.

28 Check the operation of the rear suspension before taking the machine on the road.

---

15 Swingarm - inspection and bearing replacement

Inspection

1 Thoroughly clean all components, removing all traces of dirt, corrosion and grease **(see illustration)**.

2 Inspect all components closely, looking for obvious signs of wear such as heavy scoring, and cracks or distortion due to accident damage. Inspect the wear indicator line on the front of the drive chain slider. If it is worn to the line it must be replaced. Any damaged or worn component must be replaced.

Bearing replacement

3 Lever out the dust seals, using a flat-bladed screwdriver, and inspect them for signs of wear or damage; replace them if necessary.

14.20a Install the locknut onto the adjusting bolt and tighten as much as possible by hand . . .

14.20b . . . then use the service tool as shown to tighten the locknut to the specified torque setting

14.21 Tighten the swingarm pivot nut to the specified torque setting

1 Chain front guard
2 Chain rear guard
3 Drive chain slider
4 Drive chain adjusting bolt
5 Collar
6 Dust seal
7 Dust seal
8 Snap-ring
9 Ball bearings
10 Center spacer
11 Needle roller bearing

15.1 Exploded view of swingarm components

Note that the left and right seals are a different size.

4 Using snap ring pliers, remove the snap ring from the right side of the swingarm **(see illustration)**.

5 The two right side bearings can be driven out of position simultaneously, using a hammer and suitable drift inserted from the left side of the swingarm. Move the drift around the face of the bearing whilst driving it out of position, so that the bearings leave the swingarm squarely. If difficulty is experienced in removing the bearings, a special tool is available from Honda, Pt. No. 07936-3710001. An alternative is to use an internally-expanding bearing puller which are available commercially or can be hired. Otherwise the bearings must be replaced by a dealer service agent or bike repair specialist. Once the bearings have been removed, tip out the center spacer, noting which way round it fits.

6 Wash the bearings thoroughly in a high flash-point solvent to remove all traces of the old grease.

7 Check the bearing tracks and balls for wear, pitting or damage to hardened surfaces.

A small amount of side movement in the bearing is normal, but no radial movement should be detectable.

8 Check the bearings for play and roughness when they are spun by hand. All bearings will emit a small amount of noise when spun but they should not chatter or sound rough. If there is any doubt about the condition of the bearings they should be replaced.

9 Install the center spacer, then pack the bearings with grease and drift them separately into position using a suitable tubular drift which bears only on the outer race of the bearing.

10 Secure the bearings in position with the snap ring, ensuring that it is correctly seated in its groove.

11 The needle roller bearing fitted to the left side of swingarm can, if necessary, be replaced as described in Section 11 of this Chapter.

12 Press the dust seals into position using a suitable tubular spacer which bears only on the hard outer edge of the seal **(see illustration)**. Make sure the correct size seal is fitted to each side.

15.4 Swingarm right side bearings are retained by a snap-ring (arrow)

15.12 Press the dust seals into position using a suitable tubular spacer

16 Drive chain - removal, cleaning and installation

Removal

Note: *The original equipment drive chain fitted to all models has a staked-type master (joining) link which can be disassembled using either Honda service tool, Pt No. 07HMH-MR10102 for US 1993 through 1995 models and UK N to S models, and Pt No. 07HMH-MR10103 for all later models, or one of several commercially-available drive chain cutting/staking tools. Such chains can be recognised by the master link side plate's identification marks (and usually its different color), as well as by the staked ends of the link's two pins which look as if they have been deeply center-punched, instead of peened over as with all the other pins.*

⚠ *Warning: NEVER install a drive chain which uses a clip-type master (split) link. Use ONLY the correct service tools to secure the staked-type of master link - if you do not have access to such tools, have the chain replaced by a dealer service department or bike repair shop to be sure of having it securely installed.*

1 Locate the joining link in a suitable position to work on by rotating the back wheel.

2 Slacken the drive chain as described in Chapter 1.

3 Split the chain at the joining link using the chain cutter, following carefully the manufacturer's operating instructions. **Note:** *Refer to Tools and Workshop Tips in the Reference section for more information about chains.* Remove the chain from the bike, noting its routing through the swingarm.

6

16.7 Drive chain joining link components

1 Joining link   2 O-rings   3 Side plate

Cleaning

4 Soak the chain in kerosene (paraffin) for approximately five or six minutes.

Caution: Don't use gasoline (petrol), solvent or other cleaning fluids which might damage its internal sealing properties. Don't use high-pressure water. Remove the chain, wipe it off, then blow dry it with compressed air immediately. The entire process shouldn't take longer than ten minutes - if it does, the O-rings in the chain rollers could be damaged.

Installation

5 Remove the front sprocket cover as described in Section 17, Steps 1 through 3.

6 Install the drive chain through the swingarm sections and around the front sprocket, leaving the two ends in a convenient position to work on.

17.2 Unscrew the sprocket cover retaining bolts (arrows) . . .

17.3 . . . and remove the cover and the drive chain guide plate

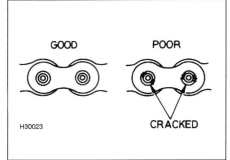

16.8 Check the joining link to make sure it is properly staked

7 Install the new joining link from the inside with the four O-rings correctly located between the link plates **(see illustration)**. Install the new side plate with its identification marks facing out. Stake the new link using the drive chain cutting/staking tool, following carefully the instructions of both the chain manufacturer and the tool manufacturer. DO NOT re-use old joining link components.

8 After staking, check the joining link and staking for any signs of cracking. If there is any evidence of cracking, the joining link, O-rings and side plate must be replaced **(see illustration)**.

9 Install the front sprocket cover as described in Section 17, Steps 11 and 12.

10 On completion, adjust and lubricate the chain following the procedures described in Chapter 1.

Caution: Use only the recommended lubricant.

---

17 Sprockets - check and replacement

Check

1 On US 1995 through 1997 models and UK R to V models, unscrew the mounting bolts and free the speedometer sensor from the sprocket cover **(see illustration)**.

2 Unscrew the two bolts securing the front sprocket cover to the engine unit, noting the position of the wiring clamp on later models **(see illustration)**.

17.9 Unscrew the front sprocket retaining bolt (arrow) . . .

17.1 On US 1995 through 1997 models and UK R to V models, unscrew the bolts (arrows) and free the speedometer sensor from the sprocket cover

3 Remove the sprocket cover and the drive chain guide plate **(see illustration)**.

4 Check the wear pattern on both sprockets (see Chapter 1). If the sprocket teeth are worn excessively, replace the chain and both sprockets as a set. Whenever the drive chain is inspected, the sprockets should be inspected also. If you are replacing the chain, replace the sprockets as well.

5 Fit the drive chain guide and sprocket cover. Fit the retaining screws, not forgetting the wiring clamp on the upper screw (if fitted), and tighten them securely.

6 On US 1995 through 1997 models and UK R to V models, engage the speedometer sensor with the sprocket bolt head then seat the sensor on the cover and securely tighten its mounting bolts.

7 Adjust and lubricate the chain following the procedures described in Chapter 1.

Caution: Use only the recommended lubricant.

Replacement

Front sprocket

8 Remove the sprocket cover as described in Steps 1 through 3 above.

9 Shift the transmission into gear and have an assistant sit on the seat and apply the rear brake hard. This will lock the transmission and enable you to slacken and remove the engine sprocket bolt **(see illustration)**.

10 Pull the engine sprocket and chain off the shaft, then separate the sprocket from the chain **(see illustration)**.

17.10 . . . and remove the front sprocket from countershaft and the drive chain

17.14 Tighten the rear sprocket retaining nuts to the specified torque setting

11 Engage the new sprocket with the chain and slide it on the shaft. Install the washer and retaining bolt and tighten it to the specified torque setting whilst locking the transmission as described above

12 Install the engine sprocket cover as described in Steps 5 through 7.

Rear sprocket

13 To remove the rear sprocket, remove the

18.4 Remove the rubber dampers from the rear wheel and inspect them for wear and damage

rear wheel as described in Chapter 7. Unscrew the nuts holding the sprocket to the wheel coupling and lift it off. Check the condition of the rubber damper under the rear wheel coupling (see Section 18).

14 Fit the new sprocket. Apply a smear of clean oil to the threads of the retaining nuts prior to fitting and tighten them to the torque setting specified at the beginning of the Chapter **(see illustration)**.

18 Rear wheel coupling/rubber damper - check and replacement

1 Remove the rear wheel as described in Chapter 7.

2 Remove the spacer from the center of the sprocket coupling.

3 Lift the sprocket coupling away from the wheel leaving the rubber dampers in position in the wheel. Take care not to lose the spacer from the inside of the coupling bearing.

4 Lift the rubber damper segments from the wheel and check them for cracks, hardening and general deterioration **(see illustration)**. Replace the rubber dampers as a set if necessary.

5 Checking and replacement procedures for the sprocket coupling bearing are described in Section 16 of Chapter 7.

6 Installation is the reverse of the removal procedure, making sure that the sprocket coupling spacers are correctly positioned.

7 Install the rear wheel as described in Chapter 7.

6

Notes

Chapter 7
Brakes, wheels and tires

Contents

Degrees of difficulty

| **Easy,** suitable for novice with little experience | **Fairly easy,** suitable for beginner with some experience | **Fairly difficult,** suitable for competent DIY mechanic 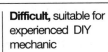 | **Difficult,** suitable for experienced DIY mechanic | **Very difficult,** suitable for expert DIY or professional |

Specifications

Brakes

Brake fluid type . . . .   See Chapter 1
Disc thickness
  Front
    New . . . .   4.5 mm (0.18 in)
    Service limit . . . .   3.5 mm (0.14 in)
  Rear
    New . . . .   5.0 mm (0.20 in)
    Service limit . . . .   4.0 mm (0.16 in)
Disc maximum runout (front and rear) . . . .   0.3 mm (0.012 in)

7

Brakes (continued)

Caliper bore ID
   Front
      US 1993 through 1997 models and UK N to V models
         Cylinder A

New	30.230 to 30.280 mm (1.1902 to 1.1921 in)
Service limit	30.290 mm (1.1930 in)

         Cylinder B

New	27.000 to 27.050 mm (1.0630 to 1.0650 in)
Service limit	27.060 mm (1.0652 in)

      US 1998 and 1999 models and UK W and X models
         Cylinder A

New	32.030 to 32.080 mm (1.2610 to 1.2630 in)
Service limit	32.090 mm (1.2634 in)

         Cylinder B

New	33.960 to 34.010 mm (1.3370 to 1.3390 in)
Service limit	34.020 mm (1.3400 in)

   Rear

New	38.180 to 38.230 mm (1.5031 to 1.5051 in)
Service limit	38.240 mm (1.5060 in)

Caliper piston OD
   Front
      US 1993 through 1997 models and UK N to V models
         Piston A

New	30.148 to 30.198 mm (1.1869 to 1.1889 in)
Service limit	30.140 mm (1.1866 in)

         Piston B

New	26.935 to 26.968 mm (1.0640 to 1.0617 in)
Service limit	26.927 mm (1.0601 in)

      US 1998 and 1999 models and UK W and X models
         Piston A

New	31.965 to 31.998 mm (1.2585 to 1.2598 in)
Service limit	31.940 mm (1.3360 in)

         Piston B

New	33.895 to 33.928 mm (1.3344 to 1.3357 in)
Service limit	33.870 mm (1.3333 in)

   Rear

New	38.115 to 38.148 mm (1.5006 to 1.5019 in)
Service limit	38.107 mm (1.5003 in)

Master cylinder bore ID
   Front
      US 1993 through 1997 models and UK N to V models

New	14.000 to 14.043 mm (0.5512 to 0.5529 in)
Service limit	14.055 mm (0.5533 in)

      US 1998 and 1999 models and UK W and X models

New	15.870 to 15.913 mm (0.6248 to 0.6265 in)
Service limit	15.925 mm (0.6270 in)

   Rear

New	15.870 to 15.913 mm (0.6248 to 0.6265 in)
Service limit	15.925 mm (0.6270 in)

Master cylinder piston OD
   Front
      US 1993 through 1997 models and UK N to V models

New	13.957 to 13.984 mm (0.5495 to 0.5506 in)
Service limit	13.945 mm (0.5490 in)

      US 1998 and 1999 models and UK W and X models

New	15.827 to 15.854 mm (0.6231 to 0.6242 in)
Service limit	15.815 mm (0.6230 in)

   Rear

New	15.827 to 15.854 mm (0.6231 to 0.6242 in)
Service limit	15.815 mm (0.6230 in)

Wheels

Maximum wheel runout (front and rear)

Axial (side-to-side)	2.0 mm (0.08 in)
Radial (out-of-round)	2.0 mm (0.08 in)
Maximum axle runout (front and rear)	0.2 mm (0.01 in)

Tires

Tire pressures . . . . See Daily (pre-ride) checks
Tire sizes*
    Front . . . . 130/70 ZR 16
    Rear . . . . 180/55 ZR 17
*Refer to the machine's handbook or the tire information label on the drive chain guard for approved tire brands

Torque settings

	Nm	ft-lbs
Front brake caliper		
Mounting bolts		
US 1993 and 1994 models and UK N and P models	27	20
US 1995 through 1999 models and UK R to X models	30	22
Joining Torx bolts		
US 1993 through 1997 models and UK N to V models	33	24
US 1998 and 1999 models and UK W and X models	23	17
Pad retaining pin	18	13
Pad retaining pin plug	2.5	1.8
Front brake disc retaining bolts	20	14
Front brake master cylinder bracket bolt	6	4.3
Front brake lever pivot bolt	1	0.7
Front brake lever pivot bolt locknut	6	4.3
Rear brake caliper		
Mounting bolt	23	17
Pad retaining pin	18	13
Pad pin plug	2.5	1.8
Slider pin	28	21
Rear brake disc retaining bolts	43	31
Brake hose banjo fitting bolts	35	25
Brake pipe flare nuts	17	12
Brake caliper bleed valves	6	4.3
Front axle bolt	60	43
Front axle clamp bolts	22	16
Rear axle nut	95	69

1 General information

The models covered in this manual are fitted with cast aluminum wheels designed to accept tubeless tires. Both front and rear brakes are hydraulically operated disc brakes, the front using a twin disc set up and the rear a single disc. The front brake calipers are of the dual opposed piston type, whilst the rear is a sliding caliper with a single piston.

Caution: Disc brake components rarely require disassembly. Do not disassemble components unless absolutely necessary. If any hydraulic brake line is loosened, the entire system must be disassembled, drained, cleaned and then properly filled and bled upon reassembly. Do not use solvents on internal brake components. Solvents will cause the seals to swell and distort. Use only clean brake fluid or alcohol for cleaning. Use care when working with brake fluid as it can injure your eyes and it will damage painted surfaces and plastic parts.

2 Front brake pads - replacement

⚠️ *Warning: When replacing the front brake pads always replace the pads in BOTH calipers - never just on one side. The dust created by the brake system may contain asbestos, which* is harmful to your health. Never blow it out with compressed air and don't inhale any of it. An approved filtering mask should be worn when working on the brakes.

US 1993 through 1997 models and UK N to V models

1 Remove the brake pad inspection cover noting its correct fitted position.
2 Unscrew the pad retaining pin plug from the caliper body to reveal the pad retaining pin **(see illustration)**.
3 Unscrew and remove the pad retaining pin from the caliper **(see illustration)**.
4 Remove the pad spring from the caliper noting its correct fitted position, and withdraw the brake pads from the caliper body **(see illustration)**.

2.2 Unscrew the plug from the caliper body

2.3 Unscrew the pad pin and withdraw it from the caliper

2.4 Note the position of the pad spring before removing it from the caliper

7

2.5 Brake pads must be replaced when the wear grooves (arrows) are no longer visible (typical pad design shown)

2.10 Insert the pads into the caliper so that their friction material faces the disc

2.11 Make sure the pad pin fits correctly through the brake pad holes and in the groove on the pad spring (arrow) before tightening to its specified torque setting

5 Inspect the surface of each pad for contamination and check that the friction material has not worn beyond its service limit groove (see illustration). If either pad is worn to or beyond the service limit groove (i.e. the grooves are no longer visible), fouled with oil or grease, or heavily scored or damaged by dirt and debris, both pads must be replaced as a set. Note that it is not possible to degrease the friction material; if the pads are contaminated in any way they must be replaced.

6 If the pads are in good condition clean them carefully, using a fine wire brush which is completely free of oil and grease to remove all traces of road dirt and corrosion. Using a pointed instrument, clean out the grooves in the friction material and dig out any embedded particles of foreign matter. Any areas of glazing may be removed using emery cloth.

7 Check the condition of the brake discs (see Section 4).

8 Remove all traces of corrosion from the pad pin. Inspect the pin for signs of damage and replace if necessary.

9 Push the pistons as far back into the caliper as possible using hand pressure only. Due to the increased friction material thickness of new pads, it may be necessary to remove the master cylinder reservoir cover, plate and diaphragm and syphon out some fluid.

10 Smear the backs of the pads with copper-based grease, making sure that none gets on the front or sides of the pads. Insert the pads into the caliper so that the friction material of each pad is facing the disc (see illustration). Insert the pad spring making sure that it is correctly fitted.

11 Insert the pad retaining pin making sure it passes through the holes in the pads and sits correctly on the pad spring, then tighten it to the torque setting specified at the beginning of the Chapter (see illustration).

12 Fit the pad pin plug and tighten to its specified torque setting, then install the pad inspection cover.

13 Top up the master cylinder reservoir if necessary (see Daily (pre-ride) checks), and

replace the reservoir cover, plate and diaphragm if removed.

14 Operate the brake lever several times to bring the pads into contact with the disc. Check the master cylinder fluid level (see Daily (pre-ride) checks) and the operation of the brake before riding the motorcycle.

US 1998 and 1999 models and UK W and X models

15 Unscrew and remove both pad retaining pins from the caliper body (see illustration).

16 Lift the pad spring away from the caliper, noting which way around it is fitted, and withdraw the brake pads from the caliper body (see illustrations).

2.15 Unscrew and remove both pad retaining pins (arrows) from the caliper

2.16b . . . and withdraw the brake pads

17 Inspect all components as described in Steps 5 to 9.

18 Smear the backs of the pads with a light coating of copper-based grease, making sure that none gets on the friction material. Insert the pads into the caliper so that the friction material of each pad is facing the disc.

19 Make sure the UP marking on the pad spring is facing upwards then locate the spring in the caliper aperture (see illustration).

20 Push down on the pad spring and install the pad lower retaining pin making sure it passes through both the holes in the pads and correctly through the pad spring. Lightly tighten the lower retaining pin then install the

2.16a Lift out the pad spring, noting which way around it is fitted . . .

2.19 Ensure the pad spring is fitted with its UP marking (highlighted) pointing upwards

upper pin, again making sure it passes correctly through the pad holes and the spring **(see illustrations)**. Check both retaining pins are correctly fitted then tighten them both to the specified torque.

21 Top up the master cylinder reservoir if necessary (see *Daily (pre-ride) checks),* and reservoir cover plate and diaphragm if removed.

22 Operate the brake lever several times to bring the pads into contact with the disc. Check the master cylinder fluid level (see *Daily (pre-ride) checks)* and the operation of the brake before riding the motorcycle.

3 Front brake calipers - removal, overhaul and installation

> ⚠️ **Warning: If a caliper indicates the need for an overhaul (usually due to leaking fluid or sticky operation), all old brake fluid should be flushed from the system. Also, the dust created by the brake system may contain asbestos, which is harmful to your health. Never blow it out with compressed air and don't inhale any of it. An approved filtering mask should be worn when working on the brakes. Do not, under any circumstances, use petroleum-based solvents to clean brake parts. Use clean brake fluid, brake cleaner or denatured alcohol only.**

Removal

1 Unscrew the reflector mounting bolt and remove the reflector (US models only).

2 Remove the brake hose banjo fitting bolt, noting its correct alignment with the boss on the caliper, and separate the hose from the caliper. Plug the hose end or wrap a plastic bag tightly around it to minimise fluid loss and prevent dirt entering the system. Discard the sealing washers; new ones must be used on installation. **Note:** *If you are planning to overhaul the caliper and don't have a source of compressed air to blow out the pistons, just loosen the banjo bolt at this stage and retighten it lightly. The bike's hydraulic system can then be used to force the pistons out of the body once the pads have been removed. Disconnect the hose once the pistons have been sufficiently displaced.*

3 Unscrew the caliper mounting bolts and slide the caliper away from the disc **(see illustration 3.20a)**. Remove the brake pads as described in Section 2.

Overhaul

4 Clean the exterior of the caliper with denatured alcohol or brake system cleaner **(see illustration)**.

5 Remove the pistons from the caliper body, either by pumping them out by operating the front brake lever until the pistons are displaced, or by forcing them out using

2.20a Install the pad lower retaining pin first, making sure it passes through both pads and the spring . . .

compressed air. Note that two sizes of piston are used (see sizes A and B in the Specifications at the beginning of this Chapter), and that different size seals are fitted accordingly. If the compressed air method is used, place a wad of rag between the pistons to act as a cushion, then use compressed air directed into the fluid inlet to force the pistons out of the body. Use only low pressure to ease the pistons out and make sure both pistons are displaced at the same time. If the air pressure is too high and the pistons are forced out, the caliper and/or pistons may be damaged.

> ⚠️ **Warning: Never place your fingers in front of the pistons in an attempt to catch or protect them when applying compressed air, as serious injury could result.**

6 Unscrew the four caliper assembly Torx bolts and split the caliper body into its two halves. On US 1993 to 1997 models and UK N to V models extract and discard the two caliper seals and on later models extract and discard the single caliper seal. The caliper seal(s) must be renewed.

2.20b . . . then install the upper pin, again making sure it passes correctly through both pads and the spring

7 Using a wooden or plastic tool, remove the dust seals from the caliper bores and discard them. New seals must be used on installation. If a metal tool is being used, take great care **not** to damage the caliper bores.

8 Remove and discard the piston seals in the same way.

9 Clean the pistons and bores with denatured alcohol, clean brake fluid or brake system cleaner.

> *Caution: Do not, under any circumstances, use a petroleum-based solvent to clean brake parts. If compressed air is available, use it to dry the parts thoroughly (make sure it's filtered and unlubricated).*

10 Inspect the caliper bores and pistons for signs of corrosion, nicks and burrs and loss of plating. If surface defects are present, the caliper assembly must be replaced. If the caliper is in bad shape the master cylinder should also be checked.

11 If the necessary measuring equipment is available, compare the dimensions of the caliper bores and pistons to those given in the Specifications Section of this Chapter, replacing any component that is worn beyond the service limit.

1 Pad inspection cover
2 Pad spring
3 Bleed valve
4 Piston A
5 Piston B
6 Dust seal A
7 Dust seal B
8 Piston seal A
9 Piston seal B
10 Caliper seals

H30024

3.4 Exploded view of a front brake caliper (US 1993 to 1997 models, UK N to V model shown)

7

3.20a Install the new caliper mounting bolts (arrow) . . .

3.20b . . . tightening them to the specified torque setting

3.21 Align the brake hose so that it butts against the boss on the caliper (arrow)

12 Lubricate the new piston seals with clean brake fluid and install them in their grooves in the caliper bores. Note that two sizes of bore and piston are used and care must therefore be taken when installing the new seals to ensure that the correct size seals are fitted to the correct bores. The same care must be taken when fitting the new dust seals and the pistons.

13 Lubricate the new dust seals with clean brake fluid and install them in their grooves in the caliper bores.

14 Lubricate the pistons with clean brake fluid and install them closed-end first into the caliper bores. Using your thumbs, push the pistons all the way in, making sure they enter the bore squarely.

15 On US 1993 through 1997 models and UK N to V models locate both the new caliper seals in the recesses in one half of the caliper body. On later models fit the new caliper seal to the recess in the caliper body half.

16 Join the two halves of the caliper body together, making sure that the caliper seals are correctly seated in their recesses.

17 Apply a drop of non-permanent locking compound to the threads of the four caliper assembly Torx bolts, then install them in the caliper body and tighten to the torque setting specified at the beginning of the Chapter.

Installation

18 Install the brake pads as described in Section 2.

19 Install the caliper on the brake disc

making sure the pads sit squarely either side of the disc.

20 Retain the caliper with two new mounting bolts and tighten them to the torque setting specified at the beginning of this Chapter (see illustrations). Note: *The mounting bolt threads contain a locking agent, necessitating that they be renewed if disturbed.*

21 Connect the brake hose to the caliper, using new sealing washers on each side of the fitting. Align the brake hose so that it butts against the boss on the caliper (see illustration). Tighten the banjo fitting bolt to the torque setting specified at the beginning of the Chapter.

22 Fit the reflector and tighten the reflector mounting bolt (US models only).

23 Fill the master cylinder with the recommended brake fluid (see *Daily (pre-ride) checks)* and bleed the hydraulic system as described in Section 11.

24 Check for leaks and thoroughly test the operation of the brake before riding the motorcycle.

4	Front brake discs - inspection, removal and installation

Inspection

1 Visually inspect the surface of the discs for score marks and other damage. Light scratches are normal after use and won't affect brake operation, but deep grooves and

heavy score marks will reduce braking efficiency and accelerate pad wear. If the discs are badly grooved they must be machined or replaced.

2 To check disc runout, the front wheel must be raised off the ground using an auxiliary stand or hoist. Always make sure that the bike is properly supported. It may be necessary to use a jack and a block of wood under the engine, in which case the fairing lower section (see Chapter 8) and the exhaust system (see Chapter 4) must be removed. Mount a dial indicator to a fork leg, with the plunger on the indicator touching the surface of the disc about 10 mm (1/2 inch) from the outer edge (see illustration). Rotate the wheel and watch the indicator needle, comparing your reading with the limit listed in this Chapter's Specifications. If the runout is greater than the service limit, check the hub bearings for play. If the bearings are worn, replace them and repeat this check. If the disc runout is still excessive, it will have to be replaced, although machining by a competent engineering shop may be possible.

3 The disc must not be machined or allowed to wear down to a thickness less than the service limit as listed in this Chapter's Specifications and stamped on the disc itself. The thickness of the disc can be checked with a micrometer (see illustrations). If the thickness of the disc is less than the service limit, it must be replaced.

Removal

4 Remove the wheel as described in Section 14.

4.2 Using a dial indicator to measure disc runout

4.3a The minimum thickness of the disc is stamped on the disc itself (arrow)

4.3b Using a micrometer to measure disc thickness

4.5 Unscrew the disc bolts a little at a time and in a criss-cross pattern to avoid distorting the disc

Caution: Do not lay the wheel down and allow it to rest on one of the discs - the disc could become warped. Set the wheel on wood blocks so the disc doesn't support the weight of the wheel.

5 Mark the relationship of the disc to the wheel, so it can be installed in the same position. Unscrew the disc retaining bolts and remove the disc from the wheel **(see illustration)**. Loosen the bolts a little at a time, in a criss-cross pattern, to avoid distorting the disc.

6 Remove the disc. If both discs are to be removed mark them LEFT and RIGHT to ensure they are correctly positioned on installation.

Installation

7 Install the disc on the wheel, aligning the previously applied matchmarks (if you're reinstalling the original disc). Make sure the arrow stamped on the disc marking the normal direction of rotation is pointing in the direction of wheel rotation and is on the outer face of the disc **(see illustration)**.

8 Install the bolts and tighten them in a criss-cross pattern evenly and progressively to the torque setting specified at the beginning of the Chapter **(see illustration 4.5)**. Clean off all grease from the brake disc(s) using acetone or brake system cleaner. If new brake discs have been installed, remove any protective coating from their working surfaces.

9 Install the wheel as described in Section 14.

10 Operate the brake lever several times to bring the pads into contact with the disc. Check the operation of the brakes carefully before riding the bike.

5 Front brake master cylinder - removal, overhaul and installation

1 If the master cylinder is leaking fluid, or if the lever does not produce a firm feel when the brake is applied, and bleeding the brakes does not help (see Section 11), and the hydraulic hoses are all in good condition, then master cylinder overhaul is recommended.

2 Before disassembling the master cylinder, read through the entire procedure and make

4.7 Make sure the directional arrow on the disc points in the direction of normal wheel rotation (arrow)

sure that you have the correct rebuild kit. Also, you will need some new, clean brake fluid of the recommended type, some clean rags and internal snap-ring pliers. **Note:** *To prevent damage to the paint from spilled brake fluid, always cover the fuel tank when working on the master cylinder.*

Caution: Disassembly, overhaul and reassembly of the brake master cylinder must be done in a spotlessly clean work area to avoid contamination and possible failure of the brake hydraulic system components.

Removal

3 Loosen, but do not remove, the screws holding the reservoir cover in place.

4 Disconnect the electrical connectors from the brake light switch.

5 Unscrew the banjo fitting bolt and separate the brake hose from the master cylinder. Note the alignment of the hose with the boss on the master cylinder. Discard the two sealing washers as these must be replaced with new ones. Wrap the end of the hose in a clean rag and suspend the hose in an upright position or bend it down carefully and place the open end in a clean container. The objective is to prevent excessive loss of brake fluid, fluid spills and system contamination.

6 Remove the locknut from the underside of the brake lever pivot bolt, then unscrew the bolt and remove the brake lever.

7 Remove the master cylinder mounting bolts to free the clamp, then lift the master cylinder and reservoir away from the handlebar. Note the "UP" mark on the clamp indicating its correct position for instalment, and the punch mark on the handlebar which must align with the mating surfaces of the clamp.

Caution: Do not tip the master cylinder upside down or brake fluid will run out.

Overhaul

8 Unscrew the reservoir cover screws and remove the reservoir cover, the diaphragm plate and the rubber diaphragm **(see illustration)**. Drain the brake fluid from the reservoir into a suitable container. Wipe any remaining fluid out of the reservoir with a clean rag.

5.8 Exploded view of the front brake master cylinder

1 Reservoir cover
2 Diaphragm plate
3 Rubber diaphragm
4 Fluid reservoir
5 Damping rubber
6 Snap-ring
7 O-ring
8 Lever pivot bolt
9 Locknut
10 Brake light switch
11 Span adjuster arm
12 Spring
13 Joint pin
14 Span adjuster wheel
15 Span adjuster rod
16 Brake lever
17 Dust boot
18 Snap-ring
19 Piston assembly
20 Spring

5.24a Install the master cylinder clamp so that the "UP" mark is the right way up (arrow)

5.24b Align the mating surfaces of the clamp with the punchmark on the handlebar (arrow)

5.25 Align the brake hose so that it butts against the boss on the master cylinder (arrow)

9 Remove the reservoir bracket bolt from the master cylinder, and release the reservoir hose clamp at the master cylinder end. Carefully pull the hose from the elbow and separate the fluid reservoir from the master cylinder. Check the hose for cracks and replace if necessary.

10 Using a pair of snap-ring pliers, remove the snap-ring from under the dust cover on the reservoir hose elbow and withdraw the elbow from the master cylinder. Remove and discard the O-ring as a new one must be fitted on installation.

11 Undo the brake light switch retaining screw and remove the switch.

12 Carefully remove the boot from the end of the piston.

13 Using snap-ring pliers, remove the snap-ring and slide out the piston assembly and the spring. Lay the parts out in the proper order to prevent confusion during reassembly.

14 Clean all of the parts with brake system cleaner (available at auto parts stores), denatured alcohol or clean brake fluid. *Caution: Do not, under any circumstances, use a petroleum-based solvent to clean brake parts. If compressed air is available, use it to dry the parts thoroughly (make sure it's filtered and unlubricated).*

15 Check the master cylinder bore for corrosion, scratches, nicks and score marks. If damage is evident, the master cylinder must be replaced with a new one. If the master cylinder is in poor condition, then the calipers should be checked as well.

16 If the necessary measuring equipment is available, compare the dimensions of the master cylinder bore and piston to those given in the Specifications Section at the beginning of this Chapter, replacing any component that it is worn beyond the service limit.

17 The boot, piston assembly and spring are included in the rebuild kit. Use all of the new parts, regardless of the apparent condition of the old ones.

18 Before reassembling the master cylinder, soak the piston and the rubber cup seals in clean brake fluid for ten or fifteen minutes. Lubricate the master cylinder bore with clean brake fluid, then carefully insert the piston and

related parts in the reverse order of disassembly. Make sure the lips on the cup seals do not turn inside out when they are slipped into the bore and ensure the spring is fitted the correct way around.

19 Depress the piston, then install the snap-ring making sure it is properly seated in the groove. Install the rubber dust boot and make sure the lip is seated properly in the piston groove.

20 Install the brake light switch and securely tighten its retaining screw.

21 Install a new O-ring on the reservoir hose elbow and insert the elbow into the master cylinder. Install the snap-ring, making sure it is properly seated in its groove, and replace the dust cover.

22 Inspect the damping rubber at the fluid reservoir mounting and replace if deteriorated.

23 Connect the reservoir hose and hose clamp and install the fluid reservoir on the master cylinder, tightening the reservoir bracket bolt securely.

Installation

24 Attach the master cylinder to the handlebar and fit the clamp making sure the "UP" mark is facing upwards. Align the upper mating surfaces of the clamp with the punch mark on the handlebar, then tighten the upper clamp bolt first followed by the lower one **(see illustrations)**.

25 Connect the brake hose to the master cylinder, using new sealing washers on each side of the fitting. Align the hose so that it

butts against the boss on the master cylinder **(see illustration)**. Tighten the banjo union bolt to the torque setting specified at the beginning of the Chapter.

26 Install the brake lever and pivot bolt and tighten the bolt to the specified torque setting. Install the pivot bolt locknut and tighten it to the specified torque setting. The front brake lever has an adjuster mechanism which alters the span of the lever from the handlebar according to the rider's requirements. Adjust this as necessary by turning the adjuster either clockwise or anti-clockwise until the desired position is achieved (see Chapter 1).

27 Connect the brake light switch wiring.

28 Fill the fluid reservoir with the specified brake fluid as described in *Daily (pre-ride) checks*. Refer to Section 11 of this Chapter and bleed the air from the system.

---

6 Rear brake pads - replacement

Warning: The dust created by the brake system may contain asbestos, which is harmful to your health. Never blow it out with compressed air and don't inhale any of it. An approved filtering mask should be worn when working on the brakes.

1 Unscrew the plug from the caliper body to reveal the pad retaining pin, then slacken and remove the pad pin **(see illustrations)**.

6.1a Unscrew the plug from the rear brake caliper body . . .

6.1b . . . then slacken the pad pin with an Allen wrench . . .

6.1c . . . and withdraw the pin from the caliper

6.2 Unscrew the caliper mounting bolt . . .

6.3a . . . then pivot the caliper away from the disc and recover the inner . . .

2 Unscrew the caliper mounting bolt then release the brake hose from its retaining clips and pivot the caliper upwards **(see illustration)**. Do not place any excess strain on the hydraulic hose.

3 Slide out the pads along with the insulating pad and shim which are fitted to the rear of each pad **(see illustrations)**.

4 Remove the anti-rattle springs from the caliper bracket and body, noting their correct fitted positions **(see illustration)**.

5 Inspect the brake pads and associated components as described in Steps 5 through 7 of Section 2.

6 Fit the small anti-rattle spring to the caliper bracket and clip the large spring into the caliper body. Make sure both springs are correctly fitted and clipped securely in position.

7 Install the insulating pad and shim to the rear of each pad backing plate **(see illustrations)**.

8 Insert the pads into the caliper, ensuring the anti-rattle springs remain correctly positioned, so that the friction material of each pad is facing the disc. Insert the pad retaining pin making sure that it passes through the hole in both pads as well as the insulating pads and shims.

9 Pivot the caliper assembly down onto the disc and fit the caliper mounting bolt, tightening it to the torque setting specified at the beginning of the chapter.

10 Check that the brake hose is located in the retaining clamp on the swingarm.

11 Tighten the pad retaining pin to the specified torque setting, then install the pad

pin plug and tighten it to the specified torque setting.

12 Refill the master cylinder reservoir (see Chapter 1) and fit the diaphragm and cap.

13 Operate the brake pedal several times to bring the pads into contact with the disc. Check the master cylinder fluid level (see *Daily (pre-ride) checks*) and the operation of the brake before riding the bike.

7 Rear brake caliper - removal, overhaul and installation

 Warning: If the caliper indicates the need for an overhaul (usually due to leaking fluid or sticky operation), all old brake fluid should be flushed from the system. Also, the dust created by the brake system may contain asbestos, which is harmful to your health. Never blow it out with compressed air and don't inhale any of it. An approved filtering mask should be worn when working on the brakes. Do not, under any circumstances, use petroleum-based solvents to clean brake parts. Use clean brake fluid, brake cleaner or denatured alcohol only.

Removal

1 Remove the brake hose banjo fitting bolt and separate the hose from the caliper. Plug the hose end or wrap a plastic bag tightly around it to minimise fluid loss and prevent dirt entering the system. Discard the sealing washers; new ones must be used on installation. **Note:** *If you are planning to overhaul the caliper and don't have a source of compressed air to blow out the pistons, just loosen the banjo bolt at this stage and retighten it lightly. The bike's hydraulic system can then be used to force the piston out of the body once the pads have been removed. Disconnect the hose once the piston has been sufficiently displaced.*

2 Remove the brake pads and anti-rattle springs as described in Section 6.

3 Slide the caliper away from its mounting bracket and recover the slider pin rubber boot.

6.3b . . . and outer pads noting the correct fitted locations of the insulating pads and shims

6.4 Remove the small anti-rattle spring from the caliper bracket

6.7a Prior to installing, fit the insulating pad . . .

6.7b . . . and shim to the rear of each rear brake pad

7

Overhaul

4 Clean the exterior of the caliper with denatured alcohol or brake system cleaner **(see illustration)**.

5 If the piston wasn't forced out using the bike's hydraulic system, place a wad of rag between the piston and caliper frame to act as a cushion, then use compressed air directed into the fluid inlet to force the piston out of the body. Use only low pressure to ease the piston out. If the air pressure is too high and the piston is forced out, the caliper and/or piston may be damaged.

⚠ *Warning: Never place your fingers in front of the piston in an attempt to catch or protect it when applying compressed air, as serious injury could result.*

6 Using a wooden or plastic tool, remove the dust seal from the caliper bore. If a metal tool is being used, take great care not to damage the caliper bore.

7 Remove the piston seal in the same way.

8 Clean the piston and bore with denatured alcohol, clean brake fluid or brake system cleaner.

Caution: Do not, under any circumstances, use a petroleum-based solvent to clean brake parts. If compressed air is available, use it to dry the parts thoroughly (make sure it's filtered and unlubricated).

9 Inspect the caliper bore and piston for signs of corrosion, nicks and burrs and loss of plating. If surface defects are present, the caliper assembly must be replaced. If the caliper is in bad shape the master cylinder should also be checked.

10 If the necessary measuring equipment is available, compare the dimensions of the caliper bore and piston to those given in the Specifications Section of this Chapter, replacing any component that is worn beyond the service limit.

11 Temporarily install the caliper to its mounting bracket. Make sure that it slides smoothly in-and-out and check that the slider pin and the slider bush are a snug fit in their bores. If not check the slider pin and bush and their bores for burrs or excessive wear, replacing worn components as necessary. The slider pin and bush boots should be replaced as a matter of course.

12 Lubricate the new piston seal with clean brake fluid and install it in the groove in the caliper bore.

13 Lubricate the new dust seal with clean brake fluid and install it in the groove in the caliper bore.

14 Lubricate the piston with clean brake fluid and install it closed-end first in the caliper bore. Using your thumbs, push the piston all the way in, making sure it enters the bore squarely.

15 If the slider pin has been removed, apply a few drops of non-permanent locking compound to its threads. Fit the pin to the caliper body and tighten it to the torque setting specified at the beginning of the Chapter.

16 Install the new slider pin and bush boots.

17 Apply a thin coat of PBC (poly butyl cuprysil) grease, or silicone grease designed for high-temperature brake applications, to the slider pin and bush. Slide the slider bush into position in the caliper body ensuring the boot is correctly seated in the groove on each end of the bush.

Installation

18 Slide the caliper into position on the mounting bracket. Make sure the slider pin boot is correctly located in its grooves on the body and bracket.

19 Install the anti-rattle springs and brake pads as described in Section 6.

20 Connect the brake hose to the caliper, using new sealing washers on each side of the fitting. Align the hose with the boss on the caliper. Tighten the banjo fitting bolt to the specified torque setting. Check that the brake hose is located in the retaining clamp on the swingarm.

21 Fill the master cylinder with the recommended brake fluid (see *Daily (pre-ride) checks*) and bleed the hydraulic system as described in Section 11.

22 Check for leaks and thoroughly test the operation of the brake before riding the motorcycle on the road.

8 Rear brake disc - inspection, removal and installation

Inspection

1 Refer to Section 4 of this Chapter, noting that the dial indicator should be attached to the swingarm.

Removal

2 Remove the wheel as described in Section 15.

Caution: Don't lay the wheel down and allow it to rest on the disc or the sprocket - they could become warped. Set the wheel on wood blocks so the disc doesn't support the weight of the wheel.

3 Mark the relationship of the disc to the wheel, so it can be installed in the same position. Remove the bolts that retain the disc to the wheel. Loosen the bolts a little at a time, in a criss-cross pattern, to avoid distorting the disc, then remove the disc **(see illustration)**.

Installation

4 Position the disc on the wheel, aligning the previously applied matchmarks (if you're reinstalling the original disc). Make sure the arrow (stamped on the disc) marking the direction of rotation is pointing in the proper direction and is on the outer face of the disc.

5 Install the bolts and tighten them in a criss-cross pattern evenly and progressively to the torque setting specified at the beginning of this Chapter. Clean off all grease from the brake disc using acetone or brake system cleaner. If a new brake disc has been installed, remove any protective coating from its working surfaces.

6 Install the wheel as described in Section 15.

7.4 Exploded view of the rear brake caliper

Labels: PISTON, SLIDER BUSHING BOOT, CALIPER BODY, BLEEDER VALVE, SLIDER PIN, DUST SEAL, PISTON SEAL, LARGE ANTI-RATTLE PAD SPRING, SLIDER BUSHING BOOT, SLIDER BUSHING

2070-7-7.5 HAYNES

8.3 Rear brake disc is retained by four bolts (arrows)

7 Operate the brake pedal several times to bring the pads into contact with the disc. Check the operation of the brake carefully before riding the bike.

9 Rear brake master cylinder - removal, overhaul and installation

1 If the master cylinder is leaking fluid, or if the pedal does not produce a firm feel when the brake is applied, and bleeding the brakes does not help (see Section 11), and the hydraulic hoses are all in good condition, then master cylinder overhaul is recommended.
2 Before disassembling the master cylinder, read through the entire procedure and make sure that you have the correct rebuild kit. Also, you will need some new, clean brake fluid of the recommended type, some clean shop towels and internal snap-ring pliers.
Caution: Disassembly, overhaul and reassembly of the brake master cylinder must be done in a spotlessly clean work area to avoid contamination and possible failure of the brake hydraulic system components.

Removal

3 Unscrew the banjo union bolt from the top of the master cylinder, noting the alignment of the hose with the boss on the cylinder. Discard the sealing washers as new ones must be fitted. Wrap the end of the hose in a clean rag and suspend the hose in an upright position or bend it down carefully and place the open end in a clean container. The objective is to prevent excessive loss of brake fluid, fluid spills and system contamination.

4 Remove the cotter pin (split pin) and withdraw the clevis pin which secures the master cylinder pushrod to the brake pedal.
5 Remove the bolt securing the master cylinder fluid reservoir to the frame. Unscrew the reservoir cap and pour the contents into a container.
6 Unscrew the master cylinder mounting bolts which pass through the step guard, and remove the step guard and master cylinder assembly.
7 Separate the fluid reservoir hose from the elbow on the master cylinder by releasing the hose clamp.

Overhaul

8 Unscrew the fluid reservoir hose elbow retaining screw from the master cylinder and remove the elbow. Discard the O-ring as a new one must be fitted on installation **(see illustration)**. Inspect the reservoir hose for cracks or splits and replace if necessary.
9 Before removing the clevis from the end of the pushrod, it is advised that note is made of its original position, either by measuring the distance from the center of the clevis pin to the base of the master cylinder body, or by a spot of paint or other identifying mark on the pushrod threads. Hold the clevis with a pair of pliers and loosen the locknut. Unscrew the clevis and locknut from the pushrod and carefully remove the rubber dust boot from the pushrod.
10 Depress the pushrod and, using snap-ring pliers, remove the snap-ring. Slide out the piston assembly and spring. Lay the parts out in the proper order to prevent confusion during reassembly.
11 Clean all of the parts with brake system cleaner (available at auto parts stores), denatured alcohol or clean brake fluid.

Caution: Do not, under any circumstances, use a petroleum-based solvent to clean brake parts. If compressed air is available, use it to dry the parts thoroughly (make sure it's filtered and unlubricated).
12 Check the master cylinder bore for corrosion, scratches, nicks and score marks. If damage is evident, the master cylinder must be replaced with a new one. If the master cylinder is in poor condition, then the caliper should be checked as well.
13 If the necessary measuring equipment is available, compare the dimensions of the master cylinder bore and piston to those given in the Specifications Section of this Chapter, replacing any component that is worn beyond the service limit.
14 A new piston and spring are included in the rebuild kit. Use them regardless of the condition of the old ones.
15 Before reassembling the master cylinder, soak the piston and the rubber cup seals in clean brake fluid for ten or fifteen minutes. Lubricate the master cylinder bore with clean brake fluid, then carefully insert the parts in the reverse order of disassembly, ensuring the tapered end of the spring is facing the piston. Make sure the lips on the cup seals do not turn inside out when they are slipped into the bore.
16 Depress the pushrod, then install the snap-ring, making sure it is properly seated in the groove. Note that the snap-ring must be fitted with its chamfered edge towards the master cylinder piston.
17 Install the rubber dust boot, making sure the lip is seated properly in the groove.
18 Install the locknut and clevis to the end of the pushrod and position them as noted on removal (see Step 9). Hold the clevis and tighten the locknut against it.
19 Fit a new O-ring to the fluid reservoir hose elbow and fit the elbow to the master cylinder. Install the retaining screw and tighten it securely. Reconnect the fluid reservoir hose and secure with its clip.

Installation

20 Install the mounting bolts into the step guard and master cylinder and attach the assembly to the frame, tightening the bolts securely **(see illustration)**.

9.20 Install the mounting bolts through the step guard and the rear master cylinder and tighten them securely

1 Reservoir cap
2 Diaphragm plate
3 Rubber diaphragm
4 Fluid reservoir
5 Connecting hose
6 Elbow
7 O-ring
8 Cotter (split) pin
9 Clevis pin
10 Clevis
11 Dust boot
12 Snap-ring
13 Pushrod
14 Piston assembly
15 Spring

H30026

9.8 Exploded view of the rear brake master cylinder

7

9.22 Fit a new cotter (split) pin to the clevis pin

9.23 Align the hose so that it butts against the boss on the master cylinder

10.4 The metal linking pipe is mounted on the lower triple clamp (arrow)

21 Secure the master cylinder reservoir to the frame with its mounting bolt.

22 Align the brake pedal with the master cylinder clevis and slide in the clevis pin. Check the pedal height at this stage. If it requires adjusting, withdraw the clevis pin, slacken off the locknut and rotate the clevis on the pushrod threads. Tighten the locknut when the pedal height is as required. Install the clevis pin and secure it in position with a new cotter pin (split pin) **(see illustration)**.

23 Connect the brake hose banjo fitting to the top of the master cylinder, using a new sealing washer on each side of the fitting. Align the hose so that it butts against the boss on the master cylinder **(see illustration)**, and tighten the banjo union bolt to the torque setting specified at the beginning of this Chapter.

24 Fill the fluid reservoir with the specified fluid (see *Daily (pre-ride) checks*) and bleed the system following the procedure in Section 11.

25 Check the position of the brake pedal and adjust the brake light switch (see Chapter 1). Check the operation of the brake carefully before riding the bike.

10 Brake pipe and hoses - inspection and replacement

Inspection

1 Once a week, or if the motorcycle is used less frequently, before every ride, check the condition of the brake hoses.

2 Twist and flex the rubber hoses while looking for cracks, bulges and seeping fluid. Check extra carefully around the areas where the hoses connect with the banjo fittings, as these are common areas for hose failure.

3 Inspect the metal banjo union fittings connected to the brake hoses. If the fittings are rusted, scratched or cracked, replace them.

4 Inspect the metal pipe attached to the front of the lower triple clamp which links the two front brake hose unions **(see illustration)**. If the plating on the metal pipe is chipped or scratched, the lines may rust. If the fittings are

rusted, scratched or cracked, replace the pipe assembly.

Replacement

5 The brake hoses have banjo union fittings on each end of the hose. Cover the surrounding area with plenty of rags and unscrew the banjo bolt on each end of the hose. Detach the hose from any clips that may be present and remove the hose. Discard the sealing washers.

6 Position the new hose, making sure it isn't twisted or otherwise strained, between the two components. Make sure the metal tube portion of the banjo fitting is located adjacent to the boss on the component it connects to. Install the banjo bolts, using new sealing washers on both sides of the fittings, and tighten them to the torque setting specified at the beginning of this Chapter.

7 The metal pipe has a flare nut at each end, and can be removed once both nuts have been slackened. Apply a few drops of non-permanent locking compound to each of the flare nut threads then install the new pipe and tighten the flare nuts to the specified torque.

8 Flush the old brake fluid from the system, refill with the recommended fluid (see *Daily (pre-ride) checks*) and bleed the air from the system (see Section 11). Check the operation of the brakes carefully before riding the bike.

11 Brake system bleeding

1 Bleeding the brakes is simply the process of removing all the air bubbles from the brake fluid reservoirs, the hoses and the brake calipers. Bleeding is necessary whenever a brake system hydraulic connection is loosened, when a component or hose is replaced, or when the master cylinder or caliper is overhauled. Leaks in the system may also allow air to enter, but leaking brake fluid will reveal their presence and warn you of the need for repair.

2 To bleed the brakes, you will need some new, clean brake fluid of the recommended type (see Chapter 1), a length of clear vinyl or plastic tubing, a small container partially filled

with clean brake fluid, some rags and a wrench to fit the brake caliper bleed valves.

3 Cover the fuel tank and other painted components to prevent damage in the event that brake fluid is spilled.

4 Remove the reservoir cap or cover and slowly pump the brake lever or pedal a few times, until no air bubbles can be seen floating up from the holes at the bottom of the reservoir. Doing this bleeds the air from the master cylinder end of the line. Reinstall the reservoir cap or cover.

5 Attach one end of the clear vinyl or plastic tubing to the bleed valve and submerge the other end in the brake fluid in the container.

6 Remove the reservoir cap or cover and check the fluid level. Do not allow the fluid level to drop below the lower mark during the bleeding process. To top up the rear master cylinder reservoir, unscrew the retaining bolt and move the reservoir away from the frame for better access, taking care not to spill any fluid.

7 Carefully pump the brake lever or pedal three or four times and hold it in (front) or down (rear) while opening the caliper bleed valve. When the valve is opened, brake fluid will flow out of the caliper into the clear tubing and the lever will move toward the handlebar or the pedal will move down.

8 Retighten the bleed valve (note the torque setting in the Specifications of this Chapter), then release the brake lever or pedal gradually. Repeat the process until no air bubbles are visible in the brake fluid leaving the caliper and the lever or pedal is firm when applied. Disconnect the bleeding equipment and install the dust cap on the bleed valve.

9 Replace the rubber diaphragm, diaphragm plate and reservoir cap or cover, wipe up any spilled brake fluid and check the entire system for leaks.

 HAYNES HiNT *If it's not possible to produce a firm feel to the lever or pedal the fluid may be aerated. Let the brake fluid in the system stabilize for a few hours and then repeat the procedure when the tiny bubbles in the system have settled out.*

12.2 Use a dial indicator to measure wheel runout

A Radial runout   B Axial runout

12 Wheels - inspection and repair

1 In order to carry out a proper inspection of the wheels, it is necessary to support the bike with an auxiliary stand or hoist so that either wheel can be raised from the ground. Clean the wheels thoroughly to remove mud and dirt that may interfere with the inspection procedure or mask defects. Make a general check of the wheels and tires as described in Chapter 1.

2 With the bike on the auxiliary stand or hoist and the wheel to be inspected in the air, attach a dial indicator to the fork slider or the swingarm and position its stem against the side of the rim **(see illustration)**. Spin the wheel slowly and check the side-to-side (axial) runout of the rim, then compare your readings with the value listed in this Chapter's Specifications. In order to accurately check radial runout with the dial indicator, the wheel would have to be removed from the machine. With the axle clamped in a vice, the wheel can be rotated to check the runout.

3 An easier, though slightly less accurate, method is to attach a stiff wire pointer to the fork slider or the swingarm and position the end a fraction of an inch from the wheel (where the wheel and tire join). If the wheel is true, the distance from the pointer to the rim will be constant as the wheel is rotated. **Note:** *If wheel runout is excessive, check the wheel bearings very carefully before replacing the wheel.*

4 The wheels should also be visually inspected for cracks, flat spots on the rim and other damage. Since tubeless tires are fitted, look very closely for dents in the area where the tire bead contacts the rim. Dents in this area may prevent complete sealing of the tire

against the rim, which leads to deflation of the tire over a period of time.

5 If damage is evident, or if runout in either direction is excessive, the wheel will have to be replaced with a new one. Never attempt to repair a damaged cast aluminum wheel.

13 Wheels - alignment check

1 Misalignment of the wheels, which may be due to a cocked rear wheel or a bent frame or triple clamps, can cause strange and possibly serious handling problems. If the frame or triple clamps are at fault, repair by a frame specialist or replacement with new parts are the only alternatives.

2 To check the alignment you will need an assistant, a length of string or a perfectly straight piece of wood and a ruler graduated in 1/64 inch increments. A plumb bob or other suitable weight will also be required.

3 In order to make a proper check of the wheels it is necessary to support the bike in an upright position with the aid of an auxiliary stand. Measure the width of both tires at their widest points. Subtract the smaller measurement from the larger measurement, then divide the difference by two. The result is the amount of offset that should exist between the front and rear tires on both sides.

4 If a string is used, have your assistant hold one end of it about half way between the floor and the rear axle, touching the rear sidewall of the tire.

5 Run the other end of the string forward and pull it tight so that it is roughly parallel to the floor. Slowly bring the string into contact with the front sidewall of the rear tire, then turn the front wheel until it is parallel with the string. Measure the distance from the front tire sidewall to the string.

6 Repeat the procedure on the other side of the motorcycle. The distance from the front tire sidewall to the string should be equal on both sides.

7 As was previously pointed out, a perfectly straight length of wood may be substituted for the string. The procedure is the same.

8 If the distance between the string and tire is

greater on one side, or if the rear wheel appears to be cocked, refer to Chapter 6, *"Swingarm bearings - check"*, and make sure the swingarm is tight.

9 If the front-to-back alignment is correct, the wheels still may be out of alignment vertically.

10 Using the plumb bob, or other suitable weight, and a length of string, check the rear wheel to make sure it is vertical. To do this, hold the string against the tire upper sidewall and allow the weight to settle just off the floor. When the string touches both the upper and lower tire sidewalls and is perfectly straight, the wheel is vertical. If it is not, place thin spacers under one leg of the auxiliary stand.

11 Once the rear wheel is vertical, check the front wheel in the same manner. If both wheels are not perfectly vertical, the frame and/or major suspension components are bent.

14 Front wheel - removal and installation

Removal

1 In order to raise the front wheel off the ground it is necessary to use an auxiliary stand or hoist. Depending on the type of stand used it may also be necessary to raise the wheel by tying down the rear of the machine. If this is not possible, remove the fairing lower section (see Chapter 8) and the exhaust system (see Chapter 4) and place a floor jack, with a wood block on the jack head, under the engine and raise the jack to lift the wheel off the ground. Always make sure the bike is properly supported.

2 Unscrew both left and right reflector mounting bolts and remove the reflectors (US models only).

3 Unscrew both left and right brake caliper mounting bolts and slide the calipers off the discs. Support each caliper with a piece of wire or a bungee cord so that no strain is placed on the hydraulic hoses. Do not disconnect the brake hoses from the calipers.

4 Unscrew the speedometer cable retaining screw and detach the cable from its drive unit in the front wheel **(see illustrations)** (early models only).

14.4a Unscrew the retaining screw . . .

14.4b . . . and detach the speedometer cable from its drive unit

14.5 Remove the axle bolt and loosen the axle clamp bolts on both sides (arrows)

14.6 Withdraw the axle from the left side of the bike

14.10 Align the speedometer drive gear slots with the driveplate tabs (arrows) when fitting the speedometer drive to the wheel - early models

14.11 Do not omit the spacer from the right side of the wheel

5 Unscrew the front axle bolt then loosen the four axle clamp bolts **(see illustration)**.
6 Support the wheel, then withdraw the axle and carefully lower the wheel **(see illustration)**.
7 Remove the spacer from the right side of the wheel. Remove the speedometer drive (early models) or spacer (later models) from the left side.
Caution: Don't lay the wheel down and allow it to rest on one of the discs - the disc could become warped. Set the wheel on wood blocks so the disc doesn't support the weight of the wheel. Note: Do not operate the front brake lever with the wheel removed.
8 Check the axle for straightness by rolling it on a flat surface such as a piece of plate glass (if the axle is corroded first remove the corrosion using fine emery cloth). If the axle is at all bent, replace it.
9 Check the condition of the wheel bearings (see Section 16).

Installation

10 On early models, fit the speedometer drive to the wheel's left side, aligning its drive gear slots with the driveplate tabs **(see illustration)**. On later models install the spacer in the left side of the wheel.
11 Install the spacer in the right side of the wheel **(see illustration)**.
12 Maneuver the wheel into position. Note the arrow cast into the wheel showing its

correct direction of rotation **(see illustration)**. Apply a thin coat of grease to the axle.
13 Lift the wheel into position making sure the spacer(s) remains in place. On early models, position the speedometer drive lug against the rear of the lug on the fork slider **(see illustration)**.
14 Slide the axle into position from the left side. Note that the groove in the axle's head should align with the outside edge of the left fork. Tighten the left axle clamp bolts to the torque setting specified at the beginning of the Chapter.
15 Install the axle bolt and tighten it to the specified torque setting.
16 Install the brake calipers making sure the pads sit squarely on either side of the disc. Retain each caliper with two new mounting bolts and tighten them to the torque setting specified at the beginning of this Chapter. **Note:** *The mounting bolt threads contain a locking agent, necessitating that they be renewed if disturbed.*
17 On early models, connect the speedometer cable to the drive, aligning inner cable slot with the drive dog, and securely tighten its retaining screw.
18 Rest the front wheel on the ground and remove the auxiliary stand or hoist. Pump the front forks a few times to settle all components in position and tighten the right axle clamp bolts to the specified torque setting.
19 Using feeler gauges, check the clearance

between each brake disc and the caliper body **(see illustration)**. There should be at least 0.7 mm (0.028 in) clearance present on each side of the disc. If not, slacken the axle clamp bolts and push or pull the fork slider inwards or outwards (as applicable) until the required clearance is present. With the slider correctly positioned, tighten the clamp bolts to the specified torque.
20 Apply the front brake, pump the forks up and down several times and check for proper brake operation.
21 Install both left and right side reflectors and tighten the mounting bolts securely (US models only).

14.12 Note the arrow on the wheel which indicates the correct direction of normal rotation (arrow)

14.13 On early models, rotate the speedometer drive unit so that its lug abuts the rear of the fork slider lug (arrow)

14.19 Use a feeler gauge to check the caliper body-to-disc clearance

1 Caliper body
2 Disc
3 0.7 mm (0.028 in) clearance

15 Rear wheel -
removal and installation

Removal

1 Use an auxiliary stand or hoist to hold the bike upright and the rear wheel off the ground. Always make sure the bike is properly supported.

2 On US 1996 through 1999 models and UK T to X models, slacken the drive chain adjuster bolts. On all other models, slacken the drive chain adjuster locknuts and rotate the bolts so that their heads release pressure on the chain adjuster blocks.

3 Unscrew and remove the rear axle nut.

4 Support the wheel then slide out the axle from the left and lower the wheel to the ground.

5 Disengage the chain from the sprocket and remove the wheel from the swingarm. Note which spacer fits on which side of the wheel, and remove them from the wheel.

Caution: Do not lay the wheel down and allow it to rest on the disc or the sprocket - they could become warped. Set the wheel on wood blocks so the disc or the sprocket doesn't support the weight of the wheel. Do not operate the brake pedal with the wheel removed.

6 Check the axle for straightness by rolling it on a flat surface such as a piece of plate glass (if the axle is corroded, first remove the corrosion with fine emery cloth). If the axle is bent at all, replace it.

7 Check the condition of the wheel bearings (see Section 16).

Installation

8 Apply a thin coat of grease to the seal lips, then slide the spacers into their proper positions on both sides of the hub, noting that the left spacer is shouldered **(see illustration)**.

9 Apply a thin coat of grease to the axle and slide the axle into position through the left chain adjuster (US 1996 to 1999 models and UK T to X models) or adjuster block (all other models) **(see illustration)**.

10 Engage the drive chain with the sprocket and lift the wheel into position. Make sure both spacers remain in the wheel and the disc fits correctly in the caliper, with the brake pads sitting squarely on each side of the disc.

11 Slide the axle into position and fit the washer (US 1996 through 1999 models and UK T to X models) or right side chain adjuster block (all other models), and the axle nut, but do not tighten it yet **(see illustrations)**.

12 Adjust the chain slack as described in Chapter 1.

13 Tighten the axle nut to the specified torque setting.

14 Remove the auxiliary stand or hoist.

15 Operate the brake pedal several times to

15.8 Install the collared spacer into the left side of the rear wheel

15.9 Position the axle in the chain adjuster block in the left side of the swingarm

15.11a Fit the right side chain adjuster block . . .

15.11b . . . followed by the axle nut

bring the pads into contact with the disc. Check the operation of the rear brake carefully before riding the bike.

16 Wheel bearings - removal, inspection and installation

Front wheel bearings

Note: *Always replace the wheel bearings in pairs. Never replace the bearings individually. Avoid using a high pressure cleaner on the wheel bearing area.*

1 Remove the wheel as described in Section 14.

2 Set the wheel on blocks so as not to allow the weight of the wheel to rest on the brake discs.

3 Using a flat-bladed screwdriver, pry out the grease seal first from the right side of the wheel then from the left side **(see illustrations)**.

4 Withdraw the speedometer driveplate from the left side of the wheel (early models only).

5 Using a metal rod (preferably a brass drift punch) inserted through the center of the hub bearing, tap evenly around the inner race of the left side bearing to drive it from the hub

16.3a Exploded view of the front wheel and associated components

16.3b Prise out the grease seal using a flat-bladed screw driver

16.5 Drift the first wheel bearing out using a metal rod passed through from the opposite side of the wheel

16.10a Install the bearing with the marked or sealed side facing out . . .

16.10b . . . then drive the bearing squarely into the hub using a drift or socket which bears only on the bearing's outer race

16.11 Install the spacer into the wheel before fitting the other bearing

16.12 Fit the speedometer driveplate to the left side of the wheel, making sure its tangs are correctly seated in the hub slots (arrows) . . .

(see illustration). The bearing spacer will also come out.

6 Lay the wheel on its other side and remove the right side bearing using the same technique.

7 If the bearings are of the unsealed type or are only sealed on one side, clean them with a high flash-point solvent (one which won't leave any residue) and blow them dry with compressed air (don't let the bearings spin as you dry them). Apply a few drops of oil to the bearing. **Note:** *If the bearing is sealed on both sides don't attempt to clean it.*

8 Hold the outer race of the bearing and rotate the inner race - if the bearing doesn't

turn smoothly, has rough spots or is noisy, replace it with a new one.

9 If the bearing is good and can be re-used, wash it in solvent once again and dry it, then pack the bearing with high-quality wheel bearing grease.

10 Thoroughly clean the hub area of the wheel. Install the right side bearing into the recess in the hub, with the marked or sealed side facing out. Using a bearing driver or a socket large enough to contact the outer race of the bearing, drive it in until it's completely seated (see illustrations).

11 Turn the wheel over and install the bearing

spacer (see illustration). Unless the bearings are sealed on both sides, pack the remaining space no more than 2/3 full of high-melting point wheel bearing grease. Once the grease is packed in, drive the left side bearing into place as described above.

12 Fit the speedometer driveplate to the left side of the wheel on early models; ensure its locating tangs are correctly located in the hub slots (see illustration).

13 Install new grease seals, using a seal driver, large socket or a flat piece of wood to drive them into place (see illustrations).

16.13a . . . then press in a new grease seal . . .

16.13b . . . and drift squarely into position using a suitably sized drift or socket

16.15 Exploded view of the rear wheel and associated components

Labels on diagram:
DISK RETAINER BOLTS
RIGHT SPACER
RIGHT WHEEL BEARING
REAR WHEEL
RUBBER DAMPER
REAR SPROCKET COUPLING
SPROCKET NUT
GREASE SEAL
LEFT SPACER
SPACER
O-RING
BRAKE DISK
GREASE SEAL
LEFT WHEEL BEARING
SPROCKET COUPLING BEARING SHOULDERED SPACER
SPROCKET COUPLING BEARING
REAR SPROCKET
2070-7-16.16HAYNES

16.16 Remove the sprocket coupling ensuring the rubber dampers remain in position in the wheel

14 Clean off all grease from the brake discs using acetone or brake system cleaner then install the wheel as described in Section 14.

Sprocket coupling bearing

15 Remove the rear wheel as described in Section 15 and remove the shouldered spacer from the left side of the wheel **(see illustration)**.
16 Lift the sprocket coupling away from the wheel leaving the rubber dampers in position in the wheel **(see illustration)**.
17 Remove the shouldered spacer from the inside of the coupling bearing and pry out the grease seal from the outside of the coupling **(see illustrations)**.
18 Support the coupling on blocks of wood and drive out the bearing with a bearing driver or socket **(see illustration)**.
19 Inspect the bearing as described above in Steps 7 through 9.
20 Thoroughly clean the bearing recess then

install the bearing into the recess in the coupling, with the marked or sealed side facing out. Using a bearing driver or a socket large enough to contact the outer race of the bearing, drive it in until it's completely seated **(see illustration)**.

16.17a Remove the spacer from inside the coupling bearing . . .

21 Install a new grease seal, using a seal driver, large socket or a flat piece of wood to drive it into place. Fit the spacer to the inside of the bearing.
22 Apply a smear of grease to the hub O-ring and fit the sprocket coupling to the wheel **(see illustration)**.
23 Clean off all grease from the brake disc using acetone or brake system cleaner then install the wheel as described in Section 15.

Rear wheel bearings

Note: *Early model grease seals were prone to wear, allowing water into the wheel bearings. This effect is accelerated by using a high*

16.17b . . . then pry out the grease seal from the coupling

16.18 Support the coupling and drive the bearing out from the inside using a hammer and bearing driver or socket

16.20 Drive the new coupling bearing into position using a large tubular drift which bears only on the bearing's outer race

16.22 Ensure the hub O-ring is in position on the wheel and apply a smear of grease to it to aid installation

7

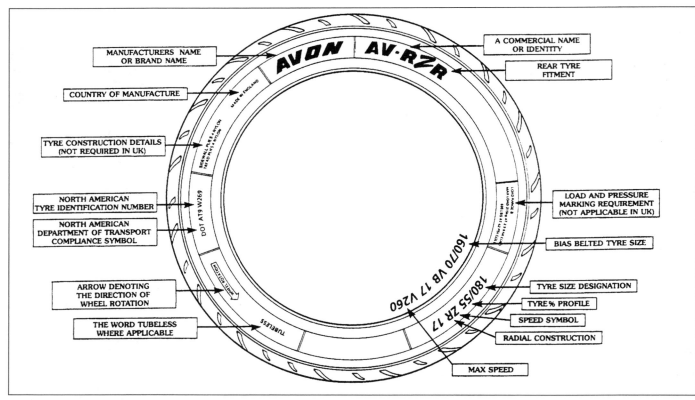

17.3 Common tire sidewall markings

pressure water cleaner directly on the rear wheel bearing area. New improved grease seals, spacers and bearings have been produced and should be used instead of the original parts when they are replaced. Always replace the wheel bearings in pairs. Never replace the bearings individually. Avoid using a high pressure cleaner on the wheel bearing area.

24 Remove the rear wheel as described in Section 15.

25 Lift the sprocket coupling away from the wheel leaving the rubber dampers in position in the wheel. Take care not to lose the spacer from inside the sprocket coupling.

26 Pry out the grease seal from the right side of the wheel.

27 Set the wheel on blocks so as not to allow the weight of the wheel to rest on the brake disc or sprocket.

28 Remove, inspect and install the bearings as described above in Steps 5 through 11.

29 Install a new grease seal to the right side of the wheel, using a seal driver, large socket or a flat piece of wood to drive it into place.

30 Install a new hub O-ring and smear it with grease **(see illustration 16.22)**. Fit the sprocket coupling to the wheel, making sure both the spacers are in position.

31 Clean off all grease from the brake disc using acetone or brake system cleaner then install the wheel as described in Section 15.

17 Tires - general information and fitting

General information

1 The wheels fitted to all models are designed to take tubeless tires only.

2 Refer to the Daily (pre-ride) checks listed at the beginning of this manual, and to the scheduled checks in Chapter 1 for tire and wheel maintenance.

Fitting new tires

3 When selecting new tires, refer to the tire information and the tire options listed in the owners handbook. Ensure that front and rear tire types are compatible, the correct size and correct speed rating; if necessary seek advice from a Honda dealer or tire fitting specialist **(see illustration)**.

4 It is recommended that tires are fitted by a motorcycle tire specialist rather than attempted in the home workshop. This is particularly relevant in the case of tubeless tires because the force required to break the seal between the wheel rim and tire bead is substantial, and is usually beyond the capabilities of an individual working with normal tire levers. Additionally, the specialist will be able to balance the wheels after tire fitting.

5 Only certain types of puncture repair are suitable for tubeless motorcycle tires. Refer to a tire fitting specialist for advice. If a tire has been repaired, Honda advise that you should not exceed 50 mph (80 kph) for the first 24 hours, and 80 mph (130 kph) thereafter.

Chapter 8
Fairing and bodywork

Contents

Degrees of difficulty

Easy, suitable for novice with little experience	Fairly easy, suitable for beginner with some experience	Fairly difficult, suitable for competent DIY mechanic	Difficult, suitable for experienced DIY mechanic	Very difficult, suitable for expert DIY or professional

1 General information

This Chapter covers the procedures necessary to remove and install the fairing and other body parts. Since many service and repair operations on these motorcycles require the removal of the fairing and/or other body parts, the procedures are grouped here and referred to from other Chapters.

In the case of damage to the fairing or other body parts, it is usually necessary to remove the broken component and replace it with a new (or used) one. The material that the fairing and other body parts are composed of doesn't lend itself to conventional repair techniques. There are however some shops that specialise in "plastic welding", so it may be worthwhile seeking the advice of one of these specialists before consigning an expensive component to the bin.

When attempting to remove any fairing section, first study it closely, noting any fasteners and associated fittings, to be sure of returning everything to its correct place on installation. In most cases the aid of an assistant will be required when removing sections, to help avoid the risk of damage to paintwork. Once the evident fasteners have

been removed, try to withdraw the section as described but DO NOT FORCE it - if it will not release, check that all fasteners have been removed and try again. Where a section engages another by means of tabs, be careful not to break the tab or its mating slot or to damage the paint work. Remember that a few moments of patience at this stage will save you a lot of money in replacing broken fairing sections!

Several types of fastener are used on the models covered here. Usually bolts or screws of varying sizes and head form are used, requiring flat-bladed or cross-head screwdrivers, or Allen wrenches. Most screw into nuts, trim nuts or threads in mounting brackets (as applicable) and are released by unscrewing them counterclockwise (anti-clockwise) in the usual way. Some small (usually cross-head) screws are threaded into plastic inserts, spreading the insert apart behind the section(s) to secure them; unscrew the screw and withdraw the insert to release it. Some types of clip, known as "quick screws" are used, which are released by turning them (either with a cross-head screwdriver or an Allen key, as appropriate) counterclockwise (anti-clockwise) through 90°; where their locations are known, this type are noted in the text, but otherwise their use will be self-evident on unscrewing them. Where trim clips are used, these are released

by pulling out the center pin, and fastened by pushing it in.

When installing a fairing section, first study it closely, noting any fasteners and associated fittings removed with it, to be sure of returning everything to its correct place. Check that all fasteners are in good condition, including all trim nuts or clips and damping/rubber mounts; any of these must be replaced if faulty before the section is reassembled. Check also that all mounting brackets are straight and repair or replace them if necessary before attempting to install the section. Where assistance was required to remove a section, make sure your assistant is on hand to install it.

Note that a small amount of lubricant (liquid soap or similar) applied to the mounting rubbers will assist the section retaining pegs to engage without the need for undue pressure. Carefully settle the section in place, following the specific instructions provided, and check that it engages correctly with its partners (where applicable) before tightening any of the fasteners. Where a section engages another by means of tabs, be careful not to break the tab or its mating slot or to damage the paint work.

Tighten the fasteners securely, but be careful not to overtighten any of them or the section may break (not always immediately) due to the uneven stress.

8

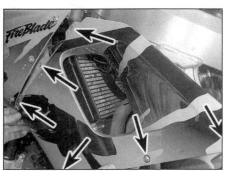

2.2a Undo the six "quick screws" to release each fairing middle section (arrows)

2 Fairing sections - removal and installation

Fairing middle sections

Removal

1 Remove the lower trim clip from the inner middle fairing panel.

2 Unscrew the six "quick screws" which secure the middle section to both the upper section and the lower section, noting the locations of the longer screws, then carefully remove the middle section, noting how it engages with both other panels **(see illustrations)**.

Installation

3 Installation is the reverse of removal. Make sure the longer "quick screws" are installed in their correct locations.

Fairing lower section

Removal

4 Remove the middle sections as described above.

5 The lower section can be removed as a single unit (see Step 8) or as independent halves (see Steps 6 and 7).

6 Unscrew the Allen bolt at the base of the assembly which secures both halves of the lower section to each other and to the inner panel **(see illustration)**.

7 Remove the fastener at the top left of the inner panel which secures it to the lower section half **(see illustration 2.9)**. Supporting the lower section half, unscrew the three Allen

bolts which secure it to the bike, and withdraw the section **(see illustrations)**.

8 To remove the entire lower fairing as an assembly, support the fairing from underneath then remove the three Allen bolts from each side which secure the assembly to the bike **(see illustrations 2.7a and 2.7b)** and lower it gently to the ground.

Installation

9 Installation is the reverse of removal. If the lower section components were separated, make sure the tabs of the inner panel engage correctly **(see illustration)**.

Fairing upper section

Removal

10 Remove both middle sections as described above.

11 Remove the rear view mirrors as described in Section 4.

12 Remove the fasteners from the left side upper fairing inner cover, carefully noting the positions of the various fasteners and collars (later models), and remove the cover **(see illustrations)**. On later models, also remove the trim clip to release the relay holder bracket

1 Middle fairing panel - right
2 Middle fairing panel - left
3 Lower fairing panel - right
4 Lower fairing panel - left
5 Inner lower fairing panel

H30030

FWD

2.2b Middle and lower fairing section assemblies

2.6 Remove the Allen bolt joining the two halves of the lower section together

2.7a Unscrew the two front bolts (arrows) . . .

2.7b . . . and single rear bolt (arrow) to free each side of the lower section

2.9 Lower section inner panel retaining screw location (A) and locating tabs (B)

2.12a Upper fairing section and associated components - US 1993 and 1994 models `and UK N and P models

1 Windshield	4 Upper stay	7 Inner cover - left	10 Lower stay
2 Rear view mirror	5 Wiring connector bracket	8 Inner middle panel - left	11 Upper fairing section
3 Rubber mounting	6 Inner cover - right	9 Inner middle panel - right	

8

2.12b Upper fairing section and associated components - US 1995 model and UK R and S models (later models similar)

1 Windshield	4 Upper stay	7 Inner cover - left	10 Inner middle panel - right
2 Rear view mirror	5 Wiring connector bracket	8 Relay bracket	11 Lower stay
3 Rubber mounting	6 Inner cover - right	9 Inner middle panel - left	12 Upper fairing section

from the fairing, noting how it fits **(see illustration)**.

13 Remove the fasteners from the right side

2.12c Release the relay holder bracket from the fairing, noting how it fits (arrows)

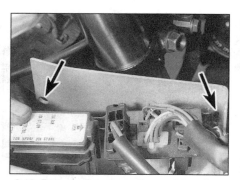

2.13 Release the connector and fuse box holder from the fairing, noting how it fits (arrows)

upper fairing inner cover, carefully noting the positions of the various fasteners and collars (later models), and remove the cover. Remove the trim clip to release the connector block holder and fuse box from the fairing, noting how they fit **(see illustration)**.

14 Trace the wiring back from each turn signal assembly and disconnect at the wiring connectors. Note the routing of the wires.

15 Disconnect the speedometer cable from the speedometer and release it from the guide in the fairing, noting its routing (early models only).

16 Disconnect the wiring plug from the rear of each headlight **(see illustration)**. Disconnect the sidelight wire connectors from the rear of each headlight on UK N and P models. On US 1995 through 1999 models

2.16 Disconnect the headlight connectors at the back of each headlight

and UK R to X models, disconnect the wiring connector to the separate sidelight unit.

17 Unscrew the bolt from the center of the front of the upper fairing and carefully remove the fairing from the bike. Note how the pegs on the rear of the headlight assembly locate in the rubbers on the lower fairing stay.

18 To separate the inner middle panels from the upper fairing, remove the turn signal assemblies (see Chapter 9), then withdraw the trim clips which fasten the panels to the fairing **(see illustration)**.

Installation

19 Installation is the reverse of removal. Make sure the pegs on the headlight are correctly aligned with the rubbers on the fairing stay and that all cables and wires are correctly routed. Note how the upper fairing

2.18 Pull out the trim clips to detach the inner middle panels from the upper fairing assembly

2.19a Align the pegs on the headlight assembly with the rubber mounts on the lower fairing stay

2.19b The inner covers mountings fit between the upper and middle sections

3.2 Having removed the rear view mirrors, unscrew the four windshield fasteners (arrows)

inner covers fit between the upper and lower fairing sections and are secured together by the longer "quick screws" **(see illustrations)**. On completion check the headlight aim as described in Chapter 9.

3 Windshield - removal and installation

Removal

1 Remove both rear view mirrors as described in Section 4.

4.1a Pull back the rubber boot to reveal the bolts, then undo the nuts

2 Remove the four fasteners securing the windshield to the upper fairing assembly, noting how they fit **(see illustration)**. Carefully withdraw the windshield from between the fairing and the fairing stay at each mirror mount, then lift the windshield away from the bike. Take care not to lose the rubber mounting dampers fitted to each side of the fairing stay.

Installation

3 Installation is the reverse of removal. Make sure the fasteners are correctly and securely fitted.

4 Rear view mirrors - removal and installation

Removal

1 Peel back the rubber cover (where fitted) and undo the nuts from the two rear view mirror retaining bolts **(see illustration)**. Remove the rear view mirror along with its mounting plate and rubber, noting the order in which they fit **(see illustration)**.

Installation

2 Installation is the reverse of removal. Make sure the components are fitted in the correct order.

5 Fairing stay - removal and installation

Upper stay

Removal

1 Remove the upper fairing assembly as described in Section 2.
2 On US 1996 through 1999 models and UK T to X models the stay is mounted on the top of the frame just behind the steering stem and is secured by the fuel tank front mounting bolts. On all other models the stay is bolted to each side of the frame **(see illustration)**. Unscrew the two bolts which secure the upper fairing stay to the frame, then carefully lift the stay away from the bike. Note the exact position of all damping rubbers and collars so that they can be returned to their original locations on installation **(see illustration)**.

Installation

3 Installation is the reverse of removal.

Lower stay

Removal

4 Remove the upper fairing assembly as described in Section 2.

5.2a On US 1993 through 1995 models and UK N to S models, the upper stay is mounted to the frame either side of the steering head

4.1b Note the order of the damping components as the mirror is removed

5.2b Note the rubber dampers fitted to each mounting point of the stay

8

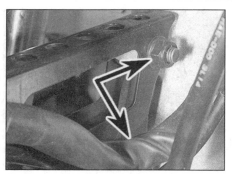

5.7 The lower stay is secured to the frame by two bolts (arrows)

6.2a The side covers are joined by two clips, one under the rider's seat . . .

6.2b . . . and one under the pillion seat

5 Remove the instrument cluster as described in Chapter 9.

6 Carefully note the correct routing of the wiring around the lower fairing stay, and release the wiring from any clips or ties.

7 Unscrew the lower stay mounting nuts and bolts, and remove the stay from the bike **(see illustration)**.

Installation

8 Installation is the reverse of removal. Make sure all the wiring is correctly routed and secured.

6 Side covers - removal and installation

Removal

1 Remove the rider's seat as described in Section 9, then open the passenger seat with the ignition key and swing it upright.

2 Remove the two joint clips which hold the two side covers together in the middle between the rider's seat and the pillion seat **(see illustrations)**.

3 Unscrew the side cover front mounting bolt **(see illustration)**.

4 Unscrew the side cover middle mounting bolt and collars, noting how they fit together **(see illustrations)**.

5 Support the side cover and unscrew the rear mounting screws. Carefully remove the side cover from the machine, noting how the slot in the rear of the cover fits into the tab on the top cover **(see illustrations)**.

Installation

6 Installation is the reverse of removal. Make sure the tab on the top cover fits correctly into the slot in the side cover, and take care not to break either.

6.3 Remove the side cover front mounting bolt . . .

6.4a . . . then the middle one . . .

6.4b . . . noting the arrangement of the collars

6.5a The rear of the side cover is secured by an upper screw . . .

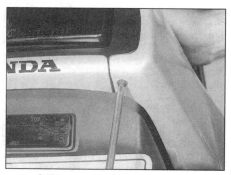

6.5b . . . and a lower screw . . .

6.5c . . . and slots into a tab on the top cover (arrow)

7.1 Note the position of the brake hose retainers

7.3a Take care not to lose the collars in the fender/mudguard mounting brackets (arrows) and note how they fit - early models

7.3b The brackets on the underside of the fender/mudguard are likely to bend and break if the mounting bolts are overtightened (arrows)

7 Front fender/mudguard - removal and installation

Removal

1 On US 1993 through 1995 models and UK N to S models, unscrew the front fender/mudguard mounting bolts (two on each side) noting the positions of the brake hose retainers on the rear mounts **(see illustration)**. Note the correct fitted position of the fender mounting brackets and, if necessary, remove them from the forks.

2 On US 1996 through 1999 models and UK T to X models, unscrew the front fender/mudguard mounting bolts (four on each side), noting the positions of the brake hose retainers on the rear mounts, and remove the fork covers. Note the correct fitted position of the fender mounting brackets (two on each side) and, if necessary, remove them from the forks.

3 Remove the fender/mudguard by withdrawing it forward from the bike. Note the two brackets on the underside of the fender/mudguard which join the mounting nuts, and take care not to lose them **(see illustrations)**.

Installation

4 Installation is the reverse of removal. Do not forget to position the brake hose retainers on the rear mounts, and take care not to overtighten the mounting bolts as this could cause the mounting nuts to rotate, breaking the bracket that joins them.

8 Rear fender/mudguard - removal and installation

Frame-mounted fender/mudguard
Removal

1 Remove the battery as described in Chapter 9.
2 Remove both side covers as described in Section 6.
3 Disconnect the wiring from the rear light assembly at the connector block, then unscrew the two rear light assembly mounting bolts and remove the assembly with the top cover attached.

4 Disconnect the wiring connectors from the rear turn signal assemblies.
5 Remove the rear shock absorber reservoir from its retaining clip on the right side of the frame and support it on the frame tube (see Chapter 6, if necessary). Do not disconnect the reservoir from its hose.
6 Unscrew the rear brake master cylinder reservoir mounting bolt and tie or support the reservoir in an upright position (see Chapter 7, if necessary). Do not disconnect the reservoir from its hose.
7 Disconnect the side stand switch wire connector, the fuel pump wire connector and the alternator wire connector, then unscrew the wire clamp from the fender/mudguard.
8 Remove the spark unit, fuel pump relay (where fitted) and starter relay from their mounting points on the rear fender/mudguard, leaving them connected to the harness and noting their locations and wiring routes. Disconnect the wiring connector from the regulator/rectifier mounted on the right side of the sub-frame, then remove the harness with the spark unit, fuel pump relay and starter relay attached.
9 Unscrew the two rear fender/mudguard mounting bolts located underneath the passenger seat rail at the rear of the sub-frame. Lower the fender/mudguard and carefully draw it back away from the machine, taking care not to snag any wiring.

Installation

10 Installation is the reverse of removal.

Make sure all wires are correctly reconnected and routed, and test the rear turn signals, rear light and brake light before riding the bike.

Swingarm-mounted fender/mudguard (where fitted)
Removal

11 Release the rear brake hose from its retaining clamp on the fender/mudguard.
12 Unscrew the drive chain guard retaining screws and remove the guard.
13 Unscrew the fender/mudguard retaining screws and carefully remove the fender/mudguard from the swingarm.

Installation

14 Installation is the reverse of removal. Make sure the brake hose is securely clamped in position.

9 Seat - removal and installation

Rider's seat
Removal

1 Unscrew the two mounting bolts located under the rear of the seat, then slide the seat back and up to release its locating hook, noting the location of the hook in its bracket **(see illustrations)**.

9.1a Pull back the rear corners of the rider's seat to access the mounting bolts

9.1b Note how the hook on the rider's seat (arrow) fits into the frame

8

Installation

2 Installation is the reverse of removal.

Passenger seat

Removal

3 Open the passenger seat with the ignition key and swing it upright.

4 Unhook the seat spring, noting how it fits, then unscrew the two seat mounting throughbolts and nuts and remove the seat from the bike **(see illustration)**.

5 To separate the seat from its mounting bracket, unscrew the two bolts which form the hinge between the seat and the bracket.

Installation

6 Installation is the reverse of removal. Make sure the spring is correctly located and that the seat moves freely on its hinges.

9.4 Unscrew the two bolts (arrows) to remove the passenger seat

Chapter 9
Electrical system

Contents

Degrees of difficulty

Easy, suitable for novice with little experience	Fairly easy, suitable for beginner with some experience	Fairly difficult, suitable for competent DIY mechanic	Difficult, suitable for experienced DIY mechanic	Very difficult, suitable for expert DIY or professional

Specifications

Battery

Capacity 12V, 8Ah

Alternator

Type . . . .   Three-phase
Output . . . .   445 watts at 5000 rpm
Charging voltage . . . .   13.0 to 15.5 volts @ 5000 rpm
Stator coil resistance . . . .   0.1 to 0.3 ohms @ 20°C (68°F)

Starter motor

Brush length
   New . . . .   12 to 13 mm (0.47 to 0.51 in)
   Service limit . . . .   4.5 mm (0.18 in)

Fuses

Main fuse (on starter relay) 30A
All other fuses (in fusebox) . . . .   4 x 10A and 1 x 20A*
See fusebox lid for circuits protected

9

Bulbs

Headlight
 US 1995 through 1999 models 12V 45/45W
 US 1993 and 1994 models and all UK models 12V 60/55W
Sidelight
 UK N and P models 12V 4W
 US 1995 through 1999 models and UK R to X models 12V 5W
Stop/taillight
 US models 12V 32/3cp
 UK models 12V 21/5W
Front turn signal/running lights
 US models 12V 32/2cp
 UK models 12V 21W
Instrument panel warning/illumination lights
 US 1998 and 1999 models and UK W and X models 12V 1.1W
 All other models 12V 1.7W
License plate light - US models only 12V 4cp

Torque settings

	Nm	ft-lbs
Ignition (main) switch bolts	24	17
Neutral switch	12	9
Oil pressure switch	12	9
Sidestand switch bolt	10	7
Alternator stator coil bolts	12	9

1 General information

The machines covered by this manual are equipped with a 12-volt electrical system. The components include a three-phase alternator and a regulator/rectifier unit.

The regulator/rectifier unit maintains the charging system output within the specified range to prevent overcharging and converts the ac (alternating current) output of the alternator to dc (direct current) to power the lights and other components and to charge the battery.

The starter motor is mounted to the crankcase behind the cylinders. The starting system includes the motor, the battery, the relay and the various wires and switches. If the engine stop switch (later models only) and the main key switch are both in the "Run" or "On" position, the circuit relay allows the starter motor to operate only if the transmission is in neutral (neutral switch on) or the clutch lever is pulled to the handlebar (clutch switch on) and the sidestand is up (sidestand switch on) **(see illustration)**.

Note: *Keep in mind that electrical parts, once purchased, can't be returned. To avoid unnecessary expense, make very sure the faulty component has been positively identified before buying a replacement part.*

2 Electrical Fault Finding

 Warning: To prevent the risk of short circuits, the ignition (main) switch must always be "OFF" and the battery negative (-) cable should be disconnected before any of the bike's other electrical components are disturbed. Don't forget to reconnect the cable securely once work is finished or if battery power is needed for circuit testing.

1 A typical electrical circuit consists of an electrical component, the switches, relays, etc. related to that component and the wiring and connectors that hook the component to both the battery and the frame. To aid in locating a problem in any electrical circuit, refer to the wiring diagrams at the end of this Chapter.

2 Before tackling any troublesome electrical circuit, first study the wiring diagram (see end of Chapter) thoroughly to get a complete picture of what makes up that individual circuit. Trouble spots, for instance, can often be narrowed down by noting if other components related to that circuit are operating properly or not. If several components or circuits fail at one time, chances are the fault lies in the fuse or earth connection, as several circuits often are

1.1 Starter circuit diagram (early model shown, later models similar)

Bl	*Black*	*G/R*	*Green and red*	*R/Bl*	*Red and black*
Bl/Br	*Black and brown*	*Lg/R*	*Light green and red*	*Y/Bl*	*Yellow and black*
G/W	*Green and white*	*R*	*Red*	*Y/R*	*Yellow and red*

3.2a Unhook the battery retaining strap to release the battery . . .

3.2b . . . and lift the battery out of its holder

routed through the same fuse and earth connections.

3 Electrical problems often stem from simple causes, such as loose or corroded connections or a blown fuse. Prior to any electrical Fault Finding, always visually check the condition of the fuse, wires and connections in the problem circuit. Intermittent failures can be especially frustrating, since you can't always duplicate the failure when it's convenient to test. In such situations, a good practice is to clean all connections in the affected circuit, whether or not they appear to be good. All of the connections and wires should also be wiggled to check for looseness which can cause intermittent failure.

4 If testing instruments are going to be utilised, use the wiring diagram to plan where you will make the necessary connections in order to accurately pinpoint the trouble spot.

5 The basic tools needed for electrical fault finding include a battery and bulb test circuit, a continuity tester, a test light, and a jumper wire. A multimeter capable of reading volts, ohms and amps is also very useful as an alternative to the above, and is necessary for performing more extensive tests and checks. Full details on the use of this test equipment are given in the *Fault Finding Equipment* section at the end of the manual.

3 Battery - inspection and maintenance

1 The battery fitted to the models covered in this manual is of the maintenance free (sealed) type and therefore requires no maintenance as such. However, the following checks should still be regularly performed.

2 Remove the rider's seat (see Chapter 8) to gain access to the battery. Disconnect the battery leads as described below and unhook the battery retaining strap **(see illustration)**. Lift the battery out of its holder **(see illustration)**.

3 Check the battery terminals and leads for tightness and corrosion. If corrosion is evident, disconnect the leads from the battery, disconnecting the negative (-) terminal first, and clean the terminals and lead ends with a wire brush or knife and emery paper. Reconnect the leads, connecting the negative (-) terminal last, and apply a thin coat of petroleum jelly to the connections to slow further corrosion.

4 The battery case should be kept clean to prevent current leakage, which can discharge the battery over a period of time (especially when it sits unused). Wash the outside of the case with a solution of baking soda and water. Rinse the battery thoroughly, then dry it.

5 Look for cracks in the case and replace the battery if any are found. If acid has been spilled on the frame or battery holder, neutralize it with a baking soda and water solution, dry it thoroughly, then touch up any damaged paint. Make sure the battery vent tube (if equipped) is directed away from the frame and is not kinked or pinched.

6 If the motorcycle sits unused for long periods of time, disconnect the cables from the battery terminals. Refer to Section 4 and charge the battery approximately once every month.

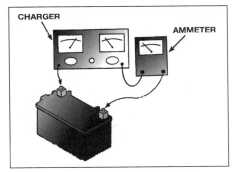

4.2 If the charger doesn't have an ammeter built in, connect one in series as shown; DO NOT connect the ammeter between the battery terminals or it will be ruined

7 The condition of the battery can be assessed by measuring the voltage present at the battery terminals. Connect the voltmeter positive (+) probe to the battery positive (+) terminal and the negative (-) probe to the battery negative (-) terminal. When fully charged there should be approximately 13 volts present. If the voltage falls below 12.3 volts the battery must be removed, disconnecting the negative (-) terminal first, and recharged as described below in Section 4.

4 Battery - charging

1 To charge the battery it is first necessary to remove it from the bike. To do this remove the rider's seat (see Chapter 8) then unhook the battery retaining strap **(see illustration 3.2a)**. Disconnect the leads from the battery, disconnecting the negative (-) terminal first, and lift the battery out of its holder **(see illustration 3.2b)**.

2 Honda recommend that the battery is charged at a rate of 0.9 amps for between 5 and 10 hours. Exceeding this figure can cause the battery to overheat, buckling the plates and rendering it useless. Few owners will have access to an expensive current controlled charger, so if a normal domestic charger is used check that after a possible initial peak, the charge rate falls to a safe level **(see illustration)**. If the battery becomes hot during charging **stop**. Further charging will cause damage. **Note:** *In emergencies Honda state that the battery can be charged at a rate of 4 amps for a period of 1 hour. However, this is not recommended and the low amp charge is by far the safer method of charging the battery.*

3 If the recharged battery discharges rapidly if left disconnected it is likely that an internal short caused by physical damage or sulphation has occurred. A new battery will be

5.2a The fusebox is located under the upper fairing right inner cover. Fuse locations and ratings are marked on the top of the fusebox lid

5.2b Unclip the fusebox lid to reveal the fuses

required. A sound item will tend to lose its charge at about 1% per day.

4 On installation, clean the battery terminals and lead ends with a wire brush or knife and emery paper. Reconnect the leads, connecting the negative (-) terminal last. Fit the battery retaining strap and install the rider's seat as described in Chapter 8.

> **HAYNES HINT** *Battery corrosion can be kept to a minimum by applying a layer of petroleum jelly to the terminals after the leads have been connected.*

5 Fuses - check and replacement

1 Most circuits are protected by fuses of different ratings. All fuses except the main fuse are located in the fusebox which is situated under the inner cover in the right side of the upper fairing. The main fuse is fitted to

5.3 A blown fuse can be identified by a break in its element

the top of the starter relay which is behind the right side cover **(see illustration 26.7)**. All fusebox fuses are labelled for easy identification.

2 To gain access to the fusebox, remove the fasteners securing the upper fairing right inner cover (see Chapter 8) then unclip and remove the fusebox lid **(see illustrations)**. To gain access to the main fuse remove the right side cover (see Chapter 8).

3 The fuses can be removed and checked visually. If you can't pull the fuse out with your fingertips, use a pair of needle-nose pliers. A blown fuse is easily identified by a break in the element **(see illustration)**. Each fuse is clearly marked with its rating and must only be replaced by a fuse of the correct rating.

Caution: Never put in a fuse of a higher rating or bridge the terminals with any other substitute, however temporary it may be. Serious damage may be done to the circuit, or a fire may start. Spare fuses of each rating are located in the fusebox, and a spare main fuse is clipped to the base of the starter relay. If the spare fuses are used, always replace them so that a spare fuse of each rating is carried on the bike at all times.

4 If a fuse blows, be sure to check the wiring circuit very carefully for evidence of a short-circuit. Look for bare wires and chafed, melted or burned insulation. If a fuse is replaced before the cause is located, the new fuse will blow immediately.

5 Occasionally a fuse will blow or cause an open-circuit for no obvious reason. Corrosion of the fuse ends and fusebox terminals may occur and cause poor fuse contact. If this happens, remove the corrosion with a wire brush or emery paper, then spray the fuse end and terminals with electrical contact cleaner.

6 Lighting system - check

1 The battery provides power for operation of the headlight, taillight, brake light, license plate light and instrument cluster lights. If none of the lights operate, always check battery voltage before proceeding. Low battery voltage indicates either a faulty battery or a defective charging system. Refer to Section 3 for battery checks and Sections 29 and 30 for charging system tests. Also, check the condition of the fuses and replace any blown fuses with new ones.

Headlight

2 If the headlight fails to work, check the fuse first with the key "ON" (see Section 5), then unplug the electrical connector for the headlight and use jumper wires to connect the bulb directly to the battery terminals. If the light comes on, the problem lies in the wiring or one of the switches in the circuit or the headlight relay. Refer to Section 18 for the switch testing procedures, and also the wiring diagrams at the end of this Chapter.

Taillight/license plate light

3 If the taillight fails to work, check the bulbs and the bulb terminals first, then the fuses, then check for battery voltage at the taillight electrical connector. If voltage is present, check the ground (earth) circuit for an open or poor connection.

4 If no voltage is indicated, check the wiring between the taillight and the ignition switch, then check the switch. On UK models, check the lighting switch as well.

Brake light

5 See Section 12 for the brake light switch checking procedure.

7.1 Disconnect the wiring connector from the headlight bulb and pull off the rubber cover

7.2a Press on the headlight bulb retaining clip to release it . . .

7.2b . . . then swing the clip away and remove the bulb

Neutral indicator light

6 If the neutral light fails to operate when the transmission is in neutral, check the fuses and the bulb (see Sections 5 and 15). If the bulb and fuses are in good condition, check for battery voltage at the connector attached to the neutral switch on the left side of the engine. If battery voltage is present, refer to Section 20 for the neutral switch check and replacement procedures.

7 If no voltage is indicated, check the wiring between the switch and the bulb for open-circuits and poor connections.

Oil pressure warning light

8 See Section 16 for the oil pressure switch check.

Sidestand switch warning light

9 If the sidestand light fails to operate when the stand is extended down, check the fuses and the bulb (see Sections 5 and 15). If the bulb and fuses are in good condition, refer to Section 21 for the sidestand switch check and replacement procedures.

10 If the switch is functioning correctly check for voltage at the switch wiring connector. If no voltage is indicated, check the wiring between the switch and the bulb for open-circuits and poor connections.

---

7 Headlight bulb and sidelight bulb - replacement

Note: The headlight bulb is of the quartz-halogen type. Do not touch the bulb glass as skin acids will shorten the bulb's service life. If the bulb is accidentally touched, it should be wiped carefully when cold with a rag soaked in stoddard solvent (methylated spirit) and dried before fitting. Allow the bulb time to cool before removing it if the headlight has been extinguished.

⚠️ **Warning: Allow the bulb time to cool before removing it if the headlight has been used.**

Headlight

1 Disconnect the wiring connector from the headlight bulb and remove the rubber dust cover **(see illustration)**.

2 Release the bulb retaining clip and swing it away, then remove the bulb **(see illustrations)**.

3 Fit the new bulb, bearing in mind the information in the note and warning at the start of this Section and secure it in position with the retaining clip.

---

4 Install the dust cover, making sure it is correctly seated and with the "TOP" mark facing up **(see illustration)**.

5 Reconnect the wiring connector and check the operation of the headlight.

Sidelight

UK N and P models

6 Pull the bulbholder out from the base of the headlight. Push the bulb inwards and twist it anti-clockwise to release it from the bulbholder. If the socket contacts are dirty or corroded, they should be scraped clean and sprayed with electrical contact cleaner before the new bulb is installed.

7 Install the new bulb in the bulbholder by pressing it in and twisting it clockwise. Press the bulbholder back into the headlight.

8 Check the operation of the sidelight.

US 1995 through 1999 models and UK R to X models

9 Unscrew the two sidelight lens retaining screws and remove the lens **(see illustration)**.

10 Pull the bulb out of the bulbholder **(see illustration)**. If the socket contacts are dirty or corroded, they should be scraped clean and sprayed with electrical contact cleaner before the new bulb is installed.

11 Carefully push the new bulb into the bulbholder.

12 Check the lens seal before fitting the lens, and replace it if damaged. Fit the lens and

---

HAYNES HINT *If the socket contacts are dirty or corroded, scrape them clean and spray them with electrical contact cleaner before a new bulb is installed.*

7.4 Install the dust cover with the "TOP" mark facing up (arrow)

7.9 Unscrew the two lens retaining screws to gain access to the sidelight bulb

7.10 Gently pull the sidelight bulb out of its holder

9

8.2 Unscrew the four screws (arrows) to release the headlight from the fairing - later model shown

install the retaining screws. Be careful not to overtighten the screws as the lens is easily damaged.

8 Headlight and sidelight - removal and installation

Headlight

Removal

1 Remove the upper fairing assembly as described in Chapter 8.
2 Unscrew the four headlight assembly retaining screws and remove the assembly from the fairing **(see illustration)**.

Installation

3 Make sure the headlight assembly is correctly seated then install the four retaining screws and washers (where fitted) and tighten them securely.
4 Install the upper fairing as described in Chapter 8.

Sidelight - US 1995 through 1999 models and UK R to X models

Removal

5 Remove the upper fairing assembly as described in Chapter 8.
6 Unscrew the two sidelight assembly

8.6 Unscrew the two screws (arrows) to release the sidelight from the fairing

retaining screws and remove the assembly from the fairing **(see illustration)**.

Installation

7 Make sure the sidelight assembly is correctly seated then install the two retaining screws and washers and tighten them securely.
8 Install the upper fairing as described in Chapter 8.

9 Turn signal, taillight and license plate bulbs - replacement

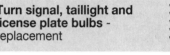

Turn signal bulbs

US 1996 through 1999 models and UK T to X models

1 Unscrew the turn signal lens retaining screw from the side of the turn signal and remove the lens.
2 Push the bulb into the holder and twist it counterclockwise (anti-clockwise) to remove it. Check the socket terminals for corrosion and clean them if necessary. Line up the pins of the new bulb with the slots in the socket, then push the bulb in and turn it clockwise until it locks into place. **Note:** *It is a good idea to use a paper towel or dry cloth when handling the new bulb to prevent injury if the bulb should break and to increase bulb life.* **Note:** *On US models, because the front turn signals double as running lights the offset pins can only be installed one way.*

9.4 Unscrew the lens retaining screw from the base of the turn signal

3 Install the lens back onto the turn signal and securely tighten the retaining screw.

All other models

4 Unscrew the turn signal lens retaining screw from the base of the turn signal and withdraw the lens **(see illustration)**.
5 Twist the bulbholder 90° in either direction to release it from the lens **(see illustration)**.
6 Push the bulb into the holder and twist it counterclockwise (anti-clockwise) to remove it **(see illustration)**. Check the socket terminals for corrosion and clean them if necessary. Line up the pins of the new bulb with the slots in the socket, then push the bulb in and turn it clockwise until it locks into place. **Note:** *It is a good idea to use a paper towel or dry cloth when handling the new bulb to prevent injury if the bulb should break and to increase bulb life.* **Note:** *On US models, because the front turn signals double as running lights the offset pins can only be installed one way.*
7 Fit the bulbholder to the lens and twist the bulbholder clockwise until it is locked into place.
8 Install the lens back into the turn signal and securely tighten the retaining screw.

Taillight bulbs

9 Unlock the passenger seat using the ignition key and swing the seat up.
10 Twist the relevant bulbholder counterclockwise (anti-clockwise) to release it from the taillight unit **(see illustration)**.

9.5 Release the bulbholder by twisting it 90° in either direction

9.6 To release the bulb gently push it into the bulbholder and twist it counterclockwise (anti-clockwise)

9.10 Twist the bulbholder counterclockwise (anti-clockwise) to release it from the taillight unit

9.11 Note the pins of the taillight bulb are offset (arrows); make sure they are correctly aligned on installation

11 Push the bulb into the holder and twist it counterclockwise (anti-clockwise) to remove it. Check the socket terminals for corrosion and clean them if necessary. Line up the pins of the new bulb with the slots in the socket, then push the bulb in and turn it clockwise until it locks into place **(see illustration)**. **Note:** *The pins on the bulb are offset so it can only be installed one way. It is a good idea to use a paper towel or dry cloth when handling the new bulb to prevent injury if the bulb should break and to increase bulb life.*
12 Install the bulbholder into the taillight unit and turn it clockwise until it is locked in place.
13 Swing the seat down into place and lock it.

License plate bulb - US models

14 Unbolt the license plate from the rear fender and ease it off the fender; if necessary disconnect the wiring under the passenger seat and pull it through the fender for improved access.
15 Unscrew the nuts from the lens holder studs and separate the license plate light components.
16 Push the bulb into the holder and twist it counterclockwise (anti-clockwise) to remove it. Check the socket terminals for corrosion and clean them if necessary. Line up the pins of the new bulb with the slots in the socket, then push the bulb in and turn it clockwise until it locks in place.
17 Install the license plate light components in a reverse of the removal sequence.

10.3 Unscrew the turn signal mounting nut and remove the collared backplate, noting how it fits

10.2 Disconnect the turn signal wiring at the connectors under the upper fairing inner cover

10 Turn signal assemblies - removal and installation

Front

Removal

1 Remove the upper fairing inner cover for the side you are working on (see Chapter 8).
2 Trace the turn signal wiring back from the turn signal and disconnect it at the connectors in the upper fairing **(see illustration)**.
3 Pull the wiring through from the fairing to the turn signal mounting, noting its routing, then unscrew the turn signal mounting nut. Remove the collared backplate, noting how it fits, then remove the turn signal from the fairing **(see illustration)**.

> **HAYNES HiNT** *When disconnecting wiring, label the connectors to avoid confusion on reconnection.*

Installation

4 Install the turn signal in the fairing, then fit the collared backplate and the nut, tightening it securely.
5 Feed the wiring through the hole in the inner fairing panel, then reconnect it at the connectors and install the upper fairing inner cover (see Chapter 8) **(see illustration)**.

10.5 Feed the wiring back through the hole in the fairing (arrow)

Rear

Removal

6 Unlock the passenger seat using the ignition key and swing the seat up.
7 Trace the wiring back from the turn signal and disconnect it at the connectors.
8 Unscrew the screw securing the turn signal assembly to the inside of the rear fender/mudguard, and remove it along with the collared backplate, noting how it fits.
9 Remove the turn signal from the fender/mudguard.

Installation

10 Install the turn signal in the rear fender/mudguard, then fit the collared backplate and the nut and tighten it securely.
11 Reconnect the wiring at the connectors, then swing the passenger seat down into place and lock it.

11 Turn signal circuit - check

1 The battery provides power for operation of the turn signal lights, so if they do not operate, always check the battery voltage first. Low battery voltage indicates either a faulty battery or a defective charging system. Refer to Section 3 for battery checks and Sections 29 and 30 for charging system tests. Also, check the fuses (see Section 5) and the switch (see Section 18).
2 Most turn signal problems are the result of a burned out bulb or corroded socket. This is especially true when the turn signals function properly in one direction, but fail to flash in the other direction. Check the bulbs and the sockets (see Section 9).
3 If the bulbs and sockets are good, check for power at the turn signal relay with the ignition "ON". The relay is mounted on the left side of the fairing mounting stay on early models, and at the front of the relay mounting bracket under the upper fairing left inner cover on later models **(see illustration)**. Refer to *wiring diagrams* at the end of the book to identify the power source terminal.

11.3 On later models the turn signal relay is mounted at the front of the relay mounting bracket under the upper fairing right inner cover (arrow)

4 If power is present, check the wiring between the relay and the turn signal lights (see the *wiring diagrams* at the end of this Chapter).
5 If the wiring is good, replace the turn signal relay.

12 Brake light switches - check and replacement

Circuit check

1 Before checking any electrical circuit, check the bulb (see Section 9) and fuses (see Section 5).
2 Using a test light connected to a good ground (earth), check for voltage at the brake light switch wiring connector (see Steps 8 and 9 for the rear brake light switch). If there's no voltage present, check the wire between the switch and the fusebox (see the *wiring diagrams* at the end of this Chapter).
3 If voltage is available, touch the probe of the test light to the other terminal of the switch, then pull the brake lever or depress the brake pedal. **Note:** *The wiring connector halves must be joined for this test and the probes inserted in the back of the connector.* If the test light doesn't light up, replace the switch.
4 If the test light does light, check the wiring between the switch and the brake lights (see the *wiring diagrams* at the end of this Chapter).

Switch replacement

Front brake lever switch

5 Remove the mounting screw and unplug the electrical connectors from the switch **(see illustration)**.
6 Detach the switch from the bottom of the front brake master cylinder.
7 Installation is the reverse of the removal procedure. The brake lever switch isn't adjustable.

Rear brake pedal switch

8 Remove the rider's seat as described in Chapter 8.

13.7 Maneuver the instrument cluster to gain access to the two wiring connectors and disconnect them

12.5 The front brake light switch (arrow) is mounted on the underside of the master cylinder

9 Trace the wiring back from the rear brake switch, located behind the rider's right footpeg bracket, and disconnect it at its wire connector. Work back along the wiring releasing it from any relevant clips and ties.
10 Unhook the spring from the switch and brake pedal and remove it from the bike.
11 Free the switch from the right footpeg bracket and remove it from the bike.
12 Install the switch by reversing the removal procedure, then adjust it by following the procedure described in Chapter 1.

13 Instrument cluster and speedometer cable/speed sensor - removal and installation

Instrument cluster

Removal

US 1993 and 1994 models and UK N and P models

1 Unscrew the speedometer cable retaining ring from the rear of the instrument cluster and detach the cable.
2 Disconnect the two instrument cluster wiring connectors.
3 Unscrew the two instrument cluster mounting bolts and remove the collars.
4 Carefully maneuver the instrument cluster away from the bike, noting the alignment of the bosses on the cluster with the rubber

13.10a Free the instrument cluster pegs from the lower mounting rubbers (arrows) . . .

13.6 Unscrew the instrument cluster mounting bolts and remove the collars

mounting grommets on the mounting bracket.
5 Inspect the cluster mounting dampers and mounting bracket grommets for signs of damage and replace if necessary.
US 1995 through 1997 models and UK R to V models
6 Unscrew the three cluster mounting bolts and remove the collars **(see illustration)**.
7 Carefully maneuver the instrument cluster out of position and disconnect the two cluster wiring connectors as they become accessible **(see illustration)**.
8 Remove the instrument cluster from the bike. Inspect the cluster mounting dampers for signs of damage and replace if necessary.
US 1998 and 1999 models and UK W and X models
9 Unscrew the instrument cluster mounting bolt and remove the collar from the rubber mounting.
10 Free the instrument cluster pegs from the lower mounting rubbers then disconnect the wiring connector and remove the instrument cluster from the bike **(see illustrations)**.
11 Inspect all mounting rubbers for signs of damage and replace if necessary.

Installation

US 1993 and 1994 models and UK N and P models
12 Maneuver the instrument cluster into position, aligning the bosses on the cluster with the rubber grommets on the mounting bracket.

13.10b . . . then disconnect the wiring connector

13.34 Disconnecting the speed sensor wiring connector

13.35 Unbolt the speed sensor from the top of the crankcase and remove it from the bike (O-ring arrowed)

13 Fit the collars to the cluster. Install the mounting bolts and tighten them securely.
14 Connect the cluster wiring connectors.
15 Connect the speedometer cable and securely tighten the retaining ring.

US 1995 through 1997 models and UK R to V models
16 Maneuver the instrument cluster into position and connect the cluster wiring connectors.
17 Fit the collars to the cluster, then install the mounting bolts and tighten them securely. US 1998 and 1999 models and UK W and X models
18 Make sure the mounting rubbers are all correctly fitted then reconnect the wiring connector to the instrument cluster.
19 Locate the cluster pegs in the lower mounting rubbers then install the collar and mounting bolt, tightening it securely.

Speedometer cable - US 1993 and 1994 models and UK N and P models

Removal
20 Unscrew the speedometer cable retaining ring from the rear of the instrument cluster and detach the cable.
21 Remove the screw securing the lower end of the cable to the drive unit on the wheel and detach the cable.
22 Free the cable from its retaining guide on the inner fairing panel and remove it from the bike, noting its correct routing.

Installation
23 Route the cable correctly and pass it through the guide on the inner fairing panel.
24 Align the inner cable slot at the lower end of the cable with the drive gear dog and connect the cable to the drive unit. Install the cable retaining screw and tighten it securely.
25 Connect the cable upper end to the instrument cluster and securely tighten the retaining ring.
26 Check that the cable doesn't restrict steering movement or interfere with any other components.

Speed sensor - US 1995 through 1997 models and UK R to V models

Removal
27 Remove the fuel tank as described in Chapter 4.
28 Trace the wiring back from the sensor to its connector on the right side of the frame. Disconnect the wiring connector and release the wiring, noting its correct routing, so its is free to be removed with the sensor.
29 Unscrew the mounting bolts and remove the sensor from the front sprocket cover **(see illustration 17.1 in Chapter 6)**.

Installation
30 Align the speed sensor drive gear with the front sprocket bolt and seat the sensor in the sprocket cover. Make sure the sensor is correctly seated then refit the retaining bolts and tighten securely.
31 Route the wiring correctly and securely reconnect the wiring connector.
32 Refit the fuel tank as described in Chapter 4.

Speed sensor - US 1998 and 1999 models and UK W and X models

Removal
33 Remove the fuel tank as described in Chapter 4.
34 Trace the wiring back from the sensor to its connector on the right side of the frame. Disconnect the wiring connector and release the wiring, noting its correct routing, so it is free to be removed with the sensor **(see illustration)**.
35 Wipe clean the area around the speed sensor then undo the retaining bolts and remove the sensor from the top of the crankcase **(see illustration)**. Remove the sensor O-ring and discard it. If the sensor is to be removed for some time, plug the crankcase aperture to prevent debris falling into it.

Installation
36 Ensure the sensor is clean and dry and fit the new O-ring to it.
37 Insert the sensor into the crankcase then screw in the retaining bolts and tighten them securely.
38 Route the sensor wiring correctly and securely reconnect the wiring connector.
39 Refit the fuel tank as described in Chapter 4.

14 Meters and gauges - check and replacement

Temperature gauge

Check
1 The temperature gauge check is described in Chapter 3.

Replacement - US 1993 through 1997 models and UK N to V models
2 Remove the instrument cluster from the bike as described in Section 13.
3 Unscrew the retaining screw from the center of the trip odometer knob and remove the knob **(see illustration)**.

14.3 Unscrew the retaining screw from the center of the trip odometer knob (arrow)

14.4a Rear view of instrument cluster - US 1993 and 1994 models, UK N and P models

1 Instrument lights
2 Warning lights
3 Temperature gauge wires
4 Tachometer wire
5 Speedometer drive gearbox

14.4b Rear view of instrument cluster - US 1995 through 1997 model, UK R to V models

1 Instrument lights
2 Warning lights
3 Tachometer wires
4 Temperature gauge wires
5 Speedometer wires

4 Unscrew the front cover retaining screws (early models have eight, later models have six) and remove the front cover. Note the position of the wiring clamp **(see illustrations)**.

5 Note the correct fitted position of the temperature gauge wires (the wiring color locations should be marked on the casing), then unscrew the wire retaining screws and detach the wires. The temperature gauge can now be removed from the casing.

6 Install the temperature gauge by reversing the removal sequence. Take care not to overtighten the retaining screws as the components are fragile and can be easily damaged.

Replacement - US 1998 and 1999 models and UK W and X models

Note: *The temperature gauge is an integral part of the instrument cluster printed circuit board.*

7 Remove the instrument cluster from the bike as described in Section 13.

8 Unscrew the seven retaining screws then lift the front cover off from the casing **(see illustrations)**.

9 Unscrew the screws securing the circuit board to the casing and separate the two **(see illustration)**.

10 Unscrew the speedometer and tachometer retaining screws and carefully ease them both away from the circuit board, taking care not to damage the wiring pins **(see illustration)**.

11 Install the circuit board by reversing the removal sequence. Make sure the speedometer and tachometer wiring pins are in good condition and all engage correctly and take care not to overtighten any retaining screws as the components are fragile and can easily be damaged.

14.8a Undo the retaining screws (arrows) . . .

14.8b . . . then lift off the instrument cluster front cover from the casing

14.9 Undo the screws (arrows) and separate the circuit board assembly from the casing

14.10 Tachometer retaining screws (A) and speedometer retaining screws (B)

Tachometer

Check

12 Disconnect the large wiring connector from the instrument cluster.

13 Remove the rider's seat as described in Chapter 8.

14 Disconnect the wiring connector from the ignition control module.

15 Using an ohmmeter or continuity tester, check for continuity between the yellow/green terminal on the instrument cluster 9-pin connector and the yellow/green terminal on the ignition control module connector. If no continuity is found, check the wiring between the connectors (see wiring diagrams at the end of the this Chapter), and repair or replace the wiring as necessary. If continuity is present but the tachometer does not work, then it is probably faulty. Before replacing the tachometer, however, take it to a Honda dealer for a more complete assessment using their specialized diagnostic equipment.

Replacement - US 1993 through 1997 models and UK N to V models

16 Carry out the operations described in Steps 2 to 4.

17 The tachometer on early models has one wire to it, whilst on later models there are two. Note the correct fitted position of the tachometer wires (the wiring color locations should be marked on the casing), then unscrew the wire retaining screws and detach the wires.

18 Unscrew the two tachometer retaining screws and lift the tachometer out of the casing.

19 Install the tachometer by reversing the removal sequence. Take care not to overtighten the retaining screws as the components are fragile and can be easily damaged.

Replacement - US 1998 and 1999 models and UK W and X models

20 Carry out the operations described in Steps 7 to 9.

21 Unscrew the tachometer retaining screws **(see illustration 14.10)** then carefully ease the tachometer away from the circuit board, taking care not to damage the wiring pins.

22 Install the tachometer by reversing the removal sequence. Make sure the wiring pins are in good condition and engage correctly with the circuit board and take care not to overtighten any retaining screws as the components are fragile and can easily be damaged.

Speedometer

Check - US 1993 and 1994 models and UK N and P models

23 Remove the cable as described in Section 13 and check its condition.

24 If the cable is in good condition, support the bike using an auxiliary stand or hoist so that the front wheel is off the ground. With the cable disconnected from the drive unit, spin the wheel and check that the drive unit gear spins, if not remove the front wheel and check the drive unit and driveplate (see Chapter 7, Section 14).

25 If both the cable and drive unit are in good condition then the speedometer itself must be faulty (either the speedometer head or the drive gearbox).

Check - US 1995 through 1999 models and UK R to X models

26 If the system malfunctions, first check that the battery is fully charged and that the terminals are clean, and that the wiring and fuses are in good condition.

27 To check the circuit, remove the fuel tank as described in Chapter 4, then trace the wiring back from the speed sensor to its connector on the right-hand side of the frame (see Section 13). Disconnect the connector and connect the positive (+) lead of a voltmeter to the black/brown terminal of the wiring harness side connector and the negative (-) lead to the green/black terminal of the connector. Switch ON the ignition and check that battery voltage (around 12 volts) is present at the connector. If no reading is obtained, check the wiring for continuity and make sure all the connectors are free from corrosion and are securely connected. Repair/replace the wiring as necessary and clean the connectors using electrical contact cleaner.

28 If battery voltage is present at the connector, reconnect the speed sensor connector then unbolt the instrument cluster from its mounting bracket (see Section 13). Support the bike using an auxiliary stand or hoist so that the rear wheel is off the ground.

29 On US 1995 through 1997 models and UK R to V models, connect the positive (+) lead of a voltmeter to the black/red (speedometer) terminal on the rear of the instrument cluster and the negative (-) lead to the green/black (speedometer) terminal of the cluster.

30 On US 1998 and 1999 models and UK W and X models, connect the positive (+) lead of a voltmeter to the pink/green terminal of the instrument cluster wiring connector and the negative (-) lead to the green/black terminal of the connector.

31 On all models, turn the ignition switch ON and, with the bike in neutral, rotate the rear wheel by hand. If the speed sensor is operating correctly, a fluctuating voltage reading between 0 to 5 volts should be measured, the rate of fluctuation depending on the speed at which the rear wheel is being rotated. If the reading obtained is correct, the speedometer itself must be faulty.

32 If no reading is obtained, check the wiring between the speedometer and speed sensor for continuity and make sure all the connectors are free from corrosion and are securely connected. Repair/replace the wiring as necessary and clean the connectors using electrical contact cleaner. If the wiring is in good condition the speed sensor is at fault and should be replaced (see Section 13).

Replacement - US 1993 and 1994 models and UK N and P models

33 Carry out the operations described in Steps 2 to 4.

34 Unscrew the three speedometer gearbox mounting screws and remove the gearbox.

35 Unscrew the speedometer retaining screws and lift the speedometer out of the casing.

36 Install the speedometer by reversing the removal sequence. Take care not to overtighten the retaining screws as the components are fragile and can be easily damaged.

Replacement - US 1995 through 1997 models and UK R to V models

37 Carry out the operations described in Steps 2 to 4.

38 Note the correct fitted position of the speedometer wires (the wiring color locations should be marked on the casing), then unscrew the wire retaining screws and detach the wires. The speedometer can now be removed from the casing.

39 Install the speedometer by reversing the removal sequence. Take care not to overtighten the retaining screws as the components are fragile and can be easily damaged.

Replacement - US 1998 and 1999 models and UK W and X models

40 Carry out the operations described in Steps 7 to 9.

41 Unscrew the speedometer retaining screws **(see illustration 14.10)** then carefully ease the speedometer away from the circuit board, taking care not to damage the wiring pins **(see illustration)**.

42 Install the speedometer by reversing the removal sequence. Make sure the wiring pins are in good condition and engage correctly with the circuit board and take care not to overtighten any retaining screws as the components are fragile and can easily be damaged.

14.41 Removing the speedometer assembly from the circuit board

9

15.2a Pull the relevant bulbholder out of the casing . . .

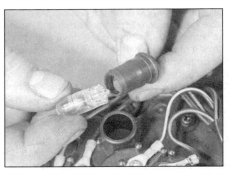

15.2b . . .and pull the bulb out of the bulbholder

15 Instrument and warning light bulbs - replacement

US 1993 through 1997 models and UK N to V models

1 Remove the instrument cluster as described in Section 13.

2 Pull the relevant bulbholder out of the back of the cluster then pull the bulb out of its holder (see illustrations). If the socket contacts are dirty or corroded, they should be scraped clean and sprayed with electrical contact cleaner before a new bulb is installed.

3 Carefully push the new bulb into position, then push the bulbholder back into the rear of the cluster.

4 Install the instrument cluster as described in Section 13.

US 1998 and 1999 models and UK W and X models

5 Remove the instrument cluster as described in Section 13.

6 Remove the rubber cap from the rear of the instrument cluster to gain access to the relevant bulb (see illustration).

7 Using a flat-bladed screwdriver, rotate the bulb 45° counterclockwise (anti-clockwise) and remove it from the instrument cluster.

8 Securely fit the new bulb to the cluster then refit the rubber cap.

9 Install the instrument cluster as described in Section 13.

15.6 Remove the rubber cap from the rear of the cluster . . .

16 Oil pressure switch - check and replacement

Check

1 The oil pressure warning light should come on when the ignition (main) switch is turned ON and extinguish a few seconds after the engine is started. If the oil pressure light comes on whilst the engine is running, stop the engine immediately and carry out an oil pressure check as described in Chapter 2.

2 If the oil pressure warning light does not come on when the ignition is turned on, check the bulb (see Section 15) and fuses (see Section 5).

3 Remove the fairing lower section (or lower section right half only) as described in Chapter 8 to gain access to the oil pressure switch; the switch is screwed into the crankcase just below the end cover (see illustration 17.3 in Chapter 2). Peel back the rubber cover, then undo the retaining screw and detach the wiring connector from the switch. With the ignition switched ON, ground (earth) the wire on the crankcase and check that the warning light comes on. If the light comes on, the switch is defective and must be replaced.

4 If the light still does not come on, check for voltage at the wire terminal using a test light. If there is no voltage present, check the wire between the switch, the instrument cluster and fusebox for continuity (see the *wiring diagrams* at the end of this Chapter).

5 If the warning light comes on whilst the

15.7 . . . then use a screwdriver to remove the bulb by rotating it 45° counterclockwise

engine is running, yet the oil pressure is satisfactory, remove the wire from the oil pressure switch as described in Step 3. With the wire detached and the ignition switched ON the light should be out. If it is illuminated, the wire between the switch and instrument cluster must be grounded (earthed) at some point. If the wiring checks out OK, the switch must be assumed faulty and replaced.

Replacement

6 Detach the wire from the switch as described above in Step 3.

7 Unscrew the switch from the crankcase and swiftly plug the hole to prevent the escape of oil.

8 Make sure the switch threads are clean and dry and apply a thin coat of suitable sealant to the end 3 to 4 mm of its threads.

9 Remove the plug and screw the switch into the crankcase, tightening it securely.

10 Attach the wire, tightening its retaining screw securely, then seat the rubber cover over the switch.

11 Check the operation of the oil pressure warning light, then install the fairing section as described in Chapter 8.

12 Check the oil level as described in Chapter 1 and top up if necessary.

17 Ignition (main) switch - check, removal and installation

Check

1 Remove the upper fairing right inner cover as described in Chapter 8. Trace the ignition (main) switch wiring back from the base of the switch, and disconnect it at the connector.

2 Using an ohmmeter or a continuity test light, check the continuity of the terminal pairs (see the *wiring diagrams* at the end of this Chapter). Continuity should exist between the terminals connected by a solid line on the diagram when the switch is in the indicated position.

3 If the switch fails any of the tests, replace it.

Removal

4 Remove the upper fairing right inner cover as described in Chapter 8. Trace the ignition (main) switch wiring back from the base of the switch, noting its routing and releasing it from

17.5 Unscrew the two Torx bolts (arrows) on the underside of the top triple clamp to release the ignition (main) switch

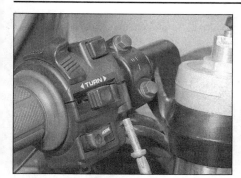

19.3 Unscrew the two left handlebar switch retaining screws

19.4 When installing the left switch, locate the peg on the switch (arrow) in the hole in the handlebar

19.6 Unscrew the two right handlebar switch retaining screws

any necessary retaining clips, and disconnect it at the connector.

5 Unscrew the two Torx bolts securing the switch to the underside of the top triple clamp and remove the switch from the bike **(see illustration)**.

Installation

6 Maneuver the switch assembly into position making sure the wiring is correctly routed.

7 Thoroughly clean the switch bolts and apply a few drops of non-permanent locking compound to their threads. Install the bolts and tighten them to the torque setting specified at the beginning of the Chapter.

8 Secure the switch wiring in position with any relevant clips or ties and reconnect it at the connector.

18 Handlebar switches - check

1 Generally speaking, the switches are reliable and trouble-free. Most troubles, when they do occur, are caused by dirty or corroded contacts, but wear and breakage of internal parts is a possibility that should not be overlooked. If breakage does occur, the entire switch and related wiring harness will have to be replaced with a new one, since individual parts are not usually available.

2 The switches can be checked for continuity

19.7 When installing the right switch, locate the peg on the switch (arrow) in the hole in the handlebar

using an ohmmeter or a continuity test light. Always disconnect the battery negative cable, which will prevent the possibility of a short circuit, before making the checks.

3 Trace the wiring harness of the switch in question back to its connector(s) which are clipped to the fairing under the right inner cover. Unplug the relevant electrical connector(s).

4 Using the ohmmeter or test light, check for continuity between the terminals of the switch harness with the switch in the various positions (see the *wiring diagrams* at the end of this Chapter).

5 If the continuity check indicates a problem exists, refer to Section 19, remove the switch and spray the switch contacts with electrical contact cleaner. If they are accessible, the contacts can be scraped clean with a knife or polished with crocus cloth. If switch components are damaged or broken, it will be obvious when the switch is disassembled.

19 Handlebar switches - removal and installation

Left handlebar switch
Removal

1 Trace the wiring harness back from the switch to the wiring connectors and unplug the relevant electrical connector.

20.2 The neutral switch is located below the front sprocket cover on the left side of the engine (arrow)

2 Work back along the harness, freeing it from all the relevant clips and ties, whilst noting its correct routing.

3 Unscrew the two switch retaining screws and remove the switch from the handlebar **(see illustration)**. Disconnect the two wires from the clutch switch.

Installation

4 Installation is a reversal of the removal procedure, making sure that the locating peg on the lower half of the switch is correctly located in the hole in the handlebar **(see illustration)**.

Right handlebar switch
Removal

5 Disconnect the switch wiring connectors as described in Steps 1 and 2 above. Disconnect the two wires from the brake light switch.

6 Unscrew the two switch retaining screws and remove the switch from the handlebar **(see illustration)**. On US 1996 through 1999 models and UK T to X models, remove the throttle cables and cable elbows from the switch (see Chapter 4 for details).

Installation

7 Installation is a reversal of the removal procedure, making sure that the locating peg on the lower half of the switch is correctly located in the hole in the handlebar **(see illustration)**. On US 1996 through 1999 models and UK T to X models, refer to Chapter 4 for details of throttle cable installation.

20 Neutral switch - check and replacement

Check

1 Before checking the electrical circuit, check the bulb (see Section 15) and fuses (see Section 5).

2 Remove the fairing lower section (or lower section left half only) as described in Chapter 8. The switch is screwed into the left side of the crankcase, below the front sprocket cover **(see illustration)**.

9

3 Disconnect the wiring connector from the switch and shift the transmission into neutral.
4 With the wire detached and the ignition switched ON, the neutral light should be out. If not, the wire between the switch and instrument cluster must be grounded (earthed) at some point.
5 Ground (earth) the wire on the crankcase and check that the neutral light comes on. If the light does come on, the switch is defective.
6 If the light does not come on when the wire is grounded (earthed), check for voltage at the wire terminal using a test light. If there's no voltage present, check the wire between the switch, the instrument cluster and fusebox (see the *wiring diagrams* at the end of this Chapter).

Replacement

7 Remove the fairing lower section (or lower section left half only) as described in Chapter 8.
8 Disconnect the wiring connector from the switch **(see illustration 20.2)**.
9 Unscrew the switch and remove it from the crankcase. Recover the sealing washer and plug the switch opening to minimise oil loss whilst the switch is removed.
10 Clean the threads of the switch and fit a new sealing washer to it.
11 Remove the plug from the crankcase and install the switch. Tighten the switch to the torque setting specified at the beginning of the Chapter, then reconnect the wiring connector.
12 Check the operation of the neutral light.
13 Check the oil level as described in Chapter 1 and top up if necessary.

21 Sidestand switch - check and replacement

Check

1 Before checking any electrical circuit, check the bulb (see Section 15) and fuses (see Section 5).
2 To gain access to the sidestand switch wiring connector remove the rider's seat as described in Chapter 8. Trace the wiring from the switch to its connector and disconnect it.
3 Check the operation of the switch using an ohmmeter or continuity test light.
4 Set the meter to the ohms x 1 scale and connect the meter to the yellow/black and green wires on the switch side of the wiring connector. With the sidestand down (extended) there should be continuity between the terminals, and with the stand up there should be no continuity (infinite resistance).
5 Connect the meter to the green/white and green wires on the switch side of the connector. With the sidestand up there should be continuity between the terminals, and with

the stand down there should be no continuity (infinite resistance).
6 If the switch does not perform as expected, it is defective and must be replaced.
7 If the switch is good, check the wiring between the wiring connector, instrument cluster and fusebox (see the *wiring diagrams* at the end of this book).

Replacement

8 Disconnect the switch wiring connector as described above in Step 2.
9 Work back along the switch wiring, freeing it from any relevant retaining clips and ties, noting its correct routing. Access to the wiring can be improved by removing the fairing lower section (or lower section left half only) as described in Chapter 8.
10 Unscrew the bolt securing the switch to the sidestand mounting bracket and remove the switch from the bike.
11 Fit the new switch to the rear of the sidestand bracket making sure the switch lug engages the hole in the sidestand, and the switch recess engages with the retaining pin **(see illustration)**. Install the switch retaining bolt and tighten it to the specified torque setting.
12 Make sure the wiring is correctly routed up to the connector and retained by all the necessary clips and ties.
13 Securely reconnect the wiring connector and check the operation of the switch and warning light as described in Chapter 1.
14 Install the rider's seat and, if removed, the fairing section as described in Chapter 8.

22 Clutch diode - check and replacement

1 On early (US 1993 through 1995 models and UK N to S models), the clutch diode is plugged into the main wiring harness clipped to the right-hand side of the frame. On later models (US 1996 through 1999 models and UK T to X models) the diode is housed in the fusebox. The diode is part of the starter safety circuit **(see illustration 1.1)** which prevents the starter motor operating whilst the transmission is in gear unless the clutch lever is pulled in. If the starter circuit is faulty, first check the fuses (see Section 5).
2 To gain access to the diode on early models, remove the fuel tank as described in Chapter 4. Remove the tape to free the diode from the wire harness, then unplug the diode **(see illustration)**. On later models open the fusebox lid (see Section 5) and unplug the diode.
3 Using an ohmmeter or a continuity test light, check for continuity between the terminals of the diode. Transpose the meter probes and check for continuity in the opposite direction. If the diode is serviceable there should be continuity in one direction

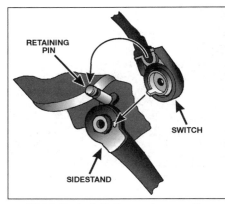

21.11 On installation make sure the sidestand switch lug engages the stand hole and the switch recess engages the retaining pin

(indicated by the arrow on the diode) and no continuity (infinite resistance) in the other. If not, the diode must be replaced.
4 If the diode is good, check the other components in the starter circuit (clutch switch, neutral switch and starter relay) as described in the relevant sections of this Chapter. If all components are good, check the wiring between the various components (see the *wiring diagrams* at the end of this book).
5 Plug the diode back into the harness and securely tape over it and around the surrounding harness wires. Install the fuel tank as described in Chapter 4.

23 Clutch switch - check and replacement

Check

1 The clutch switch is situated in the clutch lever mounting bracket. The switch is part of the starter safety circuit (see Section 1) which prevents the starter motor operating whilst the transmission is in gear unless the clutch lever is pulled in. If the starter circuit is faulty, first check the fuses (see Section 5).

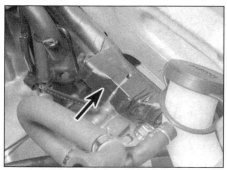

22.2 Clutch diode (arrow) is taped in wire harness on early models

23.2 The clutch switch (arrow) is mounted on the clutch lever bracket

2 To check the switch, disconnect the wiring connectors **(see illustration)**. Using an ohmmeter or a continuity test light, check for continuity between the terminals of the switch with the lever pulled into the handlebar, and no continuity (infinite resistance) with the lever released. If this is not the case, the switch is faulty and must be replaced.

3 If the switch is good, check the other components in the starter circuit (clutch diode, neutral switch and starter relay) as described in the relevant sections of this Chapter. If all components are good, check the wiring between the various components (see the *wiring diagrams* at the end of this book).

Replacement

4 Disconnect the wiring connectors from the clutch lever switch.
5 Slacken the upper adjuster to obtain maximum freeplay in the clutch cable then slacken and remove the clutch lever nut and pivot bolt.
6 Free the lever from the mounting bracket and remove the switch.
7 Install the new switch and fit the lever. Securely tighten the pivot bolt and nut then connect the switch wiring connectors.
8 Adjust the clutch cable as described in Chapter 1.

24 Horn -
check and replacement

Check

1 The horn is mounted on the underside of the lower triple clamp **(see illustration)**.
2 Unplug the wiring connectors from the horn. Using two jumper wires, apply battery voltage directly to the terminals on the horn. If the horn sounds, check the switch (see Section 18) and the wiring between the switch and the horn (see the *wiring diagrams* at the end of this Chapter).
3 If the horn doesn't sound, replace it.

Replacement

4 Unplug the wiring connectors from the horn

24.1 The horn is mounted to the underside of the lower triple clamp (arrow)

then unscrew the bolt securing the horn to its mounting bracket and remove it from the bike.
5 Connect the wiring connectors to the new horn and securely tighten its retaining bolt.

25 Fuel pump - US 1993 through 1995 models and UK N to S models

⚠ **Warning: Gasoline (petrol) is extremely flammable, so take extra precautions when you work on any part of the fuel system. Don't smoke or allow open flames or bare light bulbs near the work area, and don't work in a garage where a natural gas-type appliance (such as a water heater or clothes dryer) is present. If you spill any fuel on your skin, rinse it off immediately with soap and water. When you perform any kind of work on the fuel system, wear safety glasses and have a fire extinguisher suitable for a class B type fire (flammable liquids) on hand.**

Check

1 The fuel pump is located under the fuel tank and to the left of the coolant reservoir behind the engine. The fuel cut-off relay is located under the rider's seat behind the battery **(see illustrations)**.
2 The fuel pump is controlled through the fuel cut-off relay so that it runs whenever the ignition is switched ON and the ignition is operative (ie, only when the engine is turning

25.1a The fuel pump is located under the fuel tank

over). As soon as the ignition is killed, the relay will cut off the fuel pump's electrical supply (so that there is no risk of fuel being sprayed out under pressure in the event of an accident).
3 It should be possible to hear or feel the fuel pump running whenever the engine is turning over - either place your ear close beside the pump or feel it with your fingertips. If you can't hear or feel anything, check the circuit fuse (see Section 5). If the fuse is good, check the pump and relay for loose or corroded connections or physical damage and rectify as necessary.
4 If the circuit is fine so far, switch the ignition OFF, unplug the relay's wiring connector and connect across the relay's black and black/blue terminals with a short length of insulated jumper wire. Switch the ignition ON; the pump should operate.
5 If the pump now works, either the relay or its wiring is at fault. Test the wiring as follows.
6 Check for full battery voltage at the relay's black terminal with the ignition switch ON. If there is no battery voltage, there is a fault in the circuit between the relay and the fuse - turn off the ignition, then trace and rectify the fault as outlined in Section 2; refer to the wiring diagrams at the end of this Chapter.
7 Disconnect the wire connectors from the relay, fuel pump and ignition control module. Using an ohmmeter, check for continuity between the yellow/blue wire on the relay's wire connector and the yellow/blue wire on the control module's wire connector. Similarly, check for continuity between the blue/yellow wire on the relay's wire connector and the blue/yellow wire on the control module's wire connector. Check for continuity between the black/blue wire on the relay's wire connector and the black/blue wire on the fuel pump's wire connector. Continuity should be indicated in all tests; if not, trace and rectify the fault as described in Section 2. Reconnect all wire connectors.
8 If the pump still does not work, trace the wiring from the pump and disconnect it at the black 2-pin wiring connector. Using a fully charged 12 volt battery and two insulated jumper wires, connect the positive (+) terminal of the battery to the pump's black/blue terminal, and the negative (-) terminal of the

25.1b The fuel cut-off relay is located under the rider's seat

battery to the pump's green terminal. The pump should operate. If the pump does not operate it must be replaced.

9 If the pump works and all the relevant wiring and connectors are good, then the relay is at fault. The only definitive test of the relay is to substitute one that is known to be good. If substitution does not cure the problem, bear in mind that the ignition control module could be faulty.

10 If the pump operates but is thought to be delivering an insufficient amount of fuel, first check that the fuel tank breather hose is unobstructed (except California models), that all fuel hoses are in good condition and not pinched or trapped. Check that the fuel filters in the fuel tank and fuel delivery hose are not blocked.

11 The fuel pump's output can be checked as follows: make sure the ignition switch is OFF. Remove the rider's seat as described in Chapter 8 and the fuel tank as described in Chapter 4.

12 Disconnect the fuel hose from the carburetor T-piece **(see illustration 6.4a in Chapter 4)**.

13 Trace the wiring from the fuel pump and disconnect it at the fuel cut-off relay's 4-pin connector **(see illustration 25.1b)**. Using a short length of insulated jumper wire, connect across the black and the black/blue wire terminals of the connector **(see illustration)**.

14 Using a length of fuel hose from the fuel tank, or by using a dummy fuel tank, connect a fuel supply to the fuel filter. Place the fuel outlet hose end into a graduated beaker.

15 Turn the ignition switch ON and let fuel flow from the pump into the beaker for 5 seconds, then switch the ignition OFF.

16 Measure the amount of fuel that has flowed into the beaker, then multiply that amount by 12 to determine the fuel pump flow rate per minute. The minimum flow rate required is 900 cc (30.4 US fl oz, 31.7 Imp fl oz) per minute. If the flow rate recorded is below the minimum required, then the fuel pump must be replaced.

Removal

17 Make sure both the ignition and the fuel tap are switched OFF. Remove the rider's

25.19 Disconnect the two fuel hoses from the pump, noting which pipe fits on which nozzle

1 *Jumper wire*
2 *Relay 4-pin connector*
3 *Fuel outlet pipe*
4 *Graduated beaker*

H30033

25.13 Checking the fuel pump flow rate

seat as described in Chapter 8 and the fuel tank as described in Chapter 4.

18 Trace the wiring from the fuel pump and disconnect it at the black 2 pin connector.

19 Using a rag to mop up any spilled fuel, disconnect the two fuel hoses from the fuel pump, noting which pipe fits on which nozzle, then remove the pump with its rubber mounting sleeve from the mounting bracket, taking care not to snag the wiring **(see illustration)**.

20 To remove the fuel cut-off relay, disconnect its wiring connector and remove it from its mounting lug **(see illustration 25.1b)**.

Installation

21 Installation is a reverse of the removal procedure. Make sure the fuel hoses are correctly and securely fitted to the pump. Start the engine and look carefully for any signs of leaks at the pipe connections.

26 Starter relay - check and replacement

Check

1 If the starter circuit is faulty, first check the fuses (see Section 5). The starter relay is located behind the right side cover (see Chapter 8, if necessary).

2 With the ignition switch ON, the engine kill switch in RUN and the transmission in neutral, press the starter switch. The relay should click.

3 If the relay doesn't click, switch off the ignition and remove the relay as described below; test it as follows.

4 Set a multimeter to the ohms x 1 scale and connect it across the relay's starter motor and battery lead terminals. Using a fully-charged 12 volt battery and two insulated jumper wires, connect the positive (+) terminal of the battery to the yellow/red terminal of the relay, and the negative (-) terminal to the green/red terminal of the relay. At this point the relay should click and the multimeter read 0 ohms (continuity). If this is the case the relay is serviceable and the fault lies in the starter switch circuit (check the clutch diode, clutch switch and neutral switch as described elsewhere in this Chapter); if the relay does not click when battery voltage is applied and indicates no continuity across its terminals, it is faulty and must be replaced.

Replacement

5 Remove the seat and the right side cover as described in Chapter 8.

6 Disconnect the battery terminals, remembering to disconnect the negative (-) terminal first.

7 Unclip the red cover from the top of the relay, then unscrew the two Allen screws securing the starter motor and battery leads

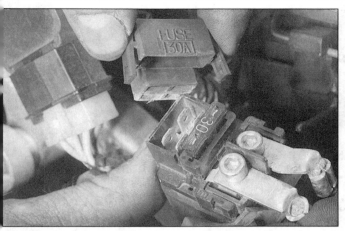

26.7 Unscrew the two Allen screws to free the starter motor and battery leads from the starter relay

27.3 Peel back the rubber cover, then unscrew the nut and disconnect the starter cable from the motor

to the relay and detach the leads **(see illustration)**.

8 Disconnect the relay wiring connector and remove the relay with its rubber sleeve from the mounting lugs.

9 Installation is the reverse of removal ensuring the terminal screws are securely tightened. Connect the negative (-) lead last when reconnecting the battery.

27 Starter motor - removal and installation

Removal

1 Remove the fuel tank as described in Chapter 4 and the fairing lower section (or lower section left half only) as described in Chapter 8.

2 Make sure the ignition is switched OFF and disconnect the battery negative (-) lead.

3 Peel back the rubber cover and unscrew the nut securing the starter cable to the motor **(see illustration)**.

4 Unscrew the starter motor retaining bolts, noting the correct fitted positions of the ground (earth) lead and wiring clamp **(see illustration)**.

5 Slide the starter motor out from the crankcase and remove it from the left side of the machine **(see illustration)**.

6 Remove the O-ring on the end of the starter motor and replace it.

Installation

7 Install a new O-ring on the end of the starter motor and ensure it is seated in its groove; apply a smear of engine oil to the O-ring to aid installation.

8 Maneuver the motor into position and slide it into the crankcase.

9 Fit the retaining bolts, making sure the wiring clip is correctly fitted underneath the front bolt and the ground (earth) lead

underneath the rear bolt, and tighten them securely.

10 Connect the cable and securely tighten its retaining nut. Make sure the rubber cover is correctly seated over the terminal.

11 Connect the battery negative lead.

12 Install the fuel tank as described in Chapter 4 and fairing section as described in Chapter 8.

28 Starter motor - disassembly, inspection and reassembly

Disassembly

1 Remove the starter motor as described in Section 27.

2 Make alignment marks between the housing and end covers **(see illustrations)**.

3 Unscrew the two long bolts then remove the rear cover from the motor along with its

27.4 Unscrew the starter motor retaining bolts, noting the correct fitted positions of the ground (earth) lead (A) and the wiring clip (B) . . .

27.5 . . . and maneuver the starter motor out from the left side of the frame

9

28.2a Exploded view of the starter motor

sealing ring. Discard the sealing ring as a new one must be used for reassembly. Remove the shim(s) from the rear end of the armature noting their correct fitted positions.

4 Remove the front cover from the motor along with its sealing ring. Discard the sealing ring as a new one must be used for reassembly. Recover the toothed washer from the cover and slide off the insulating washer and shim(s) from the front end of the armature, noting their correct fitted locations.

5 Withdraw the armature from the housing.

6 Noting the correct fitted location of each washer, unscrew the nut from the terminal bolt and remove the plain washer, the various insulating washers and the rubber ring **(see illustration)**. Withdraw the terminal bolt and brushplate assembly from the housing and recover the insulator.

7 Lift the brush springs and slide the brushes out from their holders **(see illustration)**.

Inspection

8 The parts of the starter motor that are most likely to require attention are the brushes.

Measure the length of the brushes and compare the results to the brush length listed in this Chapter's Specifications **(see illustration)**. If any of the brushes are worn beyond the service limit, replace the brushplate assembly with a new one. If the brushes are not worn excessively, nor cracked, chipped, or otherwise damaged, they may be re-used.

9 Inspect the commutator for scoring, scratches and discoloration **(see illustration)**. The commutator can be cleaned and polished

28.2b Make alignment marks between the housing and the end covers before disassembly

28.6 Unscrew the nut and remove the washers from the terminal bolt noting their correct fitted order

28.7 Lift the brush springs and slide the brushes out from their holders

28.8 Measuring brush length - replace brushes if they are worn beyond service limit

28.9 Inspect the commutator segments for wear and test as described in the text

28.14a Locate the insulator in the housing . . .

with crocus cloth, but do not use sandpaper or emery paper. After cleaning, wipe away any residue with a cloth soaked in electrical system cleaner or denatured alcohol.

10 Using an ohmmeter or a continuity test light, check for continuity between the commutator bars. Continuity should exist between each bar and all of the others. Also, check for continuity between the commutator bars and the armature shaft. There should be no continuity between the commutator and the shaft. If the checks indicate otherwise, the armature is defective.

11 Check the starter pinion gear for worn, cracked, chipped and broken teeth. If the gear is damaged or worn, replace the starter motor.

12 Inspect the insulating washers and front

cover dust seal for signs of damage and replace if necessary.

Reassembly

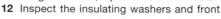

Lifting the end of the brush spring so that it is against the top of the brush holder and not pressing the brush inwards makes it much easier to install the armature.

13 Lift the brush springs and slide all the brushes back into position in their holders (see Haynes Hint).

14 Fit the insulator to the housing and install the brushplate. Insert the terminal bolt

through the brushplate and housing **(see illustrations)**.

15 Slide the rubber ring and small insulating washer(s) onto the bolt, followed by the large insulating washer(s) and the plain washer. Fit the nut to the terminal bolt and tighten it securely **(see illustrations)**.

16 Locate the brushplate assembly in the housing making sure its tab is correctly located in the housing slot **(see illustration)**.

17 Insert the armature in the front of the housing. If lifted, locate the spring ends onto the brushes and locate the brushes on the commutator bars. Check that each brush is securely pressed against the commutator by its spring and is free to move easily in its holder **(see illustrations)**.

28.14b . . . and install the brushplate assembly and terminal bolt

28.15a Slide the rubber ring onto the terminal bolt . . .

28.15b . . . followed by the insulating washers . . .

28.15c . . . and plain washer, fit the nut and tighten it securely

28.16 Make sure the brushplate tab (arrow) is correctly located in the housing slot

28.17a Insert the armature from the front of the housing . . .

9

28.17b . . . and locate the brushes on the commutator

28.18 Fit the toothed washer to the front cover so that its teeth engage with the cover ribs

28.19a Install the shims and washers on the front of the armature making sure they are fitted in the correct order

18 Fit the toothed washer to the front cover so that its teeth are correctly located with the cover ribs **(see illustration)**. Apply a smear of grease to the cover dust seal lip.

19 Slide the shim(s) onto the front end of the armature shaft then fit the insulating washer. Fit a new sealing ring to the housing and carefully slide the front cover into position, aligning the marks made on removal **(see illustrations)**.

20 Fit the shims to the rear of the armature shaft **(see illustration)**.

21 Ensure the brushplate inner tab is correctly located in the housing slot and fit a new sealing ring to the housing **(see illustration)**.

22 Align the rear cover groove with the brushplate outer tab and install the cover **(see illustration)**.

23 Check the marks made on removal are correctly aligned then fit the long bolts and tighten them securely **(see illustration)**.

24 Install the starter motor as described in Section 27.

28.19b Fit the sealing ring (arrow) and install the front cover

28.20 Fit the rear shims to the armature in the order noted on removal

29 Charging system testing - general information and precautions

1 If the performance of the charging system is suspect, the system as a whole should be checked first, followed by testing of the individual components (the alternator stator coils and the voltage regulator/rectifier). **Note:** *Before beginning the checks, make sure the battery is fully charged and that all system connections are clean and tight.*

2 Checking the output of the charging system and the performance of the various components within the charging system requires the use of a multimeter (with voltage, current and resistance checking facilities).

3 When making the checks, follow the procedures carefully to prevent incorrect connections or short circuits, as irreparable damage to electrical system components may result if short circuits occur.

4 If a multimeter is not available, the job of checking the charging system should be left to a Honda dealer.

30 Charging system - leakage and output test

1 If the charging system of the machine is thought to be faulty, remove the seat (see Chapter 8) and unhook the battery retaining strap. Perform the following checks.

Leakage test

2 Turn the ignition switch OFF and disconnect the lead from the battery negative (-) terminal.

3 Set the multimeter to the mA (milli Amps) function and connect its negative (-) probe to the battery negative (-) terminal, and positive

28.21 Make sure the brushplate tab is correctly located in the housing (arrow) . . .

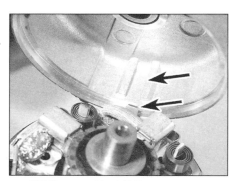

28.22 . . . and install the rear cover, aligning its groove with the brushplate outer tab (arrows)

28.23 Align the marks made on removal and install the starter motor bolts

30.3 Checking the charging system leakage rate, connect the meter as shown

(+) probe to the disconnected negative (-) lead **(see illustration)**. With the meter connected like this the reading should not exceed 0.1 mA.

4 If the reading exceeds the specified amount it is likely that there is a short circuit in the wiring. Thoroughly check the wiring between the various components (see the *wiring diagrams* at the end of this book).

5 If the reading is below the specified amount, the leakage rate is satisfactory. Disconnect the meter and connect the negative (-) lead to the battery, tightening it securely, Check the alternator output as described below.

Output test

6 Start the engine and warm it up to normal operating temperature.

7 Allow the engine to idle and connect a multimeter set to the 0-20 volts scale (voltmeter) across the terminals of the battery (positive (+) lead to battery positive (+) terminal, negative (-) lead to battery negative (-) terminal). Slowly increase the engine speed to 5000 rpm and note the reading obtained. At this speed the voltage should be 13.0 to 15.5 volts. If the voltage is below this it will be necessary to check the alternator and regulator as described in the following Sections. **Note:** *Occasionally the condition*

may arise where the charging voltage is excessive. This condition is almost certainly due to a faulty regulator/rectifier which should be tested as described in Section 32.

> **HAYNES HINT** *Clues to a faulty regulator are constantly blowing bulbs, with brightness varying considerably with engine speed, and battery overheating.*

31 Alternator stator coils - check and replacement

Check

1 Remove the rider's seat as described in Chapter 8 to gain access to the wiring connectors located in the rubber boot.

2 Disconnect the 3-pin block connector containing the yellow wires. Using a multimeter set to the ohms x 1 (ohmmeter) scale measure the resistance between each of the yellow wires on the alternator side of the connector, taking a total of three readings, then check for continuity between each terminal and ground (earth). If the stator coil windings are in good condition there should be no continuity (infinite resistance) between any of the terminals and ground (earth) and the three readings should be within the range shown in the Specifications at the start of this Chapter. If not, the alternator stator coil assembly is at fault and should be replaced. **Note:** *Before condemning the stator coils, check the fault is not due to damaged wiring between the connector and coils.*

Replacement

3 Remove the left crankcase end cover as described in Section 21 of Chapter 2. Discard the gasket as a new one must be used.

4 Unscrew the bolt and remove the wiring retaining clip from inside the cover **(see illustration)**.

5 Undo the four bolts and separate the stator coil assembly from the cover.

6 Remove all trace of sealant from the wiring grommet and apply a smear of fresh sealant to the grommet.

7 Clean the crankcase and bolt threads and apply a few drops of non-permanent locking compound to the stator retaining bolt threads. Fit the stator coil assembly to the cover and tighten the retaining bolts to the torque setting specified at the beginning of the Chapter.

8 Ensure the grommet is correctly seated in the casing then install the retaining clip and securely tighten its retaining screw.

9 Using a new gasket fit the cover to the engine as described in Section 21 of Chapter 2.

32 Regulator/rectifier unit - check and replacement

Check

1 Remove the right side cover (see Chapter 8) and disconnect the wiring connector from the regulator/rectifier unit **(see illustration)**.

2 Connect the negative (-) probe of the multimeter to a suitable ground (earth) point then switch the ignition switch ON and carry out the following checks.

3 Set the multimeter to the 0-20 dc volts setting then connect the meter positive (+) probe to the red/white terminal of the wiring connector and check for voltage. Full battery voltage should be present. Switch the ignition switch OFF.

4 Switch the multimeter to the resistance (ohms) scale. Check for continuity between the green terminal of the wiring connector and ground (earth) then check the resistance between the two yellow terminals of the wiring connector. There should be continuity between the green terminal and ground (earth) and a resistance reading of 0.1 to 0.3 ohms

31.4 Alternator stator coil retaining bolts (A) and wiring clip bolt (B)

32.1 The regulator/rectifier unit is secured to the frame behind the right side cover by two bolts

9

should be obtained between the two yellow terminals of the wiring connector.

5 If the above checks do not provide the expected results check the wiring between the battery, regulator/rectifier and alternator (see the *wiring diagrams* at the end of this book).

6 If the wiring checks out, the regulator/rectifier unit is probably faulty. Using a multimeter set to the appropriate resistance scale check the resistance between the various terminals of the regulator/rectifier **(see illustration)**. If the readings do not compare closely with those shown in the accompanying table, the regulator/rectifier unit can be considered faulty. **Note:** *The use of certain multimeters could lead to false readings being obtained. Therefore, if the above check shows the regulator/rectifier unit to be faulty take the unit to a Honda dealer for confirmation of its condition before replacing it.*

Replacement

7 Remove the right side cover (see Chapter 8).

8 Disconnect the wiring connector from the rectifier/regulator unit then unscrew the two bolts and remove the unit **(see illustration 32.1)**.

9 On installation, tighten the retaining bolts securely and connect the wiring connector. Install the side cover (see Chapter 8).

UNIT: KΩ

+ −	RED/ WHITE	YELLOW 1	YELLOW 2	YELLOW 3	GREEN
RED/WHITE		∞	∞	∞	∞
YELLOW 1	0.5-10		∞	∞	∞
YELLOW 2	0.5-10	∞		∞	∞
YELLOW 3	0.5-10	∞	∞		∞
GREEN	1-20	0.5-10	0.5-10	0.5-10	

32.6 Regulator/rectifier unit terminal identification and resistance readings

CBR900RR-N and CBR900RR-P UK models

C.J. TURK
H31010

9

CBR900RR-R and CBR900RR-S UK models

CBR900RR-T and CBR900RR-V UK models

C.J. TURK
H31012

9

CBR900RR-W and CBR900RR-X UK models

1993 and 1994 US models

US 1995 model

1996 and 1997 US models

9

Main fuse
Battery
Starter relay
Starter motor
30A
Ignition coils and spark plugs
3
2
4
1
Throttle position sensor
Rear brake switch
Rear right turn signal
Tail and brake lights
Licence light
Rear left turn signal
'99 models only
'98 models only
'99 models only
Sidestand switch
Down
Up
Alternator
C. J. TURK
H31527
Rectifier/ regulator
Pulse generator
Turn signal relay
Temp sensor
Neutral switch
Oil pressure switch
Ignition control module
Clutch diode
Fusebox
Fan motor 10A
Ignition, starter 10A
Horn, tail, side, meter 10A
Turn signal, brake lights 10A
Headlight, starter 20A
Cooling fan and switch
Front brake switch
Starter switch
Stop switch
Speed sensor
Ignition (main) switch
FAN IG BAT1 VC
ON
OFF
LOCK
Instrument cluster
Turn right (+)
Sensor (-)
(-)
(-)
Tachometer
Oil (-)
Neutral (-)
High beam (+)
Turn left (+)
Battery (+)
Illumination (+)
Speed
Ignition (+)
Temperature (-)
Horn
Horn switch
Dimmer switch
HL Lo HI
LO
N
HI
Turn signal switch
BAT3 PR PL
R
N
L
W R L
Clutch switch
'99 models only
'98 models only
LO
HI
Headlight relays
Headlights
Sidelight
'99 models only
'98 models only
Front right turn signal
Front left turn signal

1998 and 1999 US models

Dimensions and weights

Wheelbase
US models . . . . .1400 mm (55.1 in)
UK models . . . . .1405 mm (55.3 in)

Overall length
US models . . . . .2055 mm (81.0 in)
UK models
N to V models . . . . .2030 mm (80.0 in)
W and X models . . . . .2040 mm (80.3 in)

Overall width
US 1996 and 1997 models and UK T and V models . . . . . . .675 mm (26.6 in)
All other models . . . . .685 mm (27.0 in)

Overall height
US 1993 and 1994 models and UK N and P models . . . . . .1115 mm (44.0 in)
US 1995 through 1997 models and
  UK R to V models . . . . .1130 mm (44.5 in)
US 1998 and 1999 models and UK W and X models . . . . .1135 mm (44.7 in)

Seat height
US 1993 through 1995 models and UK N to S models . . . . .800 mm (31.5 in)
US 1996 through 1999 models and UK T to X models . . . . .810 mm (31.9 in)

Ground clearance
US 1993 through 1995 models and UK N to S models . . . . . .130 mm (5.1 in)
US 1996 through 1999 models and UK T to X models . . . . . .140 mm (5.5 in)

Weight (dry)
California models
  1993 through 1995 models . . . . .187 kg (412 lbs)
  1996 and 1997 models . . . . .186 kg (410 lbs)
  1998 and 1999 models . . . . .183 kg (403 lbs)
US models (except California)
  1993 through 1995 models . . . . .185 kg (408 lbs)
  1996 and 1997 models . . . . .183 kg (403 lbs)
  1998 and 1999 models . . . . .180 kg (397 lbs)
UK models
  N to S models . . . . .185 kg (408 lbs)
  T and V models . . . . .183 kg (403 lbs)
  W and X models . . . . .180 kg (397 lbs)

Weight (with oil and full fuel tank)
California models
  1993 through 1995 models . . . . .208 kg (458 lbs)
  1996 and 1997 models . . . . .207 kg (455 lbs)
  1998 and 1999 models . . . . .206 kg (454 lbs)
US models (except California)
  1993 through 1995 models . . . . .206 kg (454 lbs)
  1996 and 1997 models . . . . .205 kg (451 lbs)
  1998 and 1999 models . . . . .203 kg (448 lbs)
UK models
  N to S models . . . . .206 kg (454 lbs)
  T and V models . . . . .205 kg (451 lbs)
  W and X models . . . . .202 kg (445 lbs)

Buying tools

A toolkit is a fundamental requirement for servicing and repairing a motorcycle. Although there will be an initial expense in building up enough tools for servicing, this will soon be offset by the savings made by doing the job yourself. As experience and confidence grow, additional tools can be added to enable the repair and overhaul of the motorcycle. Many of the specialist tools are expensive and not often used so it may be preferable to hire them, or for a group of friends or motorcycle club to join in the purchase.

As a rule, it is better to buy more expensive, good quality tools. Cheaper tools are likely to wear out faster and need to be renewed more often, nullifying the original saving.

> **Warning: To avoid the risk of a poor quality tool breaking in use, causing injury or damage to the component being worked on, always aim to purchase tools which meet the relevant national safety standards.**

The following lists of tools do not represent the manufacturer's service tools, but serve as a guide to help the owner decide which tools are needed for this level of work. In addition, items such as an electric drill, hacksaw, files, soldering iron and a workbench equipped with a vice, may be needed. Although not classed as tools, a selection of bolts, screws, nuts, washers and pieces of tubing always come in useful.

For more information about tools, refer to the Haynes *Motorcycle Workshop Practice Manual* (Bk. No. 3470).

Manufacturer's service tools

Inevitably certain tasks require the use of a service tool. Where possible an alternative tool or method of approach is recommended, but sometimes there is no option if personal injury or damage to the component is to be avoided. Where required, service tools are referred to in the relevant procedure.

Service tools can usually only be purchased from a motorcycle dealer and are identified by a part number. Some of the commonly-used tools, such as rotor pullers, are available in aftermarket form from mail-order motorcycle tool and accessory suppliers.

Maintenance and minor repair tools

1 *Set of flat-bladed screwdrivers*
2 *Set of Phillips head screwdrivers*
3 *Combination open-end and ring spanners*
4 *Socket set (3/8 inch or 1/2 inch drive)*
5 *Set of Allen keys or bits*

6 *Set of Torx keys or bits*
7 *Pliers, cutters and self-locking grips (Mole grips)*
8 *Adjustable spanners*
9 *C-spanners*
10 *Tread depth gauge and tyre pressure gauge*

11 *Cable oiler clamp*
12 *Feeler gauges*
13 *Spark plug gap measuring tool*
14 *Spark plug spanner or deep plug sockets*
15 *Wire brush and emery paper*

16 *Calibrated syringe, measuring vessel and funnel*
17 *Oil filter adapters*
18 *Oil drainer can or tray*
19 *Pump type oil can*
20 *Grease gun*

21 *Straight-edge and steel rule*
22 *Continuity tester*
23 *Battery charger*
24 *Hydrometer (for battery specific gravity check)*
25 *Anti-freeze tester (for liquid-cooled engines)*

Repair and overhaul tools

1 *Torque wrench
   (small and mid-ranges)*
2 *Conventional, plastic or
   soft-faced hammers*
3 *Impact driver set*

4 *Vernier gauge*
5 *Circlip pliers (internal and
   external, or combination)*
6 *Set of cold chisels
   and punches*

7 *Selection of pullers*
8 *Breaker bars*
9 *Chain breaking/
   riveting tool set*

10 *Wire stripper and
    crimper tool*
11 *Multimeter (measures
    amps, volts and ohms)*
12 *Stroboscope (for
    dynamic timing checks)*

13 *Hose clamp
    (wingnut type shown)*
14 *Clutch holding tool*
15 *One-man brake/clutch
    bleeder kit*

Specialist tools

1 *Micrometers
   (external type)*
2 *Telescoping gauges*
3 *Dial gauge*

4 *Cylinder
   compression gauge*
5 *Vacuum gauges (left) or
   manometer (right)*
6 *Oil pressure gauge*

7 *Plastigauge kit*
8 *Valve spring compressor
   (4-stroke engines)*
9 *Piston pin drawbolt tool*

10 *Piston ring removal and
    installation tool*
11 *Piston ring clamp*
12 *Cylinder bore hone
    (stone type shown)*

13 *Stud extractor*
14 *Screw extractor set*
15 *Bearing driver set*

1 Workshop equipment and facilities

The workbench

● Work is made much easier by raising the bike up on a ramp - components are much more accessible if raised to waist level. The hydraulic or pneumatic types seen in the dealer's workshop are a sound investment if you undertake a lot of repairs or overhauls **(see illustration 1.1)**.

1.1 Hydraulic motorcycle ramp

● If raised off ground level, the bike must be supported on the ramp to avoid it falling. Most ramps incorporate a front wheel locating clamp which can be adjusted to suit different diameter wheels. When tightening the clamp, take care not to mark the wheel rim or damage the tyre - use wood blocks on each side to prevent this.

● Secure the bike to the ramp using tie-downs **(see illustration 1.2)**. If the bike has only a sidestand, and hence leans at a dangerous angle when raised, support the bike on an auxiliary stand.

1.2 Tie-downs are used around the passenger footrests to secure the bike

● Auxiliary (paddock) stands are widely available from mail order companies or motorcycle dealers and attach either to the wheel axle or swingarm pivot **(see illustration 1.3)**. If the motorcycle has a centrestand, you can support it under the crankcase to prevent it toppling whilst either wheel is removed **(see illustration 1.4)**.

1.3 This auxiliary stand attaches to the swingarm pivot

1.4 Always use a block of wood between the engine and jack head when supporting the engine in this way

Fumes and fire

● Refer to the Safety first! page at the beginning of the manual for full details. Make sure your workshop is equipped with a fire extinguisher suitable for fuel-related fires (Class B fire - flammable liquids) - it is not sufficient to have a water-filled extinguisher.

● Always ensure adequate ventilation is available. Unless an exhaust gas extraction system is available for use, ensure that the engine is run outside of the workshop.

● If working on the fuel system, make sure the workshop is ventilated to avoid a build-up of fumes. This applies equally to fume build-up when charging a battery. Do not smoke or allow anyone else to smoke in the workshop.

Fluids

● If you need to drain fuel from the tank, store it in an approved container marked as suitable for the storage of petrol (gasoline) **(see illustration 1.5)**. Do not store fuel in glass jars or bottles.

1.5 Use an approved can only for storing petrol (gasoline)

● Use proprietary engine degreasers or solvents which have a high flash-point, such as paraffin (kerosene), for cleaning off oil, grease and dirt - never use petrol (gasoline) for cleaning. Wear rubber gloves when handling solvent and engine degreaser. The fumes from certain solvents can be dangerous - always work in a well-ventilated area.

Dust, eye and hand protection

● Protect your lungs from inhalation of dust particles by wearing a filtering mask over the nose and mouth. Many frictional materials still contain asbestos which is dangerous to your health. Protect your eyes from spouts of liquid and sprung components by wearing a pair of protective goggles **(see illustration 1.6)**.

1.6 A fire extinguisher, goggles, mask and protective gloves should be at hand in the workshop

● Protect your hands from contact with solvents, fuel and oils by wearing rubber gloves. Alternatively apply a barrier cream to your hands before starting work. If handling hot components or fluids, wear suitable gloves to protect your hands from scalding and burns.

What to do with old fluids

● Old cleaning solvent, fuel, coolant and oils should not be poured down domestic drains or onto the ground. Package the fluid up in old oil containers, label it accordingly, and take it to a garage or disposal facility. Contact your local authority for location of such sites or ring the oil care hotline.

OIL CARE
FOLLOW THE CODE
OIL BANK LINE
0800 66 33 66

Note: It is antisocial and illegal to dump oil down the drain. To find the location of your local oil recycling bank, call this number free.

In the USA, note that any oil supplier must accept used oil for recycling.

2 Fasteners -
screws, bolts and nuts

Fastener types and applications

Bolts and screws

● Fastener head types are either of hexagonal, Torx or splined design, with internal and external versions of each type **(see illustrations 2.1 and 2.2)**; splined head fasteners are not in common use on motorcycles. The conventional slotted or Phillips head design is used for certain screws. Bolt or screw length is always measured from the underside of the head to the end of the item **(see illustration 2.11)**.

2.1 Internal hexagon/Allen (A), Torx (B) and splined (C) fasteners, with corresponding bits

2.2 External Torx (A), splined (B) and hexagon (C) fasteners, with corresponding sockets

● Certain fasteners on the motorcycle have a tensile marking on their heads, the higher the marking the stronger the fastener. High tensile fasteners generally carry a 10 or higher marking. Never replace a high tensile fastener with one of a lower tensile strength.

Washers **(see illustration 2.3)**

● Plain washers are used between a fastener head and a component to prevent damage to the component or to spread the load when torque is applied. Plain washers can also be used as spacers or shims in certain assemblies. Copper or aluminium plain washers are often used as sealing washers on drain plugs.

2.3 Plain washer (A), penny washer (B), spring washer (C) and serrated washer (D)

● The split-ring spring washer works by applying axial tension between the fastener head and component. If flattened, it is fatigued and must be renewed. If a plain (flat) washer is used on the fastener, position the spring washer between the fastener and the plain washer.

● Serrated star type washers dig into the fastener and component faces, preventing loosening. They are often used on electrical earth (ground) connections to the frame.

● Cone type washers (sometimes called Belleville) are conical and when tightened apply axial tension between the fastener head and component. They must be installed with the dished side against the component and often carry an OUTSIDE marking on their outer face. If flattened, they are fatigued and must be renewed.

● Tab washers are used to lock plain nuts or bolts on a shaft. A portion of the tab washer is bent up hard against one flat of the nut or bolt to prevent it loosening. Due to the tab washer being deformed in use, a new tab washer should be used every time it is disturbed.

● Wave washers are used to take up endfloat on a shaft. They provide light springing and prevent excessive side-to-side play of a component. Can be found on rocker arm shafts.

Nuts and split pins

● Conventional plain nuts are usually six-sided **(see illustration 2.4)**. They are sized by thread diameter and pitch. High tensile nuts carry a number on one end to denote their tensile strength.

2.4 Plain nut (A), shouldered locknut (B), nylon insert nut (C) and castellated nut (D)

● Self-locking nuts either have a nylon insert, or two spring metal tabs, or a shoulder which is staked into a groove in the shaft - their advantage over conventional plain nuts is a resistance to loosening due to vibration. The nylon insert type can be used a number of times, but must be renewed when the friction of the nylon insert is reduced, ie when the nut spins freely on the shaft. The spring tab type can be reused unless the tabs are damaged. The shouldered type must be renewed every time it is disturbed.

● Split pins (cotter pins) are used to lock a castellated nut to a shaft or to prevent slackening of a plain nut. Common applications are wheel axles and brake torque arms. Because the split pin arms are deformed to lock around the nut a new split pin must always be used on installation - always fit the correct size split pin which will fit snugly in the shaft hole. Make sure the split pin arms are correctly located around the nut **(see illustrations 2.5 and 2.6)**.

2.5 Bend split pin (cotter pin) arms as shown (arrows) to secure a castellated nut

2.6 Bend split pin (cotter pin) arms as shown to secure a plain nut

Caution: If the castellated nut slots do not align with the shaft hole after tightening to the torque setting, tighten the nut until the next slot aligns with the hole - never slacken the nut to align its slot.

● R-pins (shaped like the letter R), or slip pins as they are sometimes called, are sprung and can be reused if they are otherwise in good condition. Always install R-pins with their closed end facing forwards **(see illustration 2.7)**.

2.7 Correct fitting of R-pin. Arrow indicates forward direction

Circlips (see illustration 2.8)

● Circlips (sometimes called snap-rings) are used to retain components on a shaft or in a housing and have corresponding external or internal ears to permit removal. Parallel-sided (machined) circlips can be installed either way round in their groove, whereas stamped circlips (which have a chamfered edge on one face) must be installed with the chamfer facing away from the direction of thrust load **(see illustration 2.9)**.

2.8 External stamped circlip (A), internal stamped circlip (B), machined circlip (C) and wire circlip (D)

● Always use circlip pliers to remove and install circlips; expand or compress them just enough to remove them. After installation, rotate the circlip in its groove to ensure it is securely seated. If installing a circlip on a splined shaft, always align its opening with a shaft channel to ensure the circlip ends are well supported and unlikely to catch **(see illustration 2.10)**.

2.9 Correct fitting of a stamped circlip

THRUST LOAD

THRUST WASHER

SHARP EDGE

CHAMFERED EDGE

0650H

2.10 Align circlip opening with shaft channel

● Circlips can wear due to the thrust of components and become loose in their grooves, with the subsequent danger of becoming dislodged in operation. For this reason, renewal is advised every time a circlip is disturbed.

● Wire circlips are commonly used as piston pin retaining clips. If a removal tang is provided, long-nosed pliers can be used to dislodge them, otherwise careful use of a small flat-bladed screwdriver is necessary. Wire circlips should be renewed every time they are disturbed.

Thread diameter and pitch

● Diameter of a male thread (screw, bolt or stud) is the outside diameter of the threaded portion **(see illustration 2.11)**. Most motorcycle manufacturers use the ISO (International Standards Organisation) metric system expressed in millimetres, eg M6 refers to a 6 mm diameter thread. Sizing is the same for nuts, except that the thread diameter is measured across the valleys of the nut.

● Pitch is the distance between the peaks of the thread **(see illustration 2.11)**. It is expressed in millimetres, thus a common bolt size may be expressed as 6.0 x 1.0 mm (6 mm thread diameter and 1 mm pitch). Generally pitch increases in proportion to thread diameter, although there are always exceptions.

● Thread diameter and pitch are related for conventional fastener applications and the accompanying table can be used as a guide. Additionally, the AF (Across Flats), spanner or socket size dimension of the bolt or nut **(see illustration 2.11)** is linked to thread and pitch specification. Thread pitch can be measured with a thread gauge **(see illustration 2.12)**.

2.11 Fastener length (L), thread diameter (D), thread pitch (P) and head size (AF)

AF

L

D

P

2.12 Using a thread gauge to measure pitch

AF size	Thread diameter x pitch (mm)
8 mm	M5 x 0.8
8 mm	M6 x 1.0
10 mm	M6 x 1.0
12 mm	M8 x 1.25
14 mm	M10 x 1.25
17 mm	M12 x 1.25

● The threads of most fasteners are of the right-hand type, ie they are turned clockwise to tighten and anti-clockwise to loosen. The reverse situation applies to left-hand thread fasteners, which are turned anti-clockwise to tighten and clockwise to loosen. Left-hand threads are used where rotation of a component might loosen a conventional right-hand thread fastener.

Seized fasteners

● Corrosion of external fasteners due to water or reaction between two dissimilar metals can occur over a period of time. It will build up sooner in wet conditions or in countries where salt is used on the roads during the winter. If a fastener is severely corroded it is likely that normal methods of removal will fail and result in its head being ruined. When you attempt removal, the fastener thread should be heard to crack free and unscrew easily - if it doesn't, stop there before damaging something.

● A smart tap on the head of the fastener will often succeed in breaking free corrosion which has occurred in the threads **(see illustration 2.13)**.

● An aerosol penetrating fluid (such as WD-40) applied the night beforehand may work its way down into the thread and ease removal. Depending on the location, you may be able to make up a Plasticine well around the fastener head and fill it with penetrating fluid.

2.13 A sharp tap on the head of a fastener will often break free a corroded thread

● If you are working on an engine internal component, corrosion will most likely not be a problem due to the well lubricated environment. However, components can be very tight and an impact driver is a useful tool in freeing them **(see illustration 2.14)**.

2.14 Using an impact driver to free a fastener

● Where corrosion has occurred between dissimilar metals (eg steel and aluminium alloy), the application of heat to the fastener head will create a disproportionate expansion rate between the two metals and break the seizure caused by the corrosion. Whether heat can be applied depends on the location of the fastener - any surrounding components likely to be damaged must first be removed **(see illustration 2.15)**. Heat can be applied using a paint stripper heat gun or clothes iron, or by immersing the component in boiling water - wear protective gloves to prevent scalding or burns to the hands.

2.15 Using heat to free a seized fastener

● As a last resort, it is possible to use a hammer and cold chisel to work the fastener head unscrewed **(see illustration 2.16)**. This will damage the fastener, but more importantly extreme care must be taken not to damage the surrounding component.

Caution: Remember that the component being secured is generally of more value than the bolt, nut or screw - when the fastener is freed, do not unscrew it with force, instead work the fastener back and forth when resistance is felt to prevent thread damage.

2.16 Using a hammer and chisel to free a seized fastener

Broken fasteners and damaged heads

● If the shank of a broken bolt or screw is accessible you can grip it with self-locking grips. The knurled wheel type stud extractor tool or self-gripping stud puller tool is particularly useful for removing the long studs which screw into the cylinder mouth surface of the crankcase or bolts and screws from which the head has broken off **(see illustration 2.17)**. Studs can also be removed by locking two nuts together on the threaded end of the stud and using a spanner on the lower nut **(see illustration 2.18)**.

2.17 Using a stud extractor tool to remove a broken crankcase stud

2.18 Two nuts can be locked together to unscrew a stud from a component

● A bolt or screw which has broken off below or level with the casing must be extracted using a screw extractor set. Centre punch the fastener to centralise the drill bit, then drill a hole in the fastener **(see illustration 2.19)**. Select a drill bit which is approximately half to three-quarters the

2.19 When using a screw extractor, first drill a hole in the fastener . . .

diameter of the fastener and drill to a depth which will accommodate the extractor. Use the largest size extractor possible, but avoid leaving too small a wall thickness otherwise the extractor will merely force the fastener walls outwards wedging it in the casing thread.

● If a spiral type extractor is used, thread it anti-clockwise into the fastener. As it is screwed in, it will grip the fastener and unscrew it from the casing **(see illustration 2.20)**.

2.20 . . . then thread the extractor anti-clockwise into the fastener

● If a taper type extractor is used, tap it into the fastener so that it is firmly wedged in place. Unscrew the extractor (anti-clockwise) to draw the fastener out.

 Warning: Stud extractors are very hard and may break off in the fastener if care is not taken - ask an engineer about spark erosion if this happens.

● Alternatively, the broken bolt/screw can be drilled out and the hole retapped for an oversize bolt/screw or a diamond-section thread insert. It is essential that the drilling is carried out squarely and to the correct depth, otherwise the casing may be ruined - if in doubt, entrust the work to an engineer.

● Bolts and nuts with rounded corners cause the correct size spanner or socket to slip when force is applied. Of the types of spanner/socket available always use a six-point type rather than an eight or twelve-point type - better grip

2.21 Comparison of surface drive ring spanner (left) with 12-point type (right)

is obtained. Surface drive spanners grip the middle of the hex flats, rather than the corners, and are thus good in cases of damaged heads **(see illustration 2.21)**.

● Slotted-head or Phillips-head screws are often damaged by the use of the wrong size screwdriver. Allen-head and Torx-head screws are much less likely to sustain damage. If enough of the screw head is exposed you can use a hacksaw to cut a slot in its head and then use a conventional flat-bladed screwdriver to remove it. Alternatively use a hammer and cold chisel to tap the head of the fastener around to slacken it. Always replace damaged fasteners with new ones, preferably Torx or Allen-head type.

A dab of valve grinding compound between the screw head and screw-driver tip will often give a good grip.

Thread repair

● Threads (particularly those in aluminium alloy components) can be damaged by overtightening, being assembled with dirt in the threads, or from a component working loose and vibrating. Eventually the thread will fail completely, and it will be impossible to tighten the fastener.

● If a thread is damaged or clogged with old locking compound it can be renovated with a thread repair tool (thread chaser) **(see illustrations 2.22 and 2.23)**; special thread

2.22 A thread repair tool being used to correct an internal thread

2.23 A thread repair tool being used to correct an external thread

chasers are available for spark plug hole threads. The tool will not cut a new thread, but clean and true the original thread. Make sure that you use the correct diameter and pitch tool. Similarly, external threads can be cleaned up with a die or a thread restorer file **(see illustration 2.24)**.

2.24 Using a thread restorer file

● It is possible to drill out the old thread and retap the component to the next thread size. This will work where there is enough surrounding material and a new bolt or screw can be obtained. Sometimes, however, this is not possible - such as where the bolt/screw passes through another component which must also be suitably modified, also in cases where a spark plug or oil drain plug cannot be obtained in a larger diameter thread size.

● The diamond-section thread insert (often known by its popular trade name of Heli-Coil) is a simple and effective method of renewing the thread and retaining the original size. A kit can be purchased which contains the tap, insert and installing tool **(see illustration 2.25)**. Drill out the damaged thread with the size drill specified **(see illustration 2.26)**. Carefully retap the thread **(see illustration 2.27)**. Install the

2.25 Obtain a thread insert kit to suit the thread diameter and pitch required

2.26 To install a thread insert, first drill out the original thread . . .

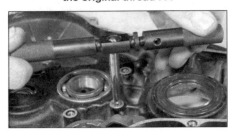

2.27 . . . tap a new thread . . .

2.28 . . . fit insert on the installing tool . . .

2.29 . . . and thread into the component . . .

2.30 . . . break off the tang when complete

insert on the installing tool and thread it slowly into place using a light downward pressure **(see illustrations 2.28 and 2.29)**. When positioned between a 1/4 and 1/2 turn below the surface withdraw the installing tool and use the break-off tool to press down on the tang, breaking it off **(see illustration 2.30)**.

● There are epoxy thread repair kits on the market which can rebuild stripped internal threads, although this repair should not be used on high load-bearing components.

Thread locking and sealing compounds

● Locking compounds are used in locations where the fastener is prone to loosening due to vibration or on important safety-related items which might cause loss of control of the motorcycle if they fail. It is also used where important fasteners cannot be secured by other means such as lockwashers or split pins.

● Before applying locking compound, make sure that the threads (internal and external) are clean and dry with all old compound removed. Select a compound to suit the component being secured - a non-permanent general locking and sealing type is suitable for most applications, but a high strength type is needed for permanent fixing of studs in castings. Apply a drop or two of the compound to the first few threads of the fastener, then thread it into place and tighten to the specified torque. Do not apply excessive thread locking compound otherwise the thread may be damaged on subsequent removal.

● Certain fasteners are impregnated with a dry film type coating of locking compound on their threads. Always renew this type of fastener if disturbed.

● Anti-seize compounds, such as copper-based greases, can be applied to protect threads from seizure due to extreme heat and corrosion. A common instance is spark plug threads and exhaust system fasteners.

3 Measuring tools and gauges

Feeler gauges

● Feeler gauges (or blades) are used for measuring small gaps and clearances **(see illustration 3.1)**. They can also be used to measure endfloat (sideplay) of a component on a shaft where access is not possible with a dial gauge.

● Feeler gauge sets should be treated with care and not bent or damaged. They are etched with their size on one face. Keep them clean and very lightly oiled to prevent corrosion build-up.

3.1 Feeler gauges are used for measuring small gaps and clearances - thickness is marked on one face of gauge

● When measuring a clearance, select a gauge which is a light sliding fit between the two components. You may need to use two gauges together to measure the clearance accurately.

Micrometers

● A micrometer is a precision tool capable of measuring to 0.01 or 0.001 of a millimetre. It should always be stored in its case and not in the general toolbox. It must be kept clean and never dropped, otherwise its frame or measuring anvils could be distorted resulting in inaccurate readings.

● External micrometers are used for measuring outside diameters of components and have many more applications than internal micrometers. Micrometers are available in different size ranges, eg 0 to 25 mm, 25 to 50 mm, and upwards in 25 mm steps; some large micrometers have interchangeable anvils to allow a range of measurements to be taken. Generally the largest precision measurement you are likely to take on a motorcycle is the piston diameter.

● Internal micrometers (or bore micrometers) are used for measuring inside diameters, such as valve guides and cylinder bores. Telescoping gauges and small hole gauges are used in conjunction with an external micrometer, whereas the more expensive internal micrometers have their own measuring device.

External micrometer

Note: *The conventional analogue type instrument is described. Although much easier to read, digital micrometers are considerably more expensive.*

● Always check the calibration of the micrometer before use. With the anvils closed (0 to 25 mm type) or set over a test gauge (for

3.2 Check micrometer calibration before use

the larger types) the scale should read zero **(see illustration 3.2)**; make sure that the anvils (and test piece) are clean first. Any discrepancy can be adjusted by referring to the instructions supplied with the tool. Remember that the micrometer is a precision measuring tool - don't force the anvils closed, use the ratchet (4) on the end of the micrometer to close it. In this way, a measured force is always applied.

● To use, first make sure that the item being measured is clean. Place the anvil of the micrometer (1) against the item and use the thimble (2) to bring the spindle (3) lightly into contact with the other side of the item **(see illustration 3.3)**. Don't tighten the thimble down because this will damage the micrometer - instead use the ratchet (4) on the end of the micrometer. The ratchet mechanism applies a measured force preventing damage to the instrument.

● The micrometer is read by referring to the linear scale on the sleeve and the annular scale on the thimble. Read off the sleeve first to obtain the base measurement, then add the fine measurement from the thimble to obtain the overall reading. The linear scale on the sleeve represents the measuring range of the micrometer (eg 0 to 25 mm). The annular scale

3.3 Micrometer component parts

1 Anvil	3 Spindle	5 Frame
2 Thimble	4 Ratchet	6 Locking lever

on the thimble will be in graduations of 0.01 mm (or as marked on the frame) - one full revolution of the thimble will move 0.5 mm on the linear scale. Take the reading where the datum line on the sleeve intersects the thimble's scale. Always position the eye directly above the scale otherwise an inaccurate reading will result.

In the example shown the item measures 2.95 mm (see illustration 3.4):

Linear scale	2.00 mm
Linear scale	0.50 mm
Annular scale	0.45 mm
Total figure	**2.95 mm**

3.5 Micrometer reading of 46.99 mm on linear and annular scales . . .

3.7 Expand the telescoping gauge in the bore, lock its position . . .

3.4 Micrometer reading of 2.95 mm

3.6 . . . and 0.004 mm on vernier scale

3.8 . . . then measure the gauge with a micrometer

Most micrometers have a locking lever (6) on the frame to hold the setting in place, allowing the item to be removed from the micrometer.
● Some micrometers have a vernier scale on their sleeve, providing an even finer measurement to be taken, in 0.001 increments of a millimetre. Take the sleeve and thimble measurement as described above, then check which graduation on the vernier scale aligns with that of the annular scale on the thimble **Note:** *The eye must be perpendicular to the scale when taking the vernier reading - if necessary rotate the body of the micrometer to ensure this.* Multiply the vernier scale figure by 0.001 and add it to the base and fine measurement figures.

In the example shown the item measures 46.994 mm (see illustrations 3.5 and 3.6):

Linear scale (base)	46.000 mm
Linear scale (base)	00.500 mm
Annular scale (fine)	00.490 mm
Vernier scale	00.004 mm
Total figure	**46.994 mm**

Internal micrometer

● Internal micrometers are available for measuring bore diameters, but are expensive and unlikely to be available for home use. It is suggested that a set of telescoping gauges and small hole gauges, both of which must be used with an external micrometer, will suffice for taking internal measurements on a motorcycle.
● Telescoping gauges can be used to

measure internal diameters of components. Select a gauge with the correct size range, make sure its ends are clean and insert it into the bore. Expand the gauge, then lock its position and withdraw it from the bore (see illustration 3.7). Measure across the gauge ends with a micrometer (see illustration 3.8).
● Very small diameter bores (such as valve guides) are measured with a small hole gauge. Once adjusted to a slip-fit inside the component, its position is locked and the gauge withdrawn for measurement with a micrometer (see illustrations 3.9 and 3.10).

Vernier caliper

Note: *The conventional linear and dial gauge type instruments are described. Digital types are easier to read, but are far more expensive.*
● The vernier caliper does not provide the precision of a micrometer, but is versatile in being able to measure internal and external diameters. Some types also incorporate a depth gauge. It is ideal for measuring clutch plate friction material and spring free lengths.
● To use the conventional linear scale vernier, slacken off the vernier clamp screws (1) and set its jaws over (2), or inside (3), the item to be measured (see illustration 3.11). Slide the jaw into contact, using the thumb-wheel (4) for fine movement of the sliding scale (5) then tighten the clamp screws (1). Read off the main scale (6) where the zero on the sliding scale (5) intersects it, taking the whole number to the left of the zero; this provides the base measurement. View along the sliding scale and select the division which

3.9 Expand the small hole gauge in the bore, lock its position . . .

3.10 . . . then measure the gauge with a micrometer

lines up exactly with any of the divisions on the main scale, noting that the divisions usually represents 0.02 of a millimetre. Add this fine measurement to the base measurement to obtain the total reading.

3.11 Vernier component parts (linear gauge)

1	Clamp screws	3	Internal jaws	5	Sliding scale	7	Depth gauge
2	External jaws	4	Thumbwheel	6	Main scale		

In the example shown the item measures 55.92 mm **(see illustration 3.12)**:

3.12 Vernier gauge reading of 55.92 mm

Base measurement	55.00 mm
Fine measurement	00.92 mm
Total figure	**55.92 mm**

● Some vernier calipers are equipped with a dial gauge for fine measurement. Before use, check that the jaws are clean, then close them fully and check that the dial gauge reads zero. If necessary adjust the gauge ring accordingly. Slacken the vernier clamp screw (1) and set its jaws over (2), or inside (3), the item to be measured **(see illustration 3.13)**. Slide the jaws into contact, using the thumbwheel (4) for fine movement. Read off the main scale (5) where the edge of the sliding scale (6) intersects it, taking the whole number to the left of the zero; this provides the base measurement. Read off the needle position on the dial gauge (7) scale to provide the fine measurement; each division represents 0.05 of a millimetre. Add this fine measurement to the base measurement to obtain the total reading.

In the example shown the item measures 55.95 mm **(see illustration 3.14)**:

Base measurement	55.00 mm
Fine measurement	00.95 mm
Total figure	55.95 mm

3.13 Vernier component parts (dial gauge)

1	Clamp screw	5	Main scale
2	External jaws	6	Sliding scale
3	Internal jaws	7	Dial gauge
4	Thumbwheel		

3.14 Vernier gauge reading of 55.95 mm

Plastigauge

● Plastigauge is a plastic material which can be compressed between two surfaces to measure the oil clearance between them. The width of the compressed Plastigauge is measured against a calibrated scale to determine the clearance.

● Common uses of Plastigauge are for measuring the clearance between crankshaft journal and main bearing inserts, between crankshaft journal and big-end bearing inserts, and between camshaft and bearing surfaces. The following example describes big-end oil clearance measurement.

● Handle the Plastigauge material carefully to prevent distortion. Using a sharp knife, cut a length which corresponds with the width of the bearing being measured and place it carefully across the journal so that it is parallel with the shaft **(see illustration 3.15)**. Carefully install both bearing shells and the connecting rod. Without rotating the rod on the journal tighten its bolts or nuts (as applicable) to the specified torque. The connecting rod and bearings are then disassembled and the crushed Plastigauge examined.

3.15 Plastigauge placed across shaft journal

● Using the scale provided in the Plastigauge kit, measure the width of the material to determine the oil clearance **(see illustration 3.16)**. Always remove all traces of Plastigauge after use using your fingernails.

Caution: Arriving at the correct clearance demands that the assembly is torqued correctly, according to the settings and sequence (where applicable) provided by the motorcycle manufacturer.

3.16 Measuring the width of the crushed Plastigauge

Dial gauge or DTI (Dial Test Indicator)

● A dial gauge can be used to accurately measure small amounts of movement. Typical uses are measuring shaft runout or shaft endfloat (sideplay) and setting piston position for ignition timing on two-strokes. A dial gauge set usually comes with a range of different probes and adapters and mounting equipment.

● The gauge needle must point to zero when at rest. Rotate the ring around its periphery to zero the gauge.

● Check that the gauge is capable of reading the extent of movement in the work. Most gauges have a small dial set in the face which records whole millimetres of movement as well as the fine scale around the face periphery which is calibrated in 0.01 mm divisions. Read off the small dial first to obtain the base measurement, then add the measurement from the fine scale to obtain the total reading.

In the example shown the gauge reads 1.48 mm **(see illustration 3.17)**:

Base measurement	1.00 mm
Fine measurement	0.48 mm
Total figure	**1.48 mm**

3.17 Dial gauge reading of 1.48 mm

● If measuring shaft runout, the shaft must be supported in vee-blocks and the gauge mounted on a stand perpendicular to the shaft. Rest the tip of the gauge against the centre of the shaft and rotate the shaft slowly whilst watching the gauge reading **(see illustration 3.18)**. Take several measurements along the length of the shaft and record the

3.18 Using a dial gauge to measure shaft runout

maximum gauge reading as the amount of runout in the shaft. **Note:** *The reading obtained will be total runout at that point - some manufacturers specify that the runout figure is halved to compare with their specified runout limit.*

● Endfloat (sideplay) measurement requires that the gauge is mounted securely to the surrounding component with its probe touching the end of the shaft. Using hand pressure, push and pull on the shaft noting the maximum endfloat recorded on the gauge **(see illustration 3.19)**.

3.19 Using a dial gauge to measure shaft endfloat

● A dial gauge with suitable adapters can be used to determine piston position BTDC on two-stroke engines for the purposes of ignition timing. The gauge, adapter and suitable length probe are installed in the place of the spark plug and the gauge zeroed at TDC. If the piston position is specified as 1.14 mm BTDC, rotate the engine back to 2.00 mm BTDC, then slowly forwards to 1.14 mm BTDC.

Cylinder compression gauges

● A compression gauge is used for measuring cylinder compression. Either the rubber-cone type or the threaded adapter type can be used. The latter is preferred to ensure a perfect seal against the cylinder head. A 0 to 300 psi (0 to 20 Bar) type gauge (for petrol/gasoline engines) will be suitable for motorcycles.

● The spark plug is removed and the gauge either held hard against the cylinder head (cone type) or the gauge adapter screwed into the cylinder head (threaded type) **(see illustration 3.20)**. Cylinder compression is measured with the engine turning over, but not running - carry out the compression test as described in

3.20 Using a rubber-cone type cylinder compression gauge

Fault Finding Equipment. The gauge will hold the reading until manually released.

Oil pressure gauge

● An oil pressure gauge is used for measuring engine oil pressure. Most gauges come with a set of adapters to fit the thread of the take-off point **(see illustration 3.21)**. If the take-off point specified by the motorcycle manufacturer is an external oil pipe union, make sure that the specified replacement union is used to prevent oil starvation.

3.21 Oil pressure gauge and take-off point adapter (arrow)

● Oil pressure is measured with the engine running (at a specific rpm) and often the manufacturer will specify pressure limits for a cold and hot engine.

Straight-edge and surface plate

● If checking the gasket face of a component for warpage, place a steel rule or precision straight-edge across the gasket face and measure any gap between the straight-edge and component with feeler gauges **(see illustration 3.22)**. Check diagonally across the component and between mounting holes **(see illustration 3.23)**.

3.22 Use a straight-edge and feeler gauges to check for warpage

3.23 Check for warpage in these directions

● Checking individual components for warpage, such as clutch plain (metal) plates, requires a perfectly flat plate or piece or plate glass and feeler gauges.

4 Torque and leverage

What is torque?

● Torque describes the twisting force about a shaft. The amount of torque applied is determined by the distance from the centre of the shaft to the end of the lever and the amount of force being applied to the end of the lever; distance multiplied by force equals torque.

● The manufacturer applies a measured torque to a bolt or nut to ensure that it will not slacken in use and to hold two components securely together without movement in the joint. The actual torque setting depends on the thread size, bolt or nut material and the composition of the components being held.

● Too little torque may cause the fastener to loosen due to vibration, whereas too much torque will distort the joint faces of the component or cause the fastener to shear off. Always stick to the specified torque setting.

Using a torque wrench

● Check the calibration of the torque wrench and make sure it has a suitable range for the job. Torque wrenches are available in Nm (Newton-metres), kgf m (kilograms-force metre), lbf ft (pounds-feet), lbf in (inch-pounds). Do not confuse lbf ft with lbf in.

● Adjust the tool to the desired torque on the scale (see illustration 4.1). If your torque wrench is not calibrated in the units specified, carefully convert the figure (see *Conversion Factors*). A manufacturer sometimes gives a torque setting as a range (8 to 10 Nm) rather than a single figure - in this case set the tool midway between the two settings. The same torque may be expressed as 9 Nm ± 1 Nm. Some torque wrenches have a method of locking the setting so that it isn't inadvertently altered during use.

4.1 Set the torque wrench index mark to the setting required, in this case 12 Nm

● Install the bolts/nuts in their correct location and secure them lightly. Their threads must be clean and free of any old locking compound. Unless specified the threads and flange should be dry - oiled threads are necessary in certain circumstances and the manufacturer will take this into account in the specified torque figure. Similarly, the manufacturer may also specify the application of thread-locking compound.

● Tighten the fasteners in the specified sequence until the torque wrench clicks, indicating that the torque setting has been reached. Apply the torque again to double-check the setting. Where different thread diameter fasteners secure the component, as a rule tighten the larger diameter ones first.

● When the torque wrench has been finished with, release the lock (where applicable) and fully back off its setting to zero - do not leave the torque wrench tensioned. Also, do not use a torque wrench for slackening a fastener.

Angle-tightening

● Manufacturers often specify a figure in degrees for final tightening of a fastener. This usually follows tightening to a specific torque setting.

● A degree disc can be set and attached to the socket (see illustration 4.2) or a protractor can be used to mark the angle of movement on the bolt/nut head and the surrounding casting (see illustration 4.3).

4.2 Angle tightening can be accomplished with a torque-angle gauge . . .

4.3 . . . or by marking the angle on the surrounding component

Loosening sequences

● Where more than one bolt/nut secures a component, loosen each fastener evenly a little at a time. In this way, not all the stress of the joint is held by one fastener and the components are not likely to distort.

● If a tightening sequence is provided, work in the REVERSE of this, but if not, work from the outside in, in a criss-cross sequence (see illustration 4.4).

4.4 When slackening, work from the outside inwards

Tightening sequences

● If a component is held by more than one fastener it is important that the retaining bolts/nuts are tightened evenly to prevent uneven stress build-up and distortion of sealing faces. This is especially important on high-compression joints such as the cylinder head.

● A sequence is usually provided by the manufacturer, either in a diagram or actually marked in the casting. If not, always start in the centre and work outwards in a criss-cross pattern (see illustration 4.5). Start off by securing all bolts/nuts finger-tight, then set the torque wrench and tighten each fastener by a small amount in sequence until the final torque is reached. By following this practice,

4.5 When tightening, work from the inside outwards

the joint will be held evenly and will not be distorted. Important joints, such as the cylinder head and big-end fasteners often have two- or three-stage torque settings.

Applying leverage

● Use tools at the correct angle. Position a socket wrench or spanner on the bolt/nut so that you pull it towards you when loosening. If this can't be done, push the spanner without curling your fingers around it **(see illustration 4.6)** - the spanner may slip or the fastener loosen suddenly, resulting in your fingers being crushed against a component.

4.6 If you can't pull on the spanner to loosen a fastener, push with your hand open

● Additional leverage is gained by extending the length of the lever. The best way to do this is to use a breaker bar instead of the regular length tool, or to slip a length of tubing over the end of the spanner or socket wrench.
● If additional leverage will not work, the fastener head is either damaged or firmly corroded in place (see *Fasteners*).

5 Bearings

Bearing removal and installation

Drivers and sockets

● Before removing a bearing, always inspect the casing to see which way it must be driven out - some casings will have retaining plates or a cast step. Also check for any identifying markings on the bearing and if installed to a certain depth, measure this at this stage. Some roller bearings are sealed on one side - take note of the original fitted position.
● Bearings can be driven out of a casing using a bearing driver tool (with the correct size head) or a socket of the correct diameter. Select the driver head or socket so that it contacts the outer race of the bearing, not the balls/rollers or inner race. Always support the casing around the bearing housing with wood blocks, otherwise there is a risk of fracture. The bearing is driven out with a few blows on the driver or socket from a heavy mallet. Unless access is severely restricted (as with wheel bearings), a pin-punch is not recommended unless it is moved around the bearing to keep it square in its housing.

● The same equipment can be used to install bearings. Make sure the bearing housing is supported on wood blocks and line up the bearing in its housing. Fit the bearing as noted on removal - generally they are installed with their marked side facing outwards. Tap the bearing squarely into its housing using a driver or socket which bears only on the bearing's outer race - contact with the bearing balls/rollers or inner race will destroy it **(see illustrations 5.1 and 5.2).**
● Check that the bearing inner race and balls/rollers rotate freely.

5.1 Using a bearing driver against the bearing's outer race

5.2 Using a large socket against the bearing's outer race

Pullers and slide-hammers

● Where a bearing is pressed on a shaft a puller will be required to extract it **(see illustration 5.3).** Make sure that the puller clamp or legs fit securely behind the bearing and are unlikely to slip out. If pulling a bearing

5.3 This bearing puller clamps behind the bearing and pressure is applied to the shaft end to draw the bearing off

off a gear shaft for example, you may have to locate the puller behind a gear pinion if there is no access to the race and draw the gear pinion off the shaft as well **(see illustration 5.4).**

> *Caution: Ensure that the puller's centre bolt locates securely against the end of the shaft and will not slip when pressure is applied. Also ensure that puller does not damage the shaft end.*

5.4 Where no access is available to the rear of the bearing, it is sometimes possible to draw off the adjacent component

● Operate the puller so that its centre bolt exerts pressure on the shaft end and draws the bearing off the shaft.
● When installing the bearing on the shaft, tap only on the bearing's inner race - contact with the balls/rollers or outer race with destroy the bearing. Use a socket or length of tubing as a drift which fits over the shaft end **(see illustration 5.5).**

5.5 When installing a bearing on a shaft use a piece of tubing which bears only on the bearing's inner race

● Where a bearing locates in a blind hole in a casing, it cannot be driven or pulled out as described above. A slide-hammer with knife-edged bearing puller attachment will be required. The puller attachment passes through the bearing and when tightened expands to fit firmly behind the bearing **(see illustration 5.6).** By operating the slide-hammer part of the tool the bearing is jarred out of its housing **(see illustration 5.7).**
● It is possible, if the bearing is of reasonable weight, for it to drop out of its housing if the casing is heated as described opposite. If this

5.6 Expand the bearing puller so that it locks behind the bearing . . .

5.7 . . . attach the slide hammer to the bearing puller

method is attempted, first prepare a work surface which will enable the casing to be tapped face down to help dislodge the bearing - a wood surface is ideal since it will not damage the casing's gasket surface. Wearing protective gloves, tap the heated casing several times against the work surface to dislodge the bearing under its own weight **(see illustration 5.8)**.

5.8 Tapping a casing face down on wood blocks can often dislodge a bearing

● Bearings can be installed in blind holes using the driver or socket method described above.

Drawbolts

● Where a bearing or bush is set in the eye of a component, such as a suspension linkage arm or connecting rod small-end, removal by drift may damage the component. Furthermore, a rubber bushing in a shock absorber eye cannot successfully be driven out of position. If access is available to a engineering press, the task is straightforward. If not, a drawbolt can be fabricated to extract the bearing or bush.

5.9 Drawbolt component parts assembled on a suspension arm

1 Bolt or length of threaded bar
2 Nuts
3 Washer (external diameter greater than tubing internal diameter)
4 Tubing (internal diameter sufficient to accommodate bearing)
5 Suspension arm with bearing
6 Tubing (external diameter slightly smaller than bearing)
7 Washer (external diameter slightly smaller than bearing)

5.10 Drawing the bearing out of the suspension arm

● To extract the bearing/bush you will need a long bolt with nut (or piece of threaded bar with two nuts), a piece of tubing which has an internal diameter larger than the bearing/bush, another piece of tubing which has an external diameter slightly smaller than the bearing/bush, and a selection of washers **(see illustrations 5.9 and 5.10)**. Note that the pieces of tubing must be of the same length, or longer, than the bearing/bush.
● The same kit (without the pieces of tubing) can be used to draw the new bearing/bush back into place **(see illustration 5.11)**.

5.11 Installing a new bearing (1) in the suspension arm

Temperature change

● If the bearing's outer race is a tight fit in the casing, the aluminium casing can be heated to release its grip on the bearing. Aluminium will expand at a greater rate than the steel bearing outer race. There are several ways to do this, but avoid any localised extreme heat (such as a blow torch) - aluminium alloy has a low melting point.
● Approved methods of heating a casing are using a domestic oven (heated to 100°C) or immersing the casing in boiling water **(see illustration 5.12)**. Low temperature range localised heat sources such as a paint stripper heat gun or clothes iron can also be used **(see illustration 5.13)**. Alternatively, soak a rag in boiling water, wring it out and wrap it around the bearing housing.

> ⚠ **Warning: All of these methods require care in use to prevent scalding and burns to the hands. Wear protective gloves when handling hot components.**

5.12 A casing can be immersed in a sink of boiling water to aid bearing removal

5.13 Using a localised heat source to aid bearing removal

● If heating the whole casing note that plastic components, such as the neutral switch, may suffer - remove them beforehand.
● After heating, remove the bearing as described above. You may find that the expansion is sufficient for the bearing to fall out of the casing under its own weight or with a light tap on the driver or socket.
● If necessary, the casing can be heated to aid bearing installation, and this is sometimes the recommended procedure if the motorcycle manufacturer has designed the housing and bearing fit with this intention.

● Installation of bearings can be eased by placing them in a freezer the night before installation. The steel bearing will contract slightly, allowing easy insertion in its housing. This is often useful when installing steering head outer races in the frame.

Bearing types and markings

● Plain shell bearings, ball bearings, needle roller bearings and tapered roller bearings will all be found on motorcycles (see illustrations 5.14 and 5.15). The ball and roller types are usually caged between an inner and outer race, but uncaged variations may be found.

5.14 Shell bearings are either plain or grooved. They are usually identified by colour code (arrow)

5.15 Tapered roller bearing (A), needle roller bearing (B) and ball journal bearing (C)

● Shell bearings (often called inserts) are usually found at the crankshaft main and connecting rod big-end where they are good at coping with high loads. They are made of a phosphor-bronze material and are impregnated with self-lubricating properties.
● Ball bearings and needle roller bearings consist of a steel inner and outer race with the balls or rollers between the races. They require constant lubrication by oil or grease and are good at coping with axial loads. Taper roller bearings consist of rollers set in a tapered cage set on the inner race; the outer race is separate. They are good at coping with axial loads and prevent movement along the shaft - a typical application is in the steering head.
● Bearing manufacturers produce bearings to ISO size standards and stamp one face of the bearing to indicate its internal and external diameter, load capacity and type (see illustration 5.16).
● Metal bushes are usually of phosphor-bronze material. Rubber bushes are used in suspension mounting eyes. Fibre bushes have also been used in suspension pivots.

5.16 Typical bearing marking

Bearing fault finding

● If a bearing outer race has spun in its housing, the housing material will be damaged. You can use a bearing locking compound to bond the outer race in place if damage is not too severe.
● Shell bearings will fail due to damage of their working surface, as a result of lack of lubrication, corrosion or abrasive particles in the oil (see illustration 5.17). Small particles of dirt in the oil may embed in the bearing material whereas larger particles will score the bearing and shaft journal. If a number of short journeys are made, insufficient heat will be generated to drive off condensation which has built up on the bearings.

5.17 Typical bearing failures

● Ball and roller bearings will fail due to lack of lubrication or damage to the balls or rollers. Tapered-roller bearings can be damaged by overloading them. Unless the bearing is sealed on both sides, wash it in paraffin (kerosene) to remove all old grease then allow it to dry. Make a visual inspection looking to dented balls or rollers, damaged cages and worn or pitted races (see illustration 5.18).
● A ball bearing can be checked for wear by listening to it when spun. Apply a film of light oil to the bearing and hold it close to the ear - hold the outer race with one hand and spin the inner

5.18 Example of ball journal bearing with damaged balls and cages

5.19 Hold outer race and listen to inner race when spun

race with the other hand (see illustration 5.19). The bearing should be almost silent when spun; if it grates or rattles it is worn.

6 Oil seals

Oil seal removal and installation

● Oil seals should be renewed every time a component is dismantled. This is because the seal lips will become set to the sealing surface and will not necessarily reseal.
● Oil seals can be prised out of position using a large flat-bladed screwdriver (see illustration 6.1). In the case of crankcase seals, check first that the seal is not lipped on the inside, preventing its removal with the crankcases joined.

6.1 Prise out oil seals with a large flat-bladed screwdriver

● New seals are usually installed with their marked face (containing the seal reference code) outwards and the spring side towards the fluid being retained. In certain cases, such as a two-stroke engine crankshaft seal, a double lipped seal may be used due to there being fluid or gas on each side of the joint.

● Use a bearing driver or socket which bears only on the outer hard edge of the seal to install it in the casing - tapping on the inner edge will damage the sealing lip.

Oil seal types and markings

● Oil seals are usually of the single-lipped type. Double-lipped seals are found where a liquid or gas is on both sides of the joint.

● Oil seals can harden and lose their sealing ability if the motorcycle has been in storage for a long period - renewal is the only solution.

● Oil seal manufacturers also conform to the ISO markings for seal size - these are moulded into the outer face of the seal (see illustration 6.2).

6.2 These oil seal markings indicate inside diameter, outside diameter and seal thickness

7 Gaskets and sealants

Types of gasket and sealant

● Gaskets are used to seal the mating surfaces between components and keep lubricants, fluids, vacuum or pressure contained within the assembly. Aluminium gaskets are sometimes found at the cylinder joints, but most gaskets are paper-based. If the mating surfaces of the components being joined are undamaged the gasket can be installed dry, although a dab of sealant or grease will be useful to hold it in place during assembly.

● RTV (Room Temperature Vulcanising) silicone rubber sealants cure when exposed to moisture in the atmosphere. These sealants are good at filling pits or irregular gasket faces, but will tend to be forced out of the joint under very high torque. They can be used to replace a paper gasket, but first make sure that the width of the paper gasket is not essential to the shimming of internal components. RTV sealants should not be used on components containing petrol (gasoline).

● Non-hardening, semi-hardening and hard setting liquid gasket compounds can be used with a gasket or between a metal-to-metal joint. Select the sealant to suit the application: universal non-hardening sealant can be used on virtually all joints; semi-hardening on joint faces which are rough or damaged; hard setting sealant on joints which require a permanent bond and are subjected to high temperature and pressure. **Note:** *Check first if the paper gasket has a bead of sealant*

impregnated in its surface before applying additional sealant.

● When choosing a sealant, make sure it is suitable for the application, particularly if being applied in a high-temperature area or in the vicinity of fuel. Certain manufacturers produce sealants in either clear, silver or black colours to match the finish of the engine. This has a particular application on motorcycles where much of the engine is exposed.

● Do not over-apply sealant. That which is squeezed out on the outside of the joint can be wiped off, whereas an excess of sealant on the inside can break off and clog oilways.

Breaking a sealed joint

● Age, heat, pressure and the use of hard setting sealant can cause two components to stick together so tightly that they are difficult to separate using finger pressure alone. Do not resort to using levers unless there is a pry point provided for this purpose (see illustration 7.1) or else the gasket surfaces will be damaged.

● Use a soft-faced hammer (see illustration 7.2) or a wood block and conventional hammer to strike the component near the mating surface. Avoid hammering against cast extremities since they may break off. If this method fails, try using a wood wedge between the two components.

Caution: If the joint will not separate, double-check that you have removed all the fasteners.

7.1 If a pry point is provided, apply gently pressure with a flat-bladed screwdriver

7.2 Tap around the joint with a soft-faced mallet if necessary - don't strike cooling fins

Removal of old gasket and sealant

● Paper gaskets will most likely come away complete, leaving only a few traces stuck on

Most components have one or two hollow locating dowels between the two gasket faces. If a dowel cannot be removed, do not resort to gripping it with pliers - it will almost certainly be distorted. Install a close-fitting socket or Phillips screwdriver into the dowel and then grip the outer edge of the dowel to free it.

the sealing faces of the components. It is imperative that all traces are removed to ensure correct sealing of the new gasket.

● Very carefully scrape all traces of gasket away making sure that the sealing surfaces are not gouged or scored by the scraper (see illustrations 7.3, 7.4 and 7.5). Stubborn deposits can be removed by spraying with an aerosol gasket remover. Final preparation of

7.3 Paper gaskets can be scraped off with a gasket scraper tool . . .

7.4 . . . a knife blade . . .

7.5 . . . or a household scraper

7.6 Fine abrasive paper is wrapped around a flat file to clean up the gasket face

7.7 A kitchen scourer can be used on stubborn deposits

the gasket surface can be made with very fine abrasive paper or a plastic kitchen scourer **(see illustrations 7.6 and 7.7)**.

● Old sealant can be scraped or peeled off components, depending on the type originally used. Note that gasket removal compounds are available to avoid scraping the components clean; make sure the gasket remover suits the type of sealant used.

Breaking and joining final drive chains

● Drive chains for all but small bikes are continuous and do not have a clip-type connecting link. The chain must be broken using a chain breaker tool and the new chain securely riveted together using a new soft rivet-type link. Never use a clip-type connecting link instead of a rivet-type link, except in an emergency. Various chain breaking and riveting tools are available, either as separate tools or combined as illustrated in the accompanying photographs - read the instructions supplied with the tool carefully.

> ⚠ **Warning: The need to rivet the new link pins correctly cannot be overstressed - loss of control of the motorcycle is very likely to result if the chain breaks in use.**

● Rotate the chain and look for the soft link. The soft link pins look like they have been

8.1 Tighten the chain breaker to push the pin out of the link . . .

8.2 . . . withdraw the pin, remove the tool . . .

8.3 . . . and separate the chain link

deeply centre-punched instead of peened over like all the other pins **(see illustration 8.9)** and its sideplate may be a different colour. Position the soft link midway between the sprockets and assemble the chain breaker tool over one of the soft link pins **(see illustration 8.1)**. Operate the tool to push the pin out through the chain **(see illustration 8.2)**. On an O-ring chain, remove the O-rings **(see illustration 8.3)**. Carry out the same procedure on the other soft link pin.

> **Caution: Certain soft link pins (particularly on the larger chains) may require their ends to be filed or ground off before they can be pressed out using the tool.**

● Check that you have the correct size and strength (standard or heavy duty) new soft link - do not reuse the old link. Look for the size marking on the chain sideplates **(see illustration 8.10)**.

● Position the chain ends so that they are engaged over the rear sprocket. On an O-ring

8.4 Insert the new soft link, with O-rings, through the chain ends . . .

8.5 . . . install the O-rings over the pin ends . . .

8.6 . . . followed by the sideplate

chain, install a new O-ring over each pin of the link and insert the link through the two chain ends **(see illustration 8.4)**. Install a new O-ring over the end of each pin, followed by the sideplate (with the chain manufacturer's marking facing outwards) **(see illustrations 8.5 and 8.6)**. On an unsealed chain, insert the link through the two chain ends, then install the sideplate with the chain manufacturer's marking facing outwards.

● Note that it may not be possible to install the sideplate using finger pressure alone. If using a joining tool, assemble it so that the plates of the tool clamp the link and press the sideplate over the pins **(see illustration 8.7)**. Otherwise, use two small sockets placed over

8.7 Push the sideplate into position using a clamp

8.8 Assemble the chain riveting tool over one pin at a time and tighten it fully

8.9 Pin end correctly riveted (A), pin end unriveted (B)

the rivet ends and two pieces of the wood between a G-clamp. Operate the clamp to press the sideplate over the pins.

● Assemble the joining tool over one pin (following the maker's instructions) and tighten the tool down to spread the pin end securely **(see illustrations 8.8 and 8.9)**. Do the same on the other pin.

> ⚠ **Warning: Check that the pin ends are secure and that there is no danger of the sideplate coming loose. If the pin ends are cracked the soft link must be renewed.**

Final drive chain sizing

● Chains are sized using a three digit number, followed by a suffix to denote the chain type **(see illustration 8.10)**. Chain type is either standard or heavy duty (thicker sideplates), and also unsealed or O-ring/X-ring type.

● The first digit of the number relates to the pitch of the chain, ie the distance from the centre of one pin to the centre of the next pin **(see illustration 8.11)**. Pitch is expressed in eighths of an inch, as follows:

8.10 Typical chain size and type marking

8.11 Chain dimensions

Sizes commencing with a 4 (eg 428) have a pitch of 1/2 inch (12.7 mm)
Sizes commencing with a 5 (eg 520) have a pitch of 5/8 inch (15.9 mm)
Sizes commencing with a 6 (eg 630) have a pitch of 3/4 inch (19.1 mm)

● The second and third digits of the chain size relate to the width of the rollers, again in imperial units, eg the 525 shown has 5/16 inch (7.94 mm) rollers **(see illustration 8.11)**.

9 Hoses

Clamping to prevent flow

● Small-bore flexible hoses can be clamped to prevent fluid flow whilst a component is worked on. Whichever method is used, ensure that the hose material is not permanently distorted or damaged by the clamp.

  a) A brake hose clamp available from auto accessory shops **(see illustration 9.1)**.
  b) A wingnut type hose clamp **(see illustration 9.2)**.

9.1 Hoses can be clamped with an automotive brake hose clamp . . .

9.2 . . . a wingnut type hose clamp . . .

  c) Two sockets placed each side of the hose and held with straight-jawed self-locking grips **(see illustration 9.3)**.
  d) Thick card each side of the hose held between straight-jawed self-locking grips **(see illustration 9.4)**.

9.3 . . . two sockets and a pair of self-locking grips . . .

9.4 . . . or thick card and self-locking grips

Freeing and fitting hoses

● Always make sure the hose clamp is moved well clear of the hose end. Grip the hose with your hand and rotate it whilst pulling it off the union. If the hose has hardened due to age and will not move, slit it with a sharp knife and peel its ends off the union **(see illustration 9.5)**.

● Resist the temptation to use grease or soap on the unions to aid installation; although it helps the hose slip over the union it will equally aid the escape of fluid from the joint. It is preferable to soften the hose ends in hot water and wet the inside surface of the hose with water or a fluid which will evaporate.

9.5 Cutting a coolant hose free with a sharp knife

Conversion Factors

Length (distance)

Inches (in)	x 25.4	= Millimetres (mm)	x 0.0394	= Inches (in)
Feet (ft)	x 0.305	= Metres (m)	x 3.281	= Feet (ft)
Miles	x 1.609	= Kilometres (km)	x 0.621	= Miles

Volume (capacity)

Cubic inches (cu in; in³)	x 16.387	= Cubic centimetres (cc; cm³)	x 0.061	= Cubic inches (cu in; in³)
Imperial pints (Imp pt)	x 0.568	= Litres (l)	x 1.76	= Imperial pints (Imp pt)
Imperial quarts (Imp qt)	x 1.137	= Litres (l)	x 0.88	= Imperial quarts (Imp qt)
Imperial quarts (Imp qt)	x 1.201	= US quarts (US qt)	x 0.833	= Imperial quarts (Imp qt)
US quarts (US qt)	x 0.946	= Litres (l)	x 1.057	= US quarts (US qt)
Imperial gallons (Imp gal)	x 4.546	= Litres (l)	x 0.22	= Imperial gallons (Imp gal)
Imperial gallons (Imp gal)	x 1.201	= US gallons (US gal)	x 0.833	= Imperial gallons (Imp gal)
US gallons (US gal)	x 3.785	= Litres (l)	x 0.264	= US gallons (US gal)

Mass (weight)

Ounces (oz)	x 28.35	= Grams (g)	x 0.035	= Ounces (oz)
Pounds (lb)	x 0.454	= Kilograms (kg)	x 2.205	= Pounds (lb)

Force

Ounces-force (ozf; oz)	x 0.278	= Newtons (N)	x 3.6	= Ounces-force (ozf; oz)
Pounds-force (lbf; lb)	x 4.448	= Newtons (N)	x 0.225	= Pounds-force (lbf; lb)
Newtons (N)	x 0.1	= Kilograms-force (kgf; kg)	x 9.81	= Newtons (N)

Pressure

Pounds-force per square inch (psi; lbf/in²; lb/in²)	x 0.070	= Kilograms-force per square centimetre (kgf/cm²; kg/cm²)	x 14.223	= Pounds-force per square inch (psi; lbf/in²; lb/in²)
Pounds-force per square inch (psi; lbf/in²; lb/in²)	x 0.068	= Atmospheres (atm)	x 14.696	= Pounds-force per square inch (psi; lbf/in²; lb/in²)
Pounds-force per square inch (psi; lbf/in²; lb/in²)	x 0.069	= Bars	x 14.5	= Pounds-force per square inch (psi; lbf/in²; lb/in²)
Pounds-force per square inch (psi; lbf/in²; lb/in²)	x 6.895	= Kilopascals (kPa)	x 0.145	= Pounds-force per square inch (psi; lbf/in²; lb/in²)
Kilopascals (kPa)	x 0.01	= Kilograms-force per square centimetre (kgf/cm²; kg/cm²)	x 98.1	= Kilopascals (kPa)
Millibar (mbar)	x 100	= Pascals (Pa)	x 0.01	= Millibar (mbar)
Millibar (mbar)	x 0.0145	= Pounds-force per square inch (psi; lbf/in²; lb/in²)	x 68.947	= Millibar (mbar)
Millibar (mbar)	x 0.75	= Millimetres of mercury (mmHg)	x 1.333	= Millibar (mbar)
Millibar (mbar)	x 0.401	= Inches of water (inH₂O)	x 2.491	= Millibar (mbar)
Millimetres of mercury (mmHg)	x 0.535	= Inches of water (inH₂O)	x 1.868	= Millimetres of mercury (mmHg)
Inches of water (inH₂O)	x 0.036	= Pounds-force per square inch (psi; lbf/in²; lb/in²)	x 27.68	= Inches of water (inH₂O)

Torque (moment of force)

Pounds-force inches (lbf in; lb in)	x 1.152	= Kilograms-force centimetre (kgf cm; kg cm)	x 0.868	= Pounds-force inches (lbf in; lb in)
Pounds-force inches (lbf in; lb in)	x 0.113	= Newton metres (Nm)	x 8.85	= Pounds-force inches (lbf in; lb in)
Pounds-force inches (lbf in; lb in)	x 0.083	= Pounds-force feet (lbf ft; lb ft)	x 12	= Pounds-force inches (lbf in; lb in)
Pounds-force feet (lbf ft; lb ft)	x 0.138	= Kilograms-force metres (kgf m; kg m)	x 7.233	= Pounds-force feet (lbf ft; lb ft)
Pounds-force feet (lbf ft; lb ft)	x 1.356	= Newton metres (Nm)	x 0.738	= Pounds-force feet (lbf ft; lb ft)
Newton metres (Nm)	x 0.102	= Kilograms-force metres (kgf m; kg m)	x 9.804	= Newton metres (Nm)

Power

Horsepower (hp)	x 745.7	= Watts (W)	x 0.0013	= Horsepower (hp)

Velocity (speed)

Miles per hour (miles/hr; mph)	x 1.609	= Kilometres per hour (km/hr; kph)	x 0.621	= Miles per hour (miles/hr; mph)

Fuel consumption*

Miles per gallon (mpg)	x 0.354	= Kilometres per litre (km/l)	x 2.825	= Miles per gallon (mpg)

Temperature

Degrees Fahrenheit = (°C x 1.8) + 32   Degrees Celsius (Degrees Centigrade; °C) = (°F - 32) x 0.56

It is common practice to convert from miles per gallon (mpg) to litres/100 kilometres (l/100km), where mpg x l/100 km = 282

A number of chemicals and lubricants are available for use in motorcycle maintenance and repair. They include a wide variety of products ranging from cleaning solvents and degreasers to lubricants and protective sprays for rubber, plastic and vinyl.

● **Contact point/spark plug cleaner** is a solvent used to clean oily film and dirt from points, grime from electrical connectors and oil deposits from spark plugs. It is oil free and leaves no residue. It can also be used to remove gum and varnish from carburettor jets and other orifices.

● **Carburettor cleaner** is similar to contact point/spark plug cleaner but it usually has a stronger solvent and may leave a slight oily reside. It is not recommended for cleaning electrical components or connections.

● **Brake system cleaner** is used to remove grease or brake fluid from brake system components (where clean surfaces are absolutely necessary and petroleum-based solvents cannot be used); it also leaves no residue.

● **Silicone-based lubricants** are used to protect rubber parts such as hoses and grommets, and are used as lubricants for hinges and locks.

● **Multi-purpose grease** is an all purpose lubricant used wherever grease is more practical than a liquid lubricant such as oil. Some multi-purpose grease is coloured white and specially formulated to be more resistant to water than ordinary grease.

● **Gear oil** (sometimes called gear lube) is a specially designed oil used in transmissions and final drive units, as well as other areas where high friction, high temperature lubrication is required. It is available in a number of viscosities (weights) for various applications.

● **Motor oil**, of course, is the lubricant specially formulated for use in the engine. It normally contains a wide variety of additives to prevent corrosion and reduce foaming and wear. Motor oil comes in various weights (viscosity ratings) of from 5 to 80. The recommended weight of the oil depends on the seasonal temperature and the demands on the engine. Light oil is used in cold climates and under light load conditions; heavy oil is used in hot climates and where high loads are encountered. Multi-viscosity oils are designed to have characteristics of both light and heavy oils and are available in a number of weights from 5W-20 to 20W-50.

● **Petrol additives** perform several functions, depending on their chemical makeup. They usually contain solvents that help dissolve gum and varnish that build up on carburettor and inlet parts. They also serve to break down carbon deposits that form on the inside surfaces of the combustion chambers. Some additives contain upper cylinder lubricants for valves and piston rings.

● **Brake and clutch fluid** is a specially formulated hydraulic fluid that can withstand the heat and pressure encountered in brake/clutch systems. Care must be taken that this fluid does not come in contact with painted surfaces or plastics. An opened container should always be resealed to prevent contamination by water or dirt.

● **Chain lubricants** are formulated especially for use on motorcycle final drive chains. A good chain lube should adhere well and have good penetrating qualities to be effective as a lubricant inside the chain and on the side plates, pins and rollers. Most chain lubes are either the foaming type or quick drying type and are usually marketed as sprays. Take care to use a lubricant marked as being suitable for O-ring chains.

● **Degreasers** are heavy duty solvents used to remove grease and grime that may accumulate on engine and frame components. They can be sprayed or brushed on and, depending on the type, are rinsed with either water or solvent.

● **Solvents** are used alone or in combination with degreasers to clean parts and assemblies during repair and overhaul. The home mechanic should use only solvents that are non-flammable and that do not produce irritating fumes.

● **Gasket sealing compounds** may be used in conjunction with gaskets, to improve their sealing capabilities, or alone, to seal metal-to-metal joints. Many gasket sealers can withstand extreme heat, some are impervious to petrol and lubricants, while others are capable of filling and sealing large cavities. Depending on the intended use, gasket sealers either dry hard or stay relatively soft and pliable. They are usually applied by hand, with a brush, or are sprayed on the gasket sealing surfaces.

● **Thread locking compound** is an adhesive locking compound that prevents threaded fasteners from loosening because of vibration. It is available in a variety of types for different applications.

● **Moisture dispersants** are usually sprays that can be used to dry out electrical components such as the fuse block and wiring connectors. Some types can also be used as treatment for rubber and as a lubricant for hinges, cables and locks.

● **Waxes and polishes** are used to help protect painted and plated surfaces from the weather. Different types of paint may require the use of different types of wax polish. Some polishes utilise a chemical or abrasive cleaner to help remove the top layer of oxidised (dull) paint on older vehicles. In recent years, many non-wax polishes (that contain a wide variety of chemicals such as polymers and silicones) have been introduced. These non-wax polishes are usually easier to apply and last longer than conventional waxes and polishes.

About the MOT Test

In the UK, all vehicles more than three years old are subject to an annual test to ensure that they meet minimum safety requirements. A current test certificate must be issued before a machine can be used on public roads, and is required before a road fund licence can be issued. Riding without a current test certificate will also invalidate your insurance.

For most owners, the MOT test is an annual cause for anxiety, and this is largely due to owners not being sure what needs to be checked prior to submitting the motorcycle for testing. The simple answer is that a fully roadworthy motorcycle will have no difficulty in passing the test.

This is a guide to getting your motorcycle through the MOT test. Obviously it will not be possible to examine the motorcycle to the same standard as the professional MOT tester, particularly in view of the equipment required for some of the checks. However, working through the following procedures will enable you to identify any problem areas before submitting the motorcycle for the test.

It has only been possible to summarise the test requirements here, based on the regulations in force at the time of printing. Test standards are becoming increasingly stringent, although there are some exemptions for older vehicles. More information about the MOT test can be obtained from the TSO publications, *How Safe is your Motorcycle* and *The MOT Inspection Manual for Motorcycle Testing*.

Many of the checks require that one of the wheels is raised off the ground. If the motorcycle doesn't have a centre stand, note that an auxiliary stand will be required. Additionally, the help of an assistant may prove useful.

Certain exceptions apply to machines under 50 cc, machines without a lighting system, and Classic bikes - if in doubt about any of the requirements listed below seek confirmation from an MOT tester prior to submitting the motorcycle for the test.

Check that the frame number is clearly visible.

> **HAYNES HiNT**
> *If a component is in borderline condition, the tester has discretion in deciding whether to pass or fail it. If the motorcycle presented is clean and evidently well cared for, the tester may be more inclined to pass a borderline component than if the motorcycle is scruffy and apparently neglected.*

Electrical System

Lights, turn signals, horn and reflector

✔ With the ignition on, check the operation of the following electrical components. **Note:** *The electrical components on certain small-capacity machines are powered by the generator, requiring that the engine is run for this check.*

a) Headlight and tail light. Check that both illuminate in the low and high beam switch positions.

b) Position lights. Check that the front position (or sidelight) and tail light illuminate in this switch position.

c) Turn signals. Check that all flash at the correct rate, and that the warning light(s) function correctly. Check that the turn signal switch works correctly.

d) Hazard warning system (where fitted). Check that all four turn signals flash in this switch position.

e) Brake stop light. Check that the light comes on when the front and rear brakes are independently applied. Models first used on or after 1st April 1986 must have a brake light switch on each brake.

f) Horn. Check that the sound is continuous and of reasonable volume.

✔ Check that there is a red reflector on the rear of the machine, either mounted separately or as part of the tail light lens.

✔ Check the condition of the headlight, tail light and turn signal lenses.

Headlight beam height

✔ The MOT tester will perform a headlight beam height check using specialised beam setting equipment **(see illustration 1)**. This equipment will not be available to the home mechanic, but if you suspect that the headlight is incorrectly set or may have been maladjusted in the past, you can perform a rough test as follows.

✔ Position the bike in a straight line facing a brick wall. The bike must be off its stand, upright and with a rider seated. Measure the height from the ground to the centre of the headlight and mark a horizontal line on the wall at this height. Position the motorcycle 3.8 metres from the wall and draw a vertical

Headlight beam height checking equipment

line up the wall central to the centreline of the motorcycle. Switch to dipped beam and check that the beam pattern falls slightly lower than the horizontal line and to the left of the vertical line **(see illustration 2)**.

Home workshop beam alignment check

Exhaust System and Final Drive

Exhaust

✔ Check that the exhaust mountings are secure and that the system does not foul any of the rear suspension components.
✔ Start the motorcycle. When the revs are increased, check that the exhaust is neither holed nor leaking from any of its joints. On a linked system, check that the collector box is not leaking due to corrosion.

✔ Note that the exhaust decibel level ("loudness" of the exhaust) is assessed at the discretion of the tester. If the motorcycle was first used on or after 1st January 1985 the silencer must carry the BSAU 193 stamp, or a marking relating to its make and model, or be of OE (original equipment) manufacture. If the silencer is marked NOT FOR ROAD USE, RACING USE ONLY or similar, it will fail the MOT.

Final drive

✔ On chain or belt drive machines, check that the chain/belt is in good condition and does not have excessive slack. Also check that the sprocket is securely mounted on the rear wheel hub. Check that the chain/belt guard is in place.
✔ On shaft drive bikes, check for oil leaking from the drive unit and fouling the rear tyre.

Steering and Suspension

Steering

✔ With the front wheel raised off the ground, rotate the steering from lock to lock. The handlebar or switches must not contact the fuel tank or be close enough to trap the rider's hand. Problems can be caused by damaged lock stops on the lower yoke and frame, or by the fitting of non-standard handlebars.
✔ When performing the lock to lock check, also ensure that the steering moves freely without drag or notchiness. Steering movement can be impaired by poorly routed cables, or by overtight head bearings or worn bearings. The tester will perform a check of the steering head bearing lower race by mounting the front wheel on a surface plate, then performing a lock to

lock check with the weight of the machine on the lower bearing **(see illustration 3)**.
✔ Grasp the fork sliders (lower legs) and attempt to push and pull on the forks **(see**

Front wheel mounted on a surface plate for steering head bearing lower race check

illustration 4). Any play in the steering head bearings will be felt. Note that in extreme cases, wear of the front fork bushes can be misinterpreted for head bearing play.
✔ Check that the handlebars are securely mounted.
✔ Check that the handlebar grip rubbers are secure. They should by bonded to the bar left end and to the throttle cable pulley on the right end.

Front suspension

✔ With the motorcycle off the stand, hold the front brake on and pump the front forks up and down **(see illustration 5)**. Check that they are adequately damped.

Checking the steering head bearings for freeplay

Hold the front brake on and pump the front forks up and down to check operation

Inspect the area around the fork dust seal for oil leakage (arrow)

Bounce the rear of the motorcycle to check rear suspension operation

Checking for rear suspension linkage play

✔ Inspect the area above and around the front fork oil seals **(see illustration 6)**. There should be no sign of oil on the fork tube (stanchion) nor leaking down the slider (lower leg). On models so equipped, check that there is no oil leaking from the anti-dive units.

✔ On models with swingarm front suspension, check that there is no freeplay in the linkage when moved from side to side.

Rear suspension

✔ With the motorcycle off the stand and an assistant supporting the motorcycle by its handlebars, bounce the rear suspension **(see illustration 7)**. Check that the suspension components do not foul on any of the cycle parts and check that the shock absorber(s) provide adequate damping.

✔ Visually inspect the shock absorber(s) and check that there is no sign of oil leakage from its damper. This is somewhat restricted on certain single shock models due to the location of the shock absorber.

✔ With the rear wheel raised off the ground, grasp the wheel at the highest point and attempt to pull it up **(see illustration 8)**. Any play in the swingarm pivot or suspension linkage bearings will be felt as movement. **Note:** *Do not confuse play with actual suspension movement.* Failure to lubricate suspension linkage bearings can lead to bearing failure **(see illustration 9)**.

✔ With the rear wheel raised off the ground, grasp the swingarm ends and attempt to move the swingarm from side to side and forwards and backwards - any play indicates wear of the swingarm pivot bearings **(see illustration 10)**.

Worn suspension linkage pivots (arrows) are usually the cause of play in the rear suspension

Grasp the swingarm at the ends to check for play in its pivot bearings

Brake pad wear can usually be viewed without removing the caliper. Most pads have wear indicator grooves (1) and some also have indicator tangs (2)

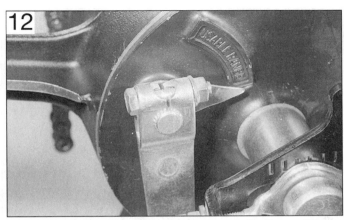

On drum brakes, check the angle of the operating lever with the brake fully applied. Most drum brakes have a wear indicator pointer and scale.

Brakes, Wheels and Tyres

Brakes

✔ With the wheel raised off the ground, apply the brake then free it off, and check that the wheel is about to revolve freely without brake drag.

✔ On disc brakes, examine the disc itself. Check that it is securely mounted and not cracked.

✔ On disc brakes, view the pad material through the caliper mouth and check that the pads are not worn down beyond the limit **(see illustration 11)**.

✔ On drum brakes, check that when the brake is applied the angle between the operating lever and cable or rod is not too great **(see illustration 12)**. Check also that the operating lever doesn't foul any other components.

✔ On disc brakes, examine the flexible hoses from top to bottom. Have an assistant hold the brake on so that the fluid in the hose is under pressure, and check that there is no sign of fluid leakage, bulges or cracking. If there are any metal brake pipes or unions, check that these are free from corrosion and damage. Where a brake-linked anti-dive system is fitted, check the hoses to the anti-dive in a similar manner.

✔ Check that the rear brake torque arm is secure and that its fasteners are secured by self-locking nuts or castellated nuts with split-pins or R-pins **(see illustration 13)**.

✔ On models with ABS, check that the self-check warning light in the instrument panel works.

✔ The MOT tester will perform a test of the motorcycle's braking efficiency based on a calculation of rider and motorcycle weight. Although this cannot be carried out at home, you can at least ensure that the braking systems are properly maintained. For hydraulic disc brakes, check the fluid level, lever/pedal feel (bleed of air if its spongy) and pad material. For drum brakes, check adjustment, cable or rod operation and shoe lining thickness.

Wheels and tyres

✔ Check the wheel condition. Cast wheels should be free from cracks and if of the built-up design, all fasteners should be secure. Spoked wheels should be checked for broken, corroded, loose or bent spokes.

✔ With the wheel raised off the ground, spin the wheel and visually check that the tyre and wheel run true. Check that the tyre does not foul the suspension or mudguards.

✔ With the wheel raised off the ground, grasp the wheel and attempt to move it about the axle (spindle) **(see illustration 14)**. Any play felt here indicates wheel bearing failure.

Brake torque arm must be properly secured at both ends

Check for wheel bearing play by trying to move the wheel about the axle (spindle)

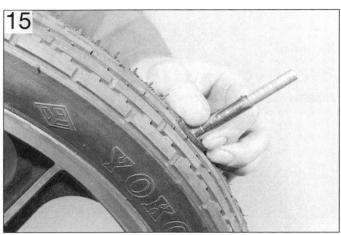

Checking the tyre tread depth

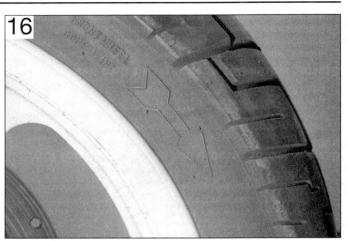

Tyre direction of rotation arrow can be found on tyre sidewall

Castellated type wheel axle (spindle) nut must be secured by a split pin or R-pin

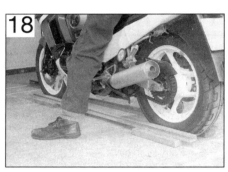

Two straightedges are used to check wheel alignment

✔ Check the tyre tread depth, tread condition and sidewall condition **(see illustration 15)**.
✔ Check the tyre type. Front and rear tyre types must be compatible and be suitable for road use. Tyres marked NOT FOR ROAD USE, COMPETITION USE ONLY or similar, will fail the MOT.

✔ If the tyre sidewall carries a direction of rotation arrow, this must be pointing in the direction of normal wheel rotation **(see illustration 16)**.
✔ Check that the wheel axle (spindle) nuts (where applicable) are properly secured. A self-locking nut or castellated nut with a split-pin or R-pin can be used **(see illustration 17)**.
✔ Wheel alignment is checked with the motorcycle off the stand and a rider seated. With the front wheel pointing straight ahead, two perfectly straight lengths of metal or wood and placed against the sidewalls of both tyres **(see illustration 18)**. The gap each side of the front tyre must be equidistant on both sides. Incorrect wheel alignment may be due to a cocked rear wheel (often as the result of poor chain adjustment) or in extreme cases, a bent frame.

General checks and condition

✔ Check the security of all major fasteners, bodypanels, seat, fairings (where fitted) and mudguards.

✔ Check that the rider and pillion footrests, handlebar levers and brake pedal are securely mounted.

✔ Check for corrosion on the frame or any load-bearing components. If severe, this may affect the structure, particularly under stress.

Sidecars

A motorcycle fitted with a sidecar requires additional checks relating to the stability of the machine and security of attachment and swivel joints, plus specific wheel alignment (toe-in) requirements. Additionally, tyre and lighting requirements differ from conventional motorcycle use. Owners are advised to check MOT test requirements with an official test centre.

Preparing for storage

Before you start

If repairs or an overhaul is needed, see that this is carried out now rather than left until you want to ride the bike again.

Give the bike a good wash and scrub all dirt from its underside. Make sure the bike dries completely before preparing for storage.

Engine

● Remove the spark plug(s) and lubricate the cylinder bores with approximately a teaspoon of motor oil using a spout-type oil can (see illustration 1). Reinstall the spark plug(s). Crank the engine over a couple of times to coat the piston rings and bores with oil. If the bike has a kickstart, use this to turn the engine over. If not, flick the kill switch to the OFF position and crank the engine over on the starter (see illustration 2). If the nature on the ignition system prevents the starter operating with the kill switch in the OFF position,

remove the spark plugs and fit them back in their caps; ensure that the plugs are earthed (grounded) against the cylinder head when the starter is operated (see illustration 3).

⚠️ **Warning: It is important that the plugs are earthed (grounded) away from the spark plug holes otherwise there is a risk of atomised fuel from the cylinders igniting.**

HAYNES HiNT *On a single cylinder four-stroke engine, you can seal the combustion chamber completely by positioning the piston at TDC on the compression stroke.*

● Drain the carburettor(s) otherwise there is a risk of jets becoming blocked by gum deposits from the fuel (see illustration 4).

● If the bike is going into long-term storage, consider adding a fuel stabiliser to the fuel in the tank. If the tank is drained completely, corrosion of its internal surfaces may occur if left unprotected for a long period. The tank can be treated with a rust preventative especially for this purpose. Alternatively, remove the tank and pour half a litre of motor oil into it, install the filler cap and shake the tank to coat its internals with oil before draining off the excess. The same effect can also be achieved by spraying WD40 or a similar water-dispersant around the inside of the tank via its flexible nozzle.

● Make sure the cooling system contains the correct mix of antifreeze. Antifreeze also contains important corrosion inhibitors.

● The air intakes and exhaust can be sealed off by covering or plugging the openings. Ensure that you do not seal in any condensation; run the engine until it is hot,

Squirt a drop of motor oil into each cylinder

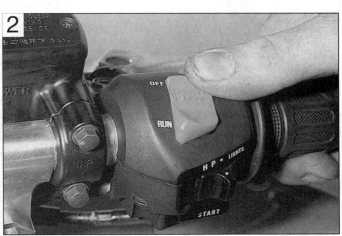

Flick the kill switch to OFF . . .

. . . and ensure that the metal bodies of the plugs (arrows) are earthed against the cylinder head

Connect a hose to the carburettor float chamber drain stub (arrow) and unscrew the drain screw

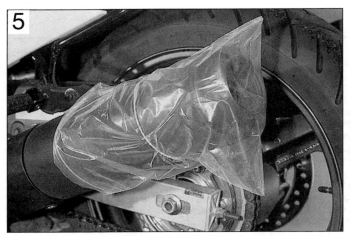

Exhausts can be sealed off with a plastic bag

Disconnect the negative lead (A) first, followed by the positive lead (B)

Use a suitable battery charger - this kit also assess battery condition

then switch off and allow to cool. Tape a piece of thick plastic over the silencer end(s) **(see illustration 5)**. Note that some advocate pouring a tablespoon of motor oil into the silencer(s) before sealing them off.

Battery

● Remove it from the bike - in extreme cases of cold the battery may freeze and crack its case **(see illustration 6)**.

● Check the electrolyte level and top up if necessary (conventional refillable batteries). Clean the terminals.
● Store the battery off the motorcycle and away from any sources of fire. Position a wooden block under the battery if it is to sit on the ground.
● Give the battery a trickle charge for a few hours every month **(see illustration 7)**.

Tyres

● Place the bike on its centrestand or an auxiliary stand which will support the motorcycle in an upright position. Position wood blocks under the tyres to keep them off the ground and to provide insulation from damp. If the bike is being put into long-term storage, ideally both tyres should be off the ground; not only will this protect the tyres, but will also ensure that no load is placed on the steering head or wheel bearings.
● Deflate each tyre by 5 to 10 psi, no more or the beads may unseat from the rim, making subsequent inflation difficult on tubeless tyres.

Pivots and controls

● Lubricate all lever, pedal, stand and

footrest pivot points. If grease nipples are fitted to the rear suspension components, apply lubricant to the pivots.
● Lubricate all control cables.

Cycle components

● Apply a wax protectant to all painted and plastic components. Wipe off any excess, but don't polish to a shine. Where fitted, clean the screen with soap and water.
● Coat metal parts with Vaseline (petroleum jelly). When applying this to the fork tubes, do not compress the forks otherwise the seals will rot from contact with the Vaseline.
● Apply a vinyl cleaner to the seat.

Storage conditions

● Aim to store the bike in a shed or garage which does not leak and is free from damp.
● Drape an old blanket or bedspread over the bike to protect it from dust and direct contact with sunlight (which will fade paint). This also hides the bike from prying eyes. Beware of tight-fitting plastic covers which may allow condensation to form and settle on the bike.

Getting back on the road

Engine and transmission

● Change the oil and replace the oil filter. If this was done prior to storage, check that the oil hasn't emulsified - a thick whitish substance which occurs through condensation.
● Remove the spark plugs. Using a spout-type oil can, squirt a few drops of oil into the cylinder(s). This will provide initial lubrication as the piston rings and bores comes back into contact. Service the spark plugs, or fit new ones, and install them in the engine.

● Check that the clutch isn't stuck on. The plates can stick together if left standing for some time, preventing clutch operation. Engage a gear and try rocking the bike back and forth with the clutch lever held against the handlebar. If this doesn't work on cable-operated clutches, hold the clutch lever back against the handlebar with a strong elastic band or cable tie for a couple of hours **(see illustration 8)**.
● If the air intakes or silencer end(s) were blocked off, remove the bung or cover used.
● If the fuel tank was coated with a rust

Hold clutch lever back against the handlebar with elastic bands or a cable tie preventative, oil or a stabiliser added to the fuel, drain and flush the tank and dispose of the fuel sensibly. If no action was taken with the fuel tank prior to storage, it is advised that the old fuel is disposed of since it will go off over a period of time. Refill the fuel tank with fresh fuel.

Frame and running gear

● Oil all pivot points and cables.
● Check the tyre pressures. They will definitely need inflating if pressures were reduced for storage.
● Lubricate the final drive chain (where applicable).
● Remove any protective coating applied to the fork tubes (stanchions) since this may well destroy the fork seals. If the fork tubes weren't protected and have picked up rust spots, remove them with very fine abrasive paper and refinish with metal polish.
● Check that both brakes operate correctly. Apply each brake hard and check that it's not possible to move the motorcycle forwards, then check that the brake frees off again once released. Brake caliper pistons can stick due to corrosion around the piston head, or on the sliding caliper types, due to corrosion of the slider pins. If the brake doesn't free after repeated operation, take the caliper off for examination. Similarly drum brakes can stick due to a seized operating cam, cable or rod linkage.
● If the motorcycle has been in long-term storage, renew the brake fluid and clutch fluid (where applicable).
● Depending on where the bike has been stored, the wiring, cables and hoses may have been nibbled by rodents. Make a visual check and investigate disturbed wiring loom tape.

Battery

● If the battery has been previously removal and given top up charges it can simply be reconnected. Remember to connect the positive cable first and the negative cable last.
● On conventional refillable batteries, if the battery has not received any attention, remove it from the motorcycle and check its electrolyte level. Top up if necessary then charge the battery. If the battery fails to hold a charge and a visual checks show heavy white sulphation of the plates, the battery is probably defective and must be renewed. This is particularly likely if the battery is old. Confirm battery condition with a specific gravity check.
● On sealed (MF) batteries, if the battery has not received any attention, remove it from the motorcycle and charge it according to the information on the battery case - if the battery fails to hold a charge it must be renewed.

Starting procedure

● If a kickstart is fitted, turn the engine over a couple of times with the ignition OFF to distribute oil around the engine. If no kickstart is fitted, flick the engine kill switch OFF and the ignition ON and crank the engine over a couple of times to work oil around the upper cylinder components. If the nature of the ignition system is such that the starter won't work with the kill switch OFF, remove the spark plugs, fit them back into their caps and earth (ground) their bodies on the cylinder head. Reinstall the spark plugs afterwards.
● Switch the kill switch to RUN, operate the choke and start the engine. If the engine won't start don't continue cranking the engine - not only will this flatten the battery, but the starter motor will overheat. Switch the ignition off and try again later. If the engine refuses to start, go through the fault finding procedures in this manual. **Note:** *If the bike has been in storage for a long time, old fuel or a carburettor blockage may be the problem. Gum deposits in carburettors can block jets - if a carburettor cleaner doesn't prove successful the carburettors must be dismantled for cleaning.*

● Once the engine has started, check that the lights, turn signals and horn work properly.

● Treat the bike gently for the first ride and check all fluid levels on completion. Settle the bike back into the maintenance schedule.

This Section provides an easy reference-guide to the more common faults that are likely to afflict your machine. Obviously, the opportunities are almost limitless for faults to occur as a result of obscure failures, and to try and cover all eventualities would require a book. Indeed, a number have been written on the subject.

Successful troubleshooting is not a mysterious 'black art' but the application of a bit of knowledge combined with a systematic and logical approach to the problem. Approach any troubleshooting by first accurately identifying the symptom and then checking through the list of possible causes, starting with the simplest or most obvious and progressing in stages to the most complex.

Take nothing for granted, but above all apply liberal quantities of common sense.

The main symptom of a fault is given in the text as a major heading below which are listed the various systems or areas which may contain the fault. Details of each possible cause for a fault and the remedial action to be taken are given, in brief, in the paragraphs below each heading. Further information should be sought in the relevant Chapter.

1 Engine doesn't start or is difficult to start

☐ Starter motor doesn't rotate
☐ Starter motor rotates but engine does not turn over
☐ Starter works but engine won't turn over (seized)
☐ No fuel flow
☐ Engine flooded
☐ No spark or weak spark
☐ Compression low
☐ Stalls after starting
☐ Rough idle

2 Poor running at low speed

☐ Spark weak
☐ Fuel/air mixture incorrect
☐ Compression low
☐ Poor acceleration

3 Poor running or no power at high speed

☐ Firing incorrect
☐ Fuel/air mixture incorrect
☐ Compression low
☐ Knocking or pinging
☐ Miscellaneous causes

4 Overheating

☐ Engine overheats
☐ Firing incorrect
☐ Fuel/air mixture incorrect
☐ Compression too high
☐ Engine load excessive
☐ Lubrication inadequate
☐ Miscellaneous causes

5 Clutch problems

☐ Clutch slipping
☐ Clutch not disengaging completely

6 Gear shifting problems

☐ Doesn't go into gear, or lever doesn't return
☐ Jumps out of gear
☐ Overshifts

7 Abnormal engine noise

☐ Knocking or pinging
☐ Piston slap or rattling
☐ Valve noise
☐ Other noise

8 Abnormal driveline noise

☐ Clutch noise
☐ Transmission noise
☐ Final drive noise

9 Abnormal frame and suspension noise

☐ Front end noise
☐ Shock absorber noise
☐ Brake noise

10 Oil pressure indicator light comes on

☐ Engine lubrication system
☐ Electrical system

11 Excessive exhaust smoke

☐ White smoke
☐ Black smoke
☐ Brown smoke

12 Poor handling or stability

☐ Handlebar hard to turn
☐ Handlebar shakes or vibrates excessively
☐ Handlebar pulls to one side
☐ Poor shock absorbing qualities

13 Braking problems

☐ Brakes are spongy, don't hold
☐ Brake lever or pedal pulsates
☐ Brakes drag

14 Electrical problems

☐ Battery dead or weak
☐ Battery overcharged

1 Engine doesn't start or is difficult to start

Starter motor doesn't rotate

☐ Engine kill switch OFF.
☐ Fuse blown. Check main fuse and starter circuit fuse (Chapter 9).
☐ Battery voltage low. Check and recharge battery (Chapter 9).
☐ Starter motor defective. Make sure the wiring to the starter is secure. Make sure the starter relay clicks when the start button is pushed. If the relay clicks, then the fault is in the wiring or motor.
☐ Starter relay faulty. Check it according to the procedure in Chapter 9.
☐ Starter switch not contacting. The contacts could be wet, corroded or dirty. Disassemble and clean the switch (Chapter 9).
☐ Wiring open or shorted. Check all wiring connections and harnesses to make sure that they are dry, tight and not corroded. Also check for broken or frayed wires that can cause a short to ground (earth) (see wiring diagram, Chapter 9).
☐ Ignition (main) switch defective. Check the switch according to the procedure in Chapter 9. Replace the switch with a new one if it is defective.
☐ Engine kill switch defective. Check for wet, dirty or corroded contacts. Clean or replace the switch as necessary (Chapter 9).
☐ Faulty neutral, side stand or clutch switch. Check the wiring to each switch and the switch itself according to the procedures in Chapter 9.

Starter motor rotates but engine does not turn over

☐ Starter motor clutch defective. Inspect and repair or replace (Chapter 2).
☐ Damaged idler or starter gears. Inspect and replace the damaged parts (Chapter 2).

Starter works but engine won't turn over (seized)

☐ Seized engine caused by one or more internally damaged components. Failure due to wear, abuse or lack of lubrication. Damage can include seized valves, followers, camshafts, pistons, crankshaft, connecting rod bearings, or transmission gears or bearings. Refer to Chapter 2 for engine disassembly.

No fuel flow

☐ No fuel in tank.
☐ Fuel pump failure or in-line filter blockage (US 1993 to 1995 models and UK CBR900RR-N to RR-S models) (see Chapters 9 and 1 respectively).
☐ Vacuum hose detached or split, or valve in tap stuck (US 1996 and 1997 models and UK CBR900RR-T and RR-V).
☐ Fuel tank breather hose obstructed (not California models).
☐ Fuel tap filter clogged. Remove the tap and clean it and the filter (Chapter 1).
☐ Fuel line clogged. Pull the fuel line loose and carefully blow through it.
☐ Float needle valve clogged. For all of the valves to be clogged, either a very bad batch of fuel with an unusual additive has been used, or some other foreign material has entered the tank. Many times after a machine has been stored for many months without running, the fuel turns to a varnish-like liquid and forms deposits on the inlet needle valves and jets. The carburetors should be removed and overhauled if draining the float chambers doesn't solve the problem.

Engine flooded

☐ Float height too high. Check as described in Chapter 4.
☐ Float needle valve worn or stuck open. A piece of dirt, rust or other debris can cause the valve to seat improperly, causing excess fuel to be admitted to the float chamber. In this case, the float chamber should be cleaned and the needle valve and seat inspected. If the needle and seat are worn, then the leaking will persist and the parts should be replaced with new ones (Chapter 4).
☐ Starting technique incorrect. Under normal circumstances (i.e., if all the carburetor functions are sound) the machine should start with little or no throttle. When the engine is cold, the choke should be operated and the engine started without opening the throttle. When the engine is at operating temperature, only a very slight amount of throttle should be necessary. If the engine is flooded, turn the fuel tap OFF and hold the throttle open while cranking the engine. This will allow additional air to reach the cylinders. Remember to turn the fuel tap back ON after the engine starts.

No spark or weak spark

☐ Ignition switch OFF.
☐ Engine kill switch turned to the OFF position.
☐ Battery voltage low. Check and recharge the battery as necessary (Chapter 9).
☐ Spark plugs dirty, defective or worn out. Locate reason for fouled plugs using spark plug condition chart and follow the plug maintenance procedures (Chapter 1).
☐ Spark plug caps or secondary (HT) wiring faulty. Check condition. Replace either or both components if cracks or deterioration are evident (Chapter 5).
☐ Spark plug caps not making good contact. Make sure that the plug caps fit snugly over the plug ends.
☐ Ignition control module defective. Check the module, referring to Chapter 5 for details.
☐ Pulse generator defective. Check the unit, referring to Chapter 5 for details.
☐ Ignition HT coils defective. Check the coils, referring to Chapter 5.
☐ Ignition or kill switch shorted. This is usually caused by water, corrosion, damage or excessive wear. The switches can be disassembled and cleaned with electrical contact cleaner. If cleaning does not help, replace the switches (Chapter 9).
☐ Wiring shorted or broken between:
   Ignition (main) switch and engine kill switch (or blown fuse)
   Ignition control module and engine kill switch
   Ignition control module and ignition HT coils
   Ignition HT coils and spark plugs
   Ignition control module and pulse generator
☐ Make sure that all wiring connections are clean, dry and tight. Look for chafed and broken wires (Chapters 5 and 9).

1 Engine doesn't start or is difficult to start (continued)

Compression low

☐ Spark plugs loose. Remove the plugs and inspect their threads. Reinstall and tighten to the specified torque (Chapter 1).

☐ Cylinder head not sufficiently tightened down. If the cylinder head is suspected of being loose, then there's a chance that the gasket or head is damaged if the problem has persisted for any length of time. The head bolts should be tightened to the proper torque in the correct sequence (Chapter 2).

☐ Improper valve clearance. This means that the valve is not closing completely and compression pressure is leaking past the valve. Check and adjust the valve clearances (Chapter 1).

☐ Cylinder and/or piston worn. Excessive wear will cause compression pressure to leak past the rings. This is usually accompanied by worn rings as well. A top-end overhaul is necessary (Chapter 2).

☐ Piston rings worn, weak, broken, or sticking. Broken or sticking piston rings usually indicate a lubrication or carburation problem that causes excess carbon deposits or seizures to form on the pistons and rings. Top-end overhaul is necessary (Chapter 2).

☐ Piston ring-to-groove clearance excessive. This is caused by excessive wear of the piston ring lands. Piston replacement is necessary (Chapter 2).

☐ Cylinder head gasket damaged. If the head is allowed to become loose, or if excessive carbon build-up on the piston crown and combustion chamber causes extremely high compression, the head gasket may leak. Retorquing the head is not always sufficient to restore the seal, so gasket replacement is necessary (Chapter 2).

☐ Cylinder head warped. This is caused by overheating or improperly tightened head bolts. Machine shop resurfacing or head replacement is necessary (Chapter 2).

☐ Valve spring broken or weak. Caused by component failure or wear; the springs must be replaced (Chapter 2).

☐ Valve not seating properly. This is caused by a bent valve (from over-revving or improper valve adjustment), burned valve or seat (improper carburation) or an accumulation of carbon deposits on the seat (from carburation or lubrication problems). The valves must be cleaned and/or replaced and the seats serviced if possible (Chapter 2).

Stalls after starting

☐ Improper choke action. Make sure the choke linkage shaft is getting a full stroke and staying in the out position (Chapter 4).

☐ Ignition malfunction. See Chapter 5.

☐ Carburetor malfunction. See Chapter 4.

☐ Fuel contaminated. The fuel can be contaminated with either dirt or water, or can change chemically if the machine is allowed to sit for several months or more. Drain the tank and float chambers (Chapter 4).

☐ Intake air leak. Check for loose carburetor-to-intake manifold connections, loose or missing vacuum gauge adapter screws or hoses, or loose carburetor tops (Chapter 4).

☐ Engine idle speed incorrect. Turn idle adjusting screw until the engine idles at the specified rpm (Chapter 1).

Rough idle

☐ Ignition malfunction. See Chapter 5.

☐ Idle speed incorrect. See Chapter 1.

☐ Carburetors not synchronized. Adjust carburetors with vacuum gauge or manometer set as described in Chapter 1.

☐ Carburetor malfunction. See Chapter 4.

☐ Fuel contaminated. The fuel can be contaminated with either dirt or water, or can change chemically if the machine is allowed to sit for several months or more. Drain the tank and float chambers (Chapter 4).

☐ Intake air leak. Check for loose carburetor-to-intake manifold connections, loose or missing vacuum gauge adapter screws or hoses, or loose carburetor tops (Chapter 4).

☐ Air filter clogged. Replace the air filter element (Chapter 1).

2 Poor running at low speeds

Spark weak

☐ Battery voltage low. Check and recharge battery (Chapter 9).

☐ Spark plugs fouled, defective or worn out. Refer to Chapter 1 for spark plug maintenance.

☐ Spark plug cap or HT wiring defective. Refer to Chapters 1 and 5 for details on the ignition system.

☐ Spark plug caps not making contact.

☐ Incorrect spark plugs. Wrong type, heat range or cap configuration. Check and install correct plugs listed in Chapter 1.

☐ Ignition control module defective. See Chapter 5.

☐ Pulse generator defective. See Chapter 5.

☐ Ignition HT coils defective. See Chapter 5.

Fuel/air mixture incorrect

☐ Pilot screws out of adjustment (Chapter 4).

☐ Pilot jet or air passage clogged. Remove and overhaul the carburetors (Chapter 4).

☐ Air bleed holes clogged. Remove carburetor and blow out all passages (Chapter 4).

☐ Air filter clogged, poorly sealed or missing (Chapter 1).

☐ Air filter housing poorly sealed. Look for cracks, holes or loose clamps and replace or repair defective parts.

☐ Fuel level too high or too low. Check the float height (Chapter 4).

☐ Fuel pump faulty. Check output rate (Chapter 9).

☐ Fuel tank breather hose obstructed (not California models).

☐ Carburetor intake manifolds loose. Check for cracks, breaks, tears or loose clamps. Replace the rubber intake manifold joints if split or perished.

Compression low

☐ Spark plugs loose. Remove the plugs and inspect their threads. Reinstall and tighten to the specified torque (Chapter 1).

☐ Cylinder head not sufficiently tightened down. If the cylinder head is suspected of being loose, then there's a chance that the gasket and head are damaged if the problem has persisted for any length of time. The head bolts should be tightened to the proper torque in the correct sequence (Chapter 2).

☐ Improper valve clearance. This means that the valve is not closing completely and compression pressure is leaking past the valve. Check and adjust the valve clearances (Chapter 1).

☐ Cylinder and/or piston worn. Excessive wear will cause compression pressure to leak past the rings. This is usually accompanied by worn rings as well. A top end overhaul is necessary (Chapter 2).

☐ Piston rings worn, weak, broken, or sticking. Broken or sticking piston rings usually indicate a lubrication or carburation problem that causes excess carbon deposits or seizures to form on the pistons and rings. Top-end overhaul is necessary (Chapter 2).

2 Poor running at low speeds (continued)

☐ Piston ring-to-groove clearance excessive. This is caused by excessive wear of the piston ring lands. Piston replacement is necessary (Chapter 2).

☐ Cylinder head gasket damaged. If the head is allowed to become loose, or if excessive carbon build-up on the piston crown and combustion chamber causes extremely high compression, the head gasket may leak. Retorquing the head is not always sufficient to restore the seal, so gasket replacement is necessary (Chapter 2).

☐ Cylinder head warped. This is caused by overheating or improperly tightened head bolts. Machine shop resurfacing or head replacement is necessary (Chapter 2).

☐ Valve spring broken or weak. Caused by component failure or wear; the springs must be replaced (Chapter 2).

☐ Valve not seating properly. This is caused by a bent valve (from over-revving or improper valve adjustment), burned valve or seat (improper carburation) or an accumulation of carbon deposits on the seat (from carburation, lubrication problems). The valves must be cleaned and/or replaced and the seats serviced if possible (Chapter 2).

Poor acceleration

☐ Carburetors leaking or dirty. Overhaul the carburetors (Chapter 4).

☐ Timing not advancing. The pulse generator or the ignition control module may be defective. If so, they must be replaced with new ones, as they can't be repaired.

☐ Carburetors not synchronized. Adjust them with a vacuum gauge set or manometer (Chapter 1).

☐ Engine oil viscosity too high. Using a heavier oil than that recommended in Chapter 1 can damage the oil pump or lubrication system and cause drag on the engine.

☐ Brakes dragging. Usually caused by debris which has entered the brake piston seals, or from a warped disc or bent axle. Repair as necessary (Chapter 7).

3 Poor running or no power at high speed

Firing incorrect

☐ Air filter restricted. Clean or replace filter (Chapter 1).

☐ Spark plugs fouled, defective or worn out. See Chapter 1 for spark plug maintenance.

☐ Spark plug caps or HT wiring defective. See Chapters 1 and 5 for details of the ignition system.

☐ Spark plug caps not in good contact. See Chapter 5.

☐ Incorrect spark plugs. Wrong type, heat range or cap configuration. Check and install correct plugs listed in Chapter 1.

☐ Ignition control module defective. See Chapter 5.

☐ Ignition coils defective. See Chapter 5.

Fuel/air mixture incorrect

☐ Main jet clogged. Dirt, water or other contaminants can clog the main jets. Clean the fuel tap filter, the in-line filter, the float chamber area, and the jets and carburetor orifices (Chapter 4).

☐ Main jet wrong size. The standard jetting is for sea level atmospheric pressure and oxygen content.

☐ Throttle shaft-to-carburetor body clearance excessive. Refer to Chapter 4 for inspection and part replacement procedures.

☐ Air bleed holes clogged. Remove and overhaul carburetors (Chapter 4).

☐ Air filter clogged, poorly sealed, or missing (Chapter 1).

☐ Air filter housing poorly sealed. Look for cracks, holes or loose clamps, and replace or repair defective parts.

☐ Fuel level too high or too low. Check the float height (Chapter 4).

☐ Fuel pump faulty. Check output rate (Chapter 9).

☐ Fuel tank breather hose obstructed (not California models).

☐ Carburetor intake manifolds loose. Check for cracks, breaks, tears or loose clamps. Replace the rubber intake manifolds if they are split or perished (Chapter 4).

Compression low

☐ Spark plugs loose. Remove the plugs and inspect their threads. Reinstall and tighten to the specified torque (Chapter 1).

☐ Cylinder head not sufficiently tightened down. If the cylinder head is suspected of being loose, then there's a chance that the gasket and head are damaged if the problem has persisted for any length of time. The head bolts should be tightened to the proper torque in the correct sequence (Chapter 2).

☐ Improper valve clearance. This means that the valve is not closing completely and compression pressure is leaking past the valve. Check and adjust the valve clearances (Chapter 1).

☐ Cylinder and/or piston worn. Excessive wear will cause compression pressure to leak past the rings. This is usually accompanied by worn rings as well. A top-end overhaul is necessary (Chapter 2).

☐ Piston rings worn, weak, broken, or sticking. Broken or sticking piston rings usually indicate a lubrication or carburation problem that causes excess carbon deposits or seizures to form on the pistons and rings. Top-end overhaul is necessary (Chapter 2).

☐ Piston ring-to-groove clearance excessive. This is caused by excessive wear of the piston ring lands. Piston replacement is necessary (Chapter 2).

☐ Cylinder head gasket damaged. If the head is allowed to become loose, or if excessive carbon build-up on the piston crown and combustion chamber causes extremely high compression, the head gasket may leak. Retorquing the head is not always sufficient to restore the seal, so gasket replacement is necessary (Chapter 2).

☐ Cylinder head warped. This is caused by overheating or improperly tightened head bolts. Machine shop resurfacing or head replacement is necessary (Chapter 2).

☐ Valve spring broken or weak. Caused by component failure or wear; the springs must be replaced (Chapter 2).

☐ Valve not seating properly. This is caused by a bent valve (from over-revving or improper valve adjustment), burned valve or seat (improper carburation) or an accumulation of carbon deposits on the seat (from carburation or lubrication problems). The valves must be cleaned and/or replaced and the seats serviced if possible (Chapter 2).

3 Poor running or no power at high speed (continued)

Knocking or pinging

☐ Carbon build-up in combustion chamber. Use of a fuel additive that will dissolve the adhesive bonding the carbon particles to the crown and chamber is the easiest way to remove the build-up. Otherwise, the cylinder head will have to be removed and decarbonized (Chapter 2).

☐ Incorrect or poor quality fuel. Old or improper grades of fuel can cause detonation. This causes the piston to rattle, thus the knocking or pinging sound. Drain old fuel and always use the recommended fuel grade.

☐ Spark plug heat range incorrect. Uncontrolled detonation indicates the plug heat range is too hot. The plug in effect becomes a glow plug, raising cylinder temperatures. Install the proper heat range plug (Chapter 1).

☐ Improper air/fuel mixture. This will cause the cylinder to run hot, which leads to detonation. Clogged jets or an air leak can cause this imbalance. See Chapter 4.

Miscellaneous causes

☐ Throttle valve doesn't open fully. Adjust the throttle grip freeplay (Chapter 1).

☐ Clutch slipping. May be caused by loose or worn clutch components. Refer to Chapter 2 for clutch overhaul procedures.

☐ Timing not advancing.

☐ Engine oil viscosity too high. Using a heavier oil than the one recommended in Chapter 1 can damage the oil pump or lubrication system and cause drag on the engine.

☐ Brakes dragging. Usually caused by debris which has entered the brake piston seals, or from a warped disc or bent axle. Repair as necessary.

4 Overheating

Engine overheats

☐ Coolant level low. Check and add coolant (see "Daily (pre-ride) checks").

☐ Leak in cooling system. Check cooling system hoses and radiator for leaks and other damage. Repair or replace parts as necessary (Chapter 3).

☐ Thermostat sticking open or closed. Check and replace as described in Chapter 3.

☐ Faulty radiator cap. Remove the cap and have it pressure tested.

☐ Coolant passages clogged. Have the entire system drained and flushed, then refill with fresh coolant.

☐ Water pump defective. Remove the pump and check the components (Chapter 3).

☐ Clogged radiator fins. Clean them by blowing compressed air through the fins from the backside.

☐ Cooling fan or fan switch fault (Chapter 3).

Firing incorrect

☐ Spark plugs fouled, defective or worn out. See Chapter 1 for spark plug maintenance.

☐ Incorrect spark plugs.

☐ Faulty ignition HT coils (Chapter 5).

Fuel/air mixture incorrect

☐ Main jet clogged. Dirt, water and other contaminants can clog the main jets. Clean the fuel tap filter, the fuel pump in-line filter, the float chamber area and the jets and carburetor orifices (Chapter 4).

☐ Main jet wrong size. The standard jetting is for sea level atmospheric pressure and oxygen content.

☐ Air filter clogged, poorly sealed or missing (Chapter 1).

☐ Air filter housing poorly sealed. Look for cracks, holes or loose clamps and replace or repair.

☐ Fuel level too low. Check float height (Chapter 4).

☐ Fuel pump faulty. Check output rate (Chapter 9).

☐ Fuel tank breather hose obstructed (not California models).

☐ Carburetor intake manifolds loose. Check for cracks, breaks, tears or loose clamps. Replace the rubber intake manifold joints if split or perished.

Compression too high

☐ Carbon build-up in combustion chamber. Use of a fuel additive that will dissolve the adhesive bonding the carbon particles to the piston crown and chamber is the easiest way to remove the build-up. Otherwise, the cylinder head will have to be removed and decarbonized (Chapter 2).

☐ Improperly machined head surface or installation of incorrect gasket during engine assembly.

Engine load excessive

☐ Clutch slipping. Can be caused by damaged, loose or worn clutch components. Refer to Chapter 2 for overhaul procedures.

☐ Engine oil level too high. The addition of too much oil will cause pressurization of the crankcase and inefficient engine operation. Check Specifications and drain to proper level (Chapter 1).

☐ Engine oil viscosity too high. Using a heavier oil than the one recommended in Chapter 1 can damage the oil pump or lubrication system as well as cause drag on the engine.

☐ Brakes dragging. Usually caused by debris which has entered the brake piston seals, or from a warped disc or bent axle. Repair as necessary.

Lubrication inadequate

☐ Engine oil level too low. Friction caused by intermittent lack of lubrication or from oil that is overworked can cause overheating. The oil provides a definite cooling function in the engine. Check the oil level (see "Daily (pre-ride) checks").

☐ Poor quality engine oil or incorrect viscosity or type. Oil is rated not only according to viscosity but also according to type. Some oils are not rated high enough for use in this engine. Check the Specifications section and change to the correct oil (Chapter 1).

Miscellaneous causes

☐ Modification to exhaust system. Most aftermarket exhaust systems cause the engine to run leaner, which make them run hotter. When installing an accessory exhaust system, always rejet the carburetors.

5 Clutch problems

Clutch slipping

☐ Cable freeplay insufficient. Check and adjust cable (Chapter 1).
☐ Friction plates worn or warped. Overhaul the clutch assembly (Chapter 2).
☐ Plain plates warped (Chapter 2).
☐ Clutch springs broken or weak. Old or heat-damaged (from slipping clutch) springs should be replaced with new ones (Chapter 2).
☐ Clutch release mechanism defective. Replace any defective parts (Chapter 2).
☐ Clutch center or outer drum unevenly worn. This causes improper engagement of the plates. Replace the damaged or worn parts (Chapter 2).

Clutch not disengaging completely

☐ Cable freeplay excessive. Check and adjust cable (Chapter 1).
☐ Clutch plates warped or damaged. This will cause clutch drag, which in turn will cause the machine to creep. Overhaul the clutch assembly (Chapter 2).

☐ Clutch spring tension uneven. Usually caused by a sagged or broken spring. Check and replace the springs as a set (Chapter 2).
☐ Engine oil deteriorated. Old, thin, worn out oil will not provide proper lubrication for the plates, causing the clutch to drag. Replace the oil and filter (Chapter 1).
☐ Engine oil viscosity too high. Using a heavier oil than recommended in Chapter 1 can cause the plates to stick together, putting a drag on the engine. Change to the correct weight oil (Chapter 1).
☐ Clutch outer drum guide seized on mainshaft. Lack of lubrication, severe wear or damage can cause the guide to seize on the shaft. Overhaul of the clutch, and perhaps transmission, may be necessary to repair the damage (Chapter 2).
☐ Clutch release mechanism defective. Overhaul the clutch cover components (Chapter 2).
☐ Loose clutch center nut. Causes drum and center misalignment putting a drag on the engine. Engagement adjustment continually varies. Overhaul the clutch assembly (Chapter 2).

6 Gear shifting problems

Doesn't go into gear or lever doesn't return

☐ Clutch not disengaging. See Section 27.
☐ Shift fork(s) bent or seized. Often caused by dropping the machine or from lack of lubrication. Overhaul the transmission (Chapter 2).
☐ Gear(s) stuck on shaft. Most often caused by a lack of lubrication or excessive wear in transmission bearings and bushings. Overhaul the transmission (Chapter 2).
☐ Gearshift drum binding. Caused by lubrication failure or excessive wear. Replace the drum and bearing (Chapter 2).
☐ Gearshift lever return spring weak or broken (Chapter 2).
☐ Gearshift lever broken. Splines stripped out of lever or shaft, caused by allowing the lever to get loose or from dropping the machine. Replace necessary parts (Chapter 2).

☐ Gearshift mechanism stopper arm broken or worn. Full engagement and rotary movement of shift drum results. Replace the arm (Chapter 2).
☐ Stopper arm spring broken. Allows arm to float, causing sporadic shift operation. Replace spring (Chapter 2).

Jumps out of gear

☐ Shift fork(s) worn. Overhaul the transmission (Chapter 2).
☐ Gear groove(s) worn. Overhaul the transmission (Chapter 2).
☐ Gear dogs or dog slots worn or damaged. The gears should be inspected and replaced. No attempt should be made to service the worn parts.

Overshifts

☐ Stopper arm spring weak or broken (Chapter 2).
☐ Gearshift shaft return spring post broken or distorted (Chapter 2).

7 Abnormal engine noise

Knocking or pinging

☐ Carbon build-up in combustion chamber. Use of a fuel additive that will dissolve the adhesive bonding the carbon particles to the piston crown and chamber is the easiest way to remove the build-up. Otherwise, the cylinder head will have to be removed and decarbonized (Chapter 2).
☐ Incorrect or poor quality fuel. Old or improper fuel can cause detonation. This causes the pistons to rattle, thus the knocking or pinging sound. Drain the old fuel and always use the recommended grade fuel (Chapter 4).
☐ Spark plug heat range incorrect. Uncontrolled detonation indicates that the plug heat range is too hot. The plug in effect becomes a glow plug, raising cylinder temperatures. Install the proper heat range plug (Chapter 1).
☐ Improper air/fuel mixture. This will cause the cylinders to run hot and lead to detonation. Clogged jets or an air leak can cause this imbalance. See Chapter 4.

Piston slap or rattling

☐ Cylinder-to-piston clearance excessive. Caused by improper assembly. Inspect and overhaul top-end parts (Chapter 2).
☐ Connecting rod bent. Caused by over-revving, trying to

start a badly flooded engine or from ingesting a foreign object into the combustion chamber. Replace the damaged parts (Chapter 2).
☐ Piston pin or piston pin bore worn or seized from wear or lack of lubrication. Replace damaged parts (Chapter 2).
☐ Piston ring(s) worn, broken or sticking. Overhaul the top-end (Chapter 2).
☐ Piston seizure damage. Usually from lack of lubrication or overheating. Replace the pistons and bore the cylinders, as necessary (Chapter 2).
☐ Connecting rod upper or lower end clearance excessive. Caused by excessive wear or lack of lubrication. Replace worn parts.

Valve noise

☐ Incorrect valve clearances. Adjust the clearances by referring to Chapter 1.
☐ Valve spring broken or weak. Check and replace weak valve springs (Chapter 2).
☐ Camshaft or cylinder head worn or damaged. Lack of lubrication at high rpm is usually the cause of damage. Insufficient oil or failure to change the oil at the recommended intervals are the chief causes. Since there are no replaceable bearings in the head, the head itself will have to be replaced if there is excessive wear or damage (Chapter 2).

7 Abnormal engine noise (continued)

Other noise

- [ ] Cylinder head gasket leaking.
- [ ] Exhaust pipe leaking at cylinder head connection. Caused by improper fit of pipe(s) or loose exhaust flange. All exhaust fasteners should be tightened evenly and carefully. Failure to do this will lead to a leak.
- [ ] Crankshaft runout excessive. Caused by a bent crankshaft (from over-revving) or damage from an upper cylinder component failure.

Can also be attributed to dropping the machine on either of the crankshaft ends.
- [ ] Engine mounting bolts loose. Tighten all engine mount bolts (Chapter 2).
- [ ] Crankshaft bearings worn (Chapter 2).
- [ ] Cam chain tensioner defective. Replace according to the procedure in Chapter 2.
- [ ] Cam chain, sprockets or guides worn (Chapter 2).

8 Abnormal driveline noise

Clutch noise

- [ ] Clutch outer drum/friction plate clearance excessive (Chapter 2).
- [ ] Loose or damaged clutch pressure plate and/or bolts (Chapter 2).

Transmission noise

- [ ] Bearings worn. Also includes the possibility that the shafts are worn. Overhaul the transmission (Chapter 2).
- [ ] Gears worn or chipped (Chapter 2).
- [ ] Metal chips jammed in gear teeth. Probably pieces from a broken clutch, gear or shift mechanism that were picked up by the gears. This will cause early bearing failure (Chapter 2).

- [ ] Engine oil level too low. Causes a howl from transmission. Also affects engine power and clutch operation. Check the oil level (see "Daily (pre-ride) checks").

Final drive noise

- [ ] Chain not adjusted properly (Chapter 1).
- [ ] Engine sprocket or rear sprocket loose. Tighten fasteners (Chapter 6).
- [ ] Sprocket(s) worn. Replace sprocket(s) (Chapter 6).
- [ ] Rear sprocket warped. Replace (Chapter 6).
- [ ] Wheel coupling damper worn. Replace damper (Chapter 6).

9 Abnormal frame and suspension noise

Front end noise

- [ ] Low fluid level or improper viscosity oil in forks. This can sound like spurting and is usually accompanied by irregular fork action (Chapter 6).
- [ ] Spring weak or broken. Makes a clicking or scraping sound. Fork oil, when drained, will have a lot of metal particles in it (Chapter 6).
- [ ] Steering head bearings loose or damaged. Clicks when braking. Check and adjust or replace as necessary (Chapters 1 and 6).
- [ ] Fork triple clamps loose. Make sure all clamp pinch bolts are tight (Chapter 6).
- [ ] Fork tube bent. Good possibility if machine has been dropped. Replace tube with a new one (Chapter 6).
- [ ] Front axle or axle clamp bolt loose. Tighten them to the specified torque (Chapter 6).

Shock absorber noise

- [ ] Fluid level incorrect. Indicates a leak caused by defective seal. Shock will be covered with oil. Replace shock or seek advice on repair from a Honda dealer (Chapter 6).
- [ ] Defective shock absorber with internal damage. This is in the body of the shock and can't be remedied. The shock must be replaced with a new one (Chapter 6).

- [ ] Bent or damaged shock body. Replace the shock with a new one (Chapter 6).

Brake noise

- [ ] Squeal caused by pad shim not installed or positioned correctly - rear caliper (Chapter 7).
- [ ] Squeal caused by dust on brake pads. Usually found in combination with glazed pads. Clean using brake cleaning solvent (Chapter 7).
- [ ] Contamination of brake pads. Oil, brake fluid or dirt causing brake to chatter or squeal. Clean or replace pads (Chapter 7).
- [ ] Pads glazed. Caused by excessive heat from prolonged use or from contamination. Do not use sandpaper, emery cloth, carborundum cloth or any other abrasive to roughen the pad surfaces as abrasives will stay in the pad material and damage the disc. A very fine flat file can be used, but pad replacement is suggested as a cure (Chapter 7).
- [ ] Disc warped. Can cause a chattering, clicking or intermittent squeal. Usually accompanied by a pulsating lever and uneven braking. Replace the disc (Chapter 7).
- [ ] Loose or worn wheel bearings. Check and replace as needed (Chapter 7).

10 Oil pressure indicator light comes on

Engine lubrication system

- [ ] Engine oil pump defective, blocked oil strainer gauze or failed relief valve. Carry out oil pressure check (Chapter 2).
- [ ] Engine oil level low. Inspect for leak or other problem causing low oil level and add recommended oil (see "Daily (pre-ride)checks").
- [ ] Engine oil viscosity too low. Very old, thin oil or an improper weight of oil used in the engine. Change to correct oil (see "Daily (pre-ride)checks").
- [ ] Camshaft or journals worn. Excessive wear causing drop in oil pressure. Replace cam and/or cylinder head. Abnormal wear could

be caused by oil starvation at high rpm from low oil level or improper weight or type of oil (see "Daily (pre-ride)checks").
- [ ] Crankshaft and/or bearings worn. Same problems as paragraph 4. Check and replace crankshaft and/or bearings (Chapter 2).

Electrical system

- [ ] Oil pressure switch defective. Check the switch according to the procedure in Chapter 9. Replace it if it is defective.
- [ ] Oil pressure indicator light circuit defective. Check for pinched, shorted, disconnected or damaged wiring (Chapter 9).

11 Excessive exhaust smoke

White smoke

☐ Piston oil ring worn. The ring may be broken or damaged, causing oil from the crankcase to be pulled past the piston into the combustion chamber. Replace the rings with new ones (Chapter 2).

☐ Cylinders worn, cracked, or scored. Caused by overheating or oil starvation. The cylinders will have to be rebored and new pistons installed.

☐ Valve oil seal damaged or worn. Replace oil seals with new ones (Chapter 2).

☐ Valve guide worn. Perform a complete valve job (Chapter 2).

☐ Engine oil level too high, which causes the oil to be forced past the rings. Drain oil to the proper level (see "Daily (pre-ride)checks").

☐ Head gasket broken between oil return and cylinder. Causes oil to be pulled into the combustion chamber. Replace the head gasket and check the head for warpage (Chapter 2).

☐ Abnormal crankcase pressurization, which forces oil past the rings. Clogged breather hose is usually the cause.

Black smoke

☐ Air filter clogged. Clean or replace the element (Chapter 1).

☐ Main jet too large or loose. Compare the jet size to the Specifications (Chapter 4).

☐ Choke cable or linkage shaft stuck, causing fuel to be pulled through choke circuit (Chapter 4).

☐ Fuel level too high. Check and adjust the float height(s) as necessary (Chapter 4).

☐ Float needle valve held off needle seat. Clean the float chambers and fuel line and replace the needles and seats if necessary (Chapter 4).

Brown smoke

☐ Main jet too small or clogged. Lean condition caused by wrong size main jet or by a restricted orifice. Clean float chambers and jets and compare jet size to Specifications (Chapter 4).

☐ Fuel flow insufficient. Float needle valve stuck closed due to chemical reaction with old fuel. Float height incorrect. Restricted fuel line. Clean line and float chamber and adjust floats if necessary.

☐ Carburetor intake manifold clamps loose (Chapter 4).

☐ Air filter poorly sealed or not installed (Chapter 1).

12 Poor handling or stability

Handlebar hard to turn

☐ Steering head bearing adjuster nut too tight. Check adjustment as described in Chapter 1.

☐ Bearings damaged. Roughness can be felt as the bars are turned from side-to-side. Replace bearings and races (Chapter 6).

☐ Races dented or worn. Denting results from wear in only one position (e.g., straight ahead), from a collision or hitting a pothole or from dropping the machine. Replace races and bearings (Chapter 6)

☐ Steering stem lubrication inadequate. Causes are grease getting hard from age or being washed out by high pressure car washes. Disassemble steering head and repack bearings (Chapter 6).

☐ Steering stem bent. Caused by a collision, hitting a pothole or by dropping the machine. Replace damaged part. Don't try to straighten the steering stem (Chapter 6).

☐ Front tire air pressure too low (Chapter 1).

Handlebar shakes or vibrates excessively

☐ Tires worn or out of balance (Chapter 7).

☐ Swingarm bearings worn. Replace worn bearings by referring to Chapter 6.

☐ Rim(s) warped or damaged. Inspect wheels for runout (Chapter 7).

☐ Wheel bearings worn. Worn front or rear wheel bearings can cause poor tracking. Worn front bearings will cause wobble (Chapter 7).

☐ Handlebar clamp bolts loose (Chapter 6).

☐ Fork triple clamp bolts loose. Tighten them to the specified torque (Chapter 6).

☐ Engine mounting bolts loose. Will cause excessive vibration with increased engine rpm (Chapter 2).

Handlebar pulls to one side

☐ Frame bent. Definitely suspect this if the machine has been dropped. May or may not be accompanied by cracking near the bend. Replace the frame (Chapter 6).

☐ Wheels out of alignment. Caused by improper location of axle spacers or from bent steering stem or frame (Chapter 6).

☐ Swingarm bent or twisted. Caused by age (metal fatigue) or impact damage. Replace the arm (Chapter 6).

☐ Steering stem bent. Caused by impact damage or by dropping the motorcycle. Replace the steering stem (Chapter 6).

☐ Fork tube bent. Disassemble the forks and replace the damaged parts (Chapter 6).

☐ Fork oil level uneven. Check and add or drain as necessary (Chapter 6).

Poor shock absorbing qualities

☐ Too hard:
Fork oil level excessive (Chapter 6).
Fork oil viscosity too high. Use a lighter oil (see the Specifications in Chapter 6).
Fork tube bent. Causes a harsh, sticking feeling (Chapter 6).
Shock shaft or body bent or damaged (Chapter 6).
Fork internal damage (Chapter 6).
Shock internal damage.
Tire pressure too high (Chapter 1).

☐ Too soft:
Fork or shock oil insufficient and/or leaking (Chapter 6).
Fork oil level too low (Chapter 6).
Fork oil viscosity too light (Chapter 6).
Fork springs weak or broken (Chapter 6).
Shock internal damage or leakage (Chapter 6).

13 Braking problems

Brakes are spongy, don't hold

☐ Air in brake line. Caused by inattention to master cylinder fluid level or by leakage. Locate problem and bleed brakes (Chapter 7).
☐ Pad or disc worn (Chapters 1 and 7).
☐ Brake fluid leak. See paragraph 1.
☐ Contaminated pads. Caused by contamination with oil, grease, brake fluid, etc. Clean or replace pads. Clean disc thoroughly with brake cleaner (Chapter 7).
☐ Brake fluid deteriorated. Fluid is old or contaminated. Drain system, replenish with new fluid and bleed the system (Chapter 7).
☐ Master cylinder internal parts worn or damaged causing fluid to bypass (Chapter 7).
☐ Master cylinder bore scratched by foreign material or broken spring. Repair or replace master cylinder (Chapter 7).
☐ Disc warped. Replace disc (Chapter 7).

Brake lever or pedal pulsates

☐ Disc warped. Replace disc (Chapter 7).
☐ Axle bent. Replace axle (Chapter 7).

☐ Brake caliper bolts loose (Chapter 7).
☐ Brake caliper sliders damaged or sticking (rear caliper), causing caliper to bind. Lubricate the sliders or replace them if they are corroded or bent (Chapter 7).
☐ Wheel warped or otherwise damaged (Chapter 7).
☐ Wheel bearings damaged or worn (Chapter 7).

Brakes drag

☐ Master cylinder piston seized. Caused by wear or damage to piston or cylinder bore (Chapter 7).
☐ Lever balky or stuck. Check pivot and lubricate (Chapter 7).
☐ Brake caliper binds. Caused by inadequate lubrication or damage to caliper sliders (Chapter 7).
☐ Brake caliper piston seized in bore. Caused by wear or ingestion of dirt past deteriorated seal (Chapter 7).
☐ Brake pad damaged. Pad material separated from backing plate. Usually caused by faulty manufacturing process or from contact with chemicals. Replace pads (Chapter 7).
☐ Pads improperly installed (Chapter 7).

14 Electrical problems

Battery dead or weak

☐ Battery faulty. Caused by sulfated plates which are shorted through sedimentation. Also, broken battery terminal making only occasional contact (Chapter 9).
☐ Battery cables making poor contact (Chapter 9).
☐ Load excessive. Caused by addition of high wattage lights or other electrical accessories.
☐ Ignition (main) switch defective. Switch either grounds (earths) internally or fails to shut off system. Replace the switch (Chapter 9).
☐ Regulator/rectifier defective (Chapter 9).
☐ Alternator stator coil open or shorted (Chapter 9).
☐ Wiring faulty. Wiring grounded (earthed) or connections loose in ignition, charging or lighting circuits (Chapter 9).

Battery overcharged

☐ Regulator/rectifier defective. Overcharging is noticed when battery gets excessively warm (Chapter 9).
☐ Battery defective. Replace battery with a new one (Chapter 9).
☐ Battery amperage too low, wrong type or size. Install manufacturer's specified amp-hour battery to handle charging load (Chapter 9).

Checking engine compression

● Low compression will result in exhaust smoke, heavy oil consumption, poor starting and poor performance. A compression test will provide useful information about an engine's condition and if performed regularly, can give warning of trouble before any other symptoms become apparent.

● A compression gauge will be required, along with an adapter to suit the spark plug hole thread size. Note that the screw-in type gauge/adapter set up is preferable to the rubber cone type.

● Before carrying out the test, first check the valve clearances as described in Chapter 1.

1 Run the engine until it reaches normal operating temperature, then stop it and remove the spark plug(s), taking care not to scald your hands on the hot components.

2 Install the gauge adapter and compression gauge in No. 1 cylinder spark plug hole (see illustration 1).

Screw the compression gauge adapter into the spark plug hole, then screw the gauge into the adapter

3 On kickstart-equipped motorcycles, make sure the ignition switch is OFF, then open the throttle fully and kick the engine over a couple of times until the gauge reading stabilises.

4 On motorcycles with electric start only, the procedure will differ depending on the nature of the ignition system. Flick the engine kill switch (engine stop switch) to OFF and turn the ignition switch ON; open the throttle fully and crank the engine over on the starter motor for a couple of revolutions until the gauge reading stabilises. If the starter will not operate with the kill switch OFF, turn the ignition switch OFF and refer to the next paragraph.

5 Install the spark plugs back into their suppressor caps and arrange the plug electrodes so that their metal bodies are earthed (grounded) against the cylinder head; this is essential to prevent damage to the ignition system as the engine is spun over (see illustration 2). Position the plugs well

All spark plugs must be earthed (grounded) against the cylinder head

away from the plug holes otherwise there is a risk of atomised fuel escaping from the combustion chambers and igniting. As a safety precaution, cover the top of the valve cover with rag. Now turn the ignition switch ON and kill switch ON, open the throttle fully and crank the engine over on the starter motor for a couple of revolutions until the gauge reading stabilises.

6 After one or two revolutions the pressure should build up to a maximum figure and then stabilise. Take a note of this reading and on multi-cylinder engines repeat the test on the remaining cylinders.

7 The correct pressures are given in Chapter 2 Specifications. If the results fall within the specified range and on multi-cylinder engines all are relatively equal, the engine is in good condition. If there is a marked difference between the readings, or if the readings are lower than specified, inspection of the top-end components will be required.

8 Low compression pressure may be due to worn cylinder bores, pistons or rings, failure of the cylinder head gasket, worn valve seals, or poor valve seating.

9 To distinguish between cylinder/piston wear and valve leakage, pour a small quantity of oil into the bore to temporarily seal the piston rings, then repeat the compression tests (see illustration 3). If the readings show

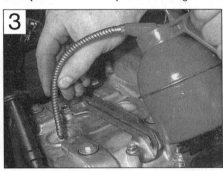

Bores can be temporarily sealed with a squirt of motor oil

a noticeable increase in pressure this confirms that the cylinder bore, piston, or rings are worn. If, however, no change is indicated, the cylinder head gasket or valves should be examined.

10 High compression pressure indicates excessive carbon build-up in the combustion chamber and on the piston crown. If this is the case the cylinder head should be removed and the deposits removed. Note that excessive carbon build-up is less likely with the used on modern fuels.

Checking battery open-circuit voltage

 Warning: The gases produced by the battery are explosive - never smoke or create any sparks in the vicinity of the battery. Never allow the electrolyte to contact your skin or clothing - if it does, wash it off and seek immediate medical attention.

Measuring open-circuit battery voltage

Float-type hydrometer for measuring battery specific gravity

● Before any electrical fault is investigated the battery should be checked.

● You'll need a dc voltmeter or multimeter to check battery voltage. Check that the leads are inserted in the correct terminals on the meter, red lead to positive (+ve), black lead to negative (-ve). Incorrect connections can damage the meter.

● A sound fully-charged 12 volt battery should produce between 12.3 and 12.6 volts across its terminals (12.8 volts for a maintenance-free battery). On machines with a 6 volt battery, voltage should be between 6.1 and 6.3 volts.

1 Set a multimeter to the 0 to 20 volts dc range and connect its probes across the battery terminals. Connect the meter's positive (+ve) probe, usually red, to the battery positive (+ve) terminal, followed by the meter's negative (-ve) probe, usually black, to the battery negative terminal (-ve) **(see illustration 4).**

2 If battery voltage is low (below 10 volts on a 12 volt battery or below 4 volts on a six volt battery), charge the battery and test the voltage again. If the battery repeatedly goes flat, investigate the motorcycle's charging system.

Checking battery specific gravity (SG)

⚠️ **Warning: The gases produced by the battery are explosive - never smoke or create any sparks in the vicinity of the battery. Never allow the electrolyte to contact your skin or clothing - if it does, wash it off and seek immediate medical attention.**

● The specific gravity check gives an indication of a battery's state of charge.

● A hydrometer is used for measuring specific gravity. Make sure you purchase one

which has a small enough hose to insert in the aperture of a motorcycle battery.

● Specific gravity is simply a measure of the electrolyte's density compared with that of water. Water has an SG of 1.000 and fully-charged battery electrolyte is about 26% heavier, at 1.260.

● Specific gravity checks are not possible on maintenance-free batteries. Testing the open-circuit voltage is the only means of determining their state of charge.

1 To measure SG, remove the battery from the motorcycle and remove the first cell cap. Draw

Digital multimeter can be used for all electrical tests

Battery-powered continuity tester

some electrolyte into the hydrometer and note the reading **(see illustration 5)**. Return the electrolyte to the cell and install the cap.

2 The reading should be in the region of 1.260 to 1.280. If SG is below 1.200 the battery needs charging. Note that SG will vary with temperature; it should be measured at 20°C (68°F). Add 0.007 to the reading for every 10°C above 20°C, and subtract 0.007 from the reading for every 10°C below 20°C. Add 0.004 to the reading for every 10°F above 68°F, and subtract 0.004 from the reading for every 10°F below 68°F.

3 When the check is complete, rinse the hydrometer thoroughly with clean water.

Checking for continuity

● The term continuity describes the uninterrupted flow of electricity through an electrical circuit. A continuity check will determine whether an **open-circuit** situation exists.

● Continuity can be checked with an ohmmeter, multimeter, continuity tester or battery and bulb test circuit **(see illustrations 6, 7 and 8)**.

Battery and bulb test circuit

Continuity check of front brake light switch using a meter - note split pins used to access connector terminals

Continuity check of rear brake light switch using a continuity tester

● All of these instruments are self-powered by a battery, therefore the checks are made with the ignition OFF.

● As a safety precaution, always disconnect the battery negative (-ve) lead before making checks, particularly if ignition switch checks are being made.

● If using a meter, select the appropriate ohms scale and check that the meter reads infinity (∞). Touch the meter probes together and check that meter reads zero; where necessary adjust the meter so that it reads zero.

● After using a meter, always switch it OFF to conserve its battery.

Switch checks

1 If a switch is at fault, trace its wiring up to the wiring connectors. Separate the wire connectors and inspect them for security and condition. A build-up of dirt or corrosion here will most likely be the cause of the problem - clean up and apply a water dispersant such as WD40.

2 If using a test meter, set the meter to the ohms x 10 scale and connect its probes across the wires from the switch **(see illustration 9)**. Simple ON/OFF type switches, such as brake light switches, only have two wires whereas combination switches, like the ignition switch, have many internal links. Study the wiring diagram to ensure that you are connecting across the correct pair of wires. Continuity (low or no measurable resistance - 0 ohms) should be indicated with the switch ON and no continuity (high resistance) with it OFF.

3 Note that the polarity of the test probes doesn't matter for continuity checks, although care should be taken to follow specific test procedures if a diode or solid-state component is being checked.

4 A continuity tester or battery and bulb circuit can be used in the same way. Connect its probes as described above **(see illustration 10)**. The light should come on to indicate continuity in the ON switch position, but should extinguish in the OFF position.

Wiring checks

● Many electrical faults are caused by damaged wiring, often due to incorrect routing or chaffing on frame components.

● Loose, wet or corroded wire connectors can also be the cause of electrical problems, especially in exposed locations.

1 A continuity check can be made on a single length of wire by disconnecting it at each end and connecting a meter or continuity tester across both ends of the wire **(see illustration 11)**.

2 Continuity (low or no resistance - 0 ohms) should be indicated if the wire is good. If no continuity (high resistance) is shown, suspect a broken wire.

Checking for voltage

● A voltage check can determine whether current is reaching a component.

● Voltage can be checked with a dc voltmeter, multimeter set on the dc volts scale, test light or buzzer **(see illustrations 12 and 13)**. A meter has the advantage of being able to measure actual voltage.

● When using a meter, check that its leads are inserted in the correct terminals on the meter, red to positive (+ve), black to negative (-ve). Incorrect connections can damage the meter.

● A voltmeter (or multimeter set to the dc volts scale) should always be connected in parallel (across the load). Connecting it in series will destroy the meter.

● Voltage checks are made with the ignition ON.

Continuity check of front brake light switch sub-harness

A simple test light can be used for voltage checks

A buzzer is useful for voltage checks

Checking for voltage at the rear brake light power supply wire using a meter . . .

1 First identify the relevant wiring circuit by referring to the wiring diagram at the end of this manual. If other electrical components share the same power supply (ie are fed from the same fuse), take note whether they are working correctly - this is useful information in deciding where to start checking the circuit.
2 If using a meter, check first that the meter leads are plugged into the correct terminals on the meter (see above). Set the meter to the dc volts function, at a range suitable for the battery voltage. Connect the meter red probe (+ve) to the power supply wire and the black probe to a good metal earth (ground) on the motorcycle's frame or directly to the battery negative (-ve) terminal **(see illustration 14)**. Battery voltage should be shown on the meter

A selection of jumper wires for making earth (ground) checks

. . . or a test light - note the earth connection to the frame (arrow)

with the ignition switched ON.
3 If using a test light or buzzer, connect its positive (+ve) probe to the power supply terminal and its negative (-ve) probe to a good earth (ground) on the motorcycle's frame or directly to the battery negative (-ve) terminal **(see illustration 15)**. With the ignition ON, the test light should illuminate or the buzzer sound.
4 If no voltage is indicated, work back towards the fuse continuing to check for voltage. When you reach a point where there is voltage, you know the problem lies between that point and your last check point.

Checking the earth (ground)

● Earth connections are made either directly to the engine or frame (such as sensors, neutral switch etc. which only have a positive feed) or by a separate wire into the earth circuit of the wiring harness. Alternatively a short earth wire is sometimes run directly from the component to the motorcycle's frame.
● Corrosion is often the cause of a poor earth connection.
● If total failure is experienced, check the security of the main earth lead from the

negative (-ve) terminal of the battery and also the main earth (ground) point on the wiring harness. If corroded, dismantle the connection and clean all surfaces back to bare metal.
1 To check the earth on a component, use an insulated jumper wire to temporarily bypass its earth connection **(see illustration 16)**. Connect one end of the jumper wire between the earth terminal or metal body of the component and the other end to the motorcycle's frame.
2 If the circuit works with the jumper wire installed, the original earth circuit is faulty. Check the wiring for open-circuits or poor connections. Clean up direct earth connections, removing all traces of corrosion and remake the joint. Apply petroleum jelly to the joint to prevent future corrosion.

Tracing a short-circuit

● A short-circuit occurs where current shorts to earth (ground) bypassing the circuit components. This usually results in a blown fuse.

● A short-circuit is most likely to occur where the insulation has worn through due to wiring chafing on a component, allowing a direct path to earth (ground) on the frame.

1 Remove any bodypanels necessary to access the circuit wiring.
2 Check that all electrical switches in the circuit are OFF, then remove the circuit fuse and connect a test light, buzzer or voltmeter (set to the dc scale) across the fuse terminals. No voltage should be shown.
3 Move the wiring from side to side whilst observing the test light or meter. When the test light comes on, buzzer sounds or meter shows voltage, you have found the cause of the short. It will usually shown up as damaged or burned insulation.
4 Note that the same test can be performed on each component in the circuit, even the switch.

A

ABS (Anti-lock braking system) A system, usually electronically controlled, that senses incipient wheel lockup during braking and relieves hydraulic pressure at wheel which is about to skid.

Aftermarket Components suitable for the motorcycle, but not produced by the motorcycle manufacturer.

Allen key A hexagonal wrench which fits into a recessed hexagonal hole.

Alternating current (ac) Current produced by an alternator. Requires converting to direct current by a rectifier for charging purposes.

Alternator Converts mechanical energy from the engine into electrical energy to charge the battery and power the electrical system.

Ampere (amp) A unit of measurement for the flow of electrical current. Current = Volts ÷ Ohms.

Ampere-hour (Ah) Measure of battery capacity.

Angle-tightening A torque expressed in degrees. Often follows a conventional tightening torque for cylinder head or main bearing fasteners **(see illustration)**.

Angle-tightening cylinder head bolts

Antifreeze A substance (usually ethylene glycol) mixed with water, and added to the cooling system, to prevent freezing of the coolant in winter. Antifreeze also contains chemicals to inhibit corrosion and the formation of rust and other deposits that would tend to clog the radiator and coolant passages and reduce cooling efficiency.

Anti-dive System attached to the fork lower leg (slider) to prevent fork dive when braking hard.

Anti-seize compound A coating that reduces the risk of seizing on fasteners that are subjected to high temperatures, such as exhaust clamp bolts and nuts.

API American Petroleum Institute. A quality standard for 4-stroke motor oils.

Asbestos A natural fibrous mineral with great heat resistance, commonly used in the composition of brake friction materials. Asbestos is a health hazard and the dust created by brake systems should never be inhaled or ingested.

ATF Automatic Transmission Fluid. Often used in front forks.

ATU Automatic Timing Unit. Mechanical device for advancing the ignition timing on early engines.

ATV All Terrain Vehicle. Often called a Quad.

Axial play Side-to-side movement.

Axle A shaft on which a wheel revolves. Also known as a spindle.

B

Backlash The amount of movement between meshed components when one component is held still. Usually applies to gear teeth.

Ball bearing A bearing consisting of a hardened inner and outer race with hardened steel balls between the two races.

Bearings Used between two working surfaces to prevent wear of the components and a build-up of heat. Four types of bearing are commonly used on motorcycles: plain shell bearings, ball bearings, tapered roller bearings and needle roller bearings.

Bevel gears Used to turn the drive through 90°. Typical applications are shaft final drive and camshaft drive **(see illustration)**.

Bevel gears are used to turn the drive through 90°

BHP Brake Horsepower. The British measurement for engine power output. Power output is now usually expressed in kilowatts (kW).

Bias-belted tyre Similar construction to radial tyre, but with outer belt running at an angle to the wheel rim.

Big-end bearing The bearing in the end of the connecting rod that's attached to the crankshaft.

Bleeding The process of removing air from an hydraulic system via a bleed nipple or bleed screw.

Bottom-end A description of an engine's crankcase components and all components contained there-in.

BTDC Before Top Dead Centre in terms of piston position. Ignition timing is often expressed in terms of degrees or millimetres BTDC.

Bush A cylindrical metal or rubber component used between two moving parts.

Burr Rough edge left on a component after machining or as a result of excessive wear.

C

Cam chain The chain which takes drive from the crankshaft to the camshaft(s).

Canister The main component in an evaporative emission control system (California market only); contains activated charcoal granules to trap vapours from the fuel system rather than allowing them to vent to the atmosphere.

Castellated Resembling the parapets along the top of a castle wall. For example, a castellated wheel axle or spindle nut.

Catalytic converter A device in the exhaust system of some machines which converts certain pollutants in the exhaust gases into less harmful substances.

Charging system Description of the components which charge the battery, ie the alternator, rectifer and regulator.

Circlip A ring-shaped clip used to prevent endwise movement of cylindrical parts and shafts. An internal circlip is installed in a groove in a housing; an external circlip fits into a groove on the outside of a cylindrical piece such as a shaft. Also known as a snap-ring.

Clearance The amount of space between two parts. For example, between a piston and a cylinder, between a bearing and a journal, etc.

Coil spring A spiral of elastic steel found in various sizes throughout a vehicle, for example as a springing medium in the suspension and in the valve train.

Compression Reduction in volume, and increase in pressure and temperature, of a gas, caused by squeezing it into a smaller space.

Compression damping Controls the speed the suspension compresses when hitting a bump.

Compression ratio The relationship between cylinder volume when the piston is at top dead centre and cylinder volume when the piston is at bottom dead centre.

Continuity The uninterrupted path in the flow of electricity. Little or no measurable resistance.

Continuity tester Self-powered bleeper or test light which indicates continuity.

Cp Candlepower. Bulb rating commonly found on US motorcycles.

Crossply tyre Tyre plies arranged in a criss-cross pattern. Usually four or six plies used, hence 4PR or 6PR in tyre size codes.

Cush drive Rubber damper segments fitted between the rear wheel and final drive sprocket to absorb transmission shocks **(see illustration)**.

Cush drive rubbers dampen out transmission shocks

D

Degree disc Calibrated disc for measuring piston position. Expressed in degrees.

Dial gauge Clock-type gauge with adapters for measuring runout and piston position. Expressed in mm or inches.

Diaphragm The rubber membrane in a master cylinder or carburettor which seals the upper chamber.

Diaphragm spring A single sprung plate often used in clutches.

Direct current (dc) Current produced by a dc generator.

Decarbonisation The process of removing carbon deposits - typically from the combustion chamber, valves and exhaust port/system.

Detonation Destructive and damaging explosion of fuel/air mixture in combustion chamber instead of controlled burning.

Diode An electrical valve which only allows current to flow in one direction. Commonly used in rectifiers and starter interlock systems.

Disc valve (or rotary valve) A induction system used on some two-stroke engines.

Double-overhead camshaft (DOHC) An engine that uses two overhead camshafts, one for the intake valves and one for the exhaust valves.

Drivebelt A toothed belt used to transmit drive to the rear wheel on some motorcycles. A drivebelt has also been used to drive the camshafts. Drivebelts are usually made of Kevlar.

Driveshaft Any shaft used to transmit motion. Commonly used when referring to the final driveshaft on shaft drive motorcycles.

E

Earth return The return path of an electrical circuit, utilising the motorcycle's frame.

ECU (Electronic Control Unit) A computer which controls (for instance) an ignition system, or an anti-lock braking system.

EGO Exhaust Gas Oxygen sensor. Sometimes called a Lambda sensor.

Electrolyte The fluid in a lead-acid battery.

EMS (Engine Management System) A computer controlled system which manages the fuel injection and the ignition systems in an integrated fashion.

Endfloat The amount of lengthways movement between two parts. As applied to a crankshaft, the distance that the crankshaft can move side-to-side in the crankcase.

Endless chain A chain having no joining link. Common use for cam chains and final drive chains.

EP (Extreme Pressure) Oil type used in locations where high loads are applied, such as between gear teeth.

Evaporative emission control system Describes a charcoal filled canister which stores fuel vapours from the tank rather than allowing them to vent to the atmosphere. Usually only fitted to California models and referred to as an EVAP system.

Expansion chamber Section of two-stroke engine exhaust system so designed to improve engine efficiency and boost power.

F

Feeler blade or gauge A thin strip or blade of hardened steel, ground to an exact thickness, used to check or measure clearances between parts.

Final drive Description of the drive from the transmission to the rear wheel. Usually by chain or shaft, but sometimes by belt.

Firing order The order in which the engine cylinders fire, or deliver their power strokes, beginning with the number one cylinder.

Flooding Term used to describe a high fuel level in the carburettor float chambers, leading to fuel overflow. Also refers to excess fuel in the combustion chamber due to incorrect starting technique.

Free length The no-load state of a component when measured. Clutch, valve and fork spring lengths are measured at rest, without any preload.

Freeplay The amount of travel before any action takes place. The looseness in a linkage, or an assembly of parts, between the initial application of force and actual movement. For example, the distance the rear brake pedal moves before the rear brake is actuated.

Fuel injection The fuel/air mixture is metered electronically and directed into the engine intake ports (indirect injection) or into the cylinders (direct injection). Sensors supply information on engine speed and conditions.

Fuel/air mixture The charge of fuel and air going into the engine. See **Stoichiometric ratio.**

Fuse An electrical device which protects a circuit against accidental overload. The typical fuse contains a soft piece of metal which is calibrated to melt at a predetermined current flow (expressed as amps) and break the circuit.

G

Gap The distance the spark must travel in jumping from the centre electrode to the side electrode in a spark plug. Also refers to the distance between the ignition rotor and the pickup coil in an electronic ignition system.

Gasket Any thin, soft material - usually cork, cardboard, asbestos or soft metal - installed between two metal surfaces to ensure a good seal. For instance, the cylinder head gasket seals the joint between the block and the cylinder head.

Gauge An instrument panel display used to monitor engine conditions. A gauge with a movable pointer on a dial or a fixed scale is an analogue gauge. A gauge with a numerical readout is called a digital gauge.

Gear ratios The drive ratio of a pair of gears in a gearbox, calculated on their number of teeth.

Glaze-busting see **Honing**

Grinding Process for renovating the valve face and valve seat contact area in the cylinder head.

Gudgeon pin The shaft which connects the connecting rod small-end with the piston. Often called a piston pin or wrist pin.

H

Helical gears Gear teeth are slightly curved and produce less gear noise that straight-cut gears. Often used for primary drives.

Installing a Helicoil thread insert in a cylinder head

Helicoil A thread insert repair system. Commonly used as a repair for stripped spark plug threads **(see illustration).**

Honing A process used to break down the glaze on a cylinder bore (also called glaze-busting). Can also be carried out to roughen a rebored cylinder to aid ring bedding-in.

HT (High Tension) Description of the electrical circuit from the secondary winding of the ignition coil to the spark plug.

Hydraulic A liquid filled system used to transmit pressure from one component to another. Common uses on motorcycles are brakes and clutches.

Hydrometer An instrument for measuring the specific gravity of a lead-acid battery.

Hygroscopic Water absorbing. In motorcycle applications, braking efficiency will be reduced if DOT 3 or 4 hydraulic fluid absorbs water from the air - care must be taken to keep new brake fluid in tightly sealed containers.

I

lbf ft Pounds-force feet. An imperial unit of torque. Sometimes written as ft-lbs.

lbf in Pound-force inch. An imperial unit of torque, applied to components where a very low torque is required. Sometimes written as in-lbs.

IC Abbreviation for Integrated Circuit.

Ignition advance Means of increasing the timing of the spark at higher engine speeds. Done by mechanical means (ATU) on early engines or electronically by the ignition control unit on later engines.

Ignition timing The moment at which the spark plug fires, expressed in the number of crankshaft degrees before the piston reaches the top of its stroke, or in the number of millimetres before the piston reaches the top of its stroke.

Infinity (∞) Description of an open-circuit electrical state, where no continuity exists.

Inverted forks (upside down forks) The sliders or lower legs are held in the yokes and the fork tubes or stanchions are connected to the wheel axle (spindle). Less unsprung weight and stiffer construction than conventional forks.

J

JASO Quality standard for 2-stroke oils.

Joule The unit of electrical energy.

Journal The bearing surface of a shaft.

K

Kickstart Mechanical means of turning the engine over for starting purposes. Only usually fitted to mopeds, small capacity motorcycles and off-road motorcycles.

Kill switch Handebar-mounted switch for emergency ignition cut-out. Cuts the ignition circuit on all models, and additionally prevent starter motor operation on others.

km Symbol for kilometre.

kmh Abbreviation for kilometres per hour.

L

Lambda (λ) sensor A sensor fitted in the exhaust system to measure the exhaust gas oxygen content (excess air factor).

Lapping see **Grinding**.
LCD Abbreviation for Liquid Crystal Display.
LED Abbreviation for Light Emitting Diode.
Liner A steel cylinder liner inserted in a aluminium alloy cylinder block.
Locknut A nut used to lock an adjustment nut, or other threaded component, in place.
Lockstops The lugs on the lower triple clamp (yoke) which abut those on the frame, preventing handlebar-to-fuel tank contact.
Lockwasher A form of washer designed to prevent an attaching nut from working loose.
LT Low Tension Description of the electrical circuit from the power supply to the primary winding of the ignition coil.

M

Main bearings The bearings between the crankshaft and crankcase.
Maintenance-free (MF) battery A sealed battery which cannot be topped up.
Manometer Mercury-filled calibrated tubes used to measure intake tract vacuum. Used to synchronise carburettors on multi-cylinder engines.
Micrometer A precision measuring instrument that measures component outside diameters **(see illustration)**.

Tappet shims are measured with a micrometer

MON (Motor Octane Number) A measure of a fuel's resistance to knock.
Monograde oil An oil with a single viscosity, eg SAE80W.
Monoshock A single suspension unit linking the swingarm or suspension linkage to the frame.
mph Abbreviation for miles per hour.
Multigrade oil Having a wide viscosity range (eg 10W40). The W stands for Winter, thus the viscosity ranges from SAE10 when cold to SAE40 when hot.
Multimeter An electrical test instrument with the capability to measure voltage, current and resistance. Some meters also incorporate a continuity tester and buzzer.

N

Needle roller bearing Inner race of caged needle rollers and hardened outer race. Examples of uncaged needle rollers can be found on some engines. Commonly used in rear suspension applications and in two-stroke engines.
Nm Newton metres.
NOx Oxides of Nitrogen. A common toxic pollutant emitted by petrol engines at higher temperatures.

O

Octane The measure of a fuel's resistance to knock.
OE (Original Equipment) Relates to components fitted to a motorcycle as standard or replacement parts supplied by the motorcycle manufacturer.
Ohm The unit of electrical resistance. Ohms = Volts ÷ Current.
Ohmmeter An instrument for measuring electrical resistance.
Oil cooler System for diverting engine oil outside of the engine to a radiator for cooling purposes.
Oil injection A system of two-stroke engine lubrication where oil is pump-fed to the engine in accordance with throttle position.
Open-circuit An electrical condition where there is a break in the flow of electricity - no continuity (high resistance).
O-ring A type of sealing ring made of a special rubber-like material; in use, the O-ring is compressed into a groove to provide the sealing action.
Oversize (OS) Term used for piston and ring size options fitted to a rebored cylinder.
Overhead cam (sohc) engine An engine with single camshaft located on top of the cylinder head.
Overhead valve (ohv) engine An engine with the valves located in the cylinder head, but with the camshaft located in the engine block or crankcase.
Oxygen sensor A device installed in the exhaust system which senses the oxygen content in the exhaust and converts this information into an electric current. Also called a Lambda sensor.

P

Plastigauge A thin strip of plastic thread, available in different sizes, used for measuring clearances. For example, a strip of Plastigauge is laid across a bearing journal. The parts are assembled and dismantled; the width of the crushed strip indicates the clearance between journal and bearing.
Polarity Either negative or positive earth (ground), determined by which battery lead is connected to the frame (earth return). Modern motorcycles are usually negative earth.
Pre-ignition A situation where the fuel/air mixture ignites before the spark plug fires. Often due to a hot spot in the combustion chamber caused by carbon build-up. Engine has a tendency to 'run-on'.
Pre-load (suspension) The amount a spring is compressed when in the unloaded state. Preload can be applied by gas, spacer or mechanical adjuster.
Premix The method of engine lubrication on older two-stroke engines. Engine oil is mixed with the petrol in the fuel tank in a specific ratio. The fuel/oil mix is sometimes referred to as "petroil".
Primary drive Description of the drive from the crankshaft to the clutch. Usually by gear or chain.
PS Pfedestärke - a German interpretation of BHP.
PSI Pounds-force per square inch. Imperial measurement of tyre pressure and cylinder pressure measurement.
PTFE Polytetrafluroethylene. A low friction substance.

Pulse secondary air injection system A process of promoting the burning of excess fuel present in the exhaust gases by routing fresh air into the exhaust ports.

Q

Quartz halogen bulb Tungsten filament surrounded by a halogen gas. Typically used for the headlight **(see illustration)**.

Quartz halogen headlight bulb construction

R

Rack-and-pinion A pinion gear on the end of a shaft that mates with a rack (think of a geared wheel opened up and laid flat). Sometimes used in clutch operating systems.
Radial play Up and down movement about a shaft.
Radial ply tyres Tyre plies run across the tyre (from bead to bead) and around the circumference of the tyre. Less resistant to tread distortion than other tyre types.
Radiator A liquid-to-air heat transfer device designed to reduce the temperature of the coolant in a liquid cooled engine.
Rake A feature of steering geometry - the angle of the steering head in relation to the vertical **(see illustration)**.

Steering geometry

Rebore Providing a new working surface to the cylinder bore by boring out the old surface. Necessitates the use of oversize piston and rings.

Rebound damping A means of controlling the oscillation of a suspension unit spring after it has been compressed. Resists the spring's natural tendency to bounce back after being compressed.

Rectifier Device for converting the ac output of an alternator into dc for battery charging.

Reed valve An induction system commonly used on two-stroke engines.

Regulator Device for maintaining the charging voltage from the generator or alternator within a specified range.

Relay A electrical device used to switch heavy current on and off by using a low current auxiliary circuit.

Resistance Measured in ohms. An electrical component's ability to pass electrical current.

RON (Research Octane Number) A measure of a fuel's resistance to knock.

rpm revolutions per minute.

Runout The amount of wobble (in-and-out movement) of a wheel or shaft as it's rotated. The amount a shaft rotates 'out-of-true'. The out-of-round condition of a rotating part.

S

SAE (Society of Automotive Engineers) A standard for the viscosity of a fluid.

Sealant A liquid or paste used to prevent leakage at a joint. Sometimes used in conjunction with a gasket.

Service limit Term for the point where a component is no longer useable and must be renewed.

Shaft drive A method of transmitting drive from the transmission to the rear wheel.

Shell bearings Plain bearings consisting of two shell halves. Most often used as big-end and main bearings in a four-stroke engine. Often called bearing inserts.

Shim Thin spacer, commonly used to adjust the clearance or relative positions between two parts. For example, shims inserted into or under tappets or followers to control valve clearances. Clearance is adjusted by changing the thickness of the shim.

Short-circuit An electrical condition where current shorts to earth (ground) bypassing the circuit components.

Skimming Process to correct warpage or repair a damaged surface, eg on brake discs or drums.

Slide-hammer A special puller that screws into or hooks onto a component such as a shaft or bearing; a heavy sliding handle on the shaft bottoms against the end of the shaft to knock the component free.

Small-end bearing The bearing in the upper end of the connecting rod at its joint with the gudgeon pin.

Spalling Damage to camshaft lobes or bearing journals shown as pitting of the working surface.

Specific gravity (SG) The state of charge of the electrolyte in a lead-acid battery. A measure of the electrolyte's density compared with water.

Straight-cut gears Common type gear used on gearbox shafts and for oil pump and water pump drives.

Stanchion The inner sliding part of the front forks, held by the yokes. Often called a fork tube.

Stoichiometric ratio The optimum chemical air/fuel ratio for a petrol engine, said to be 14.7 parts of air to 1 part of fuel.

Sulphuric acid The liquid (electrolyte) used in a lead-acid battery. Poisonous and extremely corrosive.

Surface grinding (lapping) Process to correct a warped gasket face, commonly used on cylinder heads.

T

Tapered-roller bearing Tapered inner race of caged needle rollers and separate tapered outer race. Examples of taper roller bearings can be found on steering heads.

Tappet A cylindrical component which transmits motion from the cam to the valve stem, either directly or via a pushrod and rocker arm. Also called a cam follower.

TCS Traction Control System. An electronically-controlled system which senses wheel spin and reduces engine speed accordingly.

TDC Top Dead Centre denotes that the piston is at its highest point in the cylinder.

Thread-locking compound Solution applied to fastener threads to prevent slackening. Select type to suit application.

Thrust washer A washer positioned between two moving components on a shaft. For example, between gear pinions on gearshaft.

Timing chain See **Cam Chain.**

Timing light Stroboscopic lamp for carrying out ignition timing checks with the engine running.

Top-end A description of an engine's cylinder block, head and valve gear components.

Torque Turning or twisting force about a shaft.

Torque setting A prescribed tightness specified by the motorcycle manufacturer to ensure that the bolt or nut is secured correctly. Undertightening can result in the bolt or nut coming loose or a surface not being sealed. Overtightening can result in stripped threads, distortion or damage to the component being retained.

Torx key A six-point wrench.

Tracer A stripe of a second colour applied to a wire insulator to distinguish that wire from another one with the same colour insulator. For example, Br/W is often used to denote a brown insulator with a white tracer.

Trail A feature of steering geometry. Distance from the steering head axis to the tyre's central contact point.

Triple clamps The cast components which extend from the steering head and support the fork stanchions or tubes. Often called fork yokes.

Turbocharger A centrifugal device, driven by exhaust gases, that pressurises the intake air. Normally used to increase the power output from a given engine displacement.

TWI Abbreviation for Tyre Wear Indicator. Indicates the location of the tread depth indicator bars on tyres.

U

Universal joint or U-joint (UJ) A double-pivoted connection for transmitting power from a driving to a driven shaft through an angle. Typically found in shaft drive assemblies.

Unsprung weight Anything not supported by the bike's suspension (ie the wheel, tyres, brakes, final drive and bottom (moving) part of the suspension).

V

Vacuum gauges Clock-type gauges for measuring intake tract vacuum. Used for carburettor synchronisation on multi-cylinder engines.

Valve A device through which the flow of liquid, gas or vacuum may be stopped, started or regulated by a moveable part that opens, shuts or partially obstructs one or more ports or passageways. The intake and exhaust valves in the cylinder head are of the poppet type.

Valve clearance The clearance between the valve tip (the end of the valve stem) and the rocker arm or tappet/follower. The valve clearance is measured when the valve is closed. The correct clearance is important - if too small the valve won't close fully and will burn out, whereas if too large noisy operation will result.

Valve lift The amount a valve is lifted off its seat by the camshaft lobe.

Valve timing The exact setting for the opening and closing of the valves in relation to piston position.

Vernier caliper A precision measuring instrument that measures inside and outside dimensions. Not quite as accurate as a micrometer, but more convenient.

VIN Vehicle Identification Number. Term for the bike's engine and frame numbers.

Viscosity The thickness of a liquid or its resistance to flow.

Volt A unit for expressing electrical "pressure" in a circuit. Volts = current x ohms.

W

Water pump A mechanically-driven device for moving coolant around the engine.

Watt A unit for expressing electrical power. Watts = volts x current.

Wear limit see **Service limit**

Wet liner A liquid-cooled engine design where the pistons run in liners which are directly surrounded by coolant **(see illustration)**.

Wet liner arrangement

Wheelbase Distance from the centre of the front wheel to the centre of the rear wheel.

Wiring harness or loom Describes the electrical wires running the length of the motorcycle and enclosed in tape or plastic sheathing. Wiring coming off the main harness is usually referred to as a sub harness.

Woodruff key A key of semi-circular or square section used to locate a gear to a shaft. Often used to locate the alternator rotor on the crankshaft.

Wrist pin Another name for gudgeon or piston pin.

Note: *References throughout this index relate to Chapter•page number*

Notes

Haynes Motorcycle Manuals – The Complete List

Title	Book No.
BMW	
BMW 2-valve Twins (70 - 96)	**0249**
BMW K100 & 75 2-valve Models (83 - 96)	**1373**
BMW R850 & R1100 4-valve Twins (93 - 97)	**3466**
BSA	
BSA Bantam (48 - 71)	0117
BSA Unit Singles (58 - 72)	0127
BSA Pre-unit Singles (54 - 61)	0326
BSA A7 & A10 Twins (47 - 62)	0121
BSA A50 & A65 Twins (62 - 73)	0155
DUCATI	
Ducati 600, 750 & 900 2-valve V-Twins (91 - 96)	**3290**
HARLEY-DAVIDSON	
Harley-Davidson Sportsters (70 - 99)	0702
Harley-Davidson Big Twins (70 - 99)	0703
HONDA	
Honda NB, ND, NP & NS50 Melody (81 - 85) ◊	0622
Honda NE/NB50 Vision & SA50 Vision Met-in (85 - 95) ◊	1278
Honda MB, MBX, MT & MTX50 (80 - 93)	0731
Honda C50, C70 & C90 (67 - 99)	0324
Honda CR80R & CR125R (86 - 97)	2220
Honda XR80R & XR100R (85 - 96)	2218
Honda XL/XR 80, 100, 125, 185 & 200 2-valve Models (78 - 87)	0566
Honda CB100N & CB125N (78 - 86) ◊	0569
Honda H100 & H100S Singles (80 - 92) ◊	0734
Honda CB/CD125T & CM125C Twins (77 - 88) ◊	0571
Honda CG125 (76 - 99) ◊	0433
Honda NS125 (86 - 93) ◊	3056
Honda MBX/MTX125 & MTX200 (83 - 93) ◊	1132
Honda CD/CM185 200T & CM250C 2-valve Twins (77 - 85)	0572
Honda XL/XR 250 & 500 (78 - 84)	0567
Honda XR250L, XR250R & XR400R (86 - 97)	2219
Honda CB250 & CB400N Super Dreams (78 - 84) ◊	0540
Honda CR250R & CR500R (86 - 97)	2222
Honda Elsinore 250 (73 - 75)	0217
Honda CBR400RR Fours (88 - 99)	**3552**
Honda VFR400 (NC30) & RVF400 (NC35) V-Fours (89 - 98)	**3496**
Honda CB400 & CB550 Fours (73 - 77)	0262
Honda CX/GL500 & 650 V-Twins (78 - 86)	0442
Honda CBX550 Four (82 - 86) ◊	0940
Honda XL600R & XR600R (83 - 96)	2183
Honda CBR600F1 & 1000F Fours (87 - 96)	**1730**
Honda CBR600F2 & F3 Fours (91 - 98)	**2070**
Honda CB650 sohc Fours (78 - 84)	0665
Honda NTV600 & 650 V-Twins (88 - 96)	**3243**
Honda Shadow VT600 & 750 (USA) (88 - 99)	2312
Honda CB750 sohc Four (69 - 79)	0131
Honda V45/65 Sabre & Magna (82 - 88)	0820
Honda VFR750 & 700 V-Fours (86 - 97)	**2101**
Honda VFR800 V-Fours (97 - 00)	**3703**
Honda CB750 & CB900 dohc Fours (78 - 84)	0535
Honda CBR900RR FireBlade (92 - 99)	**2161**
Honda ST1100 Pan European V-Fours (90 - 97)	**3384**
Honda Shadow VT1100 (USA) (85 - 98)	2313
Honda GL1000 Gold Wing (75 - 79)	0309
Honda GL1100 Gold Wing (79 - 81)	0669
Honda Gold Wing 1200 (USA) (84 - 87)	2199
Honda Gold Wing 1500 (USA) (88 - 98)	2225
KAWASAKI	
Kawasaki AE/AR 50 & 80 (81 - 95)	1007

Title	Book No.
Kawasaki KC, KE & KH100 (75 - 99)	1371
Kawasaki KMX125 & 200 (86 - 96) ◊	3046
Kawasaki 250, 350 & 400 Triples (72 - 79)	0134
Kawasaki 400 & 440 Twins (74 - 81)	0281
Kawasaki 400, 500 & 550 Fours (79 - 91)	0910
Kawasaki EN450 & 500 Twins (Ltd/Vulcan) (85 - 93)	2053
Kawasaki EX & ER500 (GPZ500S & ER-5) Twins (87 - 99)	**2052**
Kawasaki ZX600 (Ninja ZX-6, ZZ-R600) Fours (90 - 97)	**2146**
Kawasaki ZX-6R Ninja Fours (95 - 98)	**3541**
Kawasaki ZX600 (GPZ600R, GPX600R, Ninja 600R & RX) & ZX750 (GPX750R, Ninja 750R) Fours (85 - 97)	**1780**
Kawasaki 650 Four (76 - 78)	0373
Kawasaki 750 Air-cooled Fours (80 - 91)	0574
Kawasaki ZR550 & 750 Zephyr Fours (90 - 97)	**3382**
Kawasaki ZX750 (Ninja ZX-7 & ZXR750) Fours (89 - 96)	**2054**
Kawasaki 900 & 1000 Fours (73 - 77)	0222
Kawasaki ZX900, 1000 & 1100 Liquid-cooled Fours (83 - 97)	**1681**
MOTO GUZZI	
Moto Guzzi 750, 850 & 1000 V-Twins (74 - 78)	0339
MZ	
MZ ETZ Models (81 - 95) ◊	1680
NORTON	
Norton 500, 600, 650 & 750 Twins (57 - 70)	0187
Norton Commando (68 - 77)	0125
PIAGGIO	
Piaggio (Vespa) Scooters (91 - 98)	3492
SUZUKI	
Suzuki GT, ZR & TS50 (77 - 90) ◊	0799
Suzuki TS50X (83 - 99) ◊	1599
Suzuki 100, 125, 185 & 250 Air-cooled Trail bikes (79 - 89)	0797
Suzuki GP100 & 125 Singles (78 - 93) ◊	0576
Suzuki GS, GN, GZ & DR125 Singles (82 - 99) ◊	0888
Suzuki 250 & 350 Twins (68 - 78)	0120
Suzuki GT250X7, GT200X5 & SB200 Twins (78 - 83) ◊	0469
Suzuki GS/GSX250, 400 & 450 Twins (79 - 85)	0736
Suzuki GS500E Twin (89 - 97)	**3238**
Suzuki GS550 (77 - 82) & GS750 Fours (76 - 79)	0363
Suzuki GS/GSX550 4-valve Fours (83 - 88)	1133
Suzuki GSX-R600 & 750 (96 - 99)	**3553**
Suzuki GSF600 & 1200 Bandit Fours (95 - 97)	**3367**
Suzuki GS850 Fours (78 - 88)	0536
Suzuki GS1000 Four (77 - 79)	0484
Suzuki GSX-R750, GSX-R1100 (85 - 92), GSX600F, GSX750F, GSX1100F (Katana) Fours (88 - 96)	**2055**
Suzuki GS/GSX1000, 1100 & 1150 4-valve Fours (79 - 88)	0737
TRIUMPH	
Triumph Tiger Cub & Terrier (52 - 68)	0414
Triumph 350 & 500 Unit Twins (58 - 73)	0137
Triumph Pre-Unit Twins (47 - 62)	0251
Triumph 650 & 750 2-valve Unit Twins (63 - 83)	0122
Triumph Trident & BSA Rocket 3 (69 - 75)	0136
Triumph Triples & Fours (carburettor engines) (91 - 99)	**2162**
VESPA	
Vespa P/PX125, 150 & 200 Scooters (78 - 95)	0707
Vespa Scooters (59 - 78)	0126
YAMAHA	
Yamaha DT50 & 80 Trail Bikes (78 - 95) ◊	0800
Yamaha T50 & 80 Townmate (83 - 95) ◊	1247
Yamaha YB100 Singles (73 - 91) ◊	0474

Title	Book No.
Yamaha RS/RXS100 & 125 Singles (74 - 95)	0331
Yamaha RD & DT125LC (82 - 87) ◊	0887
Yamaha TZR125 (87 - 93) & DT125R (88 - 95) ◊	1655
Yamaha TY50, 80, 125 & 175 (74 - 84) ◊	0464
Yamaha XT & SR125 (82 - 96)	1021
Yamaha 250 & 350 Twins (70 - 79)	0040
Yamaha XS250, 360 & 400 sohc Twins (75 - 84)	0378
Yamaha RD250 & 350LC Twins (80 - 82)	0803
Yamaha RD350 YPVS Twins (83 - 95)	1158
Yamaha RD400 Twin (75 - 79)	0333
Yamaha XT, TT & SR500 Singles (75 - 83)	0342
Yamaha XZ550 Vision V-Twins (82 - 85)	0821
Yamaha FJ, FZ, XJ & YX600 Radian (84 - 92)	**2100**
Yamaha XJ600S (Diversion, Seca II) & XJ600N Fours (92 - 99)	**2145**
Yamaha YZF600R Thundercat & FZS600 Fazer (96 - 99)	**3702**
Yamaha 650 Twins (70 - 83)	0341
Yamaha XJ650 & 750 Fours (80 - 84)	0738
Yamaha XS750 & 850 Triples (76 - 85)	0340
Yamaha TDM850, TRX850 & XTZ750 (89 - 99)	**3540**
Yamaha FZR600, 750 & 1000 Fours (87 - 96)	**2056**
Yamaha XV V-Twins (81 - 96)	**0802**
Yamaha XJ900F Fours (83 - 94)	**3239**
Yamaha FJ1100 & 1200 Fours (84 - 96)	**2057**
ATVS	
Honda ATC70, 90, 110, 185 & 200 (71 - 85)	0565
Honda TRX300 Shaft Drive ATVs (88 - 95)	2125
Honda TRX300EX & TRX400EX ATVs (93 - 99)	2318
Polaris ATVs (85 to 97)	2302
Yamaha YT, YFM, YTM & YTZ ATVs (80 - 85)	1154
Yamaha YFS200 Blaster ATV (88 - 98)	2317
Yamaha YFB250 Timberwolf ATV (92 - 96)	2217
Yamaha YFM350 Big Bear and ER ATVs (87 - 95)	2126
Yamaha Warrior and Banshee ATVs (87 - 99)	2314
ATV Basics	10450
TECHNICAL TITLES	
Motorcycle Basics Manual	1083
MOTORCYCLE TECHBOOKS	
Motorcycle Electrical TechBook (3rd Edition)	3471
Motorcycle Fuel Systems TechBook	3514
Motorcycle Workshop Practice TechBook (2nd Edition)	3470

◊ = not available in the USA **Bold type** = Superbike

The manuals on this page are available through good motorcycle dealers and accessory shops.
In case of difficulty, contact: **Haynes Publishing**
(UK) +44 1963 440635   (USA) +1 805 4986703
(FR) +33 1 47 78 50 50   (SV) +46 18 124016
(Australia/New Zealand) +61 3 9763 8100

MCL08.09/99

Preserving Our Motoring Heritage

< The Model J Duesenberg Derham Tourster. Only eight of these magnificent cars were ever built – this is the only example to be found outside the United States of America

Almost every car you've ever loved, loathed or desired is gathered under one roof at the Haynes Motor Museum. Over 300 immaculately presented cars and motorbikes represent every aspect of our motoring heritage, from elegant reminders of bygone days, such as the superb Model J Duesenberg to curiosities like the bug-eyed BMW Isetta. There are also many old friends and flames. Perhaps you remember the 1959 Ford Popular that you did your courting in? The magnificent 'Red Collection' is a spectacle of classic sports cars including AC, Alfa Romeo, Austin Healey, Ferrari, Lamborghini, Maserati, MG, Riley, Porsche and Triumph.

A Perfect Day Out

Each and every vehicle at the Haynes Motor Museum has played its part in the history and culture of Motoring. Today, they make a wonderful spectacle and a great day out for all the family. Bring the kids, bring Mum and Dad, but above all bring your camera to capture those golden memories for ever. You will also find an impressive array of motoring memorabilia, a comfortable 70 seat video cinema and one of the most extensive transport book shops in Britain. The Pit Stop Cafe serves everything from a cup of tea to wholesome, home-made meals or, if you prefer, you can enjoy the large picnic area nestled in the beautiful rural surroundings of Somerset.

John Haynes O.B.E., Founder and Chairman of the museum at the wheel of a Haynes Light 12.

< The 1936 490cc sohc-engined International Norton – well known for its racing success

The Museum is situated on the A359 Yeovil to Frome road at Sparkford, just off the A303 in Somerset. It is about 40 miles south of Bristol, and 25 minutes drive from the M5 intersection at Taunton.

Open 9.30am - 5.30pm (10.00am - 4.00pm Winter) 7 days a week, *except Christmas Day, Boxing Day and New Years Day*

Special rates available for schools, coach parties and outings Charitable Trust No. 292048